LOEB CLASSICAL LIBRARY
FOUNDED BY JAMES LOEB 1911

EDITED BY
JEFFREY HENDERSON

SILIUS ITALICUS
II

LCL 278

SILIUS ITALICUS

PUNICA

BOOKS IX–XVII

WITH AN ENGLISH TRANSLATION BY

J. D. DUFF

HARVARD UNIVERSITY PRESS
CAMBRIDGE, MASSACHUSETTS
LONDON, ENGLAND

First published 1934

LOEB CLASSICAL LIBRARY® is a registered trademark of the President and Fellows of Harvard College

ISBN 978-0-674-99306-8

Printed on acid-free paper and bound by The Maple-Vail Book Manufacturing Group

CONTENTS

SILIUS ITALICUS

BOOKS IX–XVII

PUNICORUM

LIBER NONUS

ARGUMENT

Varro is eager to fight, and his boldness is increased by a successful skirmish. Paulus tries in vain to restrain his colleague (1-65). *A horrible crime committed in ignorance*

Turbato monstris Latio cladisque futurae
signa per Ausoniam prodentibus irrita divis,
haud secus ac si fausta forent et prospera pugnae
omina venturae, consul traducere noctem
exsomnis telumque manu vibrare per umbras,
ac modo segnitie Paulum increpitare, modo acres
exercere tubas nocturnaque classica velle.
nec minor in Poeno properi certaminis ardor.
erumpunt vallo, fortuna urgente sinistra,
consertaeque manus ; nam sparsi ad pabula campis
vicinis raptanda Macae fudere volucrem
telorum nubem. ante omnes invadere bella
Mancinus gaudens hostilique unguere primus
tela cruore cadit ; cadit et numerosa iuventus.
nec pecudum fibras Varro et contraria Paulo
auspicia incusante deum compesceret arma,

[a] An African people living near the river Cinyps.

PUNICA

BOOK IX

ARGUMENT (*continued*)

during the night portends disaster to the Romans (66-177). *Hannibal encourages his men and then draws them up in line of battle* (178-243). *Varro does the same* (244-277). *The battle of Cannae* (278-x. 325).

Though Italy was disturbed by these portents and the gods in vain revealed tokens of coming disaster throughout the land, yet Varro behaved as if the omens for the imminent battle were favourable and auspicious. He took no sleep that night but brandished his sword in the darkness, at one time blaming Paulus for inaction, at another seeking to sound by night the fierce war-note of his trumpets. Nor was Hannibal less eager for instant conflict. Driven on by evil fortune, our soldiers sallied out from the camp, and battle was joined. For a body of Macae,[a] foraging here and there in the neighbouring plains, discharged a cloud of winged missiles. Here Mancinus fell, while rejoicing to be the foremost fighter and first to dye his sword with the blood of an enemy; and with him fell many soldiers. Still, though Paulus objected that the entrails of the victims were ominous of the gods' disfavour, Varro would not have checked

ni sors alterni iuris, quo castra reguntur,
arbitrium pugnae properanti in fata negasset.
quae tamen haud valuit perituris milibus una
plus donasse die. rediere in castra, gemente
haud dubie Paulo, qui crastina iura videret
amenti cessura viro, frustraque suorum
servatas a caede animas. nam turbidus ira
infensusque morae dilata ob proelia ductor:
"sicine, sic," inquit, "grates pretiumque rependis,
Paule, tui capitis? meruerunt talia, qui te
legibus atque urnae dira eripuere minanti?
tradant immo hosti revocatos ilicet enses,
tradant arma iube, aut pugnantum deripe dextris.
sed vos, quorum oculos atque ora humentia vidi,
vertere cum consul terga et remeare iuberet,
ne morem et pugnae signum expectate petendae;
dux sibi quisque viam rapito, cum spargere primis
incipiet radiis Gargana cacumina Phoebus.
pandam egomet propere portas :, ruite ocius atque hunc
ereptum revocate diem." sic turbidus aegra
pestifero pugnae castra incendebat amore.
At Paulus, iam non idem nec mente nec ore,
sed qualis stratis deleto milite campis
post pugnam stetit, ante oculos atque ora futuro
obversante malo; ceu iam spe lucis adempta,
cum stupet exanimata parens natique tepentes
nequiquam fovet extremis amplexibus artus:
"per totiens," inquit, "concussae moenia Romae,

---

[a] The two consuls held command by turns on alternate days.

[b] See viii. 289 foll.

[c] See iv. 561.

the fighting, had not the rule of alternate command [a] over the army denied him the power of decision, as he rushed upon his fate. Yet this rule could give the doomed multitude a reprieve for one day only. Back they went to camp; and Paulus loudly lamented, because he saw that to-morrow the command would devolve on a madman, and that he had saved the lives of his men to no purpose. For Varro, in fierce anger and resenting the postponement of battle, addressed him thus: "Is this the way, Paulus, you show gratitude and repay me for saving your life? Is this the reward of those who rescued you from the laws and from a jury that meant mischief? [b] Better bid our men at once surrender to the foe the swords and weapons which you called back from battle; or snatch them yourself from their grasp. But you, my men, whose faces I saw wet with tears when Paulus ordered you to turn your backs in retreat, break with custom and anticipate the word of command for battle: let each man be his own commander and rush to action as soon as the first rays of the sun are thrown on the summit of Mount Garganus.[c] I shall open the gates of the camp myself with no delay. Rush ahead, and make up for the opportunity you were robbed of to-day." Thus in his excitement he tried to animate the sick hearts of his men with a fatal desire for battle.

Meanwhile Paulus underwent a change: he felt and looked now as when he stood after the battle and the field lay before him strewn with Roman corpses; for the imminent disaster pressed upon his very sight. So sits a mother stunned and senseless, when all hope of her son's life is lost, and she cherishes with a last fruitless embrace the limbs that are not yet cold. He spoke thus: "By the walls of Rome so often shaken,

perque has, nox Stygia quas iam circumvolat umbra,
insontes animas, cladi parce obvius ire.
dum transit divum furor, et consumitur ira
Fortunae, novus Hannibalis, sat, nomina ferre
si discit miles nec frigidus aspicit hostem.
nonne vides, cum vicinis auditur in arvis,
quam subitus linquat pallentia corpora sanguis ?
quamque fluant arma ante tubas ? cunctator et aeger,
ut rere, in pugnas Fabius quoscumque sub illis
culpatis duxit signis, nunc arma capessunt,
at, quos Flaminius—sed dira avertite, divi.
sin nostris animus monitis precibusque repugnat,
aures pande deo : cecinit Cymaea per orbem
haec olim vates et te praesaga tuosque
vulgavit terris proavorum aetate furores.
iamque alter tibi, nec perplexo carmine, coram
fata cano vates : sistis ni crastina signa,
firmabis nostro Phoebeae dicta Sibyllae
sanguine ; nec Graio posthac Diomede ferentur
sed te, si perstas, insignes consule campi."
haec Paulus, lacrimaeque oculis ardentibus ortae.

Necnon et noctem sceleratus polluit error.
Xanthippo captus Libycis tolerarat in oris
servitium Satricus, mox inter praemia regi
Autololum dono datus ob virtutis honorem.
huic domus et gemini fuerant Sulmone relicti
matris in uberibus nati, Mancinus et una

---

[a] " were slain at Lake Trasimene " are the words which Paulus forbears to utter.

[b] The Sibyl of Cumae: see vii. 483. [c] See viii. 241.

[d] Silius must have invented the episode that follows; but he can hardly have expected his readers to believe a story so monstrously improbable. [e] See vi. 302 foll.

[f] A city of the Peligni in N. Italy, the birthplace of Ovid.

and by these innocent lives, round whom the shadow of infernal night is now hovering, I implore you, Varro, go not to meet disaster. Until Heaven's wrath has passed away and the anger of Fortune is spent, be content, if our recruits learn to endure the name of Hannibal and cease to turn cold at sight of the enemy. See you not how the very sound of his approach drives the blood in a moment from their pale faces, how the swords drop from their hands before the trumpet sounds? You think Fabius a sick man and a dawdler; but every soldier whom he led to battle beneath the standards you blame is in the ranks to-day, whereas the troops of Flaminius [a]—but may Heaven avert the evil omen! Even if your heart is set against my warnings and entreaties, open your ears to the god. Long ago, in the time of our forefathers, the priestess of Cumae [b] foretold these things to mankind, and her foreknowledge proclaimed to the world you and your madness. Now I turn prophet too and tell you the future to your face in no riddling strain: if you move the standards to-morrow, you shall confirm by my death the prophecy of the Sibyl, Apollo's priestess, and this field shall no longer be famous because of Diomede [c] the Greek but because of you, the Roman consul." Thus Paulus spoke, and the tears sprang from his burning eyes.

That night too was stained by a terrible crime committed in error.[d] Satricus, taken prisoner by Xanthippus,[e] had endured slavery in the land of Libya, and had then been given to the king of the Autololes with other rewards conferred on him in recognition of his valour. This man was a native of Sulmo [f] and left two boys there at their mother's breast—Mancinus and one who bore the Trojan name

nomine Rhoeteo Solimus ; nam Dardana origo
et Phrygio genus a proavo, qui, sceptra secutus
Aeneae, claram muris fundaverat urbem
ex sese dictam Solimon ; celebrata colonis
mox Italis, paulatim attrito nomine, Sulmo.
at tum barbaricis Satricus cum rege catervis
advectus, quo non spretum, si posceret usus,
noscere Gaetulis Latias interprete voces,
postquam posse datum Peligna revisere tecta
et patrium sperare larem, ad conamina noctem
advocat ac furtim castris evadit iniquis.
sed fuga nuda viri ; sumpto nam prodere coepta
vitabat clipeo et dextra remeabat inermi.
exuvias igitur prostrataque corpora campo
lustrat et exutis Mancini cingitur armis.
iamque metus levior ; verum, cui dempta ferebat
exsangui spolia et cuius nudaverat artus,
natus erat, paulo ante Maca prostratus ab hoste.
  Ecce sub adventum noctis primumque soporem
alter natorum, Solimus, vestigia vallo
Ausonio vigil extulerat, dum sorte vicissim
alternat portae excubias, fratrisque petebat
Mancini stratum sparsa inter funera corpus,
furtiva cupiens miserum componere terra.
nec longum celerarat iter, cum tendere in armis
aggere Sidonio venientem conspicit hostem.
quodque dabat fors in subitis necopina, sepulcro
Aetoli condit membra occultata Thoantis.
inde, ubi nulla sequi propius pone arma virumque
incomitata videt vestigia ferre per umbras,
prosiliens tumulo contorquet nuda parentis

[a] *i.e.* Libyans.

of Solimus; for their remote ancestor was a Trojan who had followed Aeneas as his sovereign and built a famous city which he called by his own name, Solimus; but, when many Italian colonists resorted thither, the name was gradually shortened into Sulmo. And now Satricus had come with his king among the foreign invaders; and the Gaetulians [a] were willing enough, when occasion required, to use his services to interpret Latin speech. But when the chance was given him of revisiting his native town and he could hope to see his father's house again, he summoned night to aid his enterprise and stole out of the hated camp. But he fled unarmed: to carry a shield might betray his design, and he started home with no weapon in his hand. Therefore he scanned the armour of the dead who lay on the field, and armed himself with weapons taken from the corpse of Mancinus. Now he felt less fear; but it was his own son, slain a few hours before by a Libyan foe, whose limbs he had stripped, and from whose lifeless body he had taken the spoils which now he carried.

Now when night came and sleep began, his other son, Solimus, came forth from the Roman camp, to relieve in his allotted turn the watch at the gate, and searched for the body of his brother, Mancinus, among the corpses lying on the field; he wished to bury the hapless youth secretly. He had not hastened far when he saw an armed enemy coming towards him from the Carthaginian camp. Thus surprised, he took the course that chance offered him, and concealed himself behind the tomb of Thoas, an Aetolian. But then, when he saw no soldiers following close behind, but only a single man walking alone in the dark, he sprang up from the tomb and threw his javelin at his

in terga haud frustra iaculum ; Tyriamque sequentum
Satricus esse manum et Sidonia vulnera credens,
auctorem caeci trepidus circumspicit ictus.
Verum ubi victorem iuvenili robore cursus
attulit, et notis fulsit lux tristis ab armis,
fraternusque procul, luna prodente, retexit
ante oculos sese et radiavit comminus umbo,
exclamat iuvenis, subita flammatus ab ira :
" non sim equidem Sulmone satus tua, Satrice, proles
nec frater, Mancine, tuus fatearque nepotem
Pergameo indignum Solimo, si evadere detur
huic nostras impune manus. tu nobile gestes
germani spolium ante oculos referasque superba,
me spirante, domus Pelignae perfidus arma ?
haec tibi, cara parens Acca, ad solacia luctus
dona feram, nati ut figas aeterna sepulcro."
talia vociferans stricto mucrone ruebat.
Ast illi iam tela manu iamque arma fluebant,
audita patria natisque et coniuge et armis,
ac membra et sensus gelidus stupefecerat horror.
tum vox semanimi miseranda effunditur ore :
" parce, precor, dextrae, non ut mihi vita supersit,
(quippe nefas hac velle frui) sed sanguine nostro
ne damnes, o nate, manus. Carthaginis ille
captivus, patrias nunc primum advectus in oras,
ille ego sum Satricus, Solimi genus. haud tua, nate,
fraus ulla est : iaceres in me cum fervidus hastam,

father's unprotected back. His aim was true; and Satricus, believing that he was pursued by a Carthaginian force and that his wound was due to them, looked round anxiously, to discover the unseen hand that had struck him.

But when Solimus, running with youthful vigour, came up to his victim, a dismal light flashed from the familiar arms, and the shield of Mancinus, revealed by the moonlight, showed itself clear before his eyes and gleamed close beside him. Then the young man, fired with sudden wrath, cried out: 'No true son of Satricus, no native of Sulmo, should I be, and no brother of Mancinus—and I would own myself no worthy descendant of Trojan Solimus, if I suffered this man to escape unpunished! Shall he wear before my eyes the noble spoils he took from my brother? Is this traitor to carry off the glorious armour of a Pelignian house, while I am alive to prevent it? No! To you, dear mother Acca, I shall carry back this gift, to assuage your grief, and for you to fix for ever on the grave of your son." Thus shouting, he rushed on with sword unsheathed.

But already sword and shield were slipping from the grasp of Satricus, when he heard Sulmo named, and the arms, and the names of his wife and children: frozen horror had stunned him, mind and body. And then a piteous cry came forth from his half-dead lips: "Hold your hand, my son—not that I may live on (for to desire the enjoyment of such a life would be a crime), but that you may not bring a curse on your hand by shedding your father's blood. I am Satricus, son of Solimus, who was taken prisoner by Carthage long ago and have now just returned to my native land. You did no wrong, my son. When you hurled

Poenus eram. verum, castris elapsus acerbis,
ad vos et carae properabam coniugis ora.
hunc rapui exanimi clipeum ; sed iam unice nobis,
haec fratris tumulis arma excusata reporta.
curarum tibi prima tamen sit, nate, referre
ductori monitus Paulo, producere bellum
nitatur Poenoque neget certamina Martis.
augurio exultat divum immensamque propinqua
stragem acie sperat. quaeso, cohibete furentem
Varronem ; namque hunc fama est impellere signa.
sat magnum hoc miserae fuerit mihi cardine vitae
solamen, cavisse meis. nunc ultima, nate,
invento simul atque amisso redde parenti
oscula." sic fatus galeam exuit atque rigentis
invadit nati tremebundis colla lacertis,
attonitoque timens verbis sanare pudorem
vulneris impressi et telum excusare laborat :
" quis testis nostris, quis conscius affuit actis ?
non nox errorem nigranti condidit umbra ?
cur trepidas ? da, nate, magis, da iungere pectus.
absolvo pater ipse manum, atque in fine laborum
hac condas oculos dextra, precor." at miser, imo
pectore suspirans, iuvenis non verba vicesque
alloquio vocemve refert ; sed sanguinis atri
sistere festinat cursum laceroque ligare
ocius illacrimans altum velamine vulnus.
tandem inter gemitus miserae erupere querelae :

your impetuous spear at me, I was a Carthaginian. But I had slipped out of the hated camp and was hastening home, eager to see the face of my dear wife. I snatched this shield from a corpse ; but now carry it back, purged of guilt, to your brother's body ; no son but you have I now. But your first duty, my son, must be to warn Paulus, the Roman general : he must strive to prolong the war and give Hannibal no chance of a battle. Hannibal, overjoyed by the divine omens, hopes for an immediate engagement and immeasurable slaughter. Restrain, I entreat, Varro's madness ; for it is said that he is urging his standards on. For me this will be consolation enough at the end of a wretched life, to have warned my countrymen. And now, my son, give the last embrace to the father whom you have found and lost in the same hour." Thus he spoke and, doffing his helmet, embraced his son, who stood motionless in horror, with trembling arms. Fearing for his terror-stricken son, he strove by his words to heal the shame felt for the wound inflicted, and to make excuses for the stroke : " None was present to see what we have done, none was privy to it. Was not the mistake concealed by the darkness of night ? Why tremble so ? Rather suffer me to embrace you, my son. I, your father, myself pronounce you innocent, and I entreat you to end my troubles and close my eyes with your hand." The unhappy youth groaned deeply, and could find no voice or words in reply ; but he made haste to stop the flow of dark blood and bind up the deep wound with a piece torn off his own garment ; and his tears fell fast. At last the voice of his complaint forced its way through his groans : " Is it thus,

"sicine te nobis, genitor, Fortuna reducit
in patriam? sic te nato natumque parenti
impia restituit? felix o terque quaterque
frater, cui fatis genitorem agnoscere ademptum!
ast ego, Sidoniis imperditus, ecce, parentem
vulnere cognosco. saltem hoc, Fortuna, fuisset
solamen culpae, dubia ut mihi signa dedisses
infausti generis. verum linquetur iniquis
non ultra superis nostros celare labores."
Haec dum amens queritur, iam, deficiente cruore,
in vacuas senior vitam disperserat auras.
tum iuvenis, maestum attollens ad sidera vultum:
"pollutae dextrae et facti Titania testis
infandi, quae nocturno mea lumine tela
dirigis in patrium corpus, non amplius," inquit,
"his oculis et damnato violabere visu."
haec memorat, simul ense fodit praecordia et, atrum
sustentans vulnus, mananti sanguine signat
in clipeo mandata patris: FUGE PROELIA VARRO;
ac summi tegimen suspendit cuspide teli
defletumque super prosternit membra parentem.
Talia venturae mittebant omina pugnae
Ausoniis superi, sensimque abeuntibus umbris
conscia nox sceleris roseo cedebat Eoo.
ductor in arma suos Libys et Romanus in arma
excibant de more suos; Poenisque redibat,
qualis nulla dies omni surrexerit aevo.
"non verborum," inquit, "stimulantum," Poenus, "egetis,

[a] The Moon.

father, that cruel Fortune brings you back to your country and to us? is it thus she restores father to son and son to father? Thrice and four times happy was my brother, whom death prevented from recognizing his father. But I whom the enemy did not kill—behold! I recognize him by wounding him. This at least Fortune should have permitted, to comfort me for my sin—she should have spared me the clear proof of our ill-starred kinship. But the cruel gods shall no longer find it possible to hide our sufferings."

While the distracted son complained thus, the father from loss of blood breathed forth his life into empty air. Then the young man raised his sad eyes to heaven and cried: "O Queen of heaven,[a] thou that didst witness the dreadful deed wrought by my polluted hand, thou whose light guided my weapon in the night to my father's body, these eyes and this accursed countenance shall no longer profane thy deity." With these words he drove his sword into his own body; and, when the blood flowed forth from the dark wound, he checked it and wrote his father's message in letters of blood upon his shield—"Varro, beware of battle!" Then he hung the shield on the point of his spear, and threw himself down upon the body of the father he so deeply mourned.

Such were the omens for the coming battle that Heaven sent to the Romans. By degrees darkness departed, and the night that witnessed that dreadful deed gave place to rosy dawn. The generals, Carthaginian and Roman, summoned their men to arms in customary fashion; and a day began for the invaders, the like of which will never be seen again. "You need no words of encouragement," said Hannibal;

Herculeis iter a metis ad Iapygis agros
vincendo emensi ; nusquam est animosa Saguntos ;
concessere Alpes ; pater ipse superbus aquarum
Ausonidum Eridanus captivo defluit alveo.
strage virum mersus Trebia est, atque ora sepulto
Lydia Flaminio premitur, lateque refulgent
ossibus ac nullo sulcantur vomere campi.
clarior his titulus, plusque allatura cruoris
lux oritur. mihi magna satis, sat vero superque
bellandi merces sit gloria ; cetera vobis
vincantur. quicquid diti devexit Hibero,
quicquid in Aetnaeis iactavit Roma triumphis,
quin etiam Libyco si quid de litore raptum
condidit, in vestros veniet sine sortibus enses.
ferte domos, quod dextra dabit ; nil ductor honoris
ex opibus posco. raptor per saecula longa
Dardanus edomitum vobis spoliaverit orbem.
qui Tyria ducis Sarranum ab origine nomen,
seu Laurens tibi, Sigeo sulcata colono,
arridet tellus, seu sunt Byzacia cordi
rura magis, centum Cereri fruticantia culmis,
electos optare dabo inter praemia campos.
addam etiam, flava Thybris quas irrigat unda,
captivis late gregibus depascere ripas.
qui vero externo socius mihi sanguine Byrsae
signa moves, dextram Ausonia si caede cruentam

[a] *i.e.* Etruscan.
[b] *i.e.* Roman.
[c] A district in Africa near the Lesser Syrtis, of fabulous fertility.

"you have marched victorious all the way from the Pillars of Hercules to the Iapygian fields; brave Saguntum has been wiped out; the Alps have granted you a passage; and the Po, the proud father of Italian rivers, flows down now in a conquered channel. The Trebia is hidden beneath the bodies of the slain; the corpse of Flaminius lies upon the Lydian [a] land; and the fields, furrowed by no plough, are whitened far and wide by Roman bones. A greater achievement than all these is at hand; a day is dawning that shall bring with it more bloodshed. For me fame is enough, and more than enough, to repay me for the toils of war; let the other gains of victory be yours. All the treasure that Roman ships have brought down the rich Hiberus, all that Rome has displayed in her triumphs over Sicily, and also any booty from the Libyan shore that she has stored up—all this shall fall to your swords, with no casting of lots. Take home with you all the spoil that you get by the sword; I, your general, seek no fame from riches. It will be for your benefit, that the Dardan [b] robbers have for centuries past conquered and pillaged the world. To you I speak who trace your origin back to ancient Tyre and Sidon: whether the acres of Laurentum, ploughed by Roman husbandmen, are your choice, or whether you prefer the fields of Byzacium,[c] where a hundred blades of corn spring from one seed—I shall allow you to choose the land you like best, as part of your reward. I shall give you also the meadows watered by the yellow stream of the Tiber, as a wide pasture-land for the flocks taken from the enemy. Next I say to the allies of foreign blood who fight in the ranks of Carthage: if any of you lift up a hand red with Roman blood, he

attolles, hinc iam civis Carthaginis esto.
neu vos Garganus Daunique fefellerit ora;
ad muros statis Romae; licet avia longe
urbs agat et nostro procul a certamine distet,
hic hodie ruet, atque ultra te ad proelia, miles,
nulla voco; ex acie tende in Capitolia cursum."
Haec memorat. tum, propulso munimine valli,
fossarum rapuere moras, aciemque locorum
consilio curvis accommodat ordine ripis.
barbaricus laevo stetit ad certamina cornu
bellator Nasamon unaque immanior artus
Marmarides, tum Maurus atrox Garamasque Macesque
et Massylae acies et ferro vivere laetum
vulgus Adyrmachidae pariter, gens accola Nili,
corpora ab immodico servans nigrantia Phoebo;
quis positum agminibus caput imperiumque Nealces.
at parte in dextra, sinuat qua flexibus undam
Aufidus et curvo circum errat gurgite ripas,
Mago regit. subiere leves, quos horrida misit
Pyrene, populi varioque auxere tumultu
flumineum latus; effulget caetrata iuventus;
Cantaber ante alios nec tectus tempora Vasco
ac torto miscens Baliaris proelia plumbo
Baetigenaeque viri. celsus media ipse coercet
agmina, quae patrio firmavit milite quaeque
Celtarum Eridano perfusis saepe catervis.

---

[a] Apulia.

[b] Of the river Aufidus on which Cannae (lit. "The Reed-bed") stood.

[c] The Spanish troops, who formed the backbone of Hannibal's army, are meant.

[d] The Guadalquivir: the chief city on the river was Corduba.

shall be henceforth a citizen of Carthage. And do not be misled by the sight of Mount Garganus and the land of Daunus [a]: you are standing now before the walls of Rome. Although the city lies at a distance and is far removed from this battlefield, she shall fall here and now, and never again shall I summon you to arms; when the fight is over, march straight against the Capitol."

Such was his speech. Then they threw down the protecting rampart and hurried over the trenches that delayed them; and the general drew up his line in suitable order on the winding banks,[b] following the lie of the ground. On the left wing, ready for battle, stood the Nasamonians, a barbarous host, and with them the Marmaridae of giant stature; next were fierce Moors and Garamantes and Macae; Massylian warriors and a swarm of Adyrmachidae—a people who dwell by the Nile and rejoice to live by the sword, and whose skins are for ever blackened by their merciless sun. Nealces was appointed captain and commander of these troops. Then on the right wing, where the Aufidus makes bends and meanders round its own banks with circling waters, there Mago was in command. Here fought the light-armed peoples who came from the rugged Pyrenees,[c] filling the river-banks with confused noise; and their crescent-shaped shields shone in the sun. Foremost were the Cantabrians; and there were bare-headed Vascones, and Balearic slingers who fight with leaden bullets, and the sons of the Baetis.[d] The centre was commanded by Hannibal himself, conspicuous on horseback, and was composed of stout warriors from Carthage and companies of Gauls whose limbs had often been bathed in the waters of the Po. But

sed qua se fluvius retro labentibus undis
eripit et nullo cuneos munimine vallat,
turritas moles ac propugnacula dorso
belua nigranti gestans, ceu mobilis agger,
nutat et erectos attollit ad aethera muros.
cetera iam Numidis circumvolitare vagosque
ferre datur cursus et toto fervere campo.
  Dum Libys incenso dispensat milite vires
hortandoque iterum atque iterum insatiabilis urget
factis quemque suis et se cognoscere iactat,
qua dextra veniant stridentis sibila teli,
promittitque viris nulli se defore testem :
iam Varro, exacta vallo legione, movebat
cladum principia ; ac pallenti laetus in unda
laxabat sedem venturis Portitor umbris.
stant primi, quos sanguineae pendente vetabant
ire notae clipeo, defixique omine torpent.
iuxta terribilis facies : miseranda iacebant
corpora in amplexu, natusque in pectore patris
imposita vulnus dextra letale tegebat.
effusae lacrimae, Mancinique inde reversus
fraterna sub morte dolor, tum triste movebat
augurium et similes defuncto in corpore vultus.
ocius erroris culpam deflendaque facta
ductori pandunt atque arma vetantia pugnam.
ille, ardens animi : " ferte haec," ait, " omina Paulo ;
namque illum, cui femineo stant corde timores,
moverit ista manus, quae, caede imbuta nefanda,
cum Furiae expeterent poenas, fortasse paterno
signavit moriens sceleratum sanguine carmen."

[a] The dead were ferried over the Styx by Charon.
[b] See ll. 174 foll.

where the river, falling back with retreating stream, offered no protection to the combatants, there the elephants bore huge towers and upper-works on their sable backs, swaying to and fro like a moving rampart and raising the tall structures to the sky. Lastly, the Numidians had orders to ride all round about, to rove from point to point and busy themselves over all the field.

Thus Hannibal disposed his eager forces. Again and again he appealed to them and could not say enough: he roused each man by reminding him of his past exploits; he boasted that he knew the arm that launched each hissing javelin; and he promised to be the eyewitness of all that each man did. Meanwhile, Varro sent his army forth from the camp and laid the foundations of disaster; and the Ferryman of the pale river[a] rejoiced to make room for the expected ghosts. The vanguard halted, forbidden to go on by the letters of blood upon the lifted shield[b]; the portent struck them dumb and motionless. A fearful sight was before them: the ill-fated pair lay locked in an embrace, and the son had laid his hand on his father's breast, to hide the fatal wound. Tears were shed, and grief for Mancinus was renewed by his brother's death; men were affected also by the evil omen and by the resemblance between the corpses. Quickly they inform Varro of the crime committed in error, of the dreadful deed, and of the shield that forbade a battle. He cried in wrath: "Carry these omens to Paulus; for he, whose womanish heart is filled with fears, may be affected by that parricidal hand, which, when the avenging Furies came, perhaps used his father's blood to write that infamous dying message."

Tum minitans propere describit munera pugnae ;
quaque feras saevus gentes aciemque Nealces
temperat, hac sese Marso cum milite cumque
Samnitum opponit signis et Iapyge alumno.
at campi medio (namque hac in parte videbat
stare ducem Libyae) Servilius obvia adire
arma et Picentes Umbrosque inferre iubetur.
cetera Paulus habet dextro certamina cornu.
his super insidias contra Nomadumque volucrem
Scipiadae datur ire manum ; quaque arte dolisque
scindent se turmae, praedicit spargere bellum.
Iamque propinquabant acies, agilique virorum
discursu mixtoque simul calefacta per ora
cornipedum hinnitu et multum strepitantibus armis
errabat caecum turbata per agmina murmur.
sic, ubi prima movent pelago certamina venti,
inclusam rabiem ac sparsuras astra procellas
parturit unda freti fundoque emota minaces
expirat per saxa sonos atque acta cavernis
torquet anhelantem spumanti vortice pontum.
Nec vero, fati tam saevo in turbine, solum
terrarum fuit ille labor ; discordia demens
intravit caelo superosque ad bella coëgit.
hinc Mavors, hinc Gradivum comitatus Apollo
et domitor tumidi pugnat maris ; hinc Venus amens,
hinc Vesta et, captae stimulatus caede Sagunti,
Amphitryoniades, pariter veneranda Cybele
indigetesque dei Faunusque satorque Quirinus
alternusque animae mutato Castore Pollux.

---

[a] Apulians. [b] Neptune.

[c] Because she foresaw the Roman defeat.

[d] Legend said that each of the Twin Brethren spent six months of the year in Hades and six months in the upper world, the one taking the place of the other.

Then with words of menace he assigned to all their station on the field. Opposite fierce Nealces and the barbarous clans under his command Varro stood himself, with Marsians and Samnite standards and natives of Iapygia.[a] In the centre of the field, where he saw that Hannibal was stationed, Servilius had orders to face the attack and bring on the men of Picenum and Umbria. The rest of the troops were on the right wing, with Paulus in command. Finally, Scipio had orders to deal with surprise attacks by the flying troops of Numidians, and was bidden to extend his lines, wherever the enemy's cavalry laid a trap by breaking their formation.

And now the two armies closed; and the rapid movement of men, together with the neighing of hot-breathing horses and the loud clashing of weapons, sent a dull roaring noise through the moving ranks. So, when the winds begin a battle on the deep, the sea is big with pent-up fury and storms that will soon drench the stars; then, churned up from the bottom, it breathes out sounds of menace through the rocks; and, driven from its caves, torments the restless water with its foaming eddies.

Nor was the trouble confined to earth, when this crack of doom was heard: the madness of strife invaded heaven and forced the gods to fight. On one side fought Apollo and Mars with him, and the Ruler of the stormy sea[b]; with them was Venus in despair,[c] and Vesta, and Hercules, stung by the slaughter of captured Saguntum, and likewise worshipful Cybele; and the native gods of Italy—Faunus and father Quirinus; and Pollux who takes turns of life with his brother Castor.[d] On the other

contra cincta latus ferro Saturnia Iuno
et Pallas, Libycis Tritonidos edita lymphis,
ac patrius flexis per tempora cornibus Hammon
multaque praeterea divorum turba minorum.
quorum ubi mole simul venientum et gressibus alma
intremuit tellus, pars implevere propinquos
divisi montes, pars sedem nube sub alta
ceperunt ; vacuo descensum ad proelia caelo.
Tollitur immensus deserta ad sidera clamor,
Phlegraeis quantas effudit ad aethera voces
terrigena in campis exercitus ; aut sator aevi,
quanta Cyclopas nova fulmina voce poposcit,
Iupiter, exstructis vidit cum montibus ire
magnanimos raptum caelestia regna gigantas.
nec vero prima in tantis concursibus hasta
ulla fuit : stridens nimbus certante furore
telorum simul effusus, cupidaeque cruoris
hinc atque hinc animae gemina cecidere procella ;
ac prius insanus dextra quam ducitur ensis,
bellantum pars magna iacet. super ipsa suorum
corpora consistunt avidi calcantque gementes.
nec magis aut Libyco protrudi Dardana nisu
avertive potest pubes, aut ordine pelli
fixa suo Sarrana manus, quam vellere sede
si coeptet Calpen impacto gurgite pontus.
amisere ictus spatium, nec morte peracta
artatis cecidisse licet. galea horrida flictu
adversae ardescit galeae, clipeusque fatiscit

[a] See note to iii. 324.
[b] See note to i. 415.
[c] See note to iv. 275.
[d] Gibraltar.

was Juno, daughter of Saturn, with her sword girt round her, and Pallas who sprang from the Libyan waters of Lake Tritonis [a]; and Ammon,[b] the native god of Africa, whose brow bears curving horns, and a great company of lesser deities as well. When they all came on together, Mother Earth shook beneath the tread of those mighty beings. Some of them went apart and filled the mountains round with their presence, while others rested beneath a high cloud; and heaven was left empty when they came down to battle.

A tremendous shout went up to the deserted sky, loud as the challenge sent up to heaven by the army of the Earthborn on the plain of Phlegra,[c] loud as the voice with which Jupiter, creator of the universe, demanded fresh thunderbolts from the Cyclopes, when he saw the aspiring Giants coming, with mountains piled on mountains, to seize the throne of heaven. Nor was any spear the first to be thrown in that mighty conflict: a hissing storm of missiles was discharged all at once with emulous rage; and men on both sides, eager for blood, were killed themselves by the cross-fire; and, even before the furious sword was drawn, a great number of the combatants lay low. In their eagerness, men even stood on the bodies of their comrades, and trod them under foot, in spite of their groans. The pressure of the Carthaginians could not dislodge nor turn aside the Roman line; nor could the steady ranks of Carthage be broken up; the sea might as well try to wrench Calpe [d] from its seat by the impact of its waters. Blows failed for want of room; and the close-packed dead had no space to fall. Helmet, clashing fiercely against helmet of a foe, flashed fire; shield, striking

impulsu clipei, atque ensis contunditur ense;
pes pede, virque viro teritur; tellusque videri
sanguine operta nequit, caelumque et sidera pendens
abstulit ingestis nox densa sub aethere telis.
quis astare loco dederat Fortuna secundo,
contorum longo et procerae cuspidis ictu,
ceu primas agitent acies, certamina miscent.
at, quos deinde tenet retrorsum inglorius ordo,
missilibus certant pugnas aequare priorum.
ultra clamor agit bellum, milesque, cupiti
Martis inops, saevis impellit vocibus hostem.
non ullum defit teli genus: hi sude pugnas,
hi pinu flagrante cient, hi pondere pili;
at saxis fundaque alius iaculoque volucri.
interdum stridens per nubila fertur harundo,
interdumque ipsis metuenda falarica muris.

Speramusne, deae, quarum mihi sacra coluntur,
mortali totum hunc aperire in saecula voce
posse diem? tantumne datis confidere linguae,
ut Cannas uno ore sonem? si gloria vobis
nostra placet, neque vos magnis avertitis ausis,
huc omnes cantus Phoebumque vocate parentem.
verum utinam posthac animo, Romane, secunda,
quanto tunc adversa, feras! satque hactenus, oro,
nec libeat tentare deis, an Troia proles
par bellum tolerare queat. tuque, anxia fati,
pone, precor, lacrimas et adora vulnera, laudes
perpetuas paritura tibi; nam tempore, Roma,

shield, fell to pieces ; and sword broke against sword. Foot pressed against foot, and man against man. The ground was hidden from sight by a coating of blood ; and thick darkness overhead, caused by showers of missiles, concealed the starry sky. Those to whom Fortune had assigned a station in the second line fought with long poles and far-reaching spears, as if they were in the van of the host. And those who were banished to the third line and could win no glory strove to rival the prowess of those in front by hurling missiles. Behind them shouting did the work of war, and soldiers who were denied the chance of fighting assailed the enemy with volleys of abuse. Every kind of weapon was employed : some used stakes, others burning brands, and others weighty javelins, while others plied stones and slings and flying lances. Here an arrow went hissing through the sky, and there a *falarica* [a] which even city-walls must fear.

Ye goddesses,[b] whose priest I am, how can I hope with mere mortal voice to set forth for future ages all the story of that day ? Do ye grant me such bold utterance that I can sing of Cannae with but one tongue ? If my fame is dear to you, if ye frown not on a mighty enterprise, then summon hither all your music and Apollo your sire. But would that Romans would thereafter bear prosperity with as much constancy as they showed in that dark hour. I pray that Heaven may be satisfied without testing the race of Troy, whether they can endure such an ordeal again. And thou, Rome, doubtful of thy doom, weep not, I pray, but bless those wounds which shall bring thee eternal glory. For never shalt thou be greater

[a] See note to i. 351. [b] The Muses.

nullo maior eris ; mox sic labere secundis,
ut sola cladum tuearis nomina fama.
  Iamque inter varias Fortuna utrimque virorum
alternata vices incerto eluserat iras
eventu, mediaque diu pendente per ambas
spe gentes, paribus Mavors flagrabat in armis.
mitia ceu virides agitant cum flamina culmos
necdum maturas impellit ventus aristas,
huc atque huc it summa seges nutansque vicissim
alterno lente motu incurvata nitescit.
tandem barbaricis perfractam viribus acri
dissipat incurrens aciem clamore Nealces.
laxati cunei, perque intervalla citatus
irrupit trepidis hostis. tum turbine nigro
sanguinis exundat torrens ; nullumque sub una
cuspide procumbit corpus. dum vulnera tergo
bellator timet Ausonius, per pectora saevas
exceptat mortes et leto dedecus arcet.
  Stabat cum primis mediae certamine pugnae,
aspera semper amans et par cuicumque periclo,
Scaevola ; nec tanta vitam iam strage volebat,
sed dignum proavo letum et sub nomine mortem.
is postquam frangi res atque augescere vidit
exitium : " brevis hoc vitae, quodcumque relictum,
extendamus," ait ; " nam virtus futile nomen,
ni decori sat sint pariendo tempora leti."
dixit et in medios, qua dextera concita Poeni
limitem agit, vasto connixus turbine fertur.

---

[a] He means that the courage in defeat shown by the Romans was their best title to fame.

[b] To be wounded in the back was a disgrace ; to fall with wounds in front was a glorious death : see v. 594.

than then. Later victories shall sap thy strength, till naught but the story of thy defeats [a] shall preserve thy fame.

And now Fortune, shifting from side to side, had baffled the ardour of both armies by keeping the event uncertain; and the hopes of Roman and Carthaginian hung long in the balance, while the battle raged on equal terms. So when light breezes stir the green blades of corn and the wind bends the unripe ears, the tops of the wheat move this way and that, and sway and bow and shine with a gentle changing motion. But at last Nealces and his savage horde, charging with a fierce shout, broke the Roman line and scattered it. The close ranks broke up and the enemy rushed furiously through the gaps upon the frighted foe. Then torrents of blood flowed in a dark stream over the plain; and not a man who fell was pierced by one spear only. The Romans, fearing to be wounded in the back,[b] welcomed the fatal stroke to their breasts, and by death avoided dishonour.

Scaevola, ever a lover of danger and equal to any emergency, stood among the foremost in the centre of the fray; when so many had fallen, he had no wish to survive them but desired a glorious death worthy of his great ancestor.[c] When he saw that the day was lost and that ruin was spreading, "Life is short," he cried, "and little of it remains; let me prolong that little; for valour is an empty name unless the hour of death is sufficient to win glory." With these words he gathered all his strength and rushed furiously to the centre where Hannibal was clearing a path with his unresting right hand. Then, when

[a] See viii. 383 foll.

hic exultantem Caralim atque erepta volentem
induere excelso caesi gestamina trunco
ense subit, capuloque tenus ferrum impulit ira.
volvitur ille ruens atque arva hostilia morsu
appetit et mortis premit in tellure dolores.
nec Gabaris Sicchaeque virum tenuere furentes
concordi virtute manus ; sed perdidit acer,
dum stat, decisam Gabar inter proelia dextram.
at Siccha auxilium, magno turbante dolore,
dum temere accelerat, calcato improvidus ense
succidit ac nudae sero vestigia plantae
damnavit dextraque iacet morientis amici.
tandem convertit fatalia tela Nealcae
fulminei gliscens iuvenis furor. exsilit ardens,
nomine tam claro stimulante, ad praemia caedis.
tum silicem scopulo avulsum, quem montibus altis
detulerat torrens, raptum contorquet in ora
turbidus : incusso crepuerunt pondere malae,
ablatusque viro vultus ; concreta cruento
per nares cerebro sanies fluit, atraque manant
orbibus elisis et trunca lumina fronte.
sternitur unanimo Marius succurrere Capro
conatus metuensque viro superesse cadenti.
lucis idem auspicium ac patrium et commune duobus
paupertas ; sacro iuvenes Praeneste creati
miscuerant studia et iuncta tellure serebant.
velle ac nolle ambobus idem sociataque toto
mens aevo ac parvis dives concordia rebus.
occubuere simul ; votisque ex omnibus unum

[a] Trophies taken in battle were often fastened to the trunk of a leafless tree. But is it conceivable that anyone should find time to do this in the course of a desperate battle?

Caralis, in triumph, was about to fix on a tall tree [a] the armour taken from a victim, Scaevola stabbed him, and his fury drove the sword in up to the hilt. He fell and rolled over, biting that foreign soil and crushing down the pains of death upon the ground. Nor could the rage and united valour of Gabar and Siccha stop Scaevola : brave Gabar, who stood firm, lost his right hand cut off in the fight ; and while Sicca, stricken with grief, hastened to help his friend, he trod incautiously upon a sword and fell, cursing too late his unshod feet ; and there he lay on the right hand of his dying comrade. At last the increasing fury of Scaevola attracted the deadly weapons of lightning-swift Nealces. The Carthaginian sprang forward, eager for the rewards of victory, and made more eager by Scaevola's famous name. He seized a boulder torn by a torrent from a cliff and carried down from the lofty mountains, and hurled it furiously in Scaevola's face. His teeth rattled, struck by that heavy weight ; his features were destroyed ; matter, mixed with brains and blood, gushed out through the nostrils, and a black discharge from the eyes flowed down from the crushed eye-sockets and mutilated forehead. Then Marius fell, while striving to rescue his friend, Caper, and fearing to survive his fall. They were born on the same day, and poverty was the lot of both their families ; they were natives of the sacred city, Praeneste ; they had been school-fellows, and the fields they tilled lay close together. In liking and disliking they never differed ; it was a lifelong marriage of two minds ; and brotherly love made then rich in poverty. In death they were not divided ; and of all their prayers Fortune granted

id Fortuna dedit, iunctam inter proelia mortem.
arma fuere decus victori bina Symaetho.
  Sed longum tanto laetari munere casus
haud licitum Poenis. aderat terrore minaci
Scipio, conversae miseratus terga cohortis,
et cuncti fons Varro mali flavusque comarum
Curio et a primo descendens consule Brutus.
atque his fulta viris acies repararet ademptum
mole nova campum, subito ni turbine Poenus
agmina frenasset iam procurrentia ductor.
isque ut Varronem procul inter proelia vidit
et iuxta sagulo circumvolitare rubenti
lictorem : " nosco pompam atque insignia nosco ;
Flaminius modo talis," ait. tum fervidus acrem
ingentis clipei tonitru praenuntiat iram.
heu miser ! aequari potuisti funere Paulo,
si tibi non ira superum tunc esset ademptum
Hannibalis cecidisse manu. quam saepe querere,
Varro, deis, quod Sidonium defugeris ensem !
nam, rapido subitam portans in morte salutem
procursu incepta, in sese discrimina vertit
Scipio ; nec Poenum, quamquam est ereptus opimae
caedis honor, mutasse piget maiore sub hoste
proelia et erepti Ticina ad flumina patris
exigere oblato tandem certamine poenas.
stabant educti diversis orbis in oris,
quantos non alios vidit concurrere tellus

[a] The first consuls, elected after the expulsion of the kings in 509 B.C., were L. Junius Brutus and L. Tarquinius Collatinus.

[b] These were never gained except by a commander who slew the commander of the enemy ; and Varro was in command that day : see note to iii. 587.

them one only—to die in battle side by side. The armour of both became the prize of Symaethus, their conqueror.

But the Carthaginians were not permitted to enjoy for long so great a gift of Fortune. For Scipio, pitying the men whose backs were turned in flight, came up, terrible and menacing ; and with him came Varro, the cause of all the suffering, and fair-haired Curio, and Brutus whose ancestor was the first consul.[a] Supported by these warriors, the army would have regained the lost ground by a fresh effort, had not the sudden onset of Hannibal arrested the ranks as they ran forward. When he saw Varro far off on the field and the lictors in their scarlet tunics moving round him, "Ha!" he cried; "I recognize the state and the badges of a consul; even so looked Flaminius, not long ago." Then in fury he thundered on his huge shield, to signify his eager rage. Unhappy Varro! Death might have made him the equal of Paulus ; but heaven's wrath would not suffer him to fall there by Hannibal's hand. How often was he to reproach the gods for saving him from the sword of the Carthaginian! For Scipio rushed forward and quickly brought life where death was imminent, and turned the danger from Varro to himself. And Hannibal, though he lost the glory of winning the choicest spoils,[b] was not sorry to change his antagonist for one more mighty, and to punish Scipio for rescuing his father by the river Ticinus,[c] now that the chance of a duel was at last offered him. There they stood, the two mightiest warriors that earth has ever seen meet in battle ; reared in far distant lands, in

[c] See iv. 454 foll.

Marte viri dextraque pares, sed cetera ductor
anteibat Latius, melior pietate fideque.
  Desiluere cava turbati ad proelia nube,
Mavors Scipiadae metuens, Tritonia Poeno;
adventuque deum, intrepidis ductoribus, ambae
contremuere acies. ater, qua pectora flectit
Pallas, Gorgoneo late micat ignis ab ore,
sibilaque horrificis torquet serpentibus aegis.
fulgent sanguinei, geminum vibrare cometem
ut credas, oculi; summaque in casside largus
undantes volvit flammas ad sidera vertex.
at Mavors, moto proturbans aëra telo
et clipeo campum involvens, Aetnaea Cyclopum
munere fundentem loricam incendia gestat
ac pulsat fulva consurgens aethera crista.
  Ductores pugnae intenti, quantumque vicissim
auderent, propius mensi, tamen arma ferentes
sensere advenisse deos et, laetus uterque
spectari superis, addebant mentibus iras.
iamque ictu valido libratam a pectore Poeni
Pallas in obliquum dextra detorserat hastam,
et Gradivus, opem divae portare ferocis
exemplo doctus, porgebat protinus ensem
Aetnaeum in pugnas iuveni ac maiora iubebat.
tum Virgo, ignescens penitus, violenta repente
suffudit flammis ora atque, obliqua retorquens
lumina, turbato superavit Gorgona vultu.
erexere omnes immania membra chelydri

[a] The shield of Pallas, called the aegis, displayed the snaky head of the Gorgon, Medusa, in its centre.

[b] See iv. 433.

prowess they were well matched; but otherwise the Roman was superior—in sense of duty and of honour.

Then Mars, fearing for Scipio, and Pallas, fearing for Hannibal, lighted down in haste from a hollow cloud upon the battle-field. And the appearance of the gods made both armies tremble, but the champions were undismayed. Wherever Pallas turned her breast, a baleful fire flashed far and wide from the Gorgon's face,[a] and the dreadful serpents on the aegis sent forth their hissings. Her blood-shot eyes blazed—one might think that a pair of comets were flashing—and the ample crest that crowned her helmet rolled waves of flame to the sky. And Mars, driving the air before him by the movement of his spear, and covering the plain with his shield, wore a breastplate, the gift of the Cyclopes,[b] which sent forth fire of Etna; and, as he rose high, his golden plume struck the heavens.

The champions, though on battle bent and each measuring at close quarters what he could dare to do, were aware, nevertheless, that gods had come down in arms; and both rejoiced to have them for witnesses and became more eager for battle. And now Pallas turned aside with her right hand the spear strongly hurled at Hannibal's breast; and Mars, taught by the example of the fierce goddess to help Scipio, straightway put in his hand a sword forged on Aetna, and bade him do yet mightier deeds. Then the Maiden was roused to fury: a sudden flush suffused her fierce countenance; and, when she looked askance, her disordered aspect was more terrible than the Gorgon's face. She shook her aegis, and all the serpents reared up their hideous bodies;

aegide commota, primique furoris ad ictus
rettulit ipse pedem sensim a certamine Mavors.
hic dea convulsam rapido conamine partem
vicini montis scopulisque horrentia saxa
in Martem furibunda iacit, longeque relatos
expavit sonitus, tremefacto litore, Sason.
At non haec superum fallebant proelia regem.
demittit propere succinctam nubibus Irim,
quae nimios frenet motus, ac talia fatur:
"I, dea, et Oenotris velox allabere terris
germanoque truces, dic, Pallas mitiget iras
nec speret fixas Parcarum vertere leges;
dic etiam: ni desistis (nam virus et aestus
flammiferae novi mentis) nec corripis iram,
aegida praecellant quantum horrida fulmina, nosces."
Quae postquam accepit dubitans Tritonia virgo
nec sat certa diu, patriis an cederet armis,
"absistemus," ait, "campo: sed Pallade pulsa
num fata avertet? caeloque arcebit ab alto
cernere Gargani ferventia caedibus arva?"
haec effata cava Poenum in certamina nube
sublatum diversa tulit terrasque reliquit.
At Gradivus atrox remeantis in aethera divae
abscessu revocat mentes fusosque per aequor
ipse manu magna, nebulam circumdatus, acri
restituit pugnae. convertunt signa novamque
instaurant Itali, versa formidine, caedem:
cum ventis positus custos, cui flamina carcer
imperio compressa tenet caelumque ruentes

---

[a] See note to vii. 480.
[b] Italy: see note to i. 2.
[c] See note to iii. 323.
[d] Aeolus.

and her first furious onset made even Mars retreat step by step from the fray. Then the angry goddess quickly tore away part of a mountain near her and hurled the mass of rugged rock at Mars; and the noise, carried far away, terrified the isle of Saso [a] and shook its shores.

But this duel was not hidden from the King of Heaven. He made haste to send Iris down, girt about with clouds, to quell their exceeding wrath. "Go, goddess," he said, "and glide swiftly down to the land of Oenotria [b]; and bid Pallas to abate her fury against her brother, and not to hope that she can reverse the fixed laws of Fate. Tell her this also: if she persists and still cherishes her anger—for I know the fierceness and rage of her fiery heart—she shall learn how far my dreadful thunderbolts outdo her aegis."

When the maiden of Tritonis [c] heard this message, she doubted for a space, uncertain whether to yield to her father's weapons. "I shall quit the field," she said; "but can his defeat of Pallas turn destiny aside? Or can he from his height in heaven avoid seeing the fields of Garganus reek with carnage?" Thus she spoke, and caught up Hannibal in the bosom of a cloud and bore him to a distant part of the field. Then she left the earth.

But Mars, encouraged by the retreat of the goddess to the sky, renewed his purpose. Hidden in a cloud, he raised with his own mighty hand the Romans prostrate on the field and brought them back to battle. They turned their standards about and began a fresh slaughter, and fear fell upon the foe. But now the gaoler of the winds,[d] whose prison keeps the blasts under control, and who is obeyed by every wind that

Eurique et Boreae parent Caurique Notique,
Iunonis precibus, promissa haud parva ferentis,
regnantem Aetolis Vulturnum in proelia campis
effrenat: placet hic irae exitiabilis ultor.
qui, se postquam Aetnae mersit candente barathro
concepitque ignes et flammea protulit ora,
evolat horrendo stridore ac Daunia regna
perflat, agens caecam glomerato pulvere nubem.
eripuere oculos aurae vocemque manusque;
vortice harenoso candentes, flebile dictu,
torquet in ora globos Italum et bellare maniplis
iussa laetatur rabie. tum mole ruinae
sternuntur tellure et miles et arma tubaeque;
atque omnis retro flatu occursante refertur
lancea, et in tergum Rutulis cadit irritus ictus.
atque idem flatus Poenorum tela secundant,
et velut ammento contorta hastilia turbo
adiuvat ac Tyrias impellit stridulus hastas.
tum, denso fauces praeclusus pulvere, miles
ignavam mortem compresso maeret hiatu.
ipse, caput flavum caligine conditus atra,
Vulturnus, multaque comam perfusus harena,
nunc versos agit a tergo stridentibus alis,
nunc, mediam in frontem veniens clamante procella,
obvius arma quatit patuloque insibilat ore.
interdum intentos pugnae et iam iamque ferentes
hostili iugulo ferrum conamine et ictu
avertit dextramque ipso de vulnere vellit.
nec satis Ausonias passim foedare cohortes:

---

[a] An E.S.E. wind that got up daily about the same hour: it blew the dust over the plains of Apulia and blinded the Romans: see note to viii. 663. The wind is here personified.

[b] See note to i. 318.

sweeps the sky—Eurus and Boreas, Caurus and Notus—yielded to the prayer of Juno who offered him no small rewards, and unchained for battle the fury of Vulturnus,[a] the wind that is lord of the Aetolian plains. Him she chose as the instrument of her deadly wrath. First he dived into the white-hot crater of Etna and caught fire from there; then he lifted up his flaming face, and flew forth with a dreadful roaring over all the land of Daunus, driving before him a dark cloud of thick dust. The blast made the Romans blind and dumb and helpless; the wind whirled fiery masses of eddying sand—piteous to tell—into their faces, and rejoiced to obey orders and fight furiously against the ranks. Then in vast destruction down fell soldiers and weapons and trumpets; and every lance was carried backwards by the blast, and every Roman missile fell useless behind their own backs. And the same blast was of service to the Carthaginian weapons: the howling wind quickened their javelins, as if they had been launched with a thong,[b] and drove their spears onward. At last the soldiers, stifled by the thick dust, shut their mouths tight, and mourned that they must die an inglorious death. Vulturnus himself, his fair hair hidden in black darkness and covered deep with sand, at one time turned his victims round and assailed their backs with his hissing wings; at another time he attacked them in front with boisterous blast, rattling their weapons full in face, and hissing at them with open mouth. Sometimes, when they were bent on battle and just bringing their swords to an enemy's throat, the wind thwarted the intended blow and plucked away the hand in the very act of striking. Nor was he content with spreading havoc

in Martem vomit immixtas mugitibus auras
bisque dei summas vibravit turbine cristas.
  Quae dum Romuleis exercet proelia turmis
Aeolius furor et Martem succendit in iras,
affatur Virgo, socia Iunone, parentem :
"quantos Gradivus fluctus in Punica castra,
respice, agit quantisque furens se caedibus implet !
nunc, quaeso, terris descendere non placet Irim ?
quamquam ego non Teucros (nostro cum pignore regnet
Roma, et Palladio sedes hac urbe locarim)
non Teucros delere aderam ; sed lumen alumnae
Hannibalem Libyae pelli florentibus annis
vita atque extingui primordia tanta negabam."
  Excipit hic Iuno longique laboris ab ira,
" immo," ait, " ut noscant gentes, immania quantum
regna Iovis valeant, cunctisque potentia quantum
antistet, coniux, superis tua, disice telo
flagranti (nil oramus) Carthaginis arces
Sidoniamque aciem vasto telluris hiatu
Tartareis immerge vadis aut obrue ponto."
  Contra quae miti respondet Iupiter ore :
" certatis fatis et spes extenditis aegras.
ille, o nata, libens cui tela inimica ferebas,
contundet iuvenis Tyrios ac nomina gentis
induet et Libycam feret in Capitolia laurum.
at, cui tu, coniux, cui das animosque decusque
(fata cano) avertet populis Laurentibus arma.

---

[a] An image of Pallas which fell from heaven and was kept at Troy : it was brought by Aeneas to Italy and was kept in the temple of Vesta at Rome : the safety of the city was believed to depend upon its preservation. See note to i. 659.

[b] Scipio, who won the title of Africanus after the battle of Zama.

through the Roman army, but belched forth his howling blasts against Mars himself, and the hurricane twice caused the god's topmost crest to quiver.

While the fury of the wind battled thus against the Roman troops and kindled the anger of Mars, the Maiden Goddess together with Juno addressed her Father thus: "See the storms that Mars is rousing against the ranks of Carthage, and the carnage with which he gluts his fury. Say, is it not thy pleasure now that Iris should go down to earth? Yet the purpose of my presence there was not to destroy the Trojans—let Rome hold empire together with my pledge, and there I would fix the abode of the Palladium [a]—no, but I would not allow Hannibal, the glory of my Libyan birthplace, to be slain in the flower of his youth, and such promise to be nipped in the bud."

Then Juno took up the tale, wrathful at her unending task: "Nay!" she cried: "that all the world may know the immense extent of thy power and thy vast superiority over all the gods, use thy flaming bolt, my husband, to shatter the citadels of Carthage—I beg for no mercy—and bury her soldiers in a huge chasm of the earth and plunge them in the depths of Tartarus, or whelm them in the sea."

Then Jupiter made answer with gentle words: "Ye strive against destiny, and cherish unsound hopes. That young warrior,[b] against whom thou, my daughter, wert fain to fight, shall destroy the Carthaginians and assume their name and bear to the Capitol the laurel for the conquest of Libya. That other to whom thou, my wife, givest courage and glory—I tell his fortune—shall turn his sword

nec longe cladis metae : venit hora diesque,
qua nullas umquam transisse optaverit Alpes."
sic ait atque Irim propere demittit Olympo,
quae revocet Martem iubeatque abscedere pugna.
nec vetitis luctatus abit Gradivus in altas
cum fremitu nubes, quamquam lituique tubaeque
vulneraque et sanguis et clamor et arma iuvarent.

Ut patuit liber superum certamine tandem
laxatusque deo campus, ruit aequore ab imo
Poenus, quo sensim caelestia fugerat arma,
magna voce trahens equitemque virosque feraeque
turrigerae molem tormentorumque labores.
atque ubi turbantem leviores ense catervas
agnovit iuvenem, scintillavitque cruentis
ira genis : " quaenam Furiae quisve egit in hostem,
en, Minuci, deus, ut rursus te credere nobis
auderes ? " inquit. " genitor tibi natus ab armis
ille meis, ubi nunc Fabius ? semel, improbe, nostras
sit satis evasisse manus." atque inde superbis
hasta comes dictis murali turbine pectus
transforat et voces venturas occupat ictu.

Nec ferro saevire sat est : appellitur atra
mole fera, et monstris componitur Itala pubes.
nam, praevectus equo, moderantem cuspide Lucas
Maurum in bella boves stimulis maioribus ire
ac raptare iubet Libycarum armenta ferarum.

---

[a] See vii. 736 foll.

[b] This name was given to elephants, when the Romans first saw them in Lucania about 280 B.C. in the army of Pyrrhus, king of Epirus.

away from the Italian nation. The date of disaster is not distant: the day and hour are coming, when he shall regret that he ever crossed the Alps." Thus Jupiter spoke and sent Iris down in haste from Olympus, to recall Mars and bid him leave the battle. And Mars did not refuse to obey: he departed, loudly protesting, to high heaven, delighting as he did in clarions and trumpets, in wounds and blood and the shouting of the warriors.

When the field was free at last from the contending gods, and Mars no longer filled the plain, Hannibal rushed up from the remotest part of the battle, whither he had fled step by step before the divine weapons. With a great shout he brought with him horsemen and footmen and heavy siege-engines, and the huge beasts that carry towers on their backs. And when he recognized a warrior harassing the light-armed troops with his sword, anger flashed from his blood-stained features: "What Fury," he cried, "what god has driven you to battle, Minucius, that you should dare to face me a second time?[a] Where is Fabius now, he who was once a father to you and saved you from my spear? You ask too much: be content with having escaped once from my hand." Then, together with his insults his spear went forth and pierced the breast of Minucius with the force of a battering-ram, and cut off the reply he would have uttered.

Nor was the steel enough to gratify his rage. The huge black beasts were brought up, and the Roman soldiers were matched against monsters. For Hannibal rode along the line, and ordered the Moors, whose goads controlled the Lucan kine[b] in battle, to prick their charges to speed, and to hasten forward

immane stridens agitur, crebroque coacta
vulnere, bellatrix properos fert belua gressus.
liventi dorso turris, flammaque virisque
et iaculis armata, sedet; procul aspera grando
saxorum super arma ruit, passimque volanti
celsus telorum fundit Libys aggere nimbum.
stat niveis longum stipata per agmina vallum
dentibus, atque ebori praefixa comminus hasta
fulget ab incurvo derecta cacumine cuspis.
hic, inter trepidos rerum, per membra, per arma
exigit Ufentis sceleratum belua dentem
clamantemque ferens calcata per agmina portat.
nec levius Tadio letum: qua tegmine thorax
multiplicis lini claudit latus, improba sensim,
corpore non laeso, penetrarunt spicula dentis
et sublime virum, clipeo resonante, tulerunt.
haud excussa novi virtus terrore pericli.
utitur ad laudem casu geminumque citato
vicinus fronti lumen transverberat ense.
exstimulata gravi sese fera tollit ad auras
vulnere et erectis excussam cruribus alte
pone iacit volvens reflexo pondere turrim.
arma virique simul spoliataque belua visu
sternuntur subita, miserandum, mixta ruina.

Spargi flagrantes contra bellantia monstra
Dardanius taedas ductor iubet et facis atrae,
quos fera circumfert, compleri sulphure muros.
nec iusso mora: collectis fumantia lucent
terga elephantorum flammis; pastusque sonoro
ignis edax vento per propugnacula fertur.

the herd of elephants. Trumpeting wildly, and compelled by many a stab, the great beasts of war came quickly on. A tower, freighted with men and javelins and fire, was borne on each dusky back and discharged a fierce hail of stones over the distant ranks; and the Libyans, seated aloft, poured a shower of darts all round from their moving rampart. The line of white tusks stretched far in serried ranks; and to each tusk was fastened a blade, whose point came close and flashed down straight from the curved upper part. Here, in the general alarm, an elephant drove its murderous tusk through the armour and body of Ufens and carried him shrieking through the trampled ranks. Nor had Tadius an easier death: where the corslet with its many folds of linen protected his body, the persistent point of a tusk bored its way in by degrees and then swung the man aloft unwounded, while his shield rang. The brave man was not terrified by danger in this strange form, but turned it to glorious account: when close to the elephant's forehead, he stabbed both its eyes with quick thrusts of his sword. Maddened by the grievous wound, the beast rose on its hind legs and reared up till it threw off the heavy tower on the ground behind it. A piteous sight, when weapons and men and the blinded beast suddenly came crashing down together to the ground!

The Roman general ordered his men to hurl lighted torches against the fighting monsters, and to shower dark sulphurous brands upon the moving forts carried by the elephants. They obeyed at once: the backs of the beasts sent up smoke and flame, as the fire grew; and fed by the roaring wind, it spread over the fighting-towers and devoured them. Even so,

non aliter, Pindo Rhodopeve incendia pastor
cum iacit, et silvis spatiatur fervida pestis,
frondosi ignescunt scopuli ; subitoque per alta
collucet iuga dissultans Vulcanius ardor.
it fera candenti torrente bitumine corpus
amens et laxo diducit limite turmas.
nec cuiquam virtus propiora capessere bella :
longinquis audent iaculis et harundinis ictu.
uritur impatiens et magni corporis aestu
huc atque huc iactas accendit belua flammas,
donec vicini tandem se fluminis undis
praecipitem dedit et, tenui decepta liquore
stagnantis per plana vadi, tulit incita longis
exstantem ripis flammam ; tum denique sese
gurgitis immersit molem capiente profundo.

At qua pugna datur, necdum Maurusia pestis
igne calet, circumfusi Rhoeteia pubes
nunc iaculis, nunc et saxis, nunc alite plumbo
eminus incessunt, ut qui castella per altos
oppugnat munita locos atque assidet arces.
ausus digna viro, fortuna digna secunda,
extulerat dextram atque adversum comminus ensem
Mincius, infelix ausi ; sed stridula, anhelum
fervorem effundens, monstri manus abstulit acri
implicitum nexu diroque ligamine torsit
et superas alte miserum iaculata per auras
telluri elisis afflixit, flebile, membris.

Has inter clades viso Varrone sub armis
increpitans Paulus : " quin imus comminus," inquit,

[a] Famous mountains in Thessaly and Thrace. For improving pasture by burning see note to vii. 365.

when the shepherd burns the grass on Pindus or Rhodope,[a] and the fierce blaze spreads through the woods, the leaf-clad heights catch fire ; and suddenly the flame of fire leaps from point to point and shines over all the lofty range. Scorched by the burning pitch, the beasts ran wild and cleared a wide path through the ranks. Nor was any man bold enough to fight them at close quarters : to attack from a distance with javelins and showers of arrows was all they dared. Maddened by the heat, the huge beasts in their torment tossed the fire on all sides and spread it, till they plunged headlong into the stream beside them. But deceived by the shallow water that overflowed the level plain, they rushed far along the banks, and the flame, rising above the water, went with them. At last they dived beneath the stream, where the water was deep enough to cover their huge bodies.

But, where battle was possible, and before the Moorish monsters were set on fire, the Roman soldiers surrounded them at a distance and assailed them with javelins and stones and flying bullets, like men besieging a citadel or attacking a fortified place on high ground. Mincius showed courage worthy of a warrior and worthy of better fortune : coming close, he raised up his drawn sword ; but his brave deed miscarried ; for the trunk of the trumpeting monster, discharging hot and panting breath, wound its angry coils round him and lifted him up ; then it brandished his body in that dreadful grasp, and hurled it high in air, and dashed the crushed limbs of the poor wretch upon the ground—a mournful sight.

Amid these disasters Paulus sighted Varro on the field and thus taunted him: "Why are we not

" ductori Tyrio, quem vinctum colla catenis
staturum ante tuos currus promisimus urbi ?
heu patria, heu plebes scelerata et prava favoris !
haud umquam expedies tam dura sorte malorum,
quem tibi non nasci fuerit per vota petendum,
Varronem Hannibalemne, magis." dum talia Paulus,
urget praecipites Libys atque in terga ruentum
ante oculos cunctas ductoris concitat hastas.
pulsatur galea et quatiuntur consulis arma ;
acrius hoc Paulus medios ruit asper in hostes.
Tum vero excussus mentem, in certamina Paulo
avia diducto, convertit Varro manuque
cornipedem inflectens, "das," inquit, "patria, poenas,
quae, Fabio incolumi, Varronem ad bella vocasti.
quaenam autem mentis vel quae discordia fati ?
Parcarumne latens fraus est ? abrumpere cuncta
iamdudum cum luce libet ; sed comprimit ensem
nescio qui deus et meme ad graviora reservat.
vivamne ? et fractos sparsosque cruore meorum
hos referam populo fasces ? atque ora per urbes
iratas spectanda dabo ? et, quo saevius ipse
Hannibal haud poscat, fugiam et te, Roma, videbo ? "
plura indignantem telis propioribus hostes
egere, et sonipes rapuit laxatus habenas.

---

[a] They did this when they elected Varro consul.

[b] The towns of Italy through which he must pass on his way to Rome. The meaning of the paragraph seems to be, that the gods saved Varro from death, in order that the Romans might show magnanimity by welcoming him on his return to Rome : see x. 615 foll.

fighting Hannibal hand to hand? Did we not promise Rome that he should stand with fetters round his neck before your triumphal car? Alas for our country! Alas for our people who in their wickedness bestow their favour amiss![a] Now that they are suffering such calamities, they will find no answer to this question: was Varro's birth or Hannibal's the worse calamity? and which should they have prayed Heaven to avert?" While Paulus spoke thus, Hannibal pressed hard on the flying Romans, and discharged all the spears of Carthage against their backs, in full view of Paulus. The consul's helmet was struck and his shield battered; but on he rushed, none the less fiercely, into the centre of the foe.

But now, when Paulus had parted from him and gone to fight far away, Varro's reason tottered. He pulled at the bridle and turned his horse round and said: "Rome, thou art punished now for having put Varro in command while Fabius still lived. But what means this divided mind, this change of fortune? Is it a trap laid for me by the Fates? I long to make an instant end of all things by taking my own life. But some god arrests my sword and keeps me alive that I may suffer even worse. Can I live and carry back to Rome these rods, broken and spattered with the blood of citizens? How shall I show my hated face through the towns of Italy?[b] How shall I, a fugitive from battle, see Rome again? Hannibal himself could desire for me no more cruel punishment."

Further protest was cut short by the approach of the enemy: their attack drove him back, and his war-horse with loosened rein carried him swiftly away.

LIBER DECIMUS

ARGUMENT

Description of the battle continued : valour and death of Paulus (1-325). *Flushed with victory, Hannibal intends to march on Rome next day ; but Juno sends the god of Sleep to stop him* (326-370). *He yields, in spite of the strong protests of Mago* (371-386). *The remnant of the Roman army rally at Canusium : their miserable plight* (387-414). *Metellus proposes that the Romans should leave Italy ; but Scipio threatens death to him and his sympathizers* (415-

Paulus, ut adversam videt increbrescere pugnam,
ceu fera, quae, telis circumcingentibus, ultro
assilit in ferrum et per vulnera colligit hostem,
in medios fert arma globos seseque periclis
ingerit atque omni letum molitur ab ense.
increpat horrendum : " perstate et fortiter, oro,
pectoribus ferrum accipite ac sine vulnere terga
ad manes deferte, viri : nisi gloria mortis,
nil superest. idem sedes adeuntibus imas
hic vobis dux Paulus erit." velocius inde
Haemonio Borea pennaque citatior ibat·
quae redit in pugnas fugientis harundine Parthi ;
atque ubi certamen primi ciet immemor aevi,
plenus Gradivo mentem, Cato, fertur in hostes

---

[a] See note to ix. 367.

[b] Haemonia is a common synonym for Thessaly.

BOOK X

ARGUMENT (*continued*)

448). *Hannibal surveys the battle-field: the faithful horse of Cloelius: the story of his ancestress, Cloelia: the body of Paulus is found and buried* (449-577). *Distress at Rome* (578-591). *Fabius encourages his countrymen* (592-604). *He also calms the fury of the populace against Varro* (605-622). *Varro returns to Rome* (623-639). *The Senate adopts measures to enlist soldiers and continue the war* (640-658).

When Paulus saw that the enemy was gaining ground, even as a wild beast dashes of its own accord upon the ring of spears that surrounds it, and so, at the cost of wounds, brings its assailants closer, so he fought his way to the centre of the battle, rushing into every danger and courting death from every sword. He cried to his men with a terrible voice: "Stand firm, I implore you, and receive the steel in your breasts without flinching, and carry unwounded backs to the world below.[a] Nothing remains save a glorious death. I, Paulus, shall be your leader still as you go down to Hades." Then on he went, swifter than Thessalian[b] Boreas or the arrow that comes back to the fight from the bow of the retreating Parthian. Where Cato, full of martial spirit and forgetful of his youth,[c] was fighting, Paulus rushed

[c] Cato, born in 234 B.C., would be eighteen at this date (216 B.C.): see vii. 691.

ac iuvenem, quem Vasco levis, quem spicula densus
Cantaber urgebat, letalibus eripit armis.
abscessere retro pavidique in terga relatos
abduxere gradus ; ut, laetus valle remota
cum capream venator agit fessamque propinquo
insequitur cursu et sperat iam tangere dextra,
si ferus adverso subitum se protulit antro
et stetit ante oculos frendens leo, deserit una
et color et sanguis et tela minora periclo,
nec iam speratae cura est in pectore praedae.
nunc in restantes mucronem comminus urget,
nunc trepidos ac terga mala formidine versos
assequitur telis. furere ac decorare labores
et saevire iuvat ; cadit ingens nominis expers
uni turba viro ; atque alter si detur in armis
Paulus Dardaniis, amittant nomina Cannae.

Tandem inclinato cornu sine more ruebat
prima acies, non parca fugae. Labienus et Ocres
sternuntur leto atque Opiter, quos Setia colle
vitifero, celsis Labienum Cingula saxa
miserunt muris. iunxit fera tempora leti
Sidonius non consimili discrimine miles :
nam Labienus obit penetrante per ilia corno ;
fratres, hic humero, cecidere, hic poplite, caesis.
oppetis et Tyrio super inguina fixe veruto
Maecenas, cui Maeonia venerabile terra
et sceptris olim celebratum nomen Etruscis.
per medios agitur, proiecto lucis amore

[a] *i.e.* would not have been a defeat of the Romans.

[b] Cingulum is a town in Picenum, which T. Labienus, the officer who went over from Caesar to Pompey at the beginning of the Civil War, rebuilt at his own expense. This fact may account for the use of the name here.

upon the foe and rescued the youth from death, when he was hard pressed by nimble Vascones and Cantabrians with showers of darts. The foemen fell back and withdrew in fear. So a hunter gleefully chases a roe-deer in a distant valley, and follows close till it is weary, hoping soon to put his hand upon it; but, if a fierce lion suddenly emerges from a cave before him and stands in full view, gnashing its teeth, then the red blood leaves the hunter's cheeks, and he drops the weapon that will not serve him at such a pass, and thinks no longer of the quarry he once counted on. Now Paulus thrust his sword-point at close range against foes who held their ground; now his missiles overtook the frightened cowards who turned their backs. He finds pleasure in fierce frenzy and gains glory from defeat; a multitude of nameless enemies fall before his single sword; and, had but a second Paulus been present in the Roman host, Cannae would have lost its fame.[a]

At last the Roman wing gave way and the front rank fell to pieces in full retreat. Ocres and Opiter, who came from the vine-clad hills of Setia, were slain, and likewise Labienus, whom rocky Cingulum sent from its high walls.[b] Soldiers of Carthage slew them all at the same time but in different ways; for Labienus was run through the body by a spear; and, of the brothers, one was wounded in the shoulder, and the other in the thigh, when they fell. Maecenas too was slain by a dart that pierced his groin; his name was held in high honour in the Lydian land[c] where his ancestors once were kings over Etruria. Despising life, Paulus pressed through the centre of

[c] Etruria: see note to vii. 29.

Hannibalem lustrans, Paulus : sors una videtur
aspera, si occumbat ductore superstite Poeno.
Quam metuens molem (neque enim, certamine sumpto,
tempestas tanta et rabies impune fuisset)
in faciem pavidi Iuno conversa Metelli :
" quid vanos," inquit, " Latio spes unica consul,
incassumque moves, fato renuente, furores ?
si superest Paulus, restant Aeneia regna ;
sin secus, Ausoniam tecum trahis. ire tumentem
tu contra iuvenem et caput hoc abscidere rebus
turbatis, o Paule, paras ? nunc Hannibal ipsi
(tam laetus bello est) ausit certare Tonanti.
et iam conversis (vidi nam flectere) habenis
evasit Varro ac sese ad meliora reservat.
sit spatium fatis ; et, dum datur, eripe leto
hanc nostris maiorem animam ; mox bella capesses."
Ad quae suspirans ductor : " mortemne sub armis
cur poscam, causa ista parum est, quod talia nostrae
pertulerunt aures suadentem monstra Metellum ?
i, demens, i, carpe fugam. non hostica tela
excipias tergo, superos precor : integer, oro,
intactusque abeas atque intres moenia Romae
cum Varrone simul. talin', pavidissime, dignum
me vita pulchraque indignum morte putasti ?
quippe furit Poenus, qui nunc contraria bella
ipsi ferre Iovi valeat. pro degener altae
virtutis patrum ! quando certamen inire,

[a] L. Caecilius Metellus, who later advised the Romans to abandon Rome after the defeat at Cannae : see ll. 415 foll.

the fray, seeking Hannibal; there was but one fate he dreaded—to die and leave the Carthaginian general alive.

But Juno feared the man's might; for, if a duel began, such a storm of passion would not have ended in nothing. Therefore she took the form of cowardly Metellus[a]: "Why," she asked, "do you, the consul on whom alone the hopes of Rome depend, defy Fortune and rage furiously to no purpose? If Paulus survives, the empire of Rome still stands; if he dies, he drags down his country with him. Do you mean, Paulus, to go forth against that warrior in his pride, and to deprive us of our leader in our time of trouble? Just now, in his joy of battle, Hannibal would dare to fight the Thunderer himself. Already Varro has turned his bridle-rein—I saw him do it—and made off, reserving himself for better times. Give Fate time to work; and, while you may, snatch from death a life that matters more than ours; you will have fighting enough hereafter."

Paulus sighed and answered: "Have I not cause enough to seek death in battle, when my ears have heard such infamous counsel from a Metellus? Fly, madman, fly! I pray heaven that no weapon of the enemy may wound you in the back.[b] Untouched and unscathed may you depart and enter the gates of Rome with Varro as your companion! Worst of cowards, did you think me worthy of life on such terms and unworthy of a noble death? Hannibal forsooth is raging, he whose valour would now challenge Jupiter himself. How far have you declined from the high emprise of your ancestors! When could

[b] See note to ix. 367.

cuive virum mallem memet componere, quam qui
et victus dabit et victor per saecula nomen ? "
  Talibus increpitat mediosque aufertur in hostes
ac retro cursum tendentem ad crebra suorum
agmina et in densis furantem membra maniplis
per conferta virum et stipata umbonibus arma
consequitur, melior planta, atque obtruncat Acherram.
ut canis occultos agitat cum Belgicus apros
erroresque ferae sollers per devia mersa
nare legit tacitoque premens vestigia rostro
lustrat inaccessos venantum indagine saltus
nec sistit nisi, conceptum sectatus odorem,
deprendit spissis arcana cubilia dumis.
  At coniux Iovis, ut Paulum depellere dictis
nequiquam fuit, et consul non desinit irae,
in faciem Mauri rursus mutata Gelestae,
avocat ignarum saevo a certamine Poenum :
" huc tela, huc," inquit, " dextram implorantibus affer,
o decus aeternum Carthaginis. horrida iuxta
stagnantes consul molitur proelia ripas ;
et laus haud alio maior datur hoste perempto."
haec ait et iuvenem diversa ad proelia raptat.
  Flumineo Libycam turbabat in aggere pubem—
Cristae nomen erat. bis terni iuncta ferebant
arma senem circa nati ; pauperque penatum,
sed domus haud obscura Tuder, notusque per Umbros
bellator populos factis et caede docebat

[a] See note to vi. 645.

I prefer to fight or against whom to match myself? Hannibal, whether conqueror or conquered, will make my name famous for ever."

Uttering such reproaches, Paulus sped off to the centre of the foe. Acherras was making his way back to where the ranks of his supporters were thick, and finding a path by stealth through close-packed warriors and a hedge of shields; but Paulus, swifter of foot, overtook and slew him. So a Belgian hound pursues a boar he cannot see; never giving tongue, with nose to the ground he tracks unerringly the beast's wanderings over hill and dale, and ranges over uplands that no line of hunters has ever surrounded; nor does he cease from following the scent once caught, till he comes upon the lair hidden deep in the thorn-brakes.

But the consort of Jupiter, when Paulus would not cease from fighting and her words proved unavailing to stop him, changed her form again: she took the likeness of the Moor, Gelesta, and summoned Hannibal, who knew her not, away from the heat of battle. "Glory of Carthage," she said, "whose fame will never die, we implore you to turn hither your armed right hand; for Paulus is fighting fiercely by the banks of the swollen river; and the death of no other foeman can bring you greater fame." With these words she hastened Hannibal to a distant part of the field.

On the high bank of the river a warrior named Crista harassed the African host; and his six sons fought together round their father. The family was poor but known to fame among the Tudertes [a]; and Crista himself had a name for deeds of arms throughout Umbria, and taught all his troop of sons to bear

natorum armigeram pugnas tractare cohortem.
unanima inde phalanx, crudo ducente magistro,
postquam hominum satiata nece est, prostraverat ictu
innumero cum turre feram, facibusque secutis
ardentem monstri spectabat laeta ruinam,
cum subitus galeae fulgor conoque coruscae
maiore intremuere iubae ; nec tarda senectus
(agnovit nam luce virum) rapit agmina, natos,
saeva parens ultro in certamina et addere passim
tela iubet nec manantes ex ore feroci,
aut quae flagrarent galea, exhorrescere flammas.
armiger haud aliter magni Iovis, anxia nido
cum dignos nutrit gestanda ad fulmina fetus,
obversam spectans ora ad Phaethontia prolem,
explorat dubios Phoebea lampade natos.
iamque suis daret ut pugnae documenta vocantis,
en—medias hasta velox praetervolat auras.
haesit multiplici non alte cuspis in auro
ac senium invalido dependens prodidit ictu.
cui Poenus : " quinam ad cassos furor impulit ictus
exsanguem senio dextram ? vix prima momordit
tegmina Callaici cornus tremebunda metalli.
en, reddo tua tela tibi ; memorabilis ista
a nobis melius discet bellare iuventus."
sic propria miseri transfigit pectora corno.

At contra, horrendum, bis terna spicula dextra
torta volant, paribusque ruunt conatibus hastae.
haud secus ac Libyca fetam tellure leaenam

---

[a] The mother-eagle was supposed to throw out of the nest as spurious any eaglet that was unable to look steadily at the sun.

[b] See ii. 401 foll.

arms and fight. And now this band of brothers, led by their hardy instructor, had glutted themselves with slaughter of men, and then laid low with countless wounds an elephant with a tower on its back. Then fire-brands followed, and they were watching with joy while the fallen monster was burning, when suddenly a helmet flashed and plumes waved bright above a higher helmet. The old man, who recognized Hannibal by the light he shed, was no laggard: willingly he urged on his troop of sons into the fierce conflict, bidding them hurl their weapons thick and fast, and disregard his fire-breathing nostrils and the flames that came from his helmet. Thus the bird of mighty Jupiter, whose care brings up her eaglets in the nest to be fit carriers of the thunderbolts, turns them to face the sun and examines them, testing their genuine descent by the rays of Phoebus.[a] And now Crista was fain to set an example for the contest that summoned them : see, his spear flies swiftly past through the space between. But the point could not penetrate the many plates of the golden corslet ; the spear hung down, and the feeble blow betrayed the failing powers of the thrower. Then Hannibal accosted him : " What madness induced your hand, feeble with age, to strike such harmless blows ? Scarce did your quivering spear scratch the surface plates of Gallician gold.[b] See ! I give you back your own weapon ; your famous sons should take me rather to teach them skill in arms." And straightway he pierced the breast of hapless Crista with his own spear.

Then from the other side—terrible to see—six javelins hurled by six arms came flying, and as many spears were hurled with might. So, when Moorish hunters in the land of Libya have beset the den of

venator premit obsesso cum Maurus in antro,
invadunt rabidi iam dudum et inania tentant
nondum sat firmo catuli certamina dente.
consumit clipeo tela et, collectus in arma,
sustinet urgentes crepitantibus ictibus hastas
Sidonius ductor ; nec iam per vulnera credit
aut per tot caedes actum satis ; iraque anhelat,
ni leto det cuncta virum iungatque parenti
corpora et excidat miseros cum stirpe penates.
  Tunc Abarim affatur ; namque una hic armiger ira
flammabat Martem atque omnes comes ibat in actus :
" suppedita mihi tela. vadis liventis Averni
demitti globus ille cupit, qui nostra lacessit
tegmina ; iam stultae fructus pietatis habebit."
haec fatus iaculo Lucam, qui maximus aevi,
transadigit ; pressa iuvenis cum cuspide labens
arma super fratrum resupino concidit ore.
mortiferum inde manu properantem vellere ferrum
pilo Volsonem (namque hoc de strage iacentum
fors dabat) affixa sternit per tegmina nare.
tum Vesulum, calido lapsantem in sanguine fratrum,
ense metit rapido plenamque—heu barbara virtus !—
abscisi galeam capitis, ceu missile telum,
conversis in terga iacit. Telesinus, ad ossa
illiso saxo, qua spina interstruit artus,
occumbit ; fratrisque videt labentia membra
Quercentis, quem funda procul per inane voluta
sopierat, dum supremam Telesinus in auras

[a] See note to vi. 154.
[b] A Roman weapon : see note to v. 216.

a mother-lioness and press her hard, her cubs at once begin a furious battle but cannot prevail because their teeth are not yet grown. Hannibal parried all six darts with his shield; then, gathering himself together behind it, he withstood the impact of the spears with their crashing blows; and, not content with all the wounds and slaughter he had dealt out already, he breathed hard in wrath, if he might not slay all the six and lay their corpses beside their father's, and destroy the hapless family, root and branch.

Now he addressed Abaris, his squire, who shared his martial ardour and ever accompanied him to battle: "Give me supply of weapons. Yon band of brothers who assault my shield are eager to go down to the dark waters of Avernus [a]; and soon shall they reap the fruits of their foolish devotion to their father." As he spoke, he pierced Lucas, the eldest of them, with a javelin; the point went home, and the youth fell with upturned face on his brothers' shields. Volso's turn came next. He was trying to pluck forth the fatal steel, when Hannibal laid him low, piercing his nostrils through his shield with a pilum [b] which he had chanced to pick up from a heap of corpses. Next Vesulus, whose foot slipped in the warm blood of his brothers, was beheaded by a swift sword-cut; and then, O inhuman warfare! he hurled helmet and severed head together, using them as a weapon, at the backs of the retreating brothers. Then Telesinus, smitten to the marrow by a stone, where the backbone knits the frame together, fell prostrate; and he witnessed the fall of his brother Quercens, who was stunned by a bullet hurled from a distant sling, even while Telesinus was breathing

exhalat lucem et dubitantia lumina condit.
at fessus maerore simul cursuque metuque
et tamen haud irae vacuus, non certa per aequor
interdum insistens Perusinus membra ferebat;
hunc sude, quam raptam Libyci per terga iacentis
armiger obtulerat monstri, super inguina fixum
obtruncat quercuque premit violentus obusta.
tentarat precibus saevum lenire furorem,
sed Stygius primos implevit fervor hiatus,
et pulmone tenus demisit anhelitus ignem.
tandem cum toto cecidit grege, nomen in Umbro
clarum, Crista, diu populo. ceu fulmine celsa
aesculus aut, proavis ab origine consita,[1] quercus
cum fumat percussa Iovi, sacrosque per aevum
aetherio ramos populantur sulphure flammae,
donec victa deo late procumbit et omnem
collabens operit spatioso stipite prolem.

Atque ea dum iuxta Tyrius stagna Aufida ductor
molitur, Paulus, numerosa caede futuram
ultus iam mortem, ceu victor bella gerebat
inter mille viros. iacet ingens Phorcys ab antris
Herculeae Calpes, caelatus Gorgone parmam,
unde genus tristique deae manabat origo.
hunc obiectantem sese atque antiqua tumentem
nomina saxificae monstrosa e stirpe Medusae,
dum laevum petit incumbens violentius inguen,
detrahit, excelsi correptum vertice coni,
afflictumque premens, tergo qua balteus imo
sinuatur, coxaeque sedet munimen utrique,

[1] consita *Heinsius*: cognita *Bauer*.

---

[a] Gibraltar.

out his life and closing his swimming eyes. Perusinus was staggering over the ground and sometimes stopping, disabled at once by grief and fear and rapid movement, but not bereft of courage, when Hannibal stabbed him above the groin with a stake which his squire had snatched from the back of a dead elephant and handed to him. The fierce thrust of the scorched brand held him down. He had tried to appease that furious wrath by entreaty ; but the fatal heat filled his mouth as soon as he opened it, and the breath of it drove the fire down to the lungs. Thus at last fell Crista, a name long famous in Umbria, and all his sons with him. So a tall oak-tree, planted long ago by our forefathers, when smitten by Jupiter's thunderbolt, sends up smoke ; and the flames and sulphur of heaven make havoc of the boughs revered for centuries, until it crashes in wide ruin, conquered by the god, and the huge trunk, as it falls, covers all the scions that grow round it.

While the Tyrian leader performed these feats near the waters of Aufidus, Paulus avenged his own coming death by slaying many victims, and fought like a conqueror among a thousand foes. Down went huge Phorcys, who came from the caves of Calpe,[a] sacred to Hercules ; on his shield was engraved the Gorgon's head ; for that cruel goddess derived her birth and beginning from Calpe. Phorcys pressed forward, proud of his ancient race and descent from Medusa, the monster who turned men to stone. As he aimed a furious blow at the left groin of Paulus, the consul seized him by the crest of his tall helmet and turned the blow aside : then, dashing him down upon the ground, he drove his sword downwards through him, where the belt curves round the base

coniecto fodit ense super ; vomit ille calentem
sanguinis effundens per hiantia viscera rivum,
et subit Aetolos Atlanticus accola campos.
Has inter strages rapido terrore coorti,
invadunt terga atque averso turbine miscent
bella inopina viri, Tyrius quos fallere doctus
hanc ipsam pugnae rector formarat ad artem ;
succinctique dolis, fugerent ceu Punica castra,
dediderant dextras ; tum totis mentibus actam
in caedes aciem pone atque in terga ruentes
praecipitant. non hasta viro, non deficit ensis :
e strage est ferrum atque evulsa cadavere tela.
raptum Galba procul—neque enim virtutis amorem
adversa exemisse valent—ut vidit ab hoste
auferri signum, conixus corpore toto
victorem assequitur letalique occupat ictu.
ac dum comprensam caeso de corpore praedam
avellit, tardeque manus moribunda remittit,
transfixus gladio propere accurrentis Amorgi
occidit, immoriens magnis non prosperus ausis.
Haec inter, veluti nondum satiasset Enyo
iras saeva truces, sublatum pulvere campum
Vulturnus rotat et candentes torquet harenas.
iamque reluctantes stridens immane procella
per longum tulit ad campi suprema cavisque
afflictos ripis tumidum demersit in amnem.
hic tibi finis erat, metas hic Aufidus aevi
servabat tacito, non felix Curio, leto.
namque, furens animi dum consternata moratur

---

[a] Diomede : see note to i. 125.
[b] Another name for Bellona, the goddess of war.

of the spine and protects both the hips. A hot stream of blood gushed forth from the gaping entrails; and the dweller by Atlas went down beneath the soil of the Aetolian chief.[a]

In the midst of this carnage there was a sudden alarm. A fresh onset of war was launched, and the Roman rear was surprised by troops trained by Hannibal, a master of stratagem, for this very purpose. Pretending to desert from the Carthaginian army, they had surrendered. Now, equipped with guile, they rushed in a body upon the Roman rear, with hearts wholly bent on slaughter. They lacked not for spears and swords; for they tore weapons from the corpses. From far off Galba saw an enemy seize a standard and carry it off; defeat has no power to quench a brave man's spirit; and with an exertion of all his strength he caught up the spoiler and struck him dead ere he could escape. But while he grasped his prize and wrenched it from the dying hand that was slow to yield it up, Amorgus came up quickly and ran a sword through him; and Galba fell and died, balked of his high emprise.

Meanwhile, as if cruel Enyo[b] had not yet glutted her savage wrath, the Sirocco lifted the surface of the field in whirling clouds of dust, and drove the burning sand in all directions. And now the tempest with frightful howling blew the resisting bodies of men to a distance, as far as the limit of the plain, dashing them against the sunken banks, and sinking them in the swollen river. Such was the end of ill-starred Curio; and here the Aufidus marked the limit of his life with an inglorious death. For, while stopping with furious anger the terrified ranks and

agmina et oppositu membrorum sistere certat,
in praeceps magna propulsus mole ruentum
turbatis hauritur aquis fundoque volutus
Hadriaca iacuit sine nomine mortis harena.
Ingens ferre mala et Fortunae subdere colla
nescius, adversa fronte incurrebat in arma
vincentum consul; pereundi Martius ardor
atque animos iam sola dabat fiducia mortis;
cum Viriathus agens telis, regnator Hiberae
magnanimus terrae, iuxta atque ante ora furentis
obtruncat Pauli fessum certaminis hostem.
heu dolor, heu lacrimae! Servilius, optima belli,
post Paulum belli pars optima, corruit ictu
barbarico magnamque cadens leto addidit uno
invidiam Cannis. tristem non pertulit iram
consul et, insani quamquam contraria venti
exarmat vis atque obtendit pulvere lucem,
squalentem rumpens ingestae torvus harenae
ingreditur nimbum ac Viriathum[1] moris Hiberi
carmina pulsata fundentem barbara caetra
invadit laevaeque fodit vitalia mammae.
hic fuit extremus caedum labor: addere bello
haud ultra licuit dextram, nec tanta relictum est
uti, Roma, tibi posthac ad proelia Paulo.
saxum ingens, vasto libratum pondere, caeca
venit in ora manu et, perfractae cassidis aera
ossibus infodiens, complevit sanguine vultus.
inde pedem referens, labentia membra propinquo
imposuit scopulo atque, undanti vulnere anhelans,

[1] Viriathum *Postgate*: ritu iam *edd.*

---

[a] Cannae is near the mouth of the river Aufidus.
[b] A chief in Lusitania (Portugal).

trying to arrest them by throwing his body in the way, he was driven headlong forward by the mass of fugitives and swallowed up by the swollen stream; down he sank to the bottom and lay on the sands of the Adriatic,[a] without honour in death.

Mighty in endurance and incapable of bending the neck to Fortune, Paulus rushed right against the weapons of the victorious foe. Nothing gave him confidence now but his longing for a soldier's death, and his certainty that he must die. Then Viriathus,[b] the high-souled ruler of a Spanish kingdom, drove before him a war-wearied Roman and slew him under the eyes of the consul and close beside him. O grief! O tears! Servilius,[c] the best warrior in all the host, the best after Paulus, was slain by the sword of the barbarian, and his single death added a darker stain to the guilt of Cannae. Paulus could not contain his fierce anger. Though the wild fury of the wind in his face disabled him and veiled the daylight with dust, he broke through the thick dark cloud of sand and strode on in wrath. While Viriathus in Spanish fashion was shouting a savage song of victory and beating on his shield, Paulus attacked him and pierced the vital part in his left breast. This was his last victim, his last labour; no longer might Paulus take part in the war, nor might Rome make use of him hereafter in the great battles still to come. A huge stone, whose enormous weight was hurled by an unseen hand, struck him in the face, driving the fragments of his brazen helmet into the bone and covering his face with blood. Then he drew back and rested his failing limbs on a rock near by;

[c] As consul in 217 B.C. he had commanded an army at Lake Trasimene: see v. 98.

sedit terribilis clipeum super ore cruento :
immanis ceu, depulsis levioribus hastis,
accepit leo cum tandem per pectora ferrum,
stat teli patiens media tremebundus harena
ac, manante iubis rictuque et naribus unda
sanguinis, interdum languentia murmura torquens,
effundit patulo spumantem ex ore cruorem.
tum vero incumbunt Libyes, super ipse citato
ductor equo, qua flatus agit, qua pervius ensis,
qua sonipes, qua belligero fera belua dente.
obrutus hic telis ferri per corpora Piso
rectorem ut vidit Libyae, conixus in hastam
ilia cornipedis subrecta cuspide transit
collapsoque super nequiquam incumbere coeptat :
cum Poenus, propere collecto corpore, quamquam
cernuus inflexo sonipes effuderat armo :
" umbraene Ausoniae rediviva bella retractant
post obitum dextra ? nec in ipsa morte quiescunt ? "
sic ait atque aegrum coeptanti attollere corpus
arduus insurgens totum permiscuit ensem.
  Ecce, Cydonea violatus harundine plantam,
Lentulus effusis campum linquebat habenis,
cum videt in scopulo rorantem saxa cruore
torvoque obtutu labentem in Tartara Paulum.
mens abiit, puduitque fugae : tum visa cremari
Roma viro, tunc ad portas iam stare cruentus
Hannibal ; Aetoli tum primum ante ora fuere
sorbentes Latium campi. " Quid deinde relictum,

[a] See note to ii. 90.

gasping from his streaming wound, he sat down upon his shield, a formidable figure with his gory face. So a huge lion shakes off the lighter spears; but when at last the sword has been driven home in his breast, he stands in the centre of the arena, quivering but resigned to the blow; the blood streams from mane and mouth and nostrils, and from time to time he utters a dull roaring, and spits out blood and foam from his wide jaws. Then the Libyans came down upon Paulus; and Hannibal himself came galloping where the wind drove him, and where his sword, his charger, and the fierce beasts that fight with their tusks, had cleared a path. When Piso, buried beneath weapons, saw Hannibal riding over the dead, he raised himself with an effort on his lance and stabbed the horse's belly with his uplifted point. When the beast fell, he tried in vain to bestride it. But Hannibal picked himself up in a moment, though the horse had thrown him when it fell sprawling on its head; and thus he spoke: "Do the Roman ghosts come back again to life, to fight a second time? Can they not rest even in death?" With these words he rose to his full height and, while Piso tried to lift his wounded limbs, plunged his sword in up to the hilt.

Behold, Lentulus, wounded in the foot by a Cretan[a] arrow, was galloping off the field, when he saw Paulus seated on the rock wet with his blood, and staring with fierce eyes as he sank down to death. Lentulus changed his purpose and felt ashamed of flight. It seemed to him that he saw Rome burning now, and blood-stained Hannibal now standing at her gates; now for the first time he saw before him the Aetolian plain, the grave of Italy. "What still remains," he

crastina cur Tyrios lux non deducat ad urbem,
deseris in tantis puppim si, Paule, procellis?
testor caelicolas," inquit, " ni damna gubernas
crudelis belli vivisque in turbine tanto
invitus, plus, Paule (dolor verba aspera dictat)
plus Varrone noces. cape, quaeso, hunc, unica rerum
fessarum spes, cornipedem; languentia membra
ipse levabo humeris et dorso tuta locabo."

Haec inter, lacero manantem ex ore cruorem
eiectans, consul: " macte o virtute paterna!
nec vero spes angustae, cum talia restent
pectora Romuleo regno. calcaribus aufer,
qua vulnus permittit, equum atque hinc ocius urbis
claudantur portae: ruet haec ad moenia pestis.
dic, oro, rerum Fabio tradantur habenae.
nostris pugnavit monitis furor. amplius acta
quid superest vita, nisi caecae ostendere plebi
Paulum scire mori? feror an consumptus in urbem
vulneribus? quantine emptum velit Hannibal, ut nos
vertentes terga aspiciat? nec talia Paulo
pectora, nec manes tam parva intramus imago.
ille ego—sed vano quid enim te demoror aeger,
Lentule, conquestu? perge atque hinc cuspide fessum
eripe quadrupedem propere." tum Lentulus urbem,
magna ferens mandata, petit; nec Paulus inultum,
quod superest de luce, sinit; ceu vulnere tigris
letifero cedens tandem proiectaque corpus
luctatur morti et languentem pandit hiatum
in vanos morsus, nec sufficientibus irae

[a] See viii. 255; ix. 636.

cried, "to prevent the enemy from marching on Rome to-morrow, if you, Paulus, abandon the ship in such a storm? By Heaven I swear—if my words are harsh, grief prompts them—that, unless you take command in this terrible war and live on against your will amid the tempest, you are more guilty even than Varro. Sole hope of our suffering country, take my horse, I entreat. I will lift your weakened frame on my own shoulders and seat you safely on the saddle."

Thereupon the consul answered, spitting out the streaming blood from his mutilated mouth: "Go on and prosper, worthy son of brave ancestors! Nor is the prospect dark, when such stout hearts as yours still are found in the realm of Romulus. Spur your horse as hard as your wound will let you, and fly; bid them close the city gates instantly; the Destroyer will rush against her walls. The control of affairs must be given to Fabius. It was madness that resisted our warnings. My life is ended; and nothing remains but to prove to the ignorant populace [a] that Paulus knows how to die. Shall I be carried back to Rome, a wounded and dying man? What would not Hannibal give to see me retreating? No such intention has Paulus; and my ghost shall not go down thus humbled to the shades below. I who once—— But why should my failing accents detain you, Lentulus, with useless complaining? Away! and use your spear-point to urge your weary steed from hence." Then Lentulus made off for Rome, carrying his weighty message. Nor did Paulus suffer his last moments to pass without striking a blow. So a tigress when mortally wounded gives way at last and lying down fights against death; she opens the jaws that have no strength to bite in earnest,

ictibus extrema lambit venabula lingua.
iamque coruscanti telum propiusque ferenti
gressum exultantem et securo caedis Iertae
non expectatum surgens defixerat ensem,
Sidoniumque ducem circumspectabat, in illa
exoptans animam certantem ponere dextra.
sed vicere virum coeuntibus undique telis
et Nomas et Garamas et Celtae et Maurus et Astur.
hic finis Paulo. iacet altum pectus et ingens
dextera, quem, soli si bella agitanda darentur,
aequares forsan Fabio. mors additur urbi
pulchra decus misitque viri inter sidera nomen.
Postquam spes Italum mentesque in consule lapsae,
ceu truncus capitis, saevis exercitus armis
sternitur, et victrix toto fremit Africa campo.
hic Picentum acies, hic Umber Martius, illic
Sicana procumbit pubes, hic Hernica turma.
passim signa iacent, quae Samnis belliger, et quae
Sarrastes populi Marsaeque tulere cohortes;
transfixi clipei galeaeque et inutile ferrum
fractaque conflictu parmarum tegmina et ore
cornipedum derepta fero spumantia frena.
sanguineus tumidas in campos Aufidus undas
eiectat redditque furens sua corpora ripis.
sic Lagea ratis, vasto velut insula ponto
conspecta, illisit scopulis ubi nubifer Eurus,
naufragium spargens operit freta; iamque per undas

---

[a] See viii. 537.

[b] Lagus founded the dynasty of the Ptolemies who long ruled over Egypt: hence "Lagean" = "Egyptian."

and the tip of her tongue licks the spears with efforts that cannot gratify her rage. When Iertas came close, brandishing his weapon in triumph and sure of his victim, Paulus rose up suddenly and plunged his sword in his foe's body. Then he looked round for Hannibal, eager to yield up his life, a warrior's life, to that glorious hand. Not so: he was overcome by a shower of darts from every side, from Numidians and Garamantians, from Gauls and Moors and Asturians. Thus Paulus died. A wise heart and a mighty arm were lost in him; if he had been given sole command in the war, he might perhaps have ranked as the equal of Fabius. His noble death gave fresh glory to his country and raised his fame to the sky.

The hope and courage of the Romans fell with their general; the army, like a headless thing, was overthrown by fierce assaults; and victorious Africa raged over all the field. Here lay the men of Picenum and brave Umbrians, and there Sicilian warriors and Hernican troops. Everywhere were lying scattered the standards, borne by warlike Samnites or men from the Sarnus,[a] or by Marsian contingents; the ground was covered with battered shields and helmets and useless swords, with targets broken by collision with other targets, and with foam-covered bits, wrenched from the mouths of mettled steeds. The Aufidus, red with blood, cast up his swollen waters over the plain and in rage restored to the banks the corpses that belonged to them. So an Egyptian[b] vessel is seen like an island in the great sea; but, when the rainy East-wind has dashed her upon the rocks, she covers the sea with scattered wreckage;

et transtra et mali laceroque aplustria velo
ac miseri fluitant revomentes aequora nautae.
At Poenus, per longa diem certamina saevis
caedibus emensus, postquam eripuere furori
insignem tenebrae lucem, tum denique Martem
dimisit tandemque suis in caede pepercit.
sed mens invigilat curis noctisque quietem
ferre nequit. stimulat dona inter tanta deorum
optatas[1] nondum portas intrasse Quirini.
proxima lux placet : hinc strictos ferre ocius enses,
dum fervet cruor, et perfusae caede cohortes,
destinat, ac iam claustra manu, iam moenia flamma
occupat et iungit Tarpeia incendia Cannis.
Quo turbata viri coniux Saturnia coepto
irarumque Iovis Latiique haud inscia fati,
incautum ardorem atque avidas ad futile votum
spes iuvenis frenare parat. ciet inde quietis
regnantem tenebris Somnum, quo saepe ministro
edomita inviti componit lumina fratris.
atque huic arridens, " non te maioribus," inquit,
" ausis, dive, voco nec posco, ut mollibus alis
des victum mihi, Somne, Iovem. non mille premendi
sunt oculi tibi, nec spernens tua numina custos
Inachiae multa superandus nocte iuvencae.
ductori, precor, immittas nova somnia Poeno,

[1] optatas *Ernesti*: hortatus *edd.*

---

[a] Quirinus is the deified Romulus: hence the " gates of Quirinus " are the " gates of Rome."

[b] Juno.

[c] Jupiter.

[d] Io, daughter of Inachus, king of Argos, was loved by Zeus, who turned her into a heifer, to protect her from Juno's

the surface is strewn with floating benches and masts, with stern-ornaments with tattered sails, and with hapless sailors spitting out the brine.

Hannibal had spent the livelong day in stubborn conflict and fierce slaughter ; and, when the darkness robbed his frenzy of that glorious day, he ceased at last from fighting and spared his men from slaying yet more Romans. But he was anxious and wakeful, and resented the inaction of night. When the gods had given him so much, it stung him to think that he had not yet gained his object—to enter the gates of Quirinus.[a] Resolved to march on the morrow, he intended to hasten thence with swords still drawn, while the soldiers' blood was hot and their hands stained with carnage ; and already he sees the barriers broken and the walls on fire, and makes the burning of the Capitol follow close on Cannae.

The daughter of Saturn[b] was disturbed by Hannibal's design. Knowing well the displeasure of Jupiter and the destiny of Italy, she took steps to curb the rash ardour of Hannibal and his eager hopes of a success he could never win. At once she summoned Sleep, the regent of silent night, by whose aid she often conquers and closes her brother's[c] eyes against his will. She smiled on him and said : "I do not summon you, divine Sleep, for a burdensome task, nor do I ask of your silken wings to overcome Jupiter and place him at my mercy. Not now need you close a thousand eyes, nor conquer with deep darkness the guardian of the heifer, Inachus' daughter—the guardian who made light of your divinity.[d] I pray you to send a strange dream to the Carthaginian

jealousy ; then a guardian with a hundred eyes, named Argus, was set to watch her by Juno.

ne Romam et vetitos cupiat nunc visere muros,
quos intrare dabit numquam regnator Olympi."
Imperium celer exsequitur curvoque volucris
per tenebras portat medicata papavera cornu.
ast ubi, per tacitum allapsus, tentoria prima
Barcaei petiit iuvenis, quatit inde soporas
devexo capiti pennas oculisque quietem
irrorat, tangens Lethaea tempora virga.
exercent rabidam truculenta insomnia mentem:
iamque videbatur multo sibi milite Thybrim
cingere et insultans astare ad moenia Romae.
ipse refulgebat Tarpeiae culmine rupis,
elata torquens flagrantia fulmina dextra,
Iupiter, et lati fumabant sulphure campi,
ac gelidis Anien trepidabat caerulus undis;
et densi ante oculos iterumque iterumque tremendum
vibrabant ignes. tunc vox effusa per auras:
"sat magna, o iuvenis, prensa est tibi gloria Cannis.
siste gradum; nec enim sacris irrumpere muris,
Poene, magis dabitur, nostrum quam scandere caelum."
attonitum visis maioraque bella paventem
post confecta Sopor Iunonia iussa relinquit;
nec lux terribili purgavit imagine mentem.
Quos inter motus somni vanosque tumultus
dedita per noctem reliquo cum milite castra
nuntiat et praedam pleno trahit agmine Mago.
huic ductor laetas Tarpeio vertice mensas
spondenti, cum quinta diem nox orbe tulisset,

[a] *i.e.* "within five days."

general, that he may not be eager now to behold the forbidden walls of Rome ; for the lord of Olympus will never suffer him to enter there."

Swiftly he did her bidding and winged his way through the darkness, carrying juice of poppy-seed in a curving horn. In silence he glided on, and went first to Hannibal's tent ; then he waved his drowsy wings over the recumbent head, dropping sleep into the eyes, and touching the brows with his wand of forgetfulness. Then Hannibal's excited brain was troubled by unpeaceful dreams. He dreamed that he was even now surrounding the Tiber with a great army, and standing defiantly before the walls of Rome. Jupiter himself was seen—a shining figure on the summit of the Tarpeian rock ; his hand was raised, to launch fiery thunderbolts ; the surrounding plains smoked with sulphur, and the blue waters of cold Anio were shaken ; again and again the dreadful fire was repeated and flashed before his sight ; and at last a voice came down from the sky : " You have gained glory enough, young man, at Cannae. Stay your steps ; for the Carthaginian may as soon storm our heaven as burst his way within the sacred walls of Rome." He was appalled by the dream, and dreaded a future and more terrible war. Then Sleep, having done Juno's bidding, left him ; but daylight could not wash out the dreadful vision from his mind.

While the general's sleep was thus disturbed by groundless alarms, Mago came, reporting that the Roman camp with the remnant of the army had surrendered during the night ; and behind him came a rich array of booty. He promised that, when the fifth night was followed in succession by day,[a] Hannibal should feast and make merry on the

celatis superum monitis clausoque pavore,
vulnera et exhaustas saevo certamine vires
ac nimium laetis excusat fidere rebus.
tum spe deiectus iuvenis, ceu vertere ab ipsis
terga iuberetur muris ac signa referre,
" tanta mole," inquit, " non Roma, ut credidit ipsa,
sed Varro est victus. quonam tam prospera Martis
munera destituis fato patriamque moraris ?
mecum exultet eques ; iuro hoc caput, accipe muros
Iliacos portasque tibi sine Marte patentes."
Dumque ea Mago fremit cauto non credita fratri,
iam Latius sese Canusina in moenia miles
colligere et profugos vicino cingere vallo
coeperat. heu rebus facies inhonora sinistris !
non aquilae, non signa viris, non consulis altum
imperium, non subnixae lictore secures.
trunca atque aegra metu, ceu magna elisa ruina,
corpora debilibus nituntur sistere membris.
clamor saepe repens et saepe silentia fixis
in tellurem oculis ; nudae plerisque sinistrae
detrito clipeo ; desunt pugnacibus enses ;
saucius omnis eques ; galeis carpsere superbum
cristarum decus et damnarunt Martis honores.
at multa thorax perfossus cuspide, et haerens
loricae interdum Maurusia pendet harundo.
interdum maesto socios clamore requirunt.

Tarpeian height. Concealing the divine warning and suppressing his fears, Hannibal pleaded in excuse the wounds and weariness of the soldiers after their fierce conflict, and spoke of over-confidence due to success. Then Mago, as much disappointed as if he had been ordered to turn and march back from the very walls of Rome, thus protested: "Then our mighty effort has not defeated Rome, as Rome herself believed; it has only defeated Varro. What fate makes you throw away the bountiful gift of Mars and keep your country waiting? Let me rush forward with the cavalry, and, I swear by my head, the walls of the city will be yours and the gates will fly open before you without a battle."

While Mago spoke thus in his rage and his more cautious brother refused to believe him, the Roman soldiers had begun to rally behind the walls of Canusium and to build a rampart round the fugitives beside the town. How mean, alas, was the aspect of that beaten army, without eagles, without standards, with no consul in chief command, and no axes borne before him by lictors! Men struggle to support upon feeble limbs their frames, sick with fear and mutilated, as if they had been crushed in the fall of some great building. Sometimes a sudden shout was heard, sometimes there was silence with downcast looks. Most of them are defenceless, with no shield on the left arm; there are no swords to fight with; every horseman is wounded; rejecting the pomp and pride of war, they have plucked the splendid plumes from their helmets. Their corslets are pierced with many a spear, and in some breastplates a Moorish arrow is still sticking and hanging down. Sometimes with cries of sorrow they ask for their

hic Galba, hic Piso et, leto non dignus inerti,
Curio deflentur, gravis illic Scaevola bello.
hos passim ; at Pauli pariter ceu dira parentis
fata gemunt : ut verba mali praenuntia numquam
cessarit canere et Varronis sistere mentem,
utque diem hunc totiens nequiquam averterit urbi,
atque idem quantus dextra. sed cura futuri
quos premit, aut fossas instant praeducere muris,
aut portarum aditus, ut rerum est copia, firmant.
quaque patet campus planis ingressibus hostis,
cervorum ambustis imitantur cornua ramis,
et stilus occulitur, caecum in vestigia telum.

Ecce, super clades et non medicabile vulnus,
reliquias belli atque imperdita corpora Poenis
impia formido ac maior iactabat Erinnys.
trans aequor Tyrios enses atque arma parabant
Punica et Hannibalem mutato evadere caelo.
dux erat exilii non laetus[1] Marte Metellus,
sed stirpe haud parvi cognominis. is mala bello
pectora degeneremque manum ad deformia agebat
consulta atque alio positas spectabat in orbe,
quis sese occulerent, terras, quo nomina nulla
Poenorum, aut patriae penetraret fama relictae.

Quae postquam accepit flammata Scipio mente,
quantus Sidonium contra, fera proelia miscens,
ductorem stetit in campis, rapit ocius ensem,
atque, ubi turpe malum Latioque extrema coquebant

[1] exilii non laetus *Summers*: exilio collectis *Bauer*.

[a] These were large branches of trees, having the smaller ones left on and shortened at a certain distance from the stock, so as to present the appearance of a stag's horn. They were stuck in the ground, to impede a charge of cavalry over a plain that offered no natural obstructions.

[b] See ll. 44 foll.

lost comrades. Some weep for Galba and Piso, and for Curio who deserved to die sword in hand, while others lament Scaevola, that stout warrior. Each of these is mourned by some; but to all alike the death of Paulus is grievous as the loss of a father: "How true a prophet he was, when he foretold the evils that have come upon us, and thwarted Varro's folly! How often he tried in vain to save Rome from to-day's defeat! How brave too he was in battle!" But those who felt anxiety for the future made haste to dig trenches along the city walls, or used such materials as they had to fortify the gates. And, where the plain lay open, with nothing to obstruct the assaults of the enemy, they planted fire-hardened boughs shaped like deers' antlers,[a] whose concealed points would wound unseen the horses' feet.

But now, on the top of defeat and incurable disaster, a treasonable panic and a more dreadful madness stirred the hearts of those who had escaped the Carthaginian sword. They planned to cross the sea and by a change of clime to escape the Tyrian blades, the might of Carthage, and Hannibal. The leader of the exiles was Metellus,[b] a man who took no delight in war though his family had gained high renown. He pressed his shameful design upon cowardly spirits and degenerate hearts, and had in view a hiding place in some distant land, which the name of Carthage would never reach, nor any news of their own forsaken country.

But when Scipio heard of this plan, his wrath was kindled. He snatched up his sword—as mighty a figure as when he confronted Hannibal in deadly combat on the battle-field. He burst open the doors of the place where cowards were hatching their plot

coepta viri, ruptis foribus sese arduus infert.
tum, quatiens strictum cum voce ante ora paventum
mucronem : "Tarpeia, pater, qui templa secundam
incolis a caelo sedem, et Saturnia, nondum
Iliacis mutata malis, tuque aspera pectus
aegide Gorgoneos virgo succincta furores,
indigetesque dei, sponte en per numina vestra
perque caput, nullo levius mihi numine, patris
magnanimi iuro : numquam Lavinia regna
linquam nec linqui patiar, dum vita manebit.
ocius en testare deos, si moenia taedis
flagrabunt Libycis, nullas te ferre, Metelle,
ausurum in terras gressus. ni talia sancis,
quem tremis et cuius somnos formidine rumpis,
Hannibal hic armatus adest : moriere, nec ullo
Poenorum melior parietur gloria caeso."
his excussa incepta minis ; iamque ordine iusso
obstringunt animas patriae dictataque iurant
sacramenta deis et purgant pectora culpa.

Atque ea dum Rutulis turbata mente geruntur,
lustrabat campos et saevae tristia dextrae
facta recensebat, pertractans vulnera visu,
Hannibal et, magna circumstipante caterva,
dulcia praebebat trucibus spectacula Poenis.
quas strages inter, confossus pectora telis,
seminecem extremo vitam exhalabat in auras

---

[a] Scipio swears by Jupiter, Juno, Pallas, and the native gods of Italy, such as Quirinus.

[b] Rome.

[c] Scipio means that he himself is as dangerous to Metellus as Hannibal could be.

to bring disgrace and destruction upon Italy; he rushed towering in. Then he brandished his naked sword before their frightened eyes as he spoke: "O Father [a] that inhabitest the Tarpeian temple, next after heaven thy chosen abode; and thou, daughter of Saturn, whose heart is not yet softened by the sufferings of the Trojans; and thou, fierce Maiden Goddess, who bindest on thy breast the aegis and the terrors of the Gorgon; and ye gods of Italy—hear me when I swear voluntarily by your divinity, and by the head of my heroic father, as sacred to me as any god! I swear that never while I live shall I leave the realm of Lavinium [b] nor suffer others to leave it. Make haste, Metellus, and call heaven to witness, that, even if the walls of Rome blaze with Carthaginian brands, you will not dare to turn your steps to any foreign land. If you refuse to swear it, the Hannibal, the thought of whom terrifies you and breaks your sleep, is present here, sword in hand.[c] You shall die; and no man who slays a Carthaginian shall win more glory than your slayer." These threats put an end to their design. At once they pledged their lives to their country in the manner prescribed, and swore to heaven the oath that Scipio dictated, and so cleansed their hearts of guilt.

While the Romans were thus engaged with troubled hearts, Hannibal was riding over the battle-field, reviewing his dreadful handiwork and feasting his eyes upon wounds. A numerous staff surrounded him, and the sights he showed them were welcome to the cruel eyes of the Carthaginians. Amid these heaps of dead lay Cloelius, with many a wound in the breast and at the point of death. Sinking fast and sighing out

murmure deficiens iam Cloelius oraque nisu
languida vix aegro et dubia cervice levabat.
agnovit sonipes, arrectisque auribus acrem
hinnitum effundens, sternit tellure Bagesum,
quem tum captivo portabat in agmina dorso.
hinc, rapidum glomerans cursum, per lubrica pingui
stante cruore soli et mulcata cadavera caede
evolat ac domini consistit in ore iacentis.
inde, inclinatus colla et submissus in armos,
de more inflexis praebebat scandere terga
cruribus ac proprio quodam trepidabat amore.
milite non illo quisquam felicius acri
insultarat equo, vel si resupina citato
proiectus dorso ferretur membra, vel idem
si nudo staret tergo, dum rapta volucris
transigeret cursu sonipes certamina campi.

At Libys, humanos aequantem pectore sensus
haud parce miratus equum, quinam ille sinistrae
depugnet morti iuvenis, nomenque decusque
erogitat letique simul compendia donat.
hic Cinna (ad Tyrios namque is sua verterat arma,
credulus adversis, et tum comes ibat ovanti)
" auribus huic," inquit, "ductor fortissime, origo est
non indigna tuis. quondam sub regibus illa,
quae Libycos renuit frenos, sub regibus olim
Roma fuit ; sed enim, solium indignata Superbi,
ut sceptra exegit, confestim ingentia bella
Clusina venere domo, si Porsena fando
auditus tibi, si Cocles, si Lydia castra.
ille, ope Maeonia et populo succinctus Etrusco,
certabat pulsos per bella reponere reges.

his latest breath, he was just able with a faint effort to raise his drooping head and support it on his feeble neck. His horse knew his master; he pricked up his ears and neighed loudly; then he threw Bagaesus, his captor who was then riding him towards the battle-field. Galloping at speed, he flew over mangled corpses and ground made slippery by pools of clotted blood, and halted by the face of his stricken master. Then with sunk neck and sloping shoulders, he bent his knees, as he had been trained to do, to let his master mount; and in his anxious concern he showed an affection that was all his own.[a] No more gallant horseman than Cloelius had ever ridden that mettled steed, either reclining at full length on the flying back, or standing erect with no saddle under him, while the horse flew over the race-course and covered the distance at top speed.

Then Hannibal, marvelling much at a horse which showed the feelings of a man, asked who it was that was fighting so hard against grim death—what was his name and rank. And, as he spoke, he put Cloelius to a speedy and merciful end. Cinna answered him. Deceived by Roman reverses, he had taken sides with Carthage and now rode beside the conqueror. "Brave general," he said, "it is worth your while to hear the early history of his family. Rome, which now rejects the rule of Carthage, was herself once ruled by kings. But when she resented the reign of Superbus and expelled the tyrant, at once a great army came from Clusium's royal dome—you may have heard tell of Porsena and Horatius and the Etruscan invasion. Porsena, supported by the power and manhood of Etruria, strove to restore the exiled

[a] *i.e.* such as no other horse would have shown.

multa adeo nequiquam ausi ; pressitque tyrannus
Ianiculum[a] incumbens. ubi mox, iam pace probata,
compressere odia, et positum cum foedere bellum,
obsidibusque obstricta fides. (mansuescere corda
nescia, pro superi ! et nil non immite parata
gens Italum pro laude pati). bis Cloelia senos
nondum complerat primaevi corporis annos,
una puellarum Laurentum et pignora pacis
inter virgineas regi tramissa catervas.
facta virum sileo ; rege haec et foedere et annis
et fluvio spretis, mirantem interrita Thybrim
tranavit, frangens undam puerilibus ulnis.
cui si mutasset sexum natura, reverti
forsan Tyrrhenas[b] tibi non licuisset in oras,
Porsena. sed iuveni, ne sim tibi longior, hinc est
et genus et clara memorandum virgine nomen."

Talia dum pandit, vicinus parte sinistra
per subitum erumpit clamor. permixta ruina
inter et arma virum et lacerata cadavera Pauli
eruerant corpus media de strage iacentum.
heu quis erat ! quam non similis modo Punica telis
agmina turbanti ! vel cum Taulantia[c] regna
vertit, et Illyrico sunt addita vincla tyranno !
pulvere canities atro arentique cruore
squalebat barba, et perfracti turbine dentes
muralis saxi, tum toto corpore vulnus.

Quae postquam aspexit geminatus gaudia ductor
Sidonius : "fuge, Varro," inquit, "fuge, Varro, superstes,
dum iaceat Paulus ! patribus Fabioque sedenti

---

[a] One of the Seven Hills of Rome, on the W. of the Tiber.

[b] "Tyrrhene" is the Greek version of "Etruscan."

[c] The Taulantes were an Illyrian people : for the victory of Paulus over Illyricum in 219 B.C. see viii. 289 foll.

tell the whole story of Cannae to the Senate and the people and to Fabius, the man of inaction. Once again, Varro, if you love life so much, I shall give you leave to fly. But this hero, worthy of my enmity, whose heart beat high with valour, shall receive burial, and his grave shall be honoured. How great is Paulus in death! The fall of so many thousands gives me less joy than his alone. When fate summons me, I pray to die like him, and may Carthage survive my death!" Thus he spoke, and ordered the bodies of his soldiers to be buried when rosy Dawn should issue from her chamber on the following day, and piles of arms to be raised, as a burnt-offering to Mars. The men, though weary, made haste to do his bidding. They dispersed to the neighbouring copses and felled the trees; and the high woods on the leafy hills resounded with the axe. Here ash-trees and tall poplars with white foliage were smitten and cleft by sturdy arms, and there holm-oaks, planted by a former generation. Down came oaks and pine-trees that love the shore, and cypresses that deck the funeral train and mourn beside the pyre. And lastly they hastily built funeral pyres—a mournful duty and a tribute that means nothing to the dead—until Phoebus plunged his panting steeds in the waters of Tartessus,[a] and the moon's disk departing from the sky brought on the blind darkness of black night. Then, when the chariot of the sun shone forth with dawning fire and the earth resumed its familiar colours, they kindled the pyres and burnt the corrupting bodies of their dead on a foreign soil. They felt a dreadful apprehension of the uncertain future, and an unspoken fear invaded their inmost hearts, that, if the fortune of war turned against them later,

mox ferat, hac ipsis inimica sede iacendum.
at tibi, bellipotens, sacrum, constructus acervo
ingenti mons armorum surgebat ad astra.
ipse, manu celsam pinum flammaque comantem
attollens, ductor Gradivum in vota ciebat:
" primitias pugnae et laeti libamina belli
Hannibal Ausonio cremat haec de nomine victor,
et tibi, Mars genitor, votorum haud surde meorum,
arma electa dicat spirantum turba virorum."
tum, face coniecta, populatur fervidus ignis
flagrantem molem, et, rupta caligine, in auras
actus apex claro perfundit lumine campos.
hinc citus ad tumulum donataque funera Paulo
ibat et hostilis leti iactabat honorem.
sublimem eduxere pyram mollesque virenti
stramine composuere toros. superaddita dona,
funereum decus: expertis invisus et ensis
et clipeus, terrorque modo atque insigne superbum,
tum laceri fasces captaeque in Marte secures.
non coniux native aderant, non iuncta propinquo
sanguine turba virum, aut celsis de more feretris
praecedens prisca exequias decorabat imago
omnibus exuviis nudo, iamque Hannibal unus
sat decoris laudator erat; fulgentia pingui
murice suspirans inicit velamina et auro
intextam chlamydem ac supremo affatur honore:
" i, decus Ausoniae, quo fas est ire superbas
virtute et factis animas. tibi gloria leto
iam parta insigni: nostros Fortuna labores
versat adhuc casusque iubet nescire futuros."

---

[a] In a Roman noble's house the hall (*atrium*) was adorned by wax portrait-busts of deceased ancestors; and these were regularly carried in the funeral procession of any member of the family.

they themselves must lie in this unfriendly earth. Then, as an offering to the War-god, a huge pile of armour was raised up to the sky. Hannibal with his own hand held up a tall pine-torch with fire for foliage and called on the god to hear his prayer: "Hannibal, victorious over the Italian nation, burns these first-fruits of battle and offerings of conquest; and to thee, Father Mars, whose ears were open to my prayers, this host of surviving men dedicates the choicest armour." Then he threw the torch upon the pyre, and blazing fire made havoc of the burning mass, till the crest of flame burst through the smoke and rose to the sky, flooding the fields with bright light. From here Hannibal went quickly to witness the funeral rites granted to Paulus, proud of showing honour to a dead enemy. A tall pyre was reared, and a soft bier was made of green turf, and offerings were laid upon it, to honour the dead—the shield, the sword dreaded by those who had felt it, the rods and axes taken in the battle, broken now but once a badge of power that all men feared. No wife was there, no sons, no gathering of near kinsmen; no customary masks of ancestors were borne on high litters before the corpse to grace the funeral procession.[a] Bare was it of all trappings; but the praise of Hannibal was glory enough in itself: sighing he threw on the body a covering bright with rich purple dye and a mantle embroidered with gold, and uttered this last tribute to the dead: "Go, pride of Italy! Go whither spirits may go that exult in brave deeds! To you fame is secured already by a glorious death, but I must struggle on as Fate drives me, and she hides future events from my knowledge."

haec Libys; atque repens, crepitantibus undique flammis,
aetherias anima exultans evasit in auras.
  Fama dehinc gliscente sono iam sidera adibat;
iam maria ac terras primamque intraverat urbem.
diffidunt muris; solam pavitantibus arcem
speravisse sat est: nec enim superesse iuventam,
ac stare Ausoniae vacuum sine corpore nomen.
quodque adeo nondum portis irruperit hostis,
contemptu cessare putant. iam tecta cremari,
ac delubra rapi, caedesque ante ora nefandae
natorum, septemque arces fumare videntur.
lux una eversas bis centum in strage curules,
ac iuvenum bis tricenis orbata gemebat
milibus exhaustae nutantia moenia Romae;
atque ea post Trebiam, post Tusci stagna profundi,
nec socium numero pariter leviore perempto.
sed vero sed enim reliqui pia turba senatus
munera sortito invadunt. celer omnia lustrans
clamitat attonitis Fabius: "non ulla relicta est,
credite, cunctandi ratio: approperemus, ut hostis
nequiquam armatos ausit succedere muros.
dura inter pavidos alitur fortuna sedendo,
et gliscunt adversa metu; ite ocius, arma
deripite, o pubes, templis. vos atria raptim
nudate et clipeos in bella refigite captos.
sat patriae sumus, e numero si ad proelia nostro

[a] Livy puts the killed at 48,200: the estimate of other authorities is much higher. Eighty senators fell at Cannae.

So Hannibal spoke ; and suddenly, mid the crackling of the flames all round, the spirit of Paulus sprang forth and rose triumphant to the sky.

Meanwhile rumour waxed ever louder and louder till it reached heaven. Soon it found its way over sea and land, and came first of all to Rome. Putting no trust in their walls, the terrified citizens were content to rely upon the citadel and nothing else. For they had no fighting men left, and Italy was nothing now but an unsubstantial name. If the enemy had not yet burst in through the gates, they imputed his delay to contempt. Men thought that they saw the houses burning and the temples pillaged, their sons foully slain, and the smoke rising up from the Seven Hills. A single day mourned for the dead corpses of two hundred high magistrates, and mourned for the tottering walls of the depopulated city which had lost twice thirty thousand fighting men [a] ; and this after Trebia and the battle by Lake Trasimene ; and of the allies also an equal number had fallen at the same time. But, none the less, the surviving senators did their duty and entered upon the functions prescribed to them by lot. Fabius found speed and was everywhere, crying out to the panic-stricken people : "Believe me, there is no longer any reason for delay.[b] Let us make haste to man the walls and baffle the enemy's approach. Ill fortune is increased by the inaction of cowardice, and defeat is made worse by fear. Go quickly, ye young men, and pull down the armour in the temples. Strip the walls of your houses with speed, and take down for service the shields you took in fight. We are enough to save our country, if no one of us withdraws

[b] The policy which Fabius had followed hitherto.

nil minuit pavor. in patulis illa horrida campis
sit metuenda lues ; muros haud fregerit umquam,
exultare levis nudato corpore, Maurus."

Dum Fabius lapsas acuit formidine mentes,
Varronem adventare vagus per moenia rumor
spargit et occulto perfundit pectora motu.
haud secus ac, fractae rector si forte carinae
litoribus solus vacuis ex aequore sospes
adnatet, incerti trepidant, tendantne negentne
iactato dextras, ipsamque odere salutem
unius amissa superantis puppe magistri.
quam restare viro labem, qui accedere portis
audeat ac dirum veniat pavitantibus omen !

Hos mulcens questus Fabius deforme docebat
cladibus irasci vulgumque arcebat ab ira.
adversis etenim ferri non esse virorum
qui Martem inscribant genti, non posse dolores
condere et ex poena solacia poscere luctus.
si vero exprobrare sinant, sibi tristius illum
illuxisse diem, quo castris viderit ire
Varronem, quam quo videat remeare sine armis.
his dictis sedere minae, et conversa repente
pectora : nunc fati miseret, nunc gaudia Poeno
consulibus reputant caesis erepta duobus.
ergo omne effundit longo iam se agmine vulgus
gratantum, magnaque actum se credere mente

in fear from battle. The dreaded foe may be formidable in the open plain; but the naked Moor, for all his speed and activity, will never break down city walls."

While Fabius thus encouraged hearts that had failed for fear, a report that Varro was approaching spread up and down through the city and filled all hearts with secret uneasiness. So, when the captain of a wrecked ship is saved from the sea and swims ashore alone, men are at a loss and uncertain whether to welcome the sea-tossed man or to disown him; they cannot bear that the captain only should be saved when his ship is lost. What a stain must cling to Varro's name, when he dares to approach the gates, and presents himself, a bird of ill-omen, to his horror-stricken countrymen!

Fabius smoothed down these protests. He told them it was a shameful thing to be angry with a defeated general, and so he averted the people's indignation. Men who claimed Mars as their ancestor should not (he said) be mastered by adversity, nor be unable to hide their grief; nor should they seek solace for their mourning in punishing others. "But if I am allowed to speak a word of reproof," [a] said he, "that day on which I saw Varro proceed to the camp was more painful to me than that on which I see him return without an army." By his words their threats were silenced and their feelings underwent a sudden change: now they pity Varro's misfortune, or reflect that Hannibal has lost the satisfaction of slaying both the consuls. Therefore all the populace poured forth in long procession to thank him; and they protested that he had acted nobly,

[a] The reproof falls on the electors who chose Varro as consul.

testantur, quod, fisus avis sceptrisque superbis,
Laomedontiadum non desperaverit urbi.
Nec minus infelix culpae grandique pudore
turbatus, consul titubantem ad moenia gressum
portabat lacrimans ; deiectum attollere vultum
ac patriam aspicere et luctus renovare pigebat.
quod vero reduci tum se populusque patresque
offerrent, non gratari, sed poscere natos
quisque suos fratresque simul miseraeque parentes
ire videbantur laceranda ad consulis ora.
sic igitur muto lictore invectus in urbem,
damnatum superis aspernabatur honorem.
At patres Fabiusque, procul maerore remoto,
praecipitant curas. raptim delecta iuventa
servitia armantur, nec claudit castra saluti
postpositus pudor. infixum est Aeneia regna
Parcarum in leges quacumque reducere dextra
proque arce et sceptris et libertatis honore
vel famulas armare manus. primaeva suorum
corpora praetexto spoliant velamine et armis
insolitis cingunt : puerilis casside vultus
clauditur atque hostis pubescere caede iubetur.
idem obsecrantes, captivum vulgus ut auro
pensarent parvo (nec pauca fuere precantum
milia), miranti durarunt prodere Poeno.
cuncta adeo scelera et noxam superaverat omnem,

[a] An ancient king of Troy : here, as so often, the Romans are identified with the Trojans.

[b] It was customary for the lictors, as they marched in front of the consul, to call out, " Make way for the consul."

[c] The meaning is, that Rome virtually died on the field of Cannae.

[d] Boys and girls of free birth had, like the magistrates, a purple border round the white upper garment which they wore.

when, relying on the ancient glory and power of his country, he refused to despair of the city inhabited by the sons of Laomedon.[a]

None the less, sad at his failure and sore ashamed, Varro drew near the walls with faltering steps and weeping eyes; it was pain to him to raise his eyes from the ground and look upon his native city and recall their losses to the citizens. Though the Senate and people came out then to meet him on his return, he felt that they were not there to thank him, but that each man was demanding a lost son or brother, and that unhappy mothers were ready to tear out the consul's eyes. Thus his lictors kept silence[b] as he entered the city and he claimed no respect for the high office which the gods had condemned.

But the senators and Fabius put sorrow in the background and turned quickly to their tasks. Slaves, chosen for their strength, were armed in haste; the barracks were thrown open to them; for pride gave way to the safety of the state. They were determined to bring, by any agency, the realm of Aeneas back to the land of the living,[c] and to arm even bondsmen in defence of the Capitol and the empire and glorious freedom. They took off from their own children the purple-bordered garment of boyhood[d] and put armour on their unaccustomed shoulders. Boys hid their faces behind the helmet, and were bidden to reach manhood in slaughter of the foe. Likewise, when they were begged to ransom at an easy rate the multitude of Roman prisoners[e]—and the number of petitioners rose to many thousands—they persisted, to the astonishment of Hannibal, in their refusal to redeem them. For they held it worse than any misdeed or

[e] Livy puts their number at 8000.

armatum potuisse capi. tunc terga dedisse
damnatis Siculas longe meritare per oras
impositum, donec Latio decederet hostis.
haec tum Roma fuit ; post te cui vertere mores
si stabat fatis, potius, Carthago, maneres.

any crime for an armed man to surrender. Then sentence was passed on soldiers guilty of desertion: they were banished to distant Sicily, to serve there until the invader should retreat from Italy. Such was Rome in those days; and, if it was fated that the Roman character should change when Carthage fell, would that Carthage were still standing!

LIBER UNDECIMUS

ARGUMENT

Many peoples of Italy revolt from Rome and join Hannibal (1-27). *Capua too is inclined to go over to the Carthaginians : the wealth and luxurious habits of the citizens* (28-54). *On the motion of Pacuvius, they send Virrius and other envoys to Rome, asking that one of the two consuls should be a Campanian : this demand is indignantly refused by Torquatus, Fabius, and Marcellus* (55-129). *Capua goes over to Hannibal : Decius alone protests but in vain* (130-189). *Hannibal starts for Capua : he orders Decius to be arrested : Decius defies his threats* (190-258). *Hannibal visits the city and is entertained at a great banquet* (259-368) :

Nunc age, quos clades insignis Iapyge campo
verterit ad Libyam populos Sarranaque castra,
expediam : stat nulla diu mortalibus usquam,
Fortuna titubante, fides : adiungere dextras
certavere palam rumpenti foedera Poeno,
heu nimium faciles laesis diffidere rebus.
saevior ante alios iras servasse repostas
atque odium renovare ferox in tempore Samnis ;
mox levis et sero pressurus facta pudore
Bruttius, ambiguis fallax mox Apulus armis ;
tum gens Hirpini vana indocilisque quieti
et rupisse indigna fidem—ceu dira per omnes

[a] See note to viii. 563.

BOOK XI

ARGUMENT (*continued*)

Teuthras of Cumae, a musician, plays and sings (288-302). *The son of Pacuvius intends to stab Hannibal while feasting, but is induced by his father to give up his plan* (303-368). *Mago is sent to Carthage to announce the victory* (369-376). *Hannibal winters at Capua: Venus enfeebles the spirit of his army: he himself takes pleasure in the music of Teuthras* (377-482). *Meanwhile Mago reports at Carthage the successes of Hannibal and makes a fierce attack upon Hanno* (483-553). *Hanno replies, urging that peace should be made* (554-600). *But reinforcements are sent both to Spain and Italy* (600-611).

NEXT let me tell of the peoples who went over to the side of Libya and the camp of Hannibal after the signal victory on the plains of Apulia. Nowhere do men remain loyal for long when Fortune proves unstable. Too prone, alas, to distrust the unfortunate, the states vied with one another in open offers of friendship to faithless Carthage. Fiercest of all were the Samnites, ever ready to keep alive ancient feuds,[a] and eager to gratify their hatred afresh when occasion offered. Their example was followed by the Bruttians, a fickle folk whose late repentance was to avert their doom; by the treacherous Apulians who own no fixed alliance; and by the Hirpini, light-minded and restless men who had no reason to break faith. It

manarent populos foedi contagia morbi.
iamque Atella suas iamque et Calatia adegit,
fas superante metu, Poenorum in castra cohortes.
inde Phalanteo levitas animosa Tarento
Ausonium laxare iugum ; patefecit amicas
alta Croton portas Afrisque ad barbara iussa
Thespiadum docuit submittere colla nepotes.
idem etiam Locros habuit furor. ora vadosi
litoris, Argivos Maior qua Graecia muros
servat et Ionio luitur curvata profundo,
laetas res Libyae et fortunam in Marte secuta,
iuravit pavitans Tyrio sua proelia Marti.
iam vero, Eridani tumidissimus accola, Celtae
incubuere malis Italum veteresque doloris
tota se socios properarunt iungere mole.

Sed fas id Celtis, fas impia bella referre
Boiorum fuerit populis : Capuaene furorem,
quem Senonum genti, placuisse, et Dardana ab ortu
moenia barbarico Nomadum sociata tyranno
quisnam, mutato tantum nunc tempore, credat ?
luxus et insanis nutrita ignavia lustris
consumptusque pudor peccando unisque relictus
divitiis probrosus honor lacerabat hiantem
desidia populum ac resolutam legibus urbem.
insuper exitio truculenta superbia agebat.
nec vitiis deerant vires : non largior ulli
Ausoniae populo (sic tum Fortuna fovebat)

---

[a] Phalantus founded Tarentum, a Spartan colony and for long the chief port of South Italy.

[b] Myskelus, the founder of Crotona, was the son of Hercules by one of the daughters of Thespius, a prince in Boeotia.

[c] Here, as often in Homer, " Argive " = " Greek."

[d] For the Senones see note to i. 624.

was like a horrible plague that spread infection all over the country. Now Atella and Calatia sent their soldiers to Hannibal's camp, their fears prevailing over their sense of duty. Tarentum too, the city of Phalantus,[a] proud and fickle, threw off the Roman yoke. Crotona on the height opened her gates in friendship, and taught the descendants of the Thespiadae[b] to bow their necks to the bidding of the African barbarian. A like madness affected the Locrians. The low-lying coast, where Greater Greece preserves Argive[c] cities and bends round till it is washed by the Ionian sea, was attracted by the victories of Libya and her success in war, and swore to serve under the dreaded Carthaginians. And also the vainglorious Celts who dwell by the river Po attacked Italy in her distress; they had ancient grievances, and hastened to assist the enemy with their full strength.

It might be lawful for Celts, lawful for the tribes of the Boii, to renew impious warfare; but who could believe that Capua would take the same mad decision as the tribe of Senones,[d] and that a city of Trojan origin[e] would ally herself with a barbarous ruler of Numidians—who could believe this now, when times have changed so greatly? But luxury, and sloth fed by riotous debauchery, and utter shamelessness in sinning, and scandalous respect for wealth and wealth alone—such vices preyed upon an indolent and listless people and a city freed from the restraints of law. Their savage cruelty also bore them to their doom. And they had the means to pamper their vices. No people of Italy possessed gold and silver in more

[e] Capua was founded by Capys, one of the companions of Aeneas.

aurique argentique modus; madefacta veneno
Assyrio[a] maribus vestis medioque dierum
regales epulae atque ortu convivia solis
deprensa et nulla macula non illita vita.
tum populo saevi patres, plebesque senatus
invidia laeta, et collidens dissona corda
seditio. sed enim interea temeraria pubis
delicta augebat, pollutior ipsa, senectus.
nec, quos vile genus despectaque lucis origo
foedabat, sperare sibi et deposcere primi
deerant imperia ac patriae pereuntis habenas.
quin etiam exhilarare viris convivia caede
mos olim, et miscere epulis spectacula dira
certantum ferro, saepe et super ipsa cadentum
pocula respersis non parco sanguine mensis.

Has astu aggressus, quo verteret acrius aegras
ad Tyrios mentes, quae nulla sorte daturam
certus erat Romam (neque enim impetranda volebat)—
Pacuvio fuit haud obscurum crimine nomen—
hortatur summi partem deposcere iuris
atque alternatos sociato consule fasces;[b]
et, si partita renuant sedisse curuli
aequatumque decus geminasque videre secures,
ultorem[c] ante oculos atque ora astare repulsae.
ergo electa manus gressu fert dicta citato.
antistat cunctis praecellens Virrius ore,
sed genus obscurum nullique furore secundus.

---

[a] "Assyrian" = "Asiatic" = "Tyrian."

[b] *i.e.* that one of the two consuls should always be a citizen of Capua.

[c] Hannibal is meant.

abundance—so favoured were they then by Fortune; their garments, even those worn by men, were dyed with Assyrian[a] purple; their princely banquets began at noon, and the rising sun found them at their revels; and their way of life was defiled by every stain. Moreover, the senators oppressed the people, the masses welcomed the unpopularity of the senate, and civil discord made the parties clash. Meanwhile the old men, more corrupt themselves, outdid the headstrong follies of the young. Men notorious for humble birth and obscure origin asserted their claims, expecting and demanding to hold office before others, and to rule the sinking state. Then too, it was their ancient custom to enliven their banquets with bloodshed, and to combine with their feasting the horrid sight of armed men fighting; often the combatants fell dead above the very cups of the revellers, and the tables were stained with streams of blood.

Thus demoralized was Capua, when Pacuvius, a man whose name is known only because of his misdeeds, worked cunningly upon the minds of the citizens, in order to make them more eager to join the Carthaginians. He urged them to demand of Rome what he knew that Rome would never grant—indeed he did not wish it to be granted—that Capua should claim an equal share in the highest office[b] and that the rods should pass in turn from one consul to the other. And, if the Romans refused to share their curule chair and to admit a partner, with a second set of axes, to the high office, then one who would avenge the rebuff was near and in full view.[c] Therefore a chosen body made haste to carry the message. Their chief was Virrius, an eloquent speaker but a man of low origin and second to none in violence.

qui postquam coetu patrum ingentique senatu
impia dementis vulgi ac vix tota profudit
consulta et tumidis incendit vocibus aures,
concordi fremitu renuentum effunditur asper
toto e concilio clamor ; tum quisque fatigat
increpitans, vocumque tremit certamine templum.
Hic Torquatus, avum fronte aequavisse severa
nobilis : " heu Capua portantes talia dicta
Romuleis durastis," ait, " succedere muris ?
ad quos non ausi Carthago atque Hannibal arma
post Cannas afferre suas ? numquamne per aures
it vestras, in Tarpeia cum sede Latini
orarent paria, haud verbis, haud voce, sed acri
propulsum dextra, qui tum mandata superbo
ore apportabat, tanto per limina templi
turbine praecipitem revoluti corporis actum,
ut, saevo afflictus saxo, spectante piaret
tristia dicta Iove et lueret verba impia leto ?
en ego progenies eius, qui sede Tonantis
expulit orantem et nuda Capitolia consul
defendit dextra." rabidum hinc palmasque virorum
intentantem oculis proavitaque facta parantem
ut vidit maiore adeo crudescere motu,
excipit his frendens Fabius : " pro cuncta pudendi !
sedes, ecce, vacat, belli viduata procella ;
quem, quaeso, e vobis huic imposuisse paratis ?
inque locum Pauli quemnam datis ? an tua, Virri,
prima atque ante alias sors, concedente senatu,

---

[a] In 340 B.C. T. Manlius Torquatus was consul for the third time, when the envoys of the Latins made their insolent request.

When he had set forth the outrageous proposals of a brainsick mob at a great meeting where all the Roman senators were assembled, and even before he had ceased to enrage his hearers by his high-flown eloquence, a unanimous shout of angry refusal rose from the whole assembly; and then each separate senator rebuked him, till the building shook with their contending voices.

Then Torquatus rose. His brow severe recalled that of his noble ancestor.[a] "How now?" he asked. "Have you dared to bring such a message from Capua to the walls of Rome—these walls which Carthage and Hannibal, even after their victory at Cannae, dared not attack? Have you never heard how it fared with the insolent spokesman of the Latins, when they came to the Capitol and made a like request? Not a word was spoken: he was flung forth from the temple doors and rolled down with such violence that he was dashed against the pitiless rock. Thus he atoned, under the eyes of Jupiter, for his insolence; and the penalty for his blasphemous speech was death. Look at me! I am descended from that consul who drove the speaker forth from the Thunderer's temple, and whose unarmed hand defended the Capitol." Then in his rage he shook his fist in the faces of the envoys and was about to repeat the action of his ancestor; but when Fabius saw him proceeding to actual violence, he spoke next, grinding his teeth as he spoke: "Out on such utter shamelessness! See! a consul's seat is vacant, deprived of its occupant by the stress of war. Which, pray, of your number do you intend to place there? Whom do you propose, to fill the room of Paulus? Are you perhaps, Virrius, summoned first and foremost by the lot with the permission of

te citat ac nostris aequat iam purpura Brutis ?
i, demens, i, quo tendis ; tibi perfida fasces
det Carthago suos." medio fervore loquentis,
impatiens ultra gemitu cohibere furorem,
fulminea torvum exclamat Marcellus ab ira :
" quae tandem et quam lenta tenet patientia mentem,
o confuse nimis Gradivi turbine Varro,
ut perferre queas furibunda insomnia consul ?
nonne exturbatos iam dudum limine templi
praecipites agis ad portas, et discere cogis
semiviros, quod sit nostro de more creati
consulis imperium ? non umquam sobria pubes
et peritura brevi, moneo, ocius urbe facesse.
muros ante tuos, ut par est, debita ductor
armatus responsa dabit." consurgere cuncti
hinc pariter magnoque viros clamore premebant.
necnon et foribus propere Campana iuventus
extulit ipsa gradum, tantaeque dolore repulsae
concitus, Hannibalem volvebat Virrius ore.
Fulvius (huic nam spondebant praesagia mentis
venturum decus, et Capuae pereuntis imago
iam tum erat ante oculos) : "non si Carthaginis," inquit,
" ductorem vestris devinctum colla catenis
Romam victor agis, posthac intrare Quirini
sacratas dabitur sedes : tende ocius, oro,
quo mens aegra vocat." referunt haec inde citati
mixta minis et torva trucis responsa senatus.

---

[a] As Brutus was the first Roman to hold the office of consul, so Virrius perhaps intends to be the first Campanian to hold the same office.

[b] M. Claudius Marcellus : see note to i. 133.

[c] Q. Fulvius Flaccus, when consul for the third time, took Capua in 212 B.C.

the Senate? and does the purple robe put you on a level with our Brutus?[a] Go, poor fool, to the mark you are aiming at: let treacherous Carthage make you her ruler." His fiery speech was not finished when Marcellus,[b] no longer content to groan and hold his peace, burst out in fury and blazing wrath: "Are you, Varro, so utterly stunned by the fierce ordeal of battle? What sluggish endurance ties your tongue, so that you, the consul, can put up with the dreams of these madmen? Will you not instantly turn them out from the temple, drive them headlong to the city gates, and compel these effeminate wretches to learn the power of a consul elected in Roman fashion? I warn you to depart at once from Rome—you who are never sober and are doomed soon to perish. A general at the head of an army shall give you the answer you deserve in the right place—before the walls of Capua." Then all the House rose as one man and loudly threatened the envoys. The men of Capua themselves hastened to go forth; and Virrius, resenting so sharp a rebuff, had the name of Hannibal on his lips. Thereupon Fulvius,[c] whose prophetic soul assured him of future glory, and who could already see with his mind's eye the ruin of Capua, spoke thus: "Even if you conquer Hannibal and bring him here to Rome as your captive, never again shall you be permitted to enter the sacred dwelling-place of Quirinus.[d] I beg you will hasten to the goal,[e] whither your folly summons you." Then the envoys took back this threatening message in haste to Capua, and reported the grim reply of the angry Senate.

[d] Rome. [e] Hannibal's camp.

Tantane, omnipotens, caligine mersa latere
fata placet? veniet quondam felicior aetas,
cum pia Campano gaudebit consule Roma
et per bella diu fasces perque arma negatos
ultro ad magnanimos referet secura nepotes.
poena superborum tamen haec durabit avorum,
quod non ante suos Capua ad suffragia mittet,
quam Carthago suos. postquam nunc dicta senatus,
nunc facta exposuit, tum veris falsa per artem
Virrius admiscens cecinit fatale cruenti
turbatis signum belli. furiata iuventus
arma, arma Hannibalemque volunt; ruit undique vulgus
et Poenos in tecta vocant; ingentia facta
Sidonii iuvenis celebrant, ut ruperit Alpes
Herculei socius decoris divisque propinquas
transierit cursu rupes; ut caede referta
clauserit Eridani victor vada; victor ut idem
Lydia Romano turbarit stagna cruore;
ut Trebiae ripas aeterno nomine famae
tradiderit Paulumque idem inter proelia et idem
Flaminium, proceres rerum, demiserit umbris.
his super excisam primori Marte Saguntum
et iuga Pyrenes et Hiberum et sacra parentis
iuratumque viro bellum puerilibus annis
accumulant. unum, ducibus tot caede peremptis,
tot fusis acie, stare inter proelia nullis
attactum telis. superum cum munere detur
huic sociare viro dextras et foedere iungi,

[a] The result of the Social War (90 B.C.) was to admit all Italians as citizens; and the people of Capua, as citizens, became eligible for the consulship. Perhaps Silius is referring to some consul of his own time who was a native of Capua.

Is it your pleasure, Almighty Father, that the future shall be hidden in such utter darkness? A happier age will one day come, when loyal Rome shall welcome a consul from Capua; the rods which she long withheld from armed force she will then surrender willingly and confidently to the high-souled descendants of her foes.[a] This penalty, however, for the insolence of their ancestors shall remain, that Capua shall not send voters to Rome before Carthage sends them also.[b]—Virrius, skilfully mixing truth with falsehood, first set forth what the Senate had said and done, and then sounded to his excited hearers the fatal note of bloody war. The frantic people cried out for arms and for Hannibal. They rushed together from every quarter and invited the Carthaginians to their city. Men recalled the mighty achievements of the Tyrian youth: how, rivalling the glory of Hercules, he had burst the barrier of the Alps and overrun the peaks that reach to heaven; how he dammed the river Po with heaps of dead; how, ever victorious, he dyed the Etruscan lake[c] with Roman blood; how he gave eternal glory to the Trebia, and himself in battle sent down to Hades both Paulus and Flaminius, the Roman leaders. To all this they add his early prowess in the sacking of Saguntum, his crossing over the Pyrenees and the Ebro, and the sacrifice offered by his father when he swore in boyhood to make war against Rome. He alone, they said, was impervious in battle to all weapons, though so many leaders had been slain and so many routed. "When the goodness of Providence allows us to join hands with this hero and to ally our-

[b] A Roman colony was settled at Carthage by C. Gracchus in 122 B.C.

[c] Lake Trasimene.

fastus exsanguis populi vanumque tumorem
nimirum Capua et dominatum perferat urbis,
ceu famulis fasces aequataque iura negantis?
prorsus enim tanto potiorem nomine habendum
Varronem, ut fugiat consul fulgentior ostro.
  Talia iactantes iam lectam sorte parabant
mittere, quae Tyrios adiungat foedere, pubem.
sed non invictum ponebat pectore robur
tum solum Decius Capuae decus. isque receptus
in medios coetus—neque enim differre dabatur—
"itis," ait, "cives, violanda ad iura parentum,
damnatumque caput temerati foederis aris
iungitis hospitio? quae tanta oblivio recti?
magnum atque in magnis positum populisque virisque
adversam ostentare fidem. nunc tempus inire
proelia pro Rutulis, nunc signa aciemque movere,
dum trepidae res, et medicinam vulnera poscunt;
is locus officio, cum cessant prospera, cumque
dura ad opem Fortuna vocat. nam laeta fovere
haudquaquam magni est animi decus. huc, age, adeste.
novi dis animas similes et pectora magnis
numquam angusta malis; capiunt, mihi credite, Cannas
et Thrasymenna vada et Pauli memorabile letum.
hi sunt, qui vestris infixum moenibus hostem
deiecere manu et Capuam eripuere superbis
Samnitum iussis; hi sunt, qui iura dedere

---

[a] Decius Magius is not a fictitious character: he was a highly respected citizen of Capua.

[b] The reference is to the First Samnite War (from 343 B.C.), fought by the Romans in defence of Campania. The Sidicini had previously appealed to the Campanians for help against the Samnites.

selves with him, shall Capua, forsooth, put up with the pride and baseless insolence of an effete people, and be ruled by a state which refuses us, as if we were slaves, the rods of the consulship and equal rights? Varro, forsooth, they think more worthy of that high title, that his flight may be made more conspicuous by the consul's purple."

Talking thus wildly, they were about to send envoys, chosen by lot, to make an alliance with the Carthaginians. But Decius,[a] the sole glory of Capua in that hour, refused to put aside the firm purpose of his brave heart. When he was admitted to the conclave and temporizing was impossible, he spoke thus: "Fellow-citizens, are you about to violate the ties which our fathers cherished, and make friends with a man whom the gods have condemned for breach of treaty? How utterly you have forgotten the path of duty! It is a noble thing, and a property of noble nations and noble men, to show loyalty to the distressed. Now is the time to go to battle in defence of the Romans, and to take the field while their state is critical and their wounds call for treatment. This is the time to serve them, when success lingers and when stern Fortune summons us to help. To court the prosperous is by no means the glory of a noble mind. Hasten hither to their support! I know their godlike spirits and hearts that can bear every great disaster; they can bear, I assure you, Cannae and Lake Trasimene and the noble death of Paulus. These are the men who dislodged the enemy established in your city and rescued Capua from the tyranny of the Samnites.[b] These are the men who, when that menace was driven out, gave you a constitution and put an end to the

terrore expulso Sidicinaque bella remorunt.
quos fugitis socios? quosve additis? ille ego sanguis
Dardanius, cui sacra pater, cui nomina liquit
ab Iove ducta Capys, magno cognatus Iulo;
ille ego semihomines inter Nasamonas et inter
saevum atque aequantem ritus Garamanta ferarum
Marmarico ponam tentoria mixtus alumno?
ductoremque feram, cui nunc pro foedere proque
iustitia est ensis solaeque e sanguine laudes?
non ita, non Decio permixtum fasque nefasque,
haec ut velle queat. nullo nos invida tanto
armavit Natura bono, quam ianua mortis
quod patet et vita non aequa exire potestas."
haec vana aversas Decius iactavit ad aures.
  Ast delecta manus iungebat foedera Poeno.
iamque aderat praemissa duci turbante tumultu
Autololes numerosa cohors; ipse agmine magno
festinata citus per campos signa movebat.
et Decius: "nunc hora, viri, nunc tempus; adeste,
dum Capua dignum, dum me duce dextera vindex
molitur facinus; procumbat barbara pubes.
pro se quisque alacres rapite hoc decus. hostis adire
si parat, obstructas praebete cadavere portas
et ferro purgate nefas; hic denique solus
eluerit sanguis maculatas crimine mentes."
  Dumque ea nequiquam non ulli laeta profatur,
audita asperitate viri coeptoque feroci,

---

[a] Son of Assaracus and grandfather of Aeneas, and believed to be the founder of Capua.

[b] The corpses of the advance-guard who were now before the city.

fighting of the Sidicini. Compare the allies whom you are deserting with the new allies whom you are gaining. Shall I, with Trojan blood in my veins, I, to whom Capys [a] of old, the kinsman of great Iulus, bequeathed his sacred rites and his name derived from Jupiter—shall I consort with half-human Nasamonians and Garamantians, as cruel and savage as wild beasts, and pitch my tent cheek by jowl with a native of Marmarica? Shall I put up with a leader, whose sword now usurps the place of justice and sworn agreements, and all whose glory is derived from bloodshed? God forbid! Decius does not so confuse right and wrong that he is capable of such a choice. The greatest boon with which grudging Nature has equipped man is this—that the door of death stands open and suffers us to depart from a life that is too hard." Such was the appeal that Decius made in vain to deaf ears.

The chosen body of envoys made a treaty with Hannibal. He sent ahead a numerous troop of Autololes, and they soon arrived with noise and confusion. He himself was coming with the main body, moving in haste over the plains. Then Decius spoke: "Friends, now is the time and now the hour! Rally round me, while the arm of vengeance achieves a deed worthy of Capua and of me as leader. Lay these barbarous soldiers low. Let each man among you be eager to snatch this crown of glory. If Hannibal tries to enter, block the gates against him with corpses [b] and wipe out your guilt by the sword. That bloodshed, and nothing else, will wash away the stain with which your hearts are polluted."

While he spoke thus in vain and no man welcomed his words, Hannibal learned the hostility and des-

multa feta gerens ira praecordia, Poenus
astabat muris propereque accersere lectos
immitem castris Decium iubet. horrida virtus
armatumque fide pectus rectique cupido
et maior Capua mens imperterrita mole
invicta stabat, torvoque minacia vultu
iussa ducis verbisque etiam incessebat amaris.
quem Libyae rector tot signa, tot arma ferentes
spernentem increpitans magno clamore profatur:
"post Paulum, post Flaminium componimur eheu
vecordi Decio, mecum certasse volenti
in decus et famam leti. rapite, ite citati,
signa, duces. pateatne mihi Campana vetante
urbs Decio, explorare libet, nova bella moventi
cui patuere Alpes, saxa impellentia caelum
atque uni calcata deo." suffuderat ora
sanguis, et a torvo surgebant lumine flammae;
tum rictus spumans et anhelis faucibus acta
versabant penitus dirum suspiria murmur.
sic urbem invectus, toto comitante senatu
et vulgo ad spectanda ducis simul ora ruente,
effundit cunctam rabiem irarumque procellas.

Necnon et Decio propiora pericula mentem
flammarant, tempusque adeo cernebat adesse,
quo laudes ducis invicti superaret inermis.
non illum fuga, non clausi occuluere penates;
sed liber, veluti nullus penetrasset in urbem
Hannibal, intrepido servaverat otia vultu,

---

[a] Hercules.

[b] He had now only one eye: see note to iv. 740.

perate design of Decius. His heart swelled high with anger, and he ordered a chosen troop to bring the obstinate man at once to his camp outside the walls. That austere virtue, that breast armed with loyalty and love of justice, that heart greater than all Capua, stood there unshaken and unterrified. With frowning brows he listened to the general's threats and even assailed him with bitter speech. Then Hannibal raised his voice to a shout as he rebuked the man who defied all the standards and all the swords of Carthage. "Paulus is dead," he cried, "and Flaminius is dead; and now I am matched against this madman, Decius, who is fain to contend with me, that he may win glory and honour in death. Seize your standards, ye captains, and go forward with speed. I would fain find out whether Capua opens her gates to me in defiance of Decius, even as the Alps opened a path to me at the outset of my campaign—the Alps whose peaks strike the sky and which only a god [a] had trodden before me." His face was flushed with blood, and his angry eye [b] flashed fire; he foamed at the mouth; and the breathing that issued from his panting lungs expressed the inarticulate rage of his breast. Thus he rode into the city, escorted by all the senators and surrounded by the rabble, rushing to behold the general's face, while he gave vent to all his fury and stormy passion.

The heart of Decius also was kindled by the approach of danger. He saw that the time had come, when he, though unarmed, might win more glory than the ever-victorious general. He did not run away nor hide himself in the seclusion of his own house, but lived on his quiet life with fearless mien, as free as if Hannibal had never entered Capua. But

cum iuvenem saevis, horrendum, concitus armis
invadit globus et pedibus sublime sedentis
ductoris sistit. tonat inde ferocibus alte
incessens victor dictis : " solusne ruentem
fulcire ac revocare paras a funere Romam ?
o demens ! en, qui divum mihi munera tanta
eripiat. Decio prorsus servabar inerti
vincendus, Decio imbelli, cui femina nulla
orta in Agenoreis nostrae Carthaginis oris
cesserit. huic agedum (nam cur indigna feramus ?)
magnanimo, miles, meritas innecte catenas."
dixerat haec, necdum finem convicia norant :
illatus velut armentis super ardua colla
cum sese imposuit victorque immane sub ira
infremuit leo et immersis gravis unguibus haesit,
mandit anhelantem pendens cervice iuvencum.
at Decius, dum vincla ligant : "necte ocius," inquit,
" (nam sic Hannibalem decet intravisse) catenas,
foederis infausti pretium. sic victima prorsus
digna cadit Decius ; nec enim te, sanguine laetum
humano, sit fas caesis placasse iuvencis.
en dextra ! en foedus ! nondum tibi curia necdum
templorum intrati postes ; iam panditur acri
imperio carcer. perge ac primordia tanta
accumula paribus factis. mihi fama sub umbras
te feret oppressum Capuae cecidisse ruinis."
nec plura effari concessum. obnubitur atra
veste caput, trahiturque ferox ante ora suorum.

now, alas, a savage band of armed soldiers quickly seized him and set him down before the feet of Hannibal who sat there in state. From his high seat the conqueror thundered at him with angry speech: "Do you intend with your single hand to prop the falling building and restore a dead Rome to life? Poor fool! are you the man to snatch from me the great gifts of the gods? They kept me alive merely that I might be conquered by Decius, Decius the carpet-knight, weaker than any woman born on the Tyrian shores of our native Carthage. But why should I submit to insult? Hasten, soldiers, to fasten round the neck of this hero the fetters he deserves." Thus he spoke, and the flow of his abuse was still unchecked. So, when a lion springs upon the herd and settles aloft upon their necks, he roars terribly in his victorious rage; then he drives in his claws to keep his great weight steady, and devours the panting steer, perched high upon its neck. But Decius, while they bound him, said: "Put on the fetters with all speed: they are a fitting symbol of Hannibal's entrance and the just reward for this ill-starred alliance. Decius is indeed the fit victim to be slain. For Hannibal delights in human blood, and we should do wrong to appease him by the sacrifice of oxen. Look at his friendship! look at his alliance! He has not yet entered the senate-house or the temple doors, but already the cruel tyrant opens the prison. Proceed, and follow up your noble beginning with like deeds! In the nether world I shall have news of your fall, crushed beneath the ruins of Capua." No more was he suffered to say: his head was veiled in a black mantle, and he was carried off still defiant in the sight of his countrymen.

Exin victor ovans sedato pectore tandem
spectandis urbis tectis templisque serenos
laetus circumfert oculos et singula discit:
quis muris sator, et pubes sit quanta sub armis,
quot bello pateant argenti aerisque talenta;
nunc qualis frenata acies, nunc deinde pedestris
copia quanta viris. monstrant capitolia celsa
Stellatesque docent campos Cereremque benignam.
iamque diem ad metas defessis Phoebus Olympo
impellebat equis, fuscabat et Hesperos umbra
paulatim infusa properantem ad litora currum.
instituunt de more epulas festamque per urbem
regifice extructis celebrant convivia mensis.
ipse, deum cultu et sacro dignatus honore,
praecipuis multoque procul splendentibus ostro
accipitur sublime toris. non una ministri
turba gregis; posuisse dapes his addita cura,
his adolere focos, his ordine pocula ferre;
necnon et certis struitur penus. aspera mensa
pondera caelati fulgent antiquitus auri.
eripiunt flammae noctem, strepituque moventum
murmurat alta domus. stupet inconsuetus opimae
Sidonius mensae miles faciemque superbi
ignotam luxus oculis mirantibus haurit.
vescitur ipse silens et tantos damnat honores
esse epulis facilesque coli tanto agmine mensas,
donec pulsa fames et Bacchi munera duram

---

[a] A district in the centre of Campania, famous for fertility.
[b] Wine.

Thereupon the conqueror's rage at last sank to rest. Calm and well-pleased, in triumph he turned his gaze upon the buildings and temples of the city, and learned one thing and another—who was the founder of the city, how many men they had under arms, how many talents of silver and copper were available for war, the quality of their cavalry, and lastly the number of their infantry. They showed him their lofty citadel and told him of the Stellatian [a] plain with its bountiful harvests. By now Phoebus was driving his weary steeds down the sky to their goal, and Evening spread her gradual shade and darkened his car in its course to the sea. Then the citizens made a feast as their manner was; the city kept holiday, and banquets were held at tables piled with regal splendour. Hannibal himself, adorned like a god and received with divine honours, was placed high upon a seat of honour covered with far-shining purple. Those who served at the meal were divided into many companies: it was the duty of some to set the dishes, of others to keep the fires alight, and of others to bring round the wine-cup in due order; and yet others were appointed to pile up the store of food. Heavy golden cups, chased in relief by craftsmen of old, sparkled on the board. The bright lighting banished night, and the lofty chamber hummed with the sound of moving attendants. The soldiers of Carthage, unaccustomed to such banquets, were astonished and drank in with wondering eyes that unfamiliar scene of lavish display. Hannibal himself kept silence while eating, disapproving the splendour of the feast and the great retinue that ministered to a need so easily satisfied; but, when he had eaten enough, the gift of Bacchus [b]

laxarunt mentem : tum frontis reddita demum
laetitia, et positae graviores pectore curae.
  Personat Euboica Teuthras testudine, Cymes
incola, et obtusas immiti murmure saevae
inter bella tubae permulcet cantibus aures.
namque chaos, caecam quondam sine sidere molem
non surgente die, ac mundum sine luce canebat.
tum deus ut liquidi discisset stagna profundi
tellurisque globum media compage locasset,
ut celsum superis habitare dedisset Olympum ;
castaque Saturni monstrabat saecula patris.[1]
iamque Iovem et laetos per furta canebat amores
Electraeque toros Atlantidos ; unde creatus,
proles digna deum, tum Dardanus ; isque Tonanti
ut det Erichthonium magna de stirpe nepotem.
hinc Tros, hinc Ilus, generis tunc ordine longo
Assaracus, nulloque minor famave manuve
tum Capys ut primus dederit sua nomina muris.
concelebrant plausu pariter Sidonia pubes
Campanaeque manus. ante omnes ductor honori
nominis augusto libat carchesia ritu ;
cetera quem sequitur Bacchique e more liquorem
irrorat mensis turba ardescitque Lyaeo.
  Interea, Tyrio resoluta in gaudia coetu
converso (neque enim, iuvenis non digne sileri,
tramittam tua coepta libens famamque negabo
quamquam imperfectis, magnae tamen indolis, ausis)
mens una, inviolata mero nullisque venenis
potando exarmata, decus pugnaeque necisque

[1] *Ll.* 453-458 *were rightly transferred to this place by Summers.*

[a] Cyme (or Cumae, in Latin) was a colony from Euboea.
[b] Perolla and his father, Pacuvius (see l. 58), are historical personages : Livy (xxiv. 9) tells the whole story at length.

softened his harsh mood. Then at last he regained a cheerful aspect and laid aside his pressing anxieties.

Now Teuthras, a citizen of Cyme, played on the Euboean[a] lyre, and his singing charmed ears deafened by the ungentle note of the fierce war-trumpet. For he sang of Chaos, once a mass lighted by no star, where dawn never rose, a benighted world. Then he told how the god had severed the expanse of sea and placed the round world in the centre of the system; how he appointed lofty Olympus to be a habitation for the gods. He told of the reign of Father Saturn over a righteous race. Next he sang of Jupiter—his sweet and secret dalliance, and his union with Electra, daughter of Atlas; how their son was Dardanus, worthy of his divine parents; and how Dardanus gave the Thunderer a grandson, Erichthonius of high descent; then the long succession passed through Tros and Ilus to Assaracus and thence to Capys, inferior to none in glory and great deeds; and how he bequeathed his name to the city. Carthaginians and men of Capua together applauded the singer. First of all Hannibal in solemn fashion poured forth a libation in honour of Capys, and the rest of the company followed his example, spilling wine on the tables in customary fashion, and growing heated as they drank.

The assembled Carthaginians gave themselves up to relaxation and revelry. But there was one young man there whom I must mention; for I will not pass over your design in silence, Perolla,[b] or fail to record your purpose, which, even though it failed, proceeded from a noble mind. He, alone unaffected by wine and not enfeebled by the poison of the wine-cup, was revolving in his mind a glorious task—

Sidoniae tacito volvebat pectore molem.
quoque esset miranda magis tam sacra libido,
Pacuvio genitus patrias damnaverat artes.
is variis oneratum epulis atque atria tardo
linquentem gressu comitatus pone parentem,
postquam posse datum meditata aperire novosque
pandere conatus, et liber parte relicta
tectorum a tergo patuit locus, " accipe digna
et Capua et nobis," inquit, "consulta," togaque
armatum amota nudat latus ; " hoc ego bellum
conficere ense paro atque avulsum ferre Tonanti
rectoris Libyci victor caput. hic erit ille,
qui polluta dolis iam foedera sanciet, ensis.
si perferre nequit spectacula tanta senectus
et tremit inceptis lasso maioribus aevo,
at tu securis concede penatibus et me
linque meae menti. summum quod credis et aequas
Hannibalem superis, o quantum nomine maior
iam Poeno tibi natus erit ! " vibrabat ab ore
ignis atrox, animusque viri iam bella gerebat,
cum senior, tanti pondus conaminis aegra
iam dudum vix aure ferens, tremebundus ibidem
sternitur et pedibus crebro pavida oscula figens :
" per si quid superest vitae, per iura parentis
perque tuam nostra potiorem, nate, salutem,
absiste inceptis, oro, ne sanguine cernam
polluta hospitia ac tabo repleta cruento
pocula et eversas pugnae certamine mensas.

---

[a] See ll. 55 foll.

to fight Hannibal and kill him. And, to make his noble desire more marvellous, he was the son of Pacuvius,[a] but had spurned his father's intrigues. When his father, burdened by a feast of many courses, walked slowly away from the hall, Perolla went out behind him; and it became possible to reveal his plan and explain his startling design, when they had left part of the dwelling behind them and came to an unoccupied space[b] at the back of the building. Then Perolla spoke: "Hearken to a plan worthy of Capua and of ourselves." Then he drew back his gown and revealed a sword by his side: "I purpose to end the war by this blade, to cut off the head of Hannibal and carry it in triumph to the Thunderer.[c] This sword shall seal the alliance which treachery has stained. If your aged eyes cannot bear to look on such a sight, if you shrink from a deed too bold for your declining age, then withdraw to the safety of your own house and leave me to my purpose. You hold Hannibal to be the chief of men, and you rank him with the gods; how much more famous than the Carthaginian shall your son be soon!" Fire flashed fiercely from his eyes, and in his thought he was already striking the blow. But his father, whose ears at once refused to hear a design of such dreadful import, fell trembling to the ground and in terror kissed his son's feet again and again. "By what remains to me of life, by a father's rights, and by your life, dearer to me than my own, I entreat you to abandon your purpose; let me not witness the hospitable board defiled with blood, the winecups filled with gore, and the tables overset in mortal

[b] A garden at the back of the house, Livy says.

[c] That is, to the Capitol at Rome.

tune illum, quem non acies, non moenia et urbes
ferre valent, cum frons propior lumenque corusco
igne micat, tune illa viri, quae vertice fundit,
fulmina pertuleris, si viso intorserit ense
diram, qua vertit per campos agmina, vocem ?
fallit te, mensas inter quod credis inermem.
tot bellis quaesita viro, tot caedibus armat
maiestas aeterna ducem. si admoveris ora,
Cannas et Trebiam ante oculos Thrasymennaque busta
et Pauli stare ingentem miraberis umbram.
quid ? tanto in casu comitum iuxtaque iacentum
torpebunt dextrae ? parce, oro, et desine velle,
cui nequeas victor superesse. an tristia vincla
et Decius non erudiunt componere mentem ? "
  Talia commemorans, famae maioris amore
flagrantem ut vidit iuvenem surdumque timori,
" nil ultra posco, refer in convivia gressum ;
approperemus," ait. " non iam tibi pectora pubis
Sidoniae fodienda manu tutantia regem :
hoc iugulo dextram explora. namque haec tibi ferrum,
si Poenum invasisse paras, per viscera ferrum
nostra est ducendum. tardam ne sperne senectam :
opponam membra atque ensem extorquere negatum
morte mea eripiam." lacrimae tunc ore profusae,
et magna superum cura servatus in arma
Scipiadae Poenus ; nec tantum fata dederunt
externa peragi dextra. pulcherrimus irae
et dignus fieri compos memorabilis ausi,

[a] At the battle of Zama (201 B.C.); but Scipio did not kill Hannibal there, as Silius seems to imply.

conflict! Will you be able to withstand him whom neither armies nor walled cities can withstand, when his frown comes close and the fire flashes from his eyes? Will you endure the thunderbolts launched from that head, if the sight of your sword calls forth the dread voice that routs whole armies on the field? If you think that he sits unarmed at table, you are wrong. His armour is the immortal glory he has gained by constant warfare and hecatombs of victims slain. If you come close to him, you will marvel to see before you Cannae and the Trebia, the dead of Lake Trasimene and the mighty shade of Paulus. Again, will his officers and those who sit at meat beside him lift no finger while such a scene is acting? Keep still, I entreat you, and abandon a plan which, if successful, must cost you your life. Does not the example of Decius and his cruel fetters teach you to cool your passions?"

Thus the father spoke. But, when he saw his son deaf to fear and burning with desire of high renown, he went on thus: "I entreat no more. Go back to the banqueting-hall; let us make haste. The task before you now is not to stab the Carthaginians when they fight in defence of their chief; mine is the throat on which you must test your blade. For, if you purpose to attack Hannibal, through my heart you must drive your weapon. Despise not my age and weakness. I shall throw my body in the way, and my death shall snatch from your hand the sword which you refused to surrender at my entreaty." Then his tears gushed forth. Thus by the high design of Providence Hannibal was saved, in order to meet Scipio in arms [a]; nor did Fate permit a foreign hand to perform so great an exploit. A splendid figure was Perolla in his wrath, and well he deserved to

amisit quantam posito conamine laudem,
cui tantum est voluisse decus ! tum reddere sese
festinant epulis et tristia fronte serenant,
donec laeta virum solvit convivia somnus.
  Postera lux Phaëthontis equos proferre parabat,
iam rapido summis curru splendente sub undis,
et iuvenis magno generatus Hamilcare duras
iam dudum exercet curas. Carthaginis arces
ire ferox Mago et patribus portare iubetur
nuntius acta ducis. praeda et captiva leguntur
corpora dereptaeque viris sub Marte cruento
exuviae, fausti superis libamina belli.
altera curarum Libycis dimittitur oris
heu Decius, reduci lentas servatus ad iras,
ni poenae iuvenem indignae miseratus ab alto
Iupiter antiquam Batti vertisset ad urbem.
hic Pellaea virum Ptolemaei sceptra vehentum
eripuere minis, resolutaque vincula collo.
atque eadem vitae custos mox deinde quieto
accepit tellus ossa inviolata sepulcro.
  Nec Venerem interea fugit exoptabile tempus
Poenorum mentes caeco per laeta premendi
exitio et luxu corda importuna domandi.
spargere tela manu passim fallentia natis
imperat et tacitas in pectora mittere flammas.
tum pueris dulce arridens : " eat improba Iuno
et nos (nec mirum, quid enim sumus ?) acta secundis
despiciat. valet illa manu, valet illa lacertis ;

---

[a] Phaëthon stands for his father, the Sun.

[b] Hannibal.

[c] Cyrene, where Decius was driven by foul weather, was then a province of the Egyptian kingdom : Decius was sent on to Alexandria and found a protector in King Ptolemy.

[d] The Cupids.

accomplish his great design. But how much fame he lost by abandoning his purpose, when the mere intention is so glorious! Then they hastened back to the feast and smoothed the trouble from their brows. At last sleep came and broke up the merry-making.

When the following day was about to reveal the steeds of Phaëthon,[a] and his swift chariot was already shining beneath the surface of the sea, the son of great Hamilcar[b] had long been busily engaged. He bade proud Mago repair to the towers of Carthage and report to the senate the exploits of their general. Booty was sent with him and chosen captives and spoils stripped from the dead in bloody warfare, as thank-offerings to the gods for success in battle. Another of Hannibal's cares was Decius; he, alas, was sent to the Libyan land, to be kept till the general returned and could inflict punishment at leisure. But Jupiter on high had pity on the innocent sufferer, and turned his course aside to the ancient city of Battus.[c] And here Ptolemy, the Macedonian king of Egypt, rescued him from the threats of the men who brought him in their ship, and released him from his bonds. And the same land that had saved his life soon afterwards received his bones, to lie undisturbed in a peaceful grave.

Meantime Venus did not miss the welcome opportunity to destroy the discipline of the Carthaginians by the insidious weapon of pleasure, and to tame their fierce hearts by luxury. She bade her children[d] scatter their invisible arrows broadcast and kindle unseen fires in every breast. Then she smiled sweetly on the boys and said: "Let Juno, elated by success, give herself airs and despise us. That is no wonder; for what are we? Strong is her hand and strong her

parvula nos arcu puerili spicula sensim
fundimus, et nullus nostro de vulnere sanguis.
verum, agite, o mea turba, precor, nunc tempus, adeste
et Tyriam pubem tacitis exurite telis.
amplexu multoque mero somnoque virorum
profliganda acies, quam non perfregerit ensis,
non ignes, non immissis Gradivus habenis.
combibat illapsos ductor per viscera luxus,
nec pudeat picto fultum iacuisse cubili,
nec crinem Assyrio perfundere pugnet amomo.
ille, sub hiberno somnos educere caelo
iactator, tectis malit consumere noctes;
ac ponat ritus vescendi saepe citato
dum residet sub casside equo, discatque Lyaeo
imbellem donare diem. tum deinde madenti
post epulas sit grata chelys, segnisque soporas
aut nostro vigiles ducat sub numine noctes."
   Haec postquam Venus, applaudit lascivus et alto
mittit se caelo niveis exercitus alis.
sentit flammiferas pubes Maurusia pennas,
et pariter fusis tepuerunt pectora telis.
Bacchi dona volunt epulasque et carmina rursus
Pieria liquefacta lyra. non acer aperto
desudat campo sonipes, non ulla per auras
lancea nudatos exercet torta lacertos.
mollitae flammis lymphae languentia somno
membra fovent, miserisque bonis perit horrida virtus.
ipse etiam, afflatus fallente Cupidine, ductor
instaurat mensas dapibus repetitque volentum
hospitia et patrias paulatim decolor artes

arm ; we but gently launch our tiny shafts from the bows of boys, and our wounds are followed by no blood. But be up and doing, my children ; the time has come for you to help me and inflame the hearts of the Tyrians with your invisible weapons. With dalliance, with excess of wine and sleep, you must rout an army that neither sword nor fire could shatter, nor the chariot of Mars with its utmost speed. Let the taste for luxury steal into Hannibal's heart ; let him drink it in, and not blush to rest his limbs on an embroidered couch, nor refuse to drench his locks with perfume of Assyria. He used to boast of sleeping under the winter sky ; now let him prefer to spend whole nights under a roof. He used often to take his food on horseback with his helmet on and the horse at speed ; let him change his habits and give up the peaceful day to the god of wine ; and then, when he has well drunk, let him welcome the lyre after the feast and either spend the night in drowsy sleep or watch and wake all night in my service."

When Venus spoke thus, her sportive infantry clapped their snowy wings and flew down from high heaven. The Moorish soldiers felt the fiery arrows, and their hearts were melted in a moment by that shower of bolts. They call for wine and dainty food, and for a repetition of song that sounds sweet to the musician's lyre. No mettled horse now sweats on the open plain ; no lance, hurled to a distance, tasks the bare arm. They bathe their limbs, drowsy with sleep, in water heated over the fire ; and their stern valour is sapped by the bane of luxury. Even Hannibal, breathed upon by a deceitful Cupid, piles high the festal board and courts the hospitality of eager hosts, till by degrees he grows degenerate

exuit, occulta mentem vitiante sagitta.
altera iam patria atque aequo sub honore vocatur
altera Carthago Capua, intactumque secundae
fortunae ingenium vitia allectantia quassant.
nec luxus ullus mersaeque libidine vitae
Campanis modus ; accumulant variasque per artes
scenarum certant epulas distinguere ludo,
ut strepit assidue ad Phrygiam Nilotica loton
Memphis Amyclaeo pariter[1] lasciva Canopo.
inprimis dulcem, Poeno laetante, per aures
nunc voce infundit Teuthras, nunc pectine, cantum.
isque ubi mirantem resonantia pollice fila
ductorem vidit Libyae, canere inde superbas
Aoniae laudes sensim testudinis orsus,
concordem citharae movit per carmina linguam,
vincere linquentes vitam quae possit olores.
atque haec e multis carpsit mollissima mensae :
" Argolicis quondam populis, mirabile dictu,
exaudita chelys, lapidem testudine felix
ducere et in muris posuisse volentia saxa.
haec Amphionio vallavit pectine Thebas
ac, silice aggeribus per se scandente vocatis,
iussit in immensum cantatas surgere turres.
altera, turbatum plectro moderata profundum,
et tenuit phocas et in omni Protea forma
traxit et aequoreo portavit Ariona dorso.

[1] pariter *ed.*: passim *edd.*

---

[a] Canopus in Egypt is called Spartan (an unsuitable epithet), because Canopus, the steersman of Menelaus, died there, and the place was named after him.

[b] Aonia, a part of Boeotia, was the dwelling-place of Apollo and the Muses.

[c] Amphion, son of Zeus and Antiope, received the lyre from Hermes who invented it. Three other famous musicians

and discards the virtues of his race; for his mind was poisoned by the unseen arrow. Capua is now a second home to him: he calls it a second Carthage and honours it as much; and the character which victory could not hurt is shattered by the seductions of vice. For the men of Capua set no limits to the luxury and profligacy of their lives: they went further and further: using various arts, they sought to set off their banquets by means of stage-plays: so Memphis on the Nile resounds ever with the Phrygian flute and matches Spartan Canopus [a] in its revelry. Teuthras above all charmed Hannibal, filling his ears with sweet music both of the voice and of the instrument; and he, when he saw the general marvelling at the sound his fingers drew from the strings, began by degrees to set forth the splendid triumphs of the Aonian [b] lyre; and he sang in unison with the music in a voice that might surpass the dying swan. And this was the song he chose out of many, as most grateful to those who sat at meat:

"Long ago the nations of Greece—marvellous to tell—heard the shell of the tortoise sound, and the shell had power to draw stones and bring them of their own accord, to make walls for a city. The lyre on which Amphion [c] played built walls round Thebes and bade the towers rise high at its music; and the stone climbed up of itself upon the ramparts that came to the call of the musician. Another lyre calmed the stormy sea with its music and arrested the seals; it drew after it Proteus in all his changes of shape,[d] and carried Arion on the sea-

are next mentioned—Arion, Cheiron, and Orpheus. The lyre of Orpheus became a constellation (l. 461).

[d] See vii. 422 foll.

iam, quae Peliaca formabat rupe canendo
heroum mentes et magni pectora Achillis,
Centauro dilecta chelys, compesceret iras,
percussa fide, vel pelagi vel tristis Averni.
sed, quos pulsabat Riphaeum ad Strymona, nervi,
auditus superis, auditus manibus Orpheus,
emerito fulgent clara inter sidera caelo.
hunc etiam mater, tota comitante sororum
Aonidum turba, mater mirata canentem.
non illo Pangaea iuga aut Mavortius Haemus,
non illo modulante sonos stetit ultima Thrace ;
cum silvis venere ferae, cum montibus amnes,
immemor et dulcis nidi positoque volatu
non mota volucris captiva pependit in aethra.
quin etiam, Pagasaea ratis cum caerula, nondum
cognita terrenae, pontumque intrare negaret,
ad puppim sacrae, cithara eliciente, carinae
adductum cantu venit mare. pallida regna
Bistonius vates flammisque Acheronta sonantem
placavit plectro et fixit revolubile saxum.
o dirae Ciconum matres Geticique furores
et damnata deis Rhodope ! tulit ora revulsa
in pontum, ripis utraque sequentibus, Hebrus.
tum quoque, cum rapidi caput a cervice recisum
portarent fluctus, subito emicuere per undas
ad murmur cete toto exultantia ponto."

[a] The Centaur who trained the young Achilles and other heroes.

[b] "Riphean" = Northern: Orpheus lived in Thrace.

[c] Calliope.

[d] Mars was the chief deity of the warlike people of Thrace.

[e] The port in Thessaly from which the Argo sailed.

[f] For *Bistonius* see ii. 76.

beast's back. A third lyre, whose strains moulded the minds of heroes and the spirit of great Achilles in the cave of Mount Pelion—the lyre that Cheiron [a] loved, could quell the raging sea or the wrath of Hell itself, when he struck the strings. But the chords which Orpheus struck beside the Riphean [b] Strymon, charming the gods above and the gods below the earth, earned a place in heaven and shine there among the bright stars. Even his mother,[c] together with the whole train of her sister Muses, marvelled at his playing. At his music neither Pangaeus nor Haemus, the mountain of Mars,[d] nor remotest Thrace, could stand still. Wild beasts and forests, rivers and mountains, followed him. The bird forgot her loved nestlings, stopped her flight, and hung arrested in the motionless air. Moreover, when the Argo at Pagasae [e] refused to launch out on the blue water which on land she had never known, the sea, summoned by the lyre, obeyed the music and came up to the stern of the sacred bark. The Thracian [f] bard charmed with his quill the sunless land and the crackling flames of Acheron, and stopped the stone from rolling.[g] Alas for the cruelty of the Ciconian [h] women and the madness of the Thracians! alas for Rhodope pronounced guilty by the gods! [i] When the Hebrus bore his severed head to the sea, both banks followed it [k]; and then, when it was carried along by the rushing waves, suddenly the sea-beasts emerged from the water and bounded high at the low sound of that voice all over the sea." Thus

[g] For Acheron see note to i. 92. The "stone" is that which was rolled uphill by Sisyphus in Hades.

[h] See ii. 75.

[i] The Thracian women tore Orpheus to pieces and threw his body into the river Hebrus.

[k] See l. 466.

sic tunc Pierius bellis durata virorum
pectora Castalio frangebat carmine Teuthras.
Interea placida attulerant iam flamina terris
Magonem Libycis. lauro redimita subibat
optatos puppis portus, pelagoque micabant
captiva arma procul celsa fulgentia prora.
at patulo surgens iam dudum ex aequore late
nauticus implebat resonantia litora clamor,
et, simul adductis percussa ad pectora tonsis,
centeno fractus spumabat verbere pontus.
nec lentum in medios rapienda ad gaudia vulgus
procurrit fluctus, elataque turba favore
certatim ingenti celebrat nova gaudia plausu.
aequatur rector divis : illum undique matres,
illum turba minor, moniti gaudere nepotes,
et senior manus et iuxta populusque patresque
mactatis superum dignantur honore iuvencis.
sic patriam Mago et portas ingressus ovantes
fraternae laudis fama. ruit inde senatus,
et multo patrum stipatur curia coetu.
tum divos veneratus avum de more vetusto,
" Martem," ait, " egregium et fractas, quis Itala tellus
nitebatur, opes, pars ipse haud parva laborum,
nuntio. pugnatum superis in vota secundis.
est locus, Aetoli signat quem gloria regis,
possessus quondam prisca inter saecula Dauno ;
umentes rapido circumdat gurgite campos
Aufidus et stagnis intercipit arva refusis ;
mox fluctus ferit Hadriacos magnoque fragore
cedentem impellit retrorsus in aequora pontum.

---

[a] Diomede : see note to i. 125.

Teuthras, votary of Castalia and the Muses, enfeebled by his music the soldiers' war-hardened hearts.

Meanwhile Mago had been wafted by gentle breezes to the Libyan land. His ship, wreathed with laurel, entered the desired harbour, and the glittering spoils on her lofty bows shone from a distance across the water. Then the shouting of the sailors, which had long been rising from the open sea, filled all the shore with its sound; and, when the rowers all together brought the oars back sharply to their breasts, the sea foamed under the stroke of a hundred blades. Eager to snatch a hasty joy, the citizens waded out into the water, and the exuberant crowd eagerly hailed the good news with a storm of applause. Hannibal is ranked with the gods. All the women, all the little children, rejoicing at their mothers' bidding, and all the older citizens—senate and people alike—think him worthy of divine honours and the slaughter of oxen. Thus Mago came back to Carthage and entered the gates that rang with the report of his brother's exploits. The senate assembled in haste, and the senate-house was packed with a great assembly. Mago prayed to the gods in the fashion of his sires and then spoke thus: "I bring news of a great victory: the strength upon which Italy relied has been shattered; and I myself played no small part in the work. The gods favoured us in the battle. There is a land which bears the name of a famous king of Aetolia [a] and was possessed by Daunus in an age long past; the rapid stream of the Aufidus flows round the watery plains and cuts off the promise of harvest by its floods; and later, dashing against the waves of the Adriatic, with a loud noise it forces the salt water to retreat seawards.

hic Varro et magnum Latia inter nomina Paulus
nomen, quis rerum ducibus permissa potestas,
vixdum depulsa nigrae caligine noctis,
invadunt campum et late fulgentibus armis
accendunt ultro lucem surgentis Eoi.
nos contra (nam germanum furor acer agebat
optatae pugnae) castris cita signa movemus.
intremit et tellus, et pulsus mugit Olympus.
hic fluvium et campos abscondit caede virorum
ductor, quo numquam maiorem ad bella tulerunt
rectorem terrae. vidi, cum turbine saevo
Ausonia et sonitu bellantis fusa per agros
uni terga daret. vidi, cum Varro citato
auferretur equo, proiectis degener armis.
quin et magnanimum, perfosso corpore telis,
strage super socium vidi te, Paule, cadentem.
Aegates ille et servilia foedera larga
ultus caede dies ; non plus optasse liberet,
quam tum concessit dexter deus : altera iam lux
si talis redeat, populis sis omnibus una
tum, Carthago, caput terrasque colare per omnes.
testes hi stragis, quos signum illustre superbis
mos laeva gestare viris." tum funditur ante
ora admirantum praefulgens anulus auro
datque fidem verbis haud parvo insignis acervo.
hinc iterum repetens, " restat nunc sedibus imis
vertenda atque aequanda solo iam subruta Roma.
annitamur," ait, " vires refovete tot haustas
casibus, et pateant non parca aeraria dextris,

---

[a] The treaty concluded at the end of the First Punic War. For the battle of the Aegatian Islands see note to i. 35.

Here the Roman commanders—Paulus, a name honoured in Latium, and Varro—took the field, when the darkness of night had hardly been dispelled; and the far-seen glitter of their weapons added a brighter light to the rising sun. We marched quickly from the camp to meet them; for my brother was driven on by a passionate desire for battle. The earth shook and the welkin rang as we fought. Then our general, as great a leader in war as this earth ever bore, hid the river and the plains with heaps of corpses. Before my eyes all Italy was routed and fled from him alone, from the fierce onset and the sound of his warfare. Before my eyes degenerate Varro threw down his arms and galloped from the field. I witnessed also the death of brave Paulus, when he fell, pierced through with many a dart, above the corpses of his men. The great slaughter of that day avenged the Aegatian Islands and the treaty of subservience [a]; we could not wish to pray for more than was granted us then by divine favour. If such a day came over again, Carthage would be the sole ruler over all nations and would be honoured over all the world. As evidence of the slaughter, behold these tokens, which it is the custom of high-born Romans to wear on their left hand." Therewith he poured forth before their astonished eyes glittering rings of gold; and the truth of his words was confirmed by the goodly heap of rings.[b] Then he began again: "Rome is undermined, and it only remains to wrench her from her foundations and level her with the ground. Let us make the effort," he cried; "recruit your armies weakened by so many losses, and open wide your

[b] See note to viii. 675.

quas emimus bello. desit iam belua, tristis
Ausoniis terror, necnon alimenta fatigant."
  Atque ea dum memorat, torvo conversus in ora
Hannonis vultu, quem gliscens gloria pravum
ductoris studio iam dudum agitabat acerbo :
" iamne tibi dextras inceptaque nostra probamus ?
iam fas Dardanio me non servire colono ?
anne iterum Hannibalem dedi placet ? atra veneno
invidiae nigroque undantia pectora felle,
tandem tot titulis totque exorata tropaeis,
infelix muta. dextra en, en dextera, quam tu
Aeneadis lacerare dabas, et litora et amnes
et stagna et latos implevit sanguine campos."
haec Mago, atque animos favor haud obscurus alebat.
  Cui, simul invidia atque ira stimulantibus, Hannon :
" talia vesani iuvenis convicia miror
haud equidem ; tumet ingenio, fraternaque corda
non tarde agnoscas et virus futile linguae.
qui ne mutatum vanis absistere credat,
nunc pacem orandum, nunc improba foedere rupto
arma reponendum et bellum exitiale cavendum
auctor ego. atque adeo vosmet perpendite, quaeso,
quid ferat ; haud aliud nobis censere relictum est.
tela, viros, aurum, classes, alimenta precatur
belligeramque feram. victus non plura petisset.
sanguine Dardanio Rutulos saturavimus agros,
et iacet in campis Latium. deponere curas
tandem ergo, bone, da, victor, liceatque sedere

---

[a] See ii. 276 foll. [b] See ii. 377.
[c] This is said to Hannibal.

treasury for the pay of mercenaries. Our elephants, so dreaded by the Romans, are now few in number; and our want of food-supplies troubles us."

While speaking thus he directed fierce looks at Hanno,[a] whose crooked mind had long been tortured by the growing fame of Hannibal: "Do you approve *now* of the deeds that our hands have wrought? Am I permitted *now* to refuse a Roman for my master? Or will you vote a second time [b] for the surrender of Hannibal? Unhappy man, be softened at last by so many glorious trophies, and change that heart, so black with the poison of jealousy and so full of bitter gall. See, that hand, that hand which you wished to give up to the Roman torturers, has filled shores and rivers, lakes and spreading plains, with Roman blood." Thus Mago spoke, and the manifest sympathy of his hearers gave him confidence.

Then Hanno answered, urged on at once by jealousy and anger: "Such abuse does not surprise me, coming from a brain-sick youth. He is proud by nature, and it is easy to recognize his brother's disposition and the stingless venom of his tongue. He need not suppose that I have changed and am giving up my policy in despair. For I propose that we should now sue for peace, should now lay down the arms that are stained by a breach of treaty, and avoid a war that will destroy us. Or rather, do you yourselves weigh well his proposals; there is no other decision for us to come to. He asks for arms, soldiers, and gold, for fleets, provisions, and elephants. Had he been defeated, he could not have asked for more. We have drenched the soil of Italy with Roman blood, and all Latium is laid low on the battle-fields. Then suffer us at last, noble conqueror,[c] to forget our

in patria ; liceat non exhaurire rapacis
impensis belli vacuatos saepe penates.
nunc en, nunc, inquam (falsa ut praesagia nostra
sint, oro, mensque augurio ludatur inani)
haud procul est funesta dies. atrocia novi
corda ac prospicio natas e cladibus iras.
vos ego, vos metuo, Cannae. submittite signa
atque adeo temptate, agedum, ac deposcite pacem :
non dabitur. parat ille dolor, mihi credite, maius
exitium accepto ; citiusque haec foedera victor
quam victus, dabit. atque adeo, qui tanta superbo
facta sonas ore et spumanti turbine perflas
ignorantum aures, dic, en, germanus in armis
ille tuus par Gradivo, per saecula tellus
cui similem numquam ductorem in bella creavit,
moenia Romuleae cur nondum viderit urbis ?
scilicet e gremio matrum rapiamus in hostem
nondum portandis habiles gravioribus armis ?
aeratas iussi texamus mille carinas,
atque omnis Libyae quaeratur belua terris,
ut longa imperia atque armatos proroget annos
Hannibal et regnum trahat usque in tempora fati ?
vos vero—neque enim occulto circumdamur astu—
ne dulces spoliate domos ; castrisque potentum
atque opibus sancite modum. pax optima rerum,
quas homini novisse datum est ; pax una triumphis
innumeris potior ; pax, custodire salutem
et cives aequare potens, revocetur in arces
tandem Sidonias ; et fama fugetur ab urbe

troubles and take our ease at home; suffer us to keep some children in the families so often thinned by the insatiable demands of war. Now, yes now, I say—I pray that my forecast may prove untrue and my mind may be the victim of a mere delusion—the fatal day is at hand. I know the stubborn hearts of the foe, and I foresee the martial ardour that defeat will breed. It is Cannae, Cannae that I fear. Lower your standards, or rather, make haste to sue for peace and demand it. You will not get it. Believe me, their resentment is hatching a worse destruction than that which they have suffered; and they will make this peace more readily when victorious than when they are defeated. Or rather tell us, you who proclaim those great deeds so proudly and fill the ears of the ignorant with your frothy flood of words—tell us, why that brother of yours, that match for Mars in battle, the greatest general whom earth has ever borne, has never yet set eyes on the walls of Rome. Shall we, forsooth, snatch from their mothers' laps boys who are not yet fit to carry heavy armour, and make them fight? Shall we, at his demand, build a thousand ships of war and ransack all Libya for elephants, in order that Hannibal may prolong his command and fight on for years and exercise a tyrant's sway till the day of his death? But I appeal to you—for the trap is set in our sight—rob not your homes of your loved ones, but set a limit to the armies and the power of these potentates. Peace is the best thing that man may know; peace alone is better than a thousand triumphs; peace has power to guard our lives and secure equality among fellow-citizens. Let us then after so long recall peace to the city of Carthage, and banish the reproach of treachery from

perfidiae, Phoenissa, tua. si tanta libido
armorum tenet atque enses non reddere perstat
poscenti patriae, nil suppeditare furori
hortor et haec fratri Magonem dicta referre."
  Plura annectentem (neque enim satiaverat iras
dicendo) clamor turbat diversa volentum :
" si Libyae decus, haud ulli superabilis armis,
Hannibal est irae tibi, destituemus ad ipsas
victorem metas ? nec opum adiumenta feremus ?
invidia unius sceptra ut iam parta retardet ? "
inde alacres tribuunt, quae belli posceret usus,
absentique suum iactant sub teste favorem.
mox eadem terris placitum traducere Hiberis,
dum malus obtrectat facta immortalia livor
nec sinit adiutas ductoris crescere laudes.

---

[a] Mago would report their goodwill to Hannibal.

Dido's city. If Hannibal has such a passion for war and disobeys his country when she bids him sheathe the sword, then I advise you to refuse all supplies to such a madman, and I move that Mago report this answer to his brother."

He would have added more; for he had not yet said enough to gratify his wrath; but loud cries of dissent confounded him: "If Hannibal, the glory of Libya, the invincible general, excites your anger, shall we leave the conqueror in the lurch just when he is reaching the goal, and refuse to send him supplies? Shall the jealousy of one man delay the imperial power which is already secured?" Then they eagerly voted the supplies required for war, and, in the presence of a witness,[a] made a show of their devotion to the absent general. Next they decided to send supplies also to Spain, though malicious envy belittled Hannibal's immortal deeds and sought to refuse the assistance needed for the increase of his fame.

LIBER DUODECIMUS

ARGUMENT

Hannibal leaves Capua: his troops have lost their vigour and fail in attacks upon Neapolis, Cumae, and Puteoli (1-103). *He visits Baiae and other famous places* (103-157). *He marches against Nola but is beaten off by Marcellus* (158-294). *The Romans become more hopeful and are further encouraged by an oracle from Delphi* (295-341). *The war in Sardinia: Torquatus defeats Hampsagoras: a tribute to the poet Ennius* (342-419). *Hannibal burns several cities and takes the city of Tarentum but not the citadel* (420-448). *He returns to defend Capua against a Roman blockade,*

Iam terra glaciale caput fecundaque nimbis
tempora et austrifero nebulosam vertice frontem
immitis condebat Hiems, blandisque salubre
ver Zephyris tepido mulcebat rura sereno:
prorumpit Capua Poenus vicinaque late
praemisso terrore quatit: ceu condita bruma,
dum Riphaea rigent Aquilonis flamine, tandem
evolvit serpens arcano membra cubili
et spondente die novus emicat atque coruscum
fert caput et saniem sublatis faucibus efflat.
at Libyci ducis ut fulserunt signa per agros,
desolata metu cuncta, et suadente pavore

---

[a] See note to xi. 459.

BOOK XII

ARGUMENT (*continued*)

beating two Roman armies on the way: he buries the body of Ti. Sempronius Gracchus (449-478). *Unable to force his way into Capua, he marches against Rome* (479-540). *Consternation at Rome* (541-557). *He examines the walls and surroundings of the city, but is driven back to his camp by Fulvius Flaccus who had hastened back from Campania* (558-573). *Two attempts to fight a battle are frustrated by a terrible storm sent by Jupiter* (574-667). *Making a third attempt, he is stopped by Juno, acting by Jupiter's command* (668-730). *Rejoicing of the Romans* (731-752).

UNKINDLY Winter was now hiding in the earth his icy head, his temples fraught with storms, and his cloud-capped brow that towers aloft with menace of gales; and healthful Spring was cheering the land with her gentle zephyrs and clear warm weather. Then the Carthaginians burst forth from Capua with terror in their van, and harassed all the surrounding country. Thus the serpent hides away in winter while the Riphaean [a] mountains are frozen by the North-wind's breath; but at last, when the season gives it confidence, it glides forth from its secret lair and glitters with a new skin, lifting up its shining head and breathing forth venom from its erected throat. When Hannibal's dreaded standards gleamed over the land, the country became a desert: driven

vallo se clausere simul trepidique salutis
expectant ipsis metuentes moenibus hostem.
Sed non ille vigor, qui ruptis Alpibus arma
intulerat dederatque vias Trebiaque potitus
Maeonios Italo sceleravit sanguine fluctus,
tunc inerat: molli luxu madefacta meroque,
illecebris somni torpentia membra fluebant.
quis gelidas suetum noctes thorace gravatis
sub Iove non aequo trahere et tentoria saepe
spernere, ubi hiberna ruerent cum grandine nimbi,
ac ne nocte quidem clipeive ensesve reposti,
non pharetrae aut iacula, et pro membris arma fuere:
tum grave cassis onus maioraque pondera visa
parmarum, ac nullis fusae stridoribus hastae.
Prima instaurantem sensit certamina mitis
Parthenope, non dives opum, non spreta vigoris;
sed portus traxere ducem secura volentem
aequora, quae peteret veniens Carthagine puppis.
nunc molles urbi ritus atque hospita Musis
otia et exemptum curis gravioribus aevum.
Sirenum dedit una suum, memorabile, nomen
Parthenope muris Acheloïas, aequore cuius
regnavere diu cantus, cum dulce per undas
exitium miseris caneret non prospera nautis.
haec pone aggressus (nam frontem clauserat aequor)
moenia, non ullas valuit perfringere Poenus
tota mole vias frustraque inglorius ausi

[a] Naples: the city kept up the customs and institutions of Greek civilization, and became, at a later date, a favourite place of retirement for Romans who could appreciate these attractions. Silius himself spent his old age there.

by fear men shut themselves up behind fortifications and awaited the enemy, trembling for their lives and distrusting even their walls.

But the former hardihood which had burst through the Alps and cleared a path for the army, which had mastered the Trebia and defiled the Etruscan lake with Italian blood, was no longer there. Their limbs were sluggish and flabby, enervated by luxury and ease, by wine and the enticements of sleep. Once they had been used to spend cold nights under a stormy sky while wearing their heavy breastplates, and had often despised a tent when the rain and hail of winter were pouring down; even at night they did not put off sword and buckler, quivers and lances, but treated their weapons as parts of their bodies. But now the helmet was a burden, the light shield felt too heavy, and their spears made no whizzing sound as they went forth.

When Hannibal renewed the strife, mild Parthenope [a] was the first to feel it, not because the city was wealthy or because he despised its courage; but the harbour was the attraction: he wanted safe anchorage for vessels coming from Carthage. That city is now an abode of peace, a resting-place where the Muses dwell, and life there is free from pressing anxieties. Parthenope, daughter of Acheloüs, gave the city its famous name. She was one of the Sirens, and her singing long ruled the waves, when her boding voice sang melodious destruction across the water to hapless sailors. The front of the city was defended by the sea, and therefore Hannibal attacked it on the landward side; but all his efforts failed to break open an entrance: he was baffled in the attempt and vainly belaboured the barred

pulsavit quatiens obstructas ariete portas.
stabat Cannarum Graia ad munimina victor
nequiquam et cautae mentis consulta probabat
eventu, qui post Dauni stagnantia regna
sanguine Tarpeias ire abstinuisset ad arces.
" en, qui nos segnes et nescire addere cursum
factis iactastis, quod vobis scandere nuper
non acie ex ipsa concessum moenia Romae,
intrate atque epulas promissas sede Tonantis
his, quae Graia manus defendit, reddite tectis."
talia iactabat famaeque pudore futurae,
irritus incepti prima si absisteret urbe,
audebat cuncta atque acuebat fraudibus enses.
sed subitae muris flammae totoque fluebant
aggeris anfractu tela improvisa per auras.
haud secus, occuluit saxi quo vertice fetus
ales fulva Iovis, tacito si ad culmina nisu
evasit serpens terretque propinquus hiatu,
illa, hostem rostro atque assuetis fulmina ferre
unguibus incessens, nidi circumvolat orbem.

Tandem ad vicinos Cumarum vertere portus
defessum subiit varioque lacessere motu
fortunam et famae turbando obstare sinistrae.
sed custos urbi Gracchus, tutela vel ipsis
certior, arcebat muris iterumque sedere
portis atque aditus iterum sperare vetabat.
lustrat inops animi rimaturque omnia circum

---

[a] See note to i. 293.

[b] It is implied that Greeks were not dangerous antagonists —a fixed conviction in the Roman mind.

[c] See x. 375 foll.

[d] The golden eagle.

[e] Ti. Sempronius Gracchus, consul in 215 B.C.

gates with the blows of his battering-rams. The victor of Cannae stood helpless before a Greek city; and the event proved the wisdom of his caution, when he refused to march from the bloody field of Daunus[a] against the citadel of Rome. "You called me a laggard who could not follow up his victory, because you were not allowed to scale the walls of Rome immediately after the battle. Well, then, enter Naples and make for me, in a city defended by Greeks,[b] the banquet which you promised to set in the abode of the Thunderer."[c] Thus he reproached his men, and, fearing for his fame in time coming if he were to fall back baffled from the first city he attacked, he shrank from no risks and used stratagems to sharpen his assault. But fire flashed suddenly from the walls, and a shower of missiles was discharged unexpectedly from the whole circuit of the ramparts. Even so, when the tawny bird of Jupiter[d] has hidden her young on the top of a cliff, if a serpent climbs noiselessly up the height and opens its dreaded jaws near the nestlings, the mother-bird flies round and round the nest, attacking the foe with her beak and the talons that are wont to carry thunderbolts.

Wearied out at last he thought to shift his quarters to the seaport of Cumae hard by, to challenge Fortune by change of place, and to prevent loss of reputation by causing unrest. But Gracchus,[e] the governor of the city, a surer defence than the walls themselves, kept the enemy away from the place, preventing them from encamping again by the gates and from hoping again to force an entrance. Hannibal lost courage: he rode about at furious speed and examined closely all the country round; and he tried

alite vectus equo rursusque hortatibus infit
laudum agitare suos : " pro di, quis terminus," inquit,
" ante urbes standi Graias, oblite tuorum
factorum miles ? quis erit modus ? Alpibus astat
nimirum maior moles, et scandere caelum
pulsantes iubeo scopulos ; quamquam altera detur
si similis tellus, aliaeque repente sub astra
exsurgant rupes, non ibis et arduus arma
me ducente feres ? tene heu Cumanus hiantem
agger adhuc murusque tenet Gracchusque, moveri
non ausus portis ? parvo in discrimine cerno,
an vobis gentes, quaecumque labore parastis,
casu gesta putent. per vos Tyrrhena faventum
stagna deum, per ego et Trebiam cineresque Sagunti
obtestor, dignos iam vosmet reddite vestra
quam trahitis fama et revocate in pectora Cannas."

Sic ductor fessas luxu attritasque secundis
erigere et verbis tentabat sistere mentes.
atque hic perlustrans aditus, fulgentia cernit
arcis templa iugo, quorum tum Virrius, altae
immitis ductor Capuae, primordia pandit :
" non est hoc," inquit, " nostri, quod suspicis, aevi ;
maiores fecere manus. cum regna timeret
Dictaei regis, sic fama est, linquere terras
Daedalus invenit nec toto signa sequenti
orbe dare, aetherias aliena tollere in auras
ausus se penna atque homini monstrare volatus.
suspensum hic librans media inter nubila corpus
enavit superosque novus conterruit ales.

---

[a] *i.e.* which still attends you from the past.

[b] See xi. 65.

[c] Minos, for whom Daedalus built the famous Labyrinth.

once more to excite his men by reminding them of their past deeds: "Great Heavens!" he cried; "soldiers, forgetful of your past, is your onward march to be stopped for ever by Greek cities? Will you nowhere draw the line? A mightier obstacle than the Alps, forsooth, blocks your way, and I bid you climb peaks that touch the sky! And yet, if a land like that were before us now and other cliffs were suddenly to rise as high as heaven, would you not go forward, if I led you, and carry your arms up the heights? Are you the men to stand and gape, barred by the ramparts and walls of Cumae, and by Gracchus who dares not stir outside the gates? I see it all but certain, that the world will impute to chance every result of your exertions. By Lake Trasimene where the gods favoured us, by the Trebia and by the ashes of Saguntum, I implore you to make yourselves once more worthy of the reputation you trail after you;[a] and remember Cannae."

Thus their leader sought to lift up and steady the hearts enfeebled by luxury and enervated by prosperity. And here, while studying all the means of approach, he saw a temple shining on the summit of the citadel; and Virrius,[b] the harsh governor of proud Capua, then explained its origin. "That building above us," he said, "was not the work of our time: it was raised by other hands in ancient days. When Daedalus—so the legend runs—feared the power of the Cretan king,[c] he found a way to escape from our world and leave no trace for Minos who pursued him over the whole earth. He dared to ascend the sky on wings not his own and to reveal to mankind the art of flying. Keeping his body poised amid the clouds, he floated on, and the strange winged creature

natum etiam docuit falsae sub imagine plumae
attentare vias volucrum; lapsumque solutis
pennarum remis et non felicibus alis
turbida plaudentem vidit freta; dumque dolori
indulget subito, motis ad pectora palmis,
nescius heu planctu duxit moderante volatus.
hic pro nubivago gratus pia templa meatu
instituit Phoebi atque audaces exuit alas."
  Virrius haec: sed enim ductor numerabat inertes
atque actos sine Marte dies ac stare pudebat.
ingemit adversis respectansque irrita tecta
urbe Dicarchea parat exsatiare dolorem.
hic quoque nunc pelagus, nunc muri saxea moles
officit audenti defensantumque labores.
dumque tenet socios dura atque obsaepta viarum
rumpere nitentes lentus labor, ipse propinqua
stagnorum terraeque simul miracula lustrat.
  Primores adsunt Capuae: docet ille, tepentes
unde ferant nomen Baiae, comitemque dedisse
Dulichiae puppis stagno sua nomina monstrat.
ast hic Lucrino mansisse vocabula quondam
Cocyti memorat medioque in gurgite ponti
Herculeum commendat iter, qua discidit aequor
Amphitryoniades, armenti victor Hiberi.
ille, olim populis dictum Styga, nomine verso
stagna inter celebrem nunc mitia monstrat Avernum;

---

[a] Icarus, who flew too near the sun.

[b] When Daedalus beat his breast in grief for his son, he found that the motion of his arms carried him along in the air.

[c] Puteoli (Pozzuoli): the real name is excluded by the metre.

[d] See note to viii. 539.

[e] One of the infernal rivers: see note to ii. 610.

alarmed the gods. He taught his son [a] also to put on a counterfeit semblance of wings and attempt the flight of birds; but, when the feathery oarage melted, he saw him fall and splash the stormy sea with his ill-starred wings. Yielding to his sudden grief, Daedalus smote his breast, and his blows steered his flight though he knew it not.[b] And here he raised a temple to Phoebus in gratitude for his voyage through the clouds, and here put off his daring wings."

So Virrius spoke; but Hannibal was counting up all the idle days that had passed without battle, and was ashamed of inactivity. He groaned at his failure; and looking back at the town he had besieged in vain, he sought to wreak his anger on the city of Dicaearchus.[c] But here too his attempts were foiled, now by the sea, now by the massive stone walls and the exertions of the defenders. And, while his men laboured on and on, endeavouring to force a difficult passage through obstruction, he himself visited the strange sights which the neighbouring waters and land presented.

The nobles of Capua attended him. One explained how the hot springs of Baiae got their name, pointing out that they were named after a mariner who sailed with Ulysses.[d] Another told how the Lucrine lake was called Cocytus [e] in former times, and praised the road which Hercules made over the sea, when the son of Amphitryon, after mastering the Spanish herd,[f] parted the waters asunder. A third pointed out Lake Avernus, formerly called Styx by the people, but now, under a new name, famous among healing waters. Once dreaded by birds and awful

[f] The oxen of Geryon: see note to i. 277.

tum, tristi nemore atque umbris nigrantibus horrens
et formidatus volucri, letale vomebat
suffuso virus caelo Stygiaque per urbes
religione sacer saevum retinebat honorem.
huic vicina palus—fama est Acherontis ad undas
pandere iter—caecas stagnante voragine fauces
laxat et horrendos aperit telluris hiatus
interdumque novo perturbat lumine manes.
at iuxta caligantes longumque per aevum
infernis pressas nebulis pallente sub umbra
Cimmerias iacuisse domos noctemque profundam
Tartareae narrant urbis. tum sulphure et igni
semper anhelantes coctoque bitumine campos
ostentant. tellus, atro exundante vapore
suspirans ustisque diu calefacta medullis,
aestuat et Stygios exhalat in aëra flatus ;
parturit et tremulis metuendum exsibilat antris,
interdumque cavas luctatus rumpere sedes
aut exire fretis, sonitu lugubre minaci
Mulciber immugit lacerataque viscera terrae
mandit et exesos labefactat murmure montes.
tradunt Herculea prostratos mole Gigantas
tellurem iniectam quatere, et spiramine anhelo
torreri late campos, quotiensque minantur
rumpere compagem impositam, expallescere caelum.
apparet Prochyte saevum sortita Mimanta,
apparet procul Inarime, quae turbine nigro
fumantem premit Iapetum flammasque rebelli

---

[a] Owing to its volcanic nature, the Campanian coast was supposed to be connected with the nether world ; hence the infernal rivers, Styx and Acheron, were placed here also.

[b] The fire-god, more often called Vulcanus.

[c] The Giants were punished for their revolt against the gods by being placed under mountains ; and volcanic action

in the gloomy shade of a dark forest, it sent up a poisonous exhalation to the lowering sky; the infernal deities were worshipped there with savage rites still kept up by the cities. A swamp, not far away—legend tells that it opens a way to the river Acheron—opens up darksome abysses of stagnant water, and reveals hideous fissures in the earth, and sometimes startles the ghosts below by a flash of light. Then his guides tell Hannibal that close at hand, wrapped in gloom and sunk for long ages in subterranean mists, the city of the Cimmerians lay deep in earth under a pall of shade; and they describe the unfathomed night of that Tartarean city. Next they point to the fields that ever breathe out fire and sulphur and boiling pitch.[a] A black steam rises from the ground; and the earth, long heated by subterranean fires, rumbles and heaves and sends up blasts from Hell into the air. Mulciber[b] is in labour and sends forth a dread sound of hissing from his uneasy caves. At times he struggles to burst his caverns or emerge from the sea: then he sends forth a mournful and menacing rumbling and devours the torn bowels of the earth, and mutters as he undermines the crumbling mountains. Men say that the Giants whom the might of Hercules overthrew shake the earth that lies piled above them[c]; the distant fields are scorched by their panting breath, and, whenever they threaten to burst the framework of their burden, the gods tremble. They could see Prochyte, the place appointed for savage Mimas, and Inarime in the distance, which stands above Iapetus, while he spouts forth black smoke and flame from his mutinous

is caused by their struggles: Mimas lies under Prochyte, and Iapetus under Inarime: see note to viii. 540.

ore eiectantem et, si quando evadere detur,
bella Iovi rursus superisque iterare volentem.
monstrantur Vesuvina iuga atque in vertice summo
depasti flammis scopuli stratusque ruina
mons circum atque Aetnae fatis certantia saxa.
necnon Misenum servantem Idaea sepulcro
nomina et Herculeos videt ipso in litore Baulos.
miratur pelagique minas terraeque labores.
  Quae postquam perspecta viro, regressus ad altos
inde Pheretiadum muros, frondentia laeto
palmite devastat Nysaea cacumina Gauri.
hinc ad Chalcidicam transfert citus agmina Nolam.
campo Nola sedet, crebris circumdata in orbem
turribus, et celso facilem tutatur adiri
planitiem vallo ; sed, qui non turribus arma
defendenda daret, verum ultro moenia dextra
protegeret, Marcellus opem auxiliumque ferebat.
isque ubi Agenoream procul adventare per aequor
et ferri ad muros nubem videt : " arma, cruentus
hostis adest, capite arma, viri," clamatque capitque.
circumstant rapidi iuvenes aptantque frementi
sanguineas de more iubas ; sonat inde, citato
agmina disponens passu : " tu limina dextrae
servabis portae, Nero ; tu converte cohortes
ad laevam patrias et Larinatia signa,
clarum Volscorum, Tulli, decus. ast ubi iusso,
per tacitum ruptis subita vi fundite portis

---

[a] Misenus, the steersman of Aeneas, died at Cumae.
[b] As a stable for the oxen of Geryon.
[c] The people of Puteoli.
[d] Nysa is the birthplace of Bacchus : hence " Nysaean " = " belonging to Bacchus."

jaws, and seeks, if he is ever suffered to get free, to renew his war against Jupiter and the gods. They showed Hannibal Mount Vesuvius, where fire has eaten away the rocks at its summit, and the wreckage of the mountain lies all around, and the discharge of stones seeks to rival the death dealt by Etna. He saw Misenum also which preserves the name of the Trojan [a] who lies buried there, and Bauli, built by Hercules [b] close by the sea. He looked with wonder at all the anger of the sea and the unrest of the land.

When he had beheld all these sights, he returned to the high walls of the Pheretiades,[c] and laid waste the Nysaean [d] heights of Gaurus where the vine-plant flourishes luxuriantly; and from there he quickly moved his army to Nola, a colony from Cumae. Nola, situated on a plain, is easy of approach, but is surrounded by a ring of many forts, whose high ramparts prevent access to the level ground. But Marcellus, who came to aid and support them, was not the man to shelter his troops behind the forts: his object was to defend the town by striking the first blow. When he saw the Carthaginians moving like a distant cloud across the plain and advancing towards the city, he shouted out: "To arms, my men! to arms! the murderous foe is at hand"; and as he shouted he took arms himself. As he cried aloud, his officers gathered round him in haste and fastened the general's blood-red plume to his helmet. Then his voice rang out, as he made a speedy disposition of his forces: "You, Nero, must guard the entrance of the right-hand gate; and you, Tullius, pride of the Volscians, march your countrymen and the soldiers of Larinum to the gate on our left; but, when I give the word, open the gates in silence and hurl a sudden shower

telorum in campos nimbum. ferar ipse revulsa
in medios equitumque traham certamina porta."
dumque ea Marcellus, iam claustra revellere Poeni
et scalis spretis tentabant rumpere muros.
  Insonuere tubae passim clamorque virorum
hinnitusque, simul litui raucoque tumultu
cornua et in membris concussa furentibus arma.
fertur acerba lues disiectis incita portis,
effusaeque ruunt inopino flumine turmae ;
improbus ut fractis exundat molibus amnis,
propulsum ut Borea scopulis impingitur aequor,
ut rupto terras invadunt carcere venti.
nec torrente Libys viso armorumque virumque
deiectus spe stare valet. dux Dardanus instat
attonito, praegressus equo, tergisque ruentum
incumbens hasta socios nunc voce fatigat :
" perge, age, fer gressus. dexter deus ; horaque nostra est.
hac iter ad muros Capuae." nunc rursus in hostem
conversus : " sta. quo raperis ? non terga tuorum,
te, ductor Libyae, increpito. sta. campus et arma
et Mars in manibus. dimitto e caede cohortes,
spectemur soli. Marcellus proelia posco."
sic rector Latius ; iuvenique invadere pugnam
Barcaeo suadebat honor pretiumque pericli.
  Sed non haec placido cernebat pectore Iuno

[a] The prison where they are confined by Aeolus.

of missiles over the plain. I myself, when the gate is opened, shall charge into their midst and the squadrons of cavalry will follow me." While Marcellus spoke thus, the Carthaginians were trying to pull down the ramparts; and, disdaining to use ladders, they sought to breach the walls.

Everywhere the trumpets brayed, the soldiers shouted, and the horses neighed; the clarion sounded together with the deep boom of the horn; and armour rang on the bodies of the eager combatants. The gates were thrown down, a fierce attack rushed forth, and the squadrons surprised the enemy as they galloped forth in a flood. So a swollen river overflows when its dykes are broken, and so the sea is dashed upon the rocks by the force of the Northern blasts, and so the winds, when they break prison,[a] make war on the earth. When Hannibal saw this avalanche of arms and men advancing, he lost courage and confidence. The Roman leader pressed hard on his dismay: as he rode in front, he bent down to spear the backs of the flying foe. At one time he plied his men with encouragement—"On! on! make haste! This is our hour and Heaven is favourable. Yonder lies the way to Capua." Then again he addressed Hannibal: "Stay! whither are you rushing? It is you, the leader of the host, and not your fugitive soldiers, that I blame. Stay! Here we have weapons and a field to fight on. Let the soldiers cease from slaughter and watch our single combat. I, Marcellus, challenge you to battle." Thus the Roman general spoke; and the Carthaginian was fain to fight, for honour's sake and for the prize of victory.

But Juno could not behold this scene with a mind

coeptoque avertit suprema in fata ruentem.
sistere perculsos ille et revocare laborat :
" talesne e gremio Capuae tectisque sinistris
egredimur ? state, o miseri, quis gloria summa
dedecori est. nil vos hodie, mihi credite, terga
vertentes fidum expectat : meruistis, ut omnis
ingruat Ausonia, et saevo Mavorte parastis,
ne qua spes fusos pacis vitaeque maneret."
vincebat clamore tubas vocisque vigore
quamvis obstructas saevus penetrabat in aures.
Polydamanteis iuvenis Pedianus in armis
bella agitabat atrox Troianaque semina et ortus
atque Antenorea sese de stirpe ferebat,
haud levior generis fama sacroque Timavo
gloria et Euganeis dilectum nomen in oris.
huic pater Eridanus Venetaeque ex ordine gentes
atque Apono gaudens populus, seu bella cieret
seu Musas placidus doctaeque silentia vitae
mallet et Aonio plectro mulcere labores,
non ullum dixere parem ; nec notior alter
Gradivo iuvenis, nec Phoebo notior alter.
qui postquam, effusis urgens vestigia frenis
Poenorum, iuxta galeam atque insigne perempti
agnovit spolium Pauli (puer illa gerebat,
non parvo laetus ductoris munere, Cinyps,
dilectus Poeno Cinyps, quo gratior ora
non fuit ac nulla nituit plus fronte decoris ;
quale micat semperque novum est quod Tiburis aura

---

[a] A Trojan warrior mentioned in the *Iliad*.

[b] Antenor, a Trojan, migrated to Italy after the Trojan war and founded several cities on the western coast of the Adriatic. The places mentioned below all belong to the same district.

[c] The river Po.

at ease, and turned Hannibal from his purpose as he was rushing upon his doom. He strove to rally and recall his panic-stricken men : "Is this the state in which we come forth from the lap of Capua and her baleful hospitality ? Stand fast, miserable men, whose fame, once so high, has become your disgrace. Believe me, if you retreat to-day, you will find safety nowhere. You deserve that all Italy should fall upon you ; and the result of all your fierce fighting is this, that, if you are beaten now, you have lost all hope of peace and of life." His shouting drowned the trumpets, and the noise of his angry rebuke made its way through the tumult to their ears.

Young Pedianus fought bravely there in the armour of Polydamas.[a] He claimed descent from Troy and Antenor[b] as his ancestor ; he was a worthy scion of his race, the pride of the sacred river Timavus ; and his name was dear to the Euganean land. Father Eridanus,[c] the Venetian clans one and all, and the men[d] who rejoice in the spring of Aponus—these declared that he had no rival, either in battle or when he preferred the peaceful company of the Muses and the obscurity of a studious life, and charmed away trouble with the music of the lyre. No youth was better known to Mars, and none better known to Apollo. He was riding at full gallop on the heels of the retreating enemy, when he recognized the helmet and plume taken from Paulus after death. The wearer was young Cinyps, proud of this great gift from his general. Cinyps was the favourite of Hannibal, and the comeliest of all the host ; and no face was radiant with more charm than his, like ivory which remains ever new and bright in the air

[d] The inhabitants of Patavium (Padua).

pascit ebur, vel qui miro candoris honore
lucet in aure lapis rubris advectus ab undis).
quem postquam egregium cristis et casside nota
fulgentem extremo Pedianus in agmine vidit,
ceu subita ante oculos Pauli emersisset imago
sedibus infernis amissaque posceret arma,
invadit frendens : " tune, ignavissime, sacri
portabis capitis, quae non sine crimine vester
invidiaque deum gestaret tegmina ductor ?
en Paulus." vocat inde viri ad spectacula manes
et fugientis agit costis penetrabile telum.
tum, delapsus equo, galeam atque insignia magni
consulis abrumpit dextra spoliatque videntem.
solvitur omne decus leto, niveosque per artus
it Stygius color et formae populatur honores.
ambrosiae cecidere comae, violataque cervix
marmoreum in iugulum collo labente recumbit.
haud secus Oceano rediens Cythereius ignis,
cum sese Veneri iactat splendore refecto,
si subita invadat nubes, hebetatur et atris
decrescens tenebris languentia lumina condit.
ipse etiam rapta Pedianus casside nudos
attonitus stupet ad vultus irasque coercet.

Tum, galeam magno socium clamore reportans,
immitem quatiebat equum, spumantia saevo
frena cruentantem morsu. cui turbidus armis
obvia Marcellus rapido tulit ora tumultu
agnoscensque decus : " macte o virtutis avitae,
macte Antenoride ! nunc," inquit, " rapta petamus,
quod superest, Libyci ductoris tegmina "—et ardens

[a] Pearls. [b] Lucifer, the morning star.
[c] It was so beautiful, even in death.

of Tibur, or the jewel[a] brought from the Red Sea which glitters in a lady's ear and dazzles the eye with its purity. When Pedianus saw him in the rear-guard, conspicuous by the plume he wore, and recognized the glittering helmet, he rushed on him in fury, as if the ghost of Paulus had risen suddenly into view from the nether world, demanding his lost armour: "How dare you, meanest of cowards, to wear that sacred head-piece, which, even if your general wore it, would make men cry out against the injustice of Heaven? Behold, Paulus!" Then he called the hero's ghost to watch, while he drove his sharp spear through the ribs of the fugitive. Next he sprang from his horse, and tore away the great consul's helmet and plume; and Cinyps saw himself stripped. Death robbed him of all his beauty: a Stygian hue spread over his snow-white skin and destroyed his comeliness. His ambrosial locks were disordered; his neck gave way, and the wounded head fell forward over the marble throat. Thus the star of Venus,[b] when it returns from Ocean and displays itself with new-spangled brightness to its mistress, grows dim if a sudden cloud comes over it, and hides its failing light, growing smaller in the darkness. Pedianus himself, when he had snatched the helmet, was struck dumb by the sight of the uncovered face,[c] and checked his fierceness.

Then he carried off the helmet amid the loud shouts of his men, and urged on his fiery steed, which champed the foaming bit till the blood came. Marcellus, fighting fiercely, met him in the haste and confusion of battle, and recognized the glorious trophy: "Well done!" he cried, "son of Antenor, and worthily of your brave ancestors! But one thing still remains: let us spoil Hannibal of his helmet." Eagerly he

terrificis saevam fundit stridoribus hastam.
nec forsan voti vanus foret, obvia ni vis
Gestaris opposito tenuisset corpore telum.
qui dum vicinis ductorem protegit armis,
transabiit non hunc sitiens gravis hasta cruorem
ingentesque minas mutata morte peregit.
avehitur raptim ductor, discrimine leti
turbatus, cursumque furens ad castra capessit.
iamque fugae immodicus tendit certamine gressum
praecipitem versis Poenorum exercitus armis.
assequitur telis hostis, longasque viritim
exsatiant iras cladum caeloque cruentos
certatim ostentant et dis ultoribus enses.
ille dies primus docuit, quod credere nemo
auderet superis, Martis certamine sisti
posse ducem Libyae. raptant currusque virosque
Massylamque feram ; et vivis avulsa reportant
tegmina bellantum atque abeunt, sub cuspide terga
contenti vidisse ducis. tum Martis adaequant
Marcellum decori : graditur comitante triumpho
maior, quam ferret cum victor opima Tonanti.

Inde furens, postquam vallo vix depulit hostem,
ductor Agenoreus : " quando hanc quantoque cruore
hostili labem eluerim ? mea terga videre
contigit Ausoniae ? mene," inquit, " summe deorum,
post Trebiam statuis tam turpi funere dignum ?
vosque, invicta diu, nunc heu sine Marte iuventus

[a] See note to i. 133.

hurled his deadly spear, and it sped with a dreadful whizzing noise. And perhaps he would have gained his end, had not brave Gestar met the weapon and stopped it by throwing his body in the way. He stood beside his general and sheltered him ; and the heavy spear, which thirsted for another's blood, pierced him through and wreaked its mighty wrath upon the wrong victim. Hannibal rode off in haste, troubled by his narrow escape from death, and galloped back in rage to the camp. And now the Carthaginian army, wholly bent on flight, turned and ran a headlong race for safety. Behind them came the Roman pursuers ; and each man glutted his long-pent resentment of defeat, and each held up his bloody sword, for Heaven and the avenging deities to see. That day first proved, what none would have dared to believe, though the gods had promised it—that the Libyan leader could be withstood in battle. They seized chariots and men and elephants ; they tore off the armour from living combatants and carried it away ; and then they left off, content to have seen Hannibal's back at the point of their spears. Then they praised Marcellus as equal to Mars in glory ; and he rode on escorted by a triumphant procession, a greater man than when after victory he bore the choice spoils [a] to the Thunder-god's temple.

When Hannibal had with difficulty repulsed the enemy from his camp, he vented his anger thus : " When can I wash away this stain, and how much Roman blood will be needed to cleanse it ? Has Italy been permitted to see me turn my back ? O mightiest of the gods, dost thou consider me, the victor of Trebia, worthy of such disgrace and defeat ? And you, so long invincible but now, alas, defeated

debellata bonis Capuae, non degener ipse
gestorum Ausoniis verti victricia signa:
vobis terga dedi. vidi, cum ad bella vocarem,
non secus atque Italo fugere a ductore paventes.
quid reliquum prisci Martis tibi, qui dare terga
me revocante potes?" fundebat talia Poenus;
at Latiae sese Nolana ad moenia turmae,
portantes spolia insigni clamore, ferebant.

At consueta graves per longum audire suorum
eventus Roma et numquam recreata secundis,
allato tandem faustae certamine pugnae,
erigitur primoque deum se munere tollit.
ante omnes pigra in Martem fugiensque laborum,
dum bellum tonat, et sese furata iuventus
dat poenas latebrae; tum, qui dulcedine vitae
invenere dolos iurataque foedera Poeno
corrupere, notant et purgant crimine gentem.
punitur patriam meditati linquere terram
consilium infelix scelerataque culpa Metelli.
talia corda virum. sed enim nec femina cessat
mentem aequare viros et laudis poscere partem.
omnis, prae sese portans capitisque manusque
antiquum decus ac derepta monilia collo,
certatim matrona ruit belloque ministrant.
haud tanta cessisse viros in tempore tali
laudis sorte piget; factoque in saecula ituro
laetantur tribuisse locum. tum celsa senatus
subsequitur turba. in medium certamine magno

---

[a] The reference is to Roman prisoners taken at Cannae, who were released by Hannibal on condition that they should return if no general exchange of prisoners took place. Some of them returned at once to the camp, pretending they had forgotten something, and then departed again: they claimed in this way to have kept their oath. [b] See x. 420 foll.

in peace by the luxury of Capua, *I* was not untrue to my past, *I* did not lower my victorious standards before the Romans: it was you who made me retreat. When I summoned you to arms, I saw you slink off in fear, as if I had been the Roman general. What is left of your former spirit, when you dare to turn your backs and neglect my call?" Thus Hannibal spoke; but the Roman troops went back to the walls of Nola, shouting loud and bearing their spoil with them.

And now Rome, so long accustomed to hear news of defeat to her armies, and never relieved by success, took heart again at this first sign of heaven's favour, when the news of a victory came at last. First of all, they punished for their slackness all those who had been slow to enlist and face hardship, and had concealed themselves amid the thunder of war; and next they condemned the men who had clung to life and therefore devised a trick to evade the sworn agreement made with the Carthaginians[a]; and so the nation was cleared of that guilt. Metellus also, who had proposed to abandon Italy,[b] was punished for his ill-advised policy and heinous crime. Such was the spirit of the men at Rome; and indeed the women were as high-hearted as the men and claimed a share of the praise. All the matrons came eagerly forward, bringing their family jewels for head or hand and ornaments torn from their necks, as a contribution for the war. Nor were the men displeased to let the women have precedence in so noble a cause and at such a crisis: they were glad to have given the opportunity for a sacrifice that will never be forgotten. The High Court of the Senate followed suit. With eager rivalry, they poured

privatae cumulantur opes : nudare penates
ac nihil arcanos vitae melioris ad usus
seposuisse iuvat. coït et sine nomine vulgus.
corpore sic toto ac membris Roma omnibus usa,
exsangues rursus tollebat ad aethera vultus.
  Addunt spem miseris dulcem Parnasia Cirrha
portantes responsa viri. nam laeta ferebant
exaudisse adytis, sacra cum voce tonaret
antrum, et mugiret Phoebo iam intrata sacerdos :
" solvite, gens Veneris, graviores corde timores ;
adversa, et quicquid duri sub Marte manebat,
exhaustum est vobis : restant leviora laborum
et sine pernicie terror. dis vota precesque
ferte modo et tepidos aris libate cruores.
neu date terga malis. aderit Gradivus, et ipse
Delius avertet propiora pericula vates,
Troianos notus semper minuisse labores.
sed vero, sed enim ante omnes altaria fument
centum festa Iovi ; centum cadat hostia cultris.
ille trucem belli nubem saevasque procellas
in Libyam violentus aget ; spectabitis ipsi
aegida turbato quatientem in proelia mundo."
atque ea Parnasi postquam clamata sub antris
allatum, vulgique deus pervenit ad aures,
in Capitolinas certatim scanditur arces,

[a] The port of Delphi. The chief of these envoys was Q. Fabius Pictor, the earliest Roman historian : his history was written in Greek.

out private wealth for public ends, rejoicing to strip their houses bare and keep back nothing for their own use in better times; and even the nameless populace were of the same mind. Thus a united Rome made use of all her members and once more raised towards heaven her sore-stricken head.

Hope, so sweet to the suffering, was also brought by the envoys who bore the answer of Apollo from Cirrha.[a] For they reported that they had heard glad tidings at the shrine, when the divine voice thundered through the grotto, and the priestess, possessed by the god, muttered her message: "Children of Venus, dismiss from your hearts all graver fears. You have done now with defeat and all the calamities of war that were appointed for you. Lighter tasks remain, and danger, but not destruction. Only make prayer and supplication to the gods and wet their altars with warm blood. And do not run away from your troubles. Mars will help you; and the Seer of Delos[b] himself, who, as men know, ever lightened the sufferings of Troy, will turn away imminent danger from you. But remember this: to Jupiter before other gods a hundred altars must smoke in his honour and victims must be slaughtered by a hundred knives. His power will drive the angry cloud and fierce storms of war away to Libya; and you yourselves shall see him shaking the aegis for battle in a stormy sky." And, when news came that this message had been proclaimed in the cavern of Parnassus, and the divine word reached the ears of the people, they made haste to climb the hill of the

[b] Apollo: Delos was his birth-place.

sternunturque Iovi et delubrum sanguine honorant.
tum paeana canunt responsaque fida precantur.
Interea assuetis senior Torquatus in armis
Sardoas patrio quatiebat milite terras.
namque, ortum Iliaca iactans ab origine nomen,
in bella Hampsagoras Tyrios renovata vocarat.
proles pulchra viro nec tali digna parente
Hostus erat; cuius fretus fulgente iuventa,
ipse asper paci crudos sine viribus annos
barbarici studio ritus refovebat in armis.
isque ubi Torquatum raptim properata ferentem
signa videt pugnaeque avidas accedere dextras,
fraude loci nota, latebrosa per avia saltus
evolat et, provisa fugae compendia captans,
virgulta tegitur valle ac frondentibus umbris.
Insula, fluctisono circumvallata profundo,
fastigatur aquis compressaque gurgite terras
enormes cohibet nudae sub imagine plantae:
inde Ichnusa prius Grais memorata colonis.
mox Libyci Sardus generoso sanguine fidens
Herculis, ex sese mutavit nomina terrae.
affluxere etiam et sedes posuere coactas
dispersi pelago post eruta Pergama Teucri.
nec parvum decus, advecto cum classe paterna
agmine Thespiadum, terris, Iolaë, dedisti.
fama est, cum laceris Actaeon flebile membris

---

[a] A hymn of praise, especially a hymn addressed to Apollo.

[b] T. Manlius Torquatus had subdued Sardinia during his first consulship in 235 B.C.

[c] Fugitives from Troy had settled in Sardinia, as in most other parts of the western world.

[d] The island is longer than it is broad, and narrows at each end, the "toe" and "heel" of the foot. "Ichnusa" is derived from *ichnos*, the Greek word for "footprint."

Capitol, and prostrated themselves before Jupiter, and honoured his shrine with the blood of beasts. Then they sang a paean,[a] and prayed that the oracle might come true.

Meanwhile Torquatus, now advanced in years, was attacking the island of Sardinia, where he had fought before,[b] with an army from Italy. For Hampsagoras, proud of the name which he had inherited from Trojan ancestors,[c] had invited the Carthaginians to start a fresh campaign in the island. His son Hostus was a goodly youth and worthy of a better father; and Hampsagoras, no friend to peace and devoted to barbarous customs, relied upon his son's youthful vigour and hoped by war to revive his own feeble old age. When Hostus saw Torquatus and his army coming on with speed and eager for battle, he eluded them by his knowledge of the country and fled through secret byways in the forest; and so, escaping by familiar short-cuts, he concealed himself in a wooded valley under the shade of trees.

The island of Sardinia, compassed about by the sound of the waves, is made narrow at the ends by the sea that shuts it in; and the land within its borders is irregular in shape, resembling the sole of a naked foot.[d] Hence it was called Ichnusa by the first colonists from Greece. But afterwards Sardus, proud of his descent from the Libyan Hercules, named it anew after himself. Then some Trojans, scattered over the seas after the sack of Troy, came and settled there against their will. Iolaüs, too, increased the fame of the island when he brought thither a band of Thespiadae[e] on ships of Thespiae. Legend also tells that, when Actaeon was torn to pieces—the

[a] See note to xi. 19.

supplicium lueret spectatae in fonte Dianae,
attonitum novitate mali fugisse parentem
per freta Aristaeum et Sardoos isse recessus ;
Cyrenen monstrasse ferunt nova litora matrem.
serpentum tellus pura ac viduata venenis,
sed tristis caelo et multa vitiata palude.
qua videt Italiam, saxoso torrida dorso
exercet scopulis late freta pallidaque intus
arva coquit nimium, Cancro fumantibus Austris.
cetera propensae Cereris nutrita favore.
  Hoc habitu terrae nemorosa per invia crebro
Torquatum eludens Hostus, Sidonia pugnae
tela expectabat sociosque laboris Hiberos.
qui postquam appulsis animos auxere carinis,
haud mora : prorumpit latebris ; adversaque late
agmina inhorrescunt, longumque coire videtur
et conferre gradum. media intervalla patentis
corripiunt campi properatis eminus hastis,
donec ad expertos enses, fidissima tela,
perventum. dira inde lues, caeduntque caduntque
alternique animas saevo in mucrone relinquunt.
  Non equidem innumeras caedes totque horrida facta
sperarim tanto digne pro nomine rerum
pandere nec dictis bellantum aequare calorem.
sed vos, Calliope, nostro donate labori,
nota parum magni longo tradantur ut aevo
facta viri, et meritum vati sacremus honorem.
Ennius, antiqua Messapi ab origine regis,

---

[a] A large part of the Roman corn-supply came from Sardinia.
[b] The Muse of epic poetry.
[c] Q. Ennius (269–139 B.C.) was the first great poet of Rome: he fought in the Second Punic War and wrote a history (*Annales*) of Rome in hexameter verse: fragments only of this work survive.

grievous penalty he suffered for seeing Diana while bathing—his father, Aristaeus, appalled by so strange a tragedy, fled across the sea to the bays of Sardinia, guided, it is said, by his mother, Cyrene, to this unknown land. The island is free from snakes and breeds no poisons; but the climate is gloomy and the air infected by the swamps that abound there. The side that looks toward Italy and defies the waves with its rocky cliffs is sultry; and inland the feeble crops are burnt up by excessive heat, when the South-winds blow at midsummer. But the rest of the island flourishes under the special favour of Ceres.[a]

Such is the nature of the land, and here Hostus slipped away from Torquatus again and again through the trackless woodlands; he was hoping for a Carthaginian army and Spaniards also to help him in the fighting. As soon as he was encouraged by the landing of their ships, he burst forth at once from his concealment; and the armies, bristling with spears, faced each other, eager to come to close quarters. Spears, hurled from a distance, speed across the open space between the hosts; and at last they take to the sword, that tried and trusty weapon. Fearful carnage followed; they slay and are slain, and death by the ruthless blade overtakes man after man on either side.

I cannot hope to tell of all these countless deaths and dreadful deeds in a manner worthy so great a theme, or find words to match the ardour of the combatants; but grant me this, Calliope,[b] in reward of my pains—that I may hand down to long ages the noble deeds, too little known, of a great man, and crown the poet's brow with the wreath he deserves. Foremost in the fight was Ennius,[c] a scion of the ancient stock

miscebat primas acies, Latiaeque superbum
vitis adornabat dextram decus; hispida tellus
miserunt Calabri; Rudiae genuere vetustae;
nunc Rudiae solo memorabile nomen alumno.
is prima in pugna (vates ut Thracius olim,
infestam bello quateret cum Cyzicus Argo,
spicula deposito Rhodopeia pectine torsit)
spectandum sese non parva strage virorum
fecerat, et dextrae gliscebat caedibus ardor.
advolat aeternum sperans fore pelleret Hostus
si tantam labem, ac perlibrat viribus hastam.
risit nube sedens vani conamina coepti
et telum procul in ventos dimisit Apollo,
ac super his: "nimium es iuvenis nimiumque superbis:
sperato absistas. sacer hic ac magna sororum
Aonidum cura est et dignus Apolline vates.
hic canet illustri primus bella Itala versu
attolletque duces caelo; resonare docebit
hic Latiis Helicona modis nec cedet honore
Ascraeo famave seni." sic Phoebus, et Hosto
ultrix per geminum transcurrit tempus harundo.
vertuntur iuvenis casu perculsa per agros
agmina, et effusae pariter dant terga catervae.
tum pater, audita nati nece turbidus irae,
barbaricum atque immane gemens, transfigit anhelum
pectus et ad manes urget vestigia nati.

At Libyae ductor, Marcello fractus et acri
contusus pugna, campos damnarat et arma

[a] Calabria was also called Messapia, after this king.

[b] See note to vi. 43.

[c] Orpheus.

[d] King of an island in the Sea of Marmora; the island eventually took the name of the king.

[e] The Homeric hexameter.

[f] A hill in Boeotia where the Muses dwelt.

[g] Hesiod was a native of Ascra in Boeotia.

of King Messapus[a]; and his right hand held the vine-staff,[b] the distinguishing badge of the Roman centurion. He came from the rugged land of Calabria, and he was a son of ancient Rudiae—Rudiae which now owes all her fame to this child of hers. He fought in the van; and, even as the Thracian bard[c] long ago dropped his lyre and hurled missiles brought from Rhodope, when Cyzicus[d] made war upon the Argo, so Ennius had made himself conspicuous by slaying many of the enemy, and his ardour in battle grew with the number of his victims. Now, hoping to win everlasting fame by disposing of such a dangerous foe, Hostus flew at Ennius and strongly hurled his spear. But Apollo, seated on a cloud, mocked his fruitless endeavour and sent the weapon wide into the distant air. Then he spoke: "Too insolent, too bold are you: give up your design. That sacred head is dearly loved by the Muses, and he is a bard worthy of Apollo. He shall be the first to sing of Roman wars in noble verse,[e] and shall exalt their commanders to the sky; he shall teach Helicon[f] to repeat the sound of Roman poetry, and he shall equal the sage of Ascra[g] in glory and honour." Thus Phoebus spoke, and Hostus was struck by an avenging arrow[h] which pierced both his temples. Panic-stricken by their prince's fall, his soldiers turned and fled, rushing all together from the field. When Hampsagoras heard of his son's death, he was distracted with rage: with hideous yells such as barbarians utter, he stabbed his own heaving breast and hastened to join his son in the nether world.

Hannibal meanwhile, beaten by Marcellus and sorely mauled in battle, had abandoned fighting in

[h] Shot apparently by Apollo.

verterat ad miseras non aequi Martis Acerras.
inde, ubi permisit flammis atque ensibus urbem,
Nuceriae, nihilo levior nec parcior ira,
incussit sese atque aequavit moenia terrae.
post Casilina sibi, multum obluctatus iniquis
defendentum armis, aegre reseraverat astu
limina et obsessis vitam pensaverat auro.
iamque, in Dauniacos transfundens agmina campos,
flectebat rabiem, quo praeda vel ira vocasset.
fumabat versis incensa Petilia tectis,
infelix fidei miseraeque secunda Sagunto,
at quondam Herculeam servare superba pharetram.
Verterat et mentem Tyria ad conata Tarentus,
portisque intrarant Poeni. sed enim arce corusca,
fisa loco, manus Ausoniae stipata sedebat.
hic, miranda movens, classem, quae condita portu
adstabat (namque angustis se faucibus aequor
irrumpit scopulos inter patuloque recessu
infundit campis secretum gurgite pontum)
inclusas igitur, quibus haud enare dabatur
arce superposita, claustris maris extulit astu
perque aversa tulit portatas arva carinas.
lubrica roboreis aderant substramina plaustris;
inque recens caesi tergo prolapsa iuvenci,
aequoream rota ducebat per gramina puppim.

---

[a] Apulia.

[b] This ancient city was founded by Philoctetes, who bequeathed to it the bow and arrows of Hercules.

[c] The citadel stood on what was virtually an island, and commanded the narrow channel connecting the inner harbour with the roadstead outside. Hannibal hoped to get command of the sea and so starve out the garrison of the citadel; but he never succeeded in taking it.

the open and turned his superior strength against hapless Acerrae. He gave the town to fire and sword, and then, hurling himself against Nuceria with as heavy a hand and as fierce an anger, razed the walls to the ground. Next came Casilinum, where he struggled long against the ill-matched efforts of the defenders, till at last he gained entrance by a stratagem and granted the besieged their lives in return for gold. Then he shifted his army to the Daunian plains [a] and turned his fury against any spot whither booty or anger drew him. Petilia,[b] unhappy in her loyalty and a second Saguntum in her fate, was set on fire, and the smoke went up from her ruined houses; yet once she had prided herself on preserving the arrows of Hercules.

Tarentum too had gone over to the invaders, and the Carthaginians had entered her gates. But a close-packed Roman garrison was quartered in the far-shining citadel,[c] confident in their strong position. Then Hannibal devised a wondrous plan. The Tarentine fleet was at anchor and hidden away in the harbour; for the sea bursts in through the rocks by a narrow entrance and floods an ample basin [d] with water separated from the main. Therefore, as the ships were shut in and prevented from sailing forth by the citadel commanding the entrance, Hannibal artfully brought them out by transporting them over dry land on the side away from the citadel. A slippery surface was laid down underneath wooden wagons, and wheels, moving easily over the hides of freshly-slain bullocks, carried the ships through the meadow-land. And soon the fleet,

[d] The great inner harbour.

et iam, per colles dumosque ad litus adacta,
innabat pelago veniens sine remige classis.
Nuntius interea vectis non more carinis
terrentem freta curarum fervoribus implet,
dum procul Oebalios amet expugnare nepotes
et primus rostris sulcet navalibus arva,
assessos Capuae muros : claustra ipsa revelli
portarum, ac totum miseris incurrere bellum.
linquit coepta ferox, pennasque addente pudore
atque ira simul, immani per proxima motu
evolat et minitans avida ad certamina fertur.
haud secus, amisso tigris si concita fetu
emicet, attonitae paucis lustratur in horis
Caucasus et saltu tramittitur alite Ganges,
donec fulmineo partus vestigia cursu
colligat et rabiem prenso consumat in hoste.
Obvius huic sparso Centenius agmine raptim
funditur, audendi pravus facilisque periclis.
sed parvum decus Hannibali. nam, vitis honore
perfunctus Latiae, subito stimularat agrestes
semermemque manum sternendam obiecerat hosti.
bis septem demissa neci (nec substitit agmen)
milia ; bis septem, quae non sollertior ense
sed genus insignis, iustis ducebat in armis
Fulvius ; ast aeque per corpora fusa iacentum
raptum iter est, victorque moram non passus eundi.

---

[a] It must be supposed that each ship would need more than one wagon to transport it. Silius exaggerates here: Livy's account says that the road used was broad and level.

[b] Oebalus was an ancient king of Sparta : Tarentum was a Spartan colony.

[c] See note to vi. 43.

moving on over hills and through thickets without the help of oarsmen, reached the shore and rode upon the waves.[a]

While Hannibal startled the sea by conveying the fleet in this strange fashion, news came that filled him with a fever of anxiety. While he was far away, trying to take their town from the descendants of Oebalus [b] and ploughing the fields for the first time in history with the beaks of ships, he heard that Capua was besieged, even her gates broken down, and her wretched inhabitants exposed to all the horrors of war. In anger he gave up his enterprise. Shame and wrath together lent him wings; he flew through the surrounding country at furious speed and rushed eagerly to the conflict, threatening vengeance. So, when a tigress has lost her cub and dashes forth in pursuit, the distracted beast traverses the whole Caucasus in a few hours and takes a flying leap over the Ganges, until her lightning speed finds the footprints of her young one; then she catches her enemy and wreaks all her fury upon him.

Centenius, foolhardy and careless in danger, faced him but was soon routed and his force dispersed. Yet Hannibal got little glory by it. For Centenius, who had once carried the vine-staff [c] of a Roman centurion, had hastily stirred up the country people and thrown his ill-armed levies against the foe to be destroyed. Twice seven thousand men were slain, nor did the victor halt: twice seven thousand more, fully armed, were led by Fulvius, no better skilled in war for all his famous name; and again the enemy dashed on over their prostrate bodies and refused to check the rate of their march. One thing only made

exequiae tantum famam nomenque volentem
mitificae mentis tenuerunt funere laeto.
namque per insidias, infandum, et ab hospite caesus,
colloquium et promissa petit dum perfida gentis
Lucanae, Gracchus, caeco circumdatus astu,
occiderat, laudemque Libys rapiebat humandi.
Sed non, ut scitum celerare ad moenia Poenum,
adstabat res ulla loco : iam consul uterque
praecipites aderant ; Nola vis omnis, et Arpis
aevi floridior Fabius rapida arma ferebat ;
hinc Nero et hinc volucris Silanus nocte dieque
impellebat agens properata ad bella cohortes.
undique conveniunt, pariterque opponere cunctos
uni ductores iuveni placet. arduus ipse
Tifata insidit, propior qua moenibus instat
collis, et e tumulis subiectam despicit urbem.
verum ubi tot sese circumfundentibus armis
vallatas socium portas unaque negari
intravisse sibi Capuaeque erumpere cernit,
anxius eventus, nunc ferro frangere coetum
obstantum meditatur, init nunc avia coepto
consilia atque astu quaerit tot milia portis
abstrahere artatis cinctosque resolvere muros.
sic igitur secum curasque ita corde fatigat :
" quo, mens aegra, vocas ? rursusne pericula sumam,
non aequus regione loci ? Capuaque vidente
terga dabo ? an, residens vicini vertice montis,

---

[a] The proconsul, Ti. Sempronius Gracchus, who commanded an army in Lucania.

[b] Q. Fulvius Flaccus and Appius Claudius. Nero and Silanus were praetors.

[c] The Capuans.

Hannibal pause: seeking a reputation for humanity, he gave burial to Gracchus,[a] though rejoicing at his death. For Gracchus, while seeking by means of a conference to gain the adherence of the false Lucanians, had been treacherously and foully slain by his host; encompassed by hidden guile he had been murdered, and Hannibal snatched at the credit of giving him burial.

But when it was known that Hannibal was hastening to Capua, no stone was left unturned. Both consuls[b] flew to the spot, and all the forces from Nola; the younger Fabius brought his men with speed from Arpi; Nero from one quarter and swift Silanus from another urged their armies on night and day for instant battle. From all sides they assembled; and Rome was resolved to pit all her generals against that one young commander. He himself encamped aloft on Mount Tifata, the height that rises close by the walls of Capua, and looked down thence upon the city below. But now, when he saw himself surrounded by so many armies, and the city of his allies[c] blockaded, so that it was impossible either for him to enter or for the Capuans to sally forth, he was troubled for the issue. At one time he thought of shattering every obstacle with the sword; or again he might swerve from his present purpose, and devise some stratagem to draw that great host away from the closed gates and set free the beleaguered city. Thus then he spoke to himself, and thus he turned over his anxious thoughts: "Whither does my wavering purpose summon me? Shall I face the risk again, though the lie of the land is against me? Shall I turn my back, with Capua looking on? Or shall I sit here close by on the mountain and suffer the city

exscindi ante oculos patiar socialia tecta ?
non ita me experti Fabius Fabiique magister
turbatum, Hesperio cum clausos milite colles
evasi victor sparsosque per arva iuvencos
iactare accensis stimulavi cornibus ignes.
haud dum omnes abiere doli : defendere nobis
si Capuam ereptum est, dabitur circumdare Romam."

Haec postquam placita, et tenuit sententia mentem,
non expectato Titan dum gurgite lucem
spirantes proferret equos, impellit in agmen
voce manuque viros et coepta immania pandit :
" perge, age, vince omnem, miles, virtute laborem
et, quantum humani possunt se tendere passus,
arduus accelera. Romam petis. hoc iter Alpes,
hoc Cannae stravere tibi. eia, incute muris
umbonem Iliacis Capuaeque repende ruinas ;
quam tanti fuerit cadere, ut Palatia cernas
et demigrantem Tarpeia sede Tonantem."

Instincti glomerant gressus. Roma auribus haeret,
Roma oculis ; creduntque ducis sollertibus actis
aptius id coeptum, quam si duxisset ab ipso
fatali Aeneadis campo. Vulturna citata
tramittunt alno vada postremique relinquunt
tardandis Italis corruptas igne carinas.
tum Sidicina legunt pernicibus arva maniplis
Threiciamque Calen, vestras a nomine nati,

---

[a] Minucius.

[b] See vii. 310 foll.

[c] Cannae.

[d] See note to viii. 514.

of my allies to be sacked before my face? That is not like me: Fabius and his Master of the Knights[a] did not find me discomfited when I escaped triumphantly through the hills beset by Roman soldiers, and forced the cattle, by setting light to their horns, to scatter through the fields tossing fire-brands.[b] Not yet have I lost all my cunning. If the defence of Capua is denied me, I shall find it possible to besiege Rome."

When this was settled and his mind made up, he did not wait until the Sun brought his fire-breathing steeds up from Ocean. With voice and gesture he urged his men to march, and revealed his daring design: "On, soldiers, on! with courage superior to every hardship, and increase your speed to the utmost limit of human endurance. Rome is your object. The Alps and Cannae paved the way for our present march. On with you, and dash your shields against the Roman walls, and take vengeance for the destruction of Capua. The fall of Capua is a price worth paying, if you see the Palatine Hill and the Thunder-god evicted from his abode on the Capitol."

Thus appealed to, they marched with speed. Rome rang in their ears, Rome stood before their eyes. They believed that, thanks to their general's adroitness, this enterprise was better timed than if he had led them there straight from the field[c] so fatal to the Aeneadae. Quickly they crossed the river Vulturnus in boats; and the rearguard, in order to delay the Romans, set fire to the boats and left them useless. Then the soldiers hurried through the territory of Sidicinum, and Thracian Cales,[d] the abode of Orithyia,

Orithyia, domos. hinc Allifanus Iaccho
haud inamatus ager nymphisque habitata Casinis
rura evastantur ; mox et vicinus Aquinas
et, quae fumantem texere Giganta, Fregellae
agmine carpuntur volucri. fert concitus inde
per iuga celsa gradum, duris qua rupibus haeret
bellator Frusino, et surgit suspensa tumenti
dorso frugiferis Cerealis Anagnia glebis.
iamque adeo est campos ingressus et arva Labici,
linquens Telegoni pulsatos ariete muros,
haud dignam inter tanta moram. nec amoena retentant
Algida nec iuxta Iunonis tecta Gabinae.
praeceps ad ripas immani turbine fertur,
sulphureis gelidus qua serpit leniter undis
ad genitorem Anio, labens sine murmure, Thybrim.
Hic ut signa ferox dimensaque castra locavit
et ripas tremefecit eques, perterrita pulsis
Ilia prima vadis sacro se coniugis antro
condidit, et cunctae fugerunt gurgite nymphae.
at matres Latiae, ceu moenia nulla supersint,
attonitae passim furibundis gressibus errant.
ante oculos adstant lacerae trepidantibus umbrae,
quaeque gravem ad Trebiam quaeque ad Ticina fluenta
oppetiere necem, Paulus Gracchusque cruenti
Flaminiusque simul miseris ante ora vagantur.
clausit turba vias. stat celsus et asper ab ira
ingentemque metum torvo domat ore senatus.

---

[a] Tusculum : see note to vii. 692.

[b] Hannibal was now within three miles of Rome : he never got nearer.

[c] Ilia, also called Rhea Silvia, was the daughter of King Amulius. When she bore Romulus and Remus to Mars,

named after her son. Next they laid waste the land of Allifae, dear to Bacchus, and the country where the nymphs of Casinum dwell ; and soon the speedy column passed Aquinum, and Fregellae where a buried Giant sends up smoke. On they rushed over the heights where the warlike men of Frusino cling to their rugged rocks, and where Anagnia rises on a swelling ridge, a fertile land for corn. And at last Hannibal set foot on the plains and corn-fields of Labicum and left behind the walls of Telegonus,[a] battered by the ram already but not worth delay at such a crisis. Nor did the beauty of Algidus detain him, nor Gabii, the city of Juno. With furious speed he rushed forwards to the banks where cold Anio, gliding noiselessly, winds smoothly with sulphurous waters towards Father Tiber.[b]

Here he proudly planted his standards and measured out his camp; and, when the banks shook beneath the trampling of his horsemen, their noise straightway drove Ilia down in fear to hide in the sacred grotto of her spouse,[c] and all the nymphs of the stream took flight. Meanwhile the Roman women, as if the walls were already levelled, ran aimlessly to and fro in their distraction like madwomen. Their terror saw ghosts standing before them—ghosts of mangled men, who met their death by the fatal streams of Trebia and Ticinus ; the bleeding forms of Paulus and Gracchus and Flaminius moved before their eyes. The streets were blocked by the crowds. But the Senators stood erect and formidable in wrath, and their grim aspect quelled the mighty panic. Yet

she was condemned to be drowned in the Anio : there she changed her earthly life for that of a goddess and wife of the river-god.

interdum tamen erumpunt sub casside fusae
per tacitum lacrimae : quidnam Fortuna minetur,
quidve parent superi ? pubes dispersa per altas
stat turres atque huc ventum sub corde volutat,
ut iam Roma satis credat defendere muros.
  Poenus ut ad somnos vix totam cursibus actae
indulsit pubi noctem, vigil ipse nec ullam
ad requiem facilis credensque abscedere vitae
quod sopor eripiat tempus, radiantibus armis
induitur Nomadumque iubet prorumpere turmas.
inde, levis frenis, circum pavitantia fertur
quadrupedante sono perculsae moenia Romae.
nunc aditus lustrat, clausas nunc cuspide pulsat
infesta portas fruiturque timore paventum.
nunc, lentus celsis adstans in collibus, intrat
urbem oculis discitque locos causasque locorum.
ac legeret visu cuncta et penetraret in omnes
spectando partes, ni magno turbine adesset
Fulvius, haud tota Capuae obsidione relicta.
tum demum castris turmas inflexit ovantes
spectata ductor satiatus pectora Roma.
atque ubi nox depulsa polo primaque rubescit
lampade Neptunus revocatque Aurora labores,
effundit rupto persultans agmina vallo
et, quantum clamare valet : " per plurima vestra,
o socii, decora et sacras in sanguine dextras,
vobis ite pares et tantum audete sub armis,

[a] The rampart of his camp on the Anio.

sometimes silent tears burst forth from beneath a helmet. "What," they asked, "does Fortune threaten us with, and what is the purpose of the gods?" The young men were distributed for service among the high towers, and each said to himself: "It has come to this, that Rome now is content if she can but defend her walls!"

Hannibal granted his men a short night's sleep, that they might rest after their furious march. He himself kept watch; he was never willing to rest, and thought that every hour claimed by sleep was so much lost to life. He put on his shining armour and ordered his Numidian horsemen to gallop in front. Then he rode swiftly round the walls, and the trampling of the horses raised panic in the city. Now he examined the approaches, now he beat on the closed gates with angry spear and enjoyed the terror of the citizens. Or again, he stood motionless on some eminence, bending his gaze upon the city, learning the name of each spot and the origin of its name. He would have surveyed it all, and his piercing eye would have left no part unseen, had not Fulvius come up in furious haste, without entirely abandoning the siege of Capua. Then only did Hannibal, having feasted his eyes on the sight of Rome, turn his triumphant squadrons towards their camp. And, when night was banished from the sky, and the sea grew red with sunrise, and Dawn called men back to their labours, he sent his army forth from the demolished rampart,[a] and, as he rode along, shouted with all the power of his voice: "Comrades, I adjure you by your countless laurels and your right hands consecrated by bloodshed, go forward and rival your former deeds; let your boldness in battle be as great

quantum Roma timet. reliquam hanc exscindite molem,
nil, quod vincatis, toto restabit in orbe.
neu populi vos Martigenae tardarit origo ;
intratam Senonum capietis milibus urbem
assuetamque capi. fortasse curulibus altis
iam vos, exemplo proavorum, ad nobile letum
expectant de more senes mortique parantur."

Talibus hic Poenus ; sed contra Oenotria pubes
non ullas voces ducis aut praecepta requirit.
sat matres stimulant natique et cara supinas
tendentum palmas lacrimantiaque ora parentum.
ostentant parvos vagituque incita pulsant
corda virum, armatis infigunt oscula dextris.
ire volunt et pro muris opponere densi
pectora respectantque suos fletumque resorbent.
ut vero impulso patefactae cardine portae
et simul erupit motis exercitus armis,
funditur immixtus gemitu precibusque per altos
ad caelum muros plangor, sparsaeque solutis
crinibus exululant matres atque ubera nudant.
Fulvius antevolans agmen : " quis nesciat," inquit,
" non sponte ad nostros Poenum venisse penates ?
a portis fugit Capuae." subnectere plura
conantem tristis caeli cum murmure vasto
turbavit fragor et subita de nube procellae.

Iupiter, Aethiopum remeans tellure, minantem

[a] He refers to the capture of Rome by Gauls in 390 B.C.

as the fear in Roman hearts. Destroy this one obstacle, and nothing will remain in the whole world for you to conquer. Nor, though they spring from Mars, let that parentage delay your attack: you will take a city that is accustomed to be taken, a city that the Senones entered in their thousands.[a] Perhaps the Senators are already duly seated on their high curule chairs, even as their ancestors sat, preparing for a glorious death and waiting for you to inflict it."

Thus spoke Hannibal; but the men of Rome, on their side, needed no speech or appeal from any leader. They found incentive enough in the sight of women and children, and of loved parents weeping and holding out their hands in supplication. Mothers hold up their infants and stir the eager hearts of the men by the children's cries, and imprint kisses on hands that grasp the sword. The men are eager to march and breast the enemy outside the walls in close array; and they look back at their dear ones and choke down their tears. But, when the opened gate turned on its hinges and the host sallied forth together in arms, the noise of beaten breasts, mingled with sobs and prayers, rose up over the high walls to heaven; and the matrons shrieked, baring their breasts and letting loose their hair. At the head of the army rode Fulvius. "It is an open secret," he said, "that Hannibal was no free agent when he came to attack our homes: he was driven in flight from the gates of Capua." He was about to say more, when he was interrupted by a fearful crash and loud rumbling in the sky; and a tempest burst suddenly from the clouds.

Jupiter was returning from the land of the Ethio-

Romuleo Poenum ut vidit succedere vallo,
caelicolis raptim excitis, defendere tecta
Dardana et in septem discurrere iusserat arces.
ipse e Tarpeio sublimis vertice cuncta,
et ventos simul et nubes et grandinis iras
fulminaque et tonitrus et nimbos conciet atros.
concussi tremuere poli, caelumque tenebris
clauditur, et terras caeco nox condit amictu.
instat tempestas oculis, hostique propinquo
Roma latet. iactae in turmas per nubila flammae
stridorem servant, membrisque insibilat ignis.
hinc Notus, hinc Boreas, hinc fuscis Africus alis
bella movent, quantis animos et pectora possint
irati satiare Iovis. fluit agmen aquarum,
turbine confusum piceo et nigrante procella,
atque omnes circa campos spumantibus undis
involvit. celsus summo de culmine montis
regnator superum sublata fulmina dextra
libravit clipeoque ducis, non cedere certi,
incussit : summa liquefacta est cuspis in hasta,
et fluxit, ceu correptus fornacibus, ensis.

Ambustis sed enim ductor Sidonius armis
sistebat socios et caecum e nubibus ignem
murmuraque a ventis misceri vana docebat.
tandem post clades socium caelique ruinam,
non hoste in nimbis viso, non ense, referri
signa iubet castris maestasque resuscitat iras :
" ventis debebis nimirum hiemisque procellis

---

[a] This is taken from the *Iliad*, where it is said that Zeus (Jupiter) was absent on one occasion when his presence was wanted, because he had gone to partake of a feast offered to him by the Ethiopians.

pians,[a] when he saw Hannibal's threatening approach to the ramparts of Romulus. At once he summoned the gods and bade them defend the Dardan city and each to take his place on the Seven Hills. He himself, raised high on the Tarpeian Mount, stirred up all his armoury—winds and clouds and angry hail, thunder and lightning and black rain-storms. The firmament was struck and trembled, darkness veiled the sky, and earth was hidden by the black robe of night. The enemy were blinded by the storm, and Rome, though close beside them, was hidden from their eyes. The flame, hurled through the clouds upon their ranks, kept roaring on, and the fire hisses against their limbs. Then the South-wind and the North, and the dark-winged South-west wind, began a war fierce enough to satisfy the anger in the breast of Jupiter. A deluge of rain came down, mingled with pitchy hurricanes and black storms, and covered all the surrounding plains with foaming waves. The Ruler of the gods, high on his hill-top, hurled a thunderbolt with his lifted arm and smote the shield of Hannibal. The general was resolved never to give way; but the point of his spear was melted, and his sword was fused, as if it had been plunged in the furnace.

But, though his weapons were scathed by the fire, Hannibal still rallied his men, telling them that the fire from heaven was blind, and the tumultuous roaring of the winds a mere empty din. At last, when his men had suffered and all heaven had come crashing down, without their seeing an enemy or an enemy's sword through the rain, he ordered a retreat to the camp, and thus revived his wrath and sorrow: "Rome, you may thank the winds and stormy

unum, Roma, diem ; sed non te crastina nobis
lux umquam eripiet, descendat Iupiter ipse
in terras licet." infrendens dum talia fatur,
ecce serenato clarum iubar emicat axe,
purgatusque nitet discussis nubibus aether.
Aeneadae sensere deum telisque repostis
summissas tendunt alta ad Capitolia dextras
et festa cingunt montis penetralia lauro.
tum vultus, modo non parvo sudore madentes,
nunc laetos Iovis aspectant : " da, summe deorum,
da, pater, ut sacro Libys inter proelia telo
concidat : haud alia potis est occumbere dextra."

Sic adeo orantes pressere silentia, postquam
abstulerat terras nigrantibus Hesperus umbris.
quem simul attollens rutilantem lampada Titan
obruit et vitae rediit mortalibus usus,
Poenus adest, nec se castris Oenotria pubes
continet. haud dum enses stricti, mediumque iacebat
tantum ad bella loci, quantum tramittere iactae
sufficerent hastae, cum fulgor hebescere caeli
per subitum coepit, densaeque subire tenebrae,
atque dies fugere, atque armari ad proelia rursus
Iupiter. incumbunt venti, crassusque rotante
Austro nimborum fervet globus. intonat ipse,
quod tremat et Rhodope Taurusque et Pindus et Atlas.
audivere lacus Erebi, mersusque profundis
agnovit tenebris caelestia bella Typhoeus.
invadit Notus ac, piceam cum grandine multa

---

[a] The face of the god's image is meant.
[b] All these are great mountain ranges.
[c] Hades.
[d] The Giant imprisoned under Inarime (Ischia): see note to viii. 540.

weather, forsooth! for a single day's reprieve; but the morrow shall never snatch you from my grasp, not if Jupiter descends to earth in person." While he spoke thus and gnashed his teeth, behold! the heavens cleared and the sun shone out, the clouds dispersed and the sky became pure and bright. The Aeneadae recognized the hand of the god: laying down their weapons, they held their hands up humbly towards the lofty Capitol and wreathed the temple on the hill with festal laurel. Then they looked at Jupiter's face,[a] cheerful now though bathed in sweat a little while ago: "O supreme Father of the gods," they prayed, "grant that Hannibal may be slain in battle by a bolt from heaven. No other hand has power to destroy him."

Thus they prayed and then kept silence, after Hesperus had hidden the earth beneath the shades of night. But when the sun raised his ruddy torch and hid the morning-star, and mortal men resumed the business of life, back the Carthaginians came, nor did the Roman soldiers remain in their camp. Swords were not yet drawn, and a space, only the length of a spear-cast, separated the armies, when suddenly the brightness of the sky grew dim, and thick darkness came on; daylight fled and Jupiter began to arm for battle a second time. On came the winds, and a thick mass of fiery cloud was whirled before the South-wind. Jupiter himself thundered, till Rhodope and Taurus, Pindus and Atlas,[b] were shaken by it. The pools of Erebus[c] heard it, and Typhoeus,[d] hidden in deep darkness, recognized the sound of war in heaven. The South-wind attacked, driving on a pitch-dark cloud with pelting hail, and

intorquens nubem, cunctantem et vana minantem
circumagit castrisque ducem succedere cogit.
 Verum ubi depositis saepsit sese aggere telis,
laeta serenati facies aperitur Olympi,
nullaque tam mitem credas habuisse Tonantem
fulmina, nec placido commota tonitrua caelo.
durat et affirmans non ultra spondet in ipsos
venturam caeli rabiem, modo patria virtus
in dextras redeat, nec Romam exscindere Poeni
credant esse nefas. ubi nam tunc fulmina tandem
invicti latuisse Iovis, cum sterneret ensis
Aetolos campos ? ubi, cum Tyrrhena natarent
stagna cruore virum ? " pugnat pro moenibus," inquit,
" si rector superum tot iactis culmine telis,
inter tot motus cur me contra arma ferentem
afflixisse piget ? ventis hiemique fugaces
terga damus ? remeet, quaeso, mens illa vigorque,
qua vobis, cum pacta patrum, cum foedera obessent,
integrare acies placitum." sic pectora flammat,
donec equum Titan spumantia frena resolvit.
nec nox composuit curas, somnusve frementem
ausus adire virum, et redeunt cum luce furores.
rursus in arma vocat trepidos clipeoque tremendum
increpat atque armis imitatur murmura caeli.
 Ut vero accepit tantum confidere divis
Ausonios patres, summissaque Baetis ad oras
auxilia, et noctu progressum moenibus agmen,

---

[a] At Cannae. [b] Lake Trasimene.
[c] This appeal would have been more suitably addressed to the Carthaginian senate than to Hannibal's army.
[d] Spain.

turned Hannibal about, forcing him to retreat to his camp, in spite of his reluctance and his idle threats.

But when the invader had laid down his arms and was protected by his ramparts, the skies cleared and the face of heaven smiled again: it was hard to believe that so benign a Jupiter had lately wielded bolts and vexed with his thunders a sky so peaceful. Hannibal held out: he promised and vowed that the fury of the elements would not again attack the army, if only they recovered their native valour and thought it no sacrilege for Carthage to sack Rome. Where, he asked, were the thunderbolts of invincible Jupiter hidden away, when the sword was strewing the Aetolian plain[a] with corpses, or when the Etruscan lake[b] was swollen with human gore? "If the Ruler of the gods," said he, "is fighting in defence of Rome and hurling bolt after bolt from his high place, why, when he is so busy, is he unwilling to strike down me, his adversary? Are we to turn our backs, and be routed by winds and rough weather? Show once more, I entreat you, that firmness of purpose with which you resolved to fight a second war, in spite of treaties and of the covenants of our senate."[c] Thus he sought to inflame their ardour, until the Sun loosed the foaming bits of his steeds. Night brought him no peace of mind, nor did sleep dare to visit his stormy breast; and his frenzy came back with the dawn. Once mcre he summoned his frightened men to arms, and clashed on his shield with a terrible din, and rivalled with his armour the roll of thunder.

But when he heard that the Roman Senate, trusting in divine aid, had sent reinforcements to the land of the Baetis,[d] and that the troops had started from

sic agitare fremens obsessos otia, tamque
securam Hannibalis Romam, violentior instat.
iamque propinquabat muro, cum Iupiter aegram
Iunonem alloquitur curis mulcetque monendo :
" nullane Sidonio iuveni, coniuxque sororque
cara mihi, non ulla umquam sine fine feroci
addes frena viro ? fuerit delere Saguntum,
exaequare Alpes, imponere vincula sacro
Eridano, foedare lacus : etiamne parabit
nostras ille domos, nostras perrumpere in arces ?
siste virum. namque, ut cernis, iam flagitat ignes
et parat accensis imitari fulmina flammis."
His dictis grates agit ac turbata per auras
devolat et prensa iuvenis Saturnia dextra
" quo ruis, o vecors ? maioraque bella capessis
mortali quam ferre datum ? " Iuno inquit et atram
dimovit nubem veroque apparuit ore.
" non tibi cum Phrygio res Laurentive colono ;
en, age (namque, oculis amota nube parumper,
cernere cuncta dabo) surgit qua celsus ad auras,
aspice, montis apex, vocitata Palatia regi
Parrhasio, plena tenet et resonante pharetra
intenditque arcum et pugnas meditatur Apollo.
at, qua vicinis tollit se collibus altae
molis Aventinus, viden', ut Latonia virgo
accensas quatiat Phlegethontis gurgite taedas,
exsertos avide pugnae nudata lacertos ?
parte alia, cerne, ut saevis Gradivus in armis

---

[a] Lake Trasimene is meant.

[b] Evander, who came originally from Pallantium in Arcadia : see note to vi. 631.

[c] Diana had her temple on the Aventine Hill.

[d] See note to ii. 610.

Rome during the night, he attacked with increased violence, indignant that Rome cared so little for Hannibal and that the besieged citizens should thus take their ease. He was nearing the walls, when Jupiter addressed Juno and soothed her fears by this warning: "Spouse and sister whom I love, will you never, never check this Carthaginian youth whose insolence knows no limit? He destroyed Saguntum and levelled the Alps; he put fetters on the sacred river Po and polluted the lakes.[a] Let that pass; but does he intend also to force his way into the habitations of the gods and into our citadels? Bring him to a halt; for, as you see, he is now calling for fire, and means to kindle flames in rivalry of my thunderbolts."

Saturn's daughter thanked him for his warning. Full of anxiety she flew down from heaven and took Hannibal by the right hand: "Madman, whither are you rushing? Are you intent on a warfare that is beyond the power of mortal man?" Thus speaking she dispersed the cloud of darkness and revealed herself in her real semblance. "You have not now to do with settlers from Troy or Laurentum. Look up and see! For I will remove the cloud for a space from your eyes and suffer you to behold all things. Where yonder peak rises high, the Palatine, so named by the Arcadian king,[b] is held by Apollo; he makes ready for battle, his full quiver rattles, and his bow is bent. Again, where the tall pile of the Aventine rises beside the other hills, see you how the maiden daughter of Latona[c] brandishes torches kindled in the stream of Phlegethon,[d] and thrusts forth her bared arms in her eagerness for battle? Then look elsewhere and see how Mars, the fierce

implerit dictum proprio de nomine campum.
hinc Ianus movet arma manu, movet inde Quirinus,
quisque suo de colle deus. sed enim aspice, quantus
aegida commoveat nimbos flammasque vomentem
Iupiter et quantis pascat ferus ignibus iras.
huc vultus flecte atque aude spectare Tonantem:
quas hiemes, quantos concusso vertice cernis
sub nutu tonitrus! oculis qui fulgurat ignis!
cede deis tandem et Titania desine bella."
sic affata virum indocilem pacisque modique,
mirantem superum vultus et flammea membra
abstrahit ac pacem terris caeloque reponit.

Respectans abit et castris avulsa moveri
signa iubet ductor remeaturumque minatur.
redditur extemplo flagrantior aethere lampas,
et tremula infuso resplendent caerula Phoebo.
at procul e muris videre ut signa revelli
Aeneadae versumque ducem, tacita ora vicissim
ostentant nutuque docent quod credere magno
non audent haerente metu; nec abire volentis
sed fraudem insidiasque putant et Punica corda,
ac tacitae natis infigunt oscula matres:
donec procedens oculis sese abstulit agmen
suspectosque dolos dempto terrore resolvit.
tum vero passim sacra in Capitolia pergunt
inque vicem amplexi permixta voce triumphum
Tarpeii clamant Iovis ac delubra coronant.

---

[a] The Campus Martius.

[b] Janus defends the Janiculum, and Quirinus the Quirinal Hill.

warrior, has filled all the field[a] named after himself. Janus from one side and Quirinus from another,[b] each god from his own hill, come forth to war. And then behold the mighty form of Jupiter—how he shakes the aegis till it vomits forth fire and storm, and how he gluts his fierce wrath with bursts of flame. Turn your face hither and dare to look at the Thunder-god. When he shakes his head, what storms, what mighty bolts you see obedient to his nod! What fire flashes from his eyes! Yield at last to Heaven, and fight no more against it like the Giants." With these words she turned him from his purpose and restored peace to earth and heaven. Though slow to learn peace and moderation, yet he was awed by the faces and fiery limbs of the immortals.

As he departed and ordered the standards to be wrenched up from the soil of the camp, Hannibal looked back and swore he would return. At once the sun in heaven shone brighter, and the quivering blue of the sky glittered in the sunlight. But when the Aeneadae from their walls saw the standards pulled up and Hannibal retreating in the distance, they exchanged looks in silence and conveyed by gestures what they dared not believe while panic still clung to their hearts: they supposed that Hannibal did not mean to depart; that this was a trick and a stratagem—an instance of Punic treachery; and mothers kept silence as they kissed their babes. But, when at last the army marched out of their sight, their fears vanished and their suspicion of a trick was lulled to rest. Then indeed they flocked to the temple on the Capitol; and, exchanging embraces, they acclaimed with mingled voices the triumph of Tarpeian Jupiter and decked his shrine

iamque omnes pandunt portas ; ruit undique laetum,
non sperata petens dudum sibi gaudia, vulgus.
hi spectant, quo fixa loco tentoria regis
adstiterint ; hi, qua celsus de sede vocatas
affatus fuerit turmas ; ubi belliger Astur
atque ubi atrox Garamas saevusque tetenderit Hammon.
corpora nunc viva sparguntur gurgitis unda ;
nunc Anienicolis statuunt altaria nymphis.
tum festam repetunt, lustratis moenibus, urbem.

---

[a] Spaniards.

with garlands. Next they threw open all the gates; and from every quarter the people came rushing with joy, seeking for pleasure that had long been beyond their hopes. Some gaze at the spot where Hannibal's pavilion had been pitched, others at the high seat whither he had summoned his army to address them, or at the camping-ground of the warlike Asturians,[a] savage Garamantians, and fierce Ammonites. Now they bathe in the running water of the river[b]; now they rear altars to the nymphs who haunt the Anio; and then, having purified the walls with sacrifice, they return to the rejoicing city.

[b] As a preparation for religious ceremonies: see viii. 125.

LIBER TERTIUS DECIMUS

ARGUMENT

Hannibal withdraws to the river Tutia, and is prevented from attacking Rome again by Dasius, a deserter, who explains that the city is impregnable so long as it contains the Palladium. He returns to the land of the Bruttii (1-93). *The Romans take Capua* (94-380). *Scipio's father and uncle*

Segne iter emenso vixdum Tarpeia videri
culmina desierant, torvos cum versus ad urbem
ductor Agenoreus vultus remeare parabat.
castra locat, nulla laedens ubi gramina ripa
Tutia deducit tenuem sine nomine rivum
et tacite Tuscis inglorius affluit undis.
hic modo primores socium, modo iussa deorum
nunc sese increpitat : " dic o, cui Lydia caede
creverunt stagna et concussa est Daunia tellus
armorum tonitru, quas exanimatus in oras
signa refers ? qui mucro tuum, quae lancea tandem
intravit pectus ? si nunc existeret alma
Carthago ante oculos, turrita celsa figura,
quas abitus, miles, causas, illaese, dedisses ?
'imbres, o patria, et mixtos cum grandine nimbos

[a] Six miles distant from Rome.

[b] The Tiber.

[c] In ancient works of art a city is often represented by a female figure wearing a crown of towers.

BOOK XIII

ARGUMENT (*continued*)

are defeated and killed in Spain (381-384). *This news induces Scipio to descend to Hades, to see the spirits of his kinsmen* (385-396). *He sees many ghosts of famous men and women in Hades. Finally, the Sibyl predicts the death of Hannibal* (397-893). *He then returns to the upper world* (894, 895).

SLOWLY Hannibal marched away, and the Tarpeian hill had hardly disappeared from his sight when he turned a threatening face towards Rome and prepared to march back again. He encamped by the Tutia,[a] a slender stream unknown to fame, which flows down noiselessly into the Tuscan river,[b] with no banks to mar the meadowland. Here he found fault, now with the captains of the host, now with the prohibition of the gods, and now with himself. "You who raised the level of the Lydian lake with bloodshed—you who shook the land of Daunus with the thunder of your warfare,—whither are you now retreating, all courage lost? No sword-point, no lance has pierced your breast. If our mother Carthage were now to appear before you, her high head crowned with towers,[c] what excuse could you give, soldiers, for retreating with no wounds to show? 'Foul weather, rain and hail together, and thunder, drove us back,

et tonitrus fugio.' procul hanc expellite, gentes,
femineam, Tyriae, labem, nisi luce serena
nescire ac liquida Mavortem agitare sub aethra."

Terror adhuc inerat superum ac redolentia in armis
fulmina et ante oculos irati pugna Tonantis.
parendi tamen et cuicumque incumbere iusso
durabat vigor, ac, sensim diffusus ad oras,
signa reportandi crescebat in agmine fervor.
sic, ubi perrupit stagnantem calculus undam,
exiguos format per prima volumina gyros,
mox, tremulum vibrans motu gliscente liquorem,
multiplicat crebros sinuati gurgitis orbes,
donec postremo laxatis circulus oris
contingat geminas patulo curvamine ripas.

At contra Argyripae pravum decus (inclita namque
semina ab Oenea ductoris stirpe trahebat
Aetoli: Dasio fuit haud ignobile nomen)
laetus opum, sed clauda fides; seseque calenti
addiderat Poeno, Latiae diffisus habenae—
is, volvens veterum memorata antiqua parentum,
"longo miles" ait, "quateret cum Teucria bello
Pergama, et ad muros staret sine sanguine Mavors,
sollicitis Calchas (nam sic fortissimus heros
poscenti socero saepe inter pocula Dauno
narrabat memori Diomedes condita mente)—
sed Calchas Danais, nisi clausum ex sedibus arcis
armisonae curent simulacrum avellere divae,
non umquam affirmat Therapnaeis Ilion armis

[a] The circles are concentric. [b] See note to iv. 554.
[c] The soothsayer of the Greek army.
[d] The Palladium: see note to ix. 531.

dear native land.' Drive out this womanish weakness, men of Tyrian race, that prevents you from fighting unless the sky is clear and the weather fine."

Dread of the gods filled their hearts; their weapons still smelt of the lightning, and the Thunder-god, the wrathful champion of Rome, was still before their eyes. Yet they had not lost the power to obey and to carry out every order they received; and the desire to carry the standards back to Rome grew stronger in the ranks and spread by degrees to the outside of the circle. So, when a pebble breaks the surface of a motionless pool, in its first movements it forms tiny rings; and next, while the water glints and shimmers under the growing force, it swells the number of the circles over the rounding pond,[a] until at last one extended circle reaches with wide-spreading compass from bank to bank.

There was one dissenting voice. This was Dasius, the glory and the shame of Argyripa[b]—a man of noble birth, who traced his origin to Diomede, son of Oeneus and king of Aetolia. A wealthy man but a faithless ally, he had joined himself to fiery Hannibal, distrusting the rule of Rome. Thus he spoke, recalling the tradition of former generations: "When an army carried on a long campaign against the citadel of Troy and warfare halted bloodless before the walls, Calchas[c] explained their difficulty. (The brave hero Diomede had kept the tale in mind and often told it, when Daunus, his father-in-law, asked to hear it over their wine.) Calchas assured the Greeks that, unless they could contrive to carry off the image of the Warrior Goddess[d] from the shrine in the citadel that guarded it, Ilium would never yield to the army of Sparta, nor

cessurum, aut Ledae rediturum nomen Amyclas.
quippe deis visum, ne cui perrumpere detur,
effigies ea quas umquam possederit, urbes.
tum meus adiuncto monstratam evadit in arcem
Tydides Ithaco et, dextra amolitus in ipso
custodes aditu templi, caeleste reportat
Palladium ac nostris aperit male Pergama fatis.
nam postquam Oenotris fundavit finibus urbem,
aeger delicti, Phrygium placare colendo
numen et Iliacos parat exorare penates.
ingens iam templum celsa surgebat in arce,
Laomedonteae sedes ingrata Minervae,
cum medios inter somnos altamque quietem
nec celata deam et minitans Tritonia virgo :
'non haec, Tydide, tantae pro laudis honore
digna paras, non Garganus nec Daunia tellus
debentur nobis : quaere in Laurentibus arvis,
qui nunc prima locat melioris moenia Troiae.
huc vittas castumque refer penetrale parentum.'
quis trepidus monitis Saturnia regna capessit.
iam Phryx condebat Lavinia Pergama victor
armaque Laurenti figebat Troia luco.
verum ubi Tyrrheni perventum ad fluminis undas
castraque Tydides posuit fulgentia ripa,
Priamidae intremuere metu. tum, pignora pacis
praetendens dextra ramum canentis olivae,

---

[a] Helen, wife of Menelaus.
[b] Argyripa.
[c] *i.e.* as mine.
[d] See note to iv. 561.
[e] The "land of Laurentum" and the "realm of Saturn" are names for Latium : see note to i. 605.
[f] The Tiber.

would Leda's child[a] return to Amyclae. For the gods had decreed that no city which was ever occupied by this image could be taken by any invader. Thereupon my ancestor, the son of Tydeus, with Ulysses as his companion, made his way into the citadel, as Calchas had indicated, and slew the guards in the very porch of the temple; then they carried off the divine Palladium and threw open Troy to our conquering fortunes, with evil result. For when Diomede had founded a city[b] within the borders of Italy, he felt uneasy because of his crime and sought by worship to appease the Trojan deity and make his peace with the household-gods of Ilium. A vast temple was already rising on the lofty citadel, a dwelling-place distasteful to the goddess from Laomedon's city, when the Maiden of Lake Tritonis appeared in her divine form amid the profound silence of the midnight, and warned him thus: 'Son of Tydeus, this work of yours is not adequate to do honour to such great glory[c]; Mount Garganus[d] and the Daunian land are no fitting place for me. Go to the land of Laurentum,[e] and seek there for the man who is now laying the foundation-stone of a happier Troy. Carry to him the fillets and chaste guardian-goddess of his ancestors.' Alarmed by this warning, Diomede went to the realm of Saturn. By this time the Trojan conqueror was founding another Troy at Lavinium and hanging up armour from Troy in a sacred grove at Laurentum. But when Diomede came to the stream of the Tuscan river[f] and pitched his glittering[g] camp on its bank, the sons of Priam trembled for fear. Then the son-in-law of Daunus held forth in his right hand a branch of silvery olive

[g] He brought with him soldiers whose weapons glittered.

sic orsus Dauni gener inter murmura Teucrum :
' pone, Anchisiade, memores irasque metusque ;
quicquid ad Idaeos Xanthum Simoentaque nobis
sanguine sudatum Scaeaeque ad limina portae,
haud nostrum est ; egere dei duraeque sorores.
nunc age, quod superest cur non melioribus aevi
ducimus auspiciis ? dextras iungamus inermes.
foederis, en, haec testis erit.' veniamque precatus
Troianam ostentat trepidis de puppe Minervam.
haec ausos Celtas irrumpere moenia Romae
corripuit leto neque tot de milibus unum
ingentis populi patrias dimisit ad aras."
His fractus ductor convelli signa maniplis
optato laetis abitu iubet. itur in agros,
dives ubi ante omnes colitur Feronia luco,
et sacer umectat Flavinia rura Capenas.
fama est intactas longaevi ab origine fani
crevisse, in medium congestis undique donis,
immensum per tempus opes, lustrisque relictum
innumeris aurum, solo servante pavore.
hac avidas mentes ac barbara corda rapina
polluit atque armat contemptu pectora divum.
avia tunc longinqua placent, quae sulcat aratro
ad freta porrectis Trinacria Bruttius arvis.
Dum Libys haud laetus Rhegina ad litora tendit,

---

[a] The Fates.

as a pledge of peace, and spoke thus while the Trojans muttered in displeasure: 'Son of Anchises, lay aside the recollections of rage and fear. For all the sweat and blood we poured out by Xanthus and Simois, rivers of Ida, and by the Scaean gate, we are not to blame: we were driven on by the gods and the inexorable Sisters.[a] Say, why should we not spend under happier auspices what yet remains of life? Let us join hands that grasp no swords. She whom you now behold shall be the witness of our alliance.' Thus he asked pardon of the Trojans, and displayed to their startled sight the image on the stern of his ship. When the Gauls dared to break through the walls of Rome, this goddess put a speedy end to them, and of that vast horde not a single man out of so many thousands returned in peace to the altars of his country."

By these words Hannibal was discouraged. He ordered his men to pull up the standards, and they rejoiced, being eager to depart. They marched to the spot where Feronia's temple of surpassing wealth stands in a sacred grove, and where the sacred river Capenas waters the fields of Flavina. Legend told that the treasure of the temple had never been rifled since its remote foundation, but had grown from time immemorial by means of offerings pouring in from all quarters; and gold, guarded by fear alone, had been left there for centuries. By plundering this temple, Hannibal steeped in guilt his greedy horde of barbarians, and steeled their hearts with contempt of the gods. Next it was decided to march far away, to where the fields ploughed by the Bruttians stretch out towards the Sicilian sea.

While Hannibal sadly bent his steps towards the

victor, summoto patriis a finibus hoste,
Fulvius infaustam Campana ad moenia clausis
portabat famam miserisque extrema movebat.
tum prensans passim, cuicumque est nomen in armis :
" dedecus hoc defende manu ; cur perfida et urbi
altera Carthago nostrae post foedera rupta
et missum ad portas Poenum, post iura petita
consulis alterni stat adhuc, et turribus altis
Hannibalem ac Libycas expectat lenta cohortes ? "
miscebat dictis facta et nunc robore celsas
educi turres, quis vinceret ardua muri,
cogebat, nunc coniunctas astringere nodis
instabat ferroque trabes, quo frangeret altos
portarum postes quateretque morantia claustra.
hic latera intextus stellatis axibus agger,
hic gravida armato surgebat vinea dorso.
at postquam properata satis, quae commonet usus,
dat signum atque alacer scalis transcendere muros
imperat ac saevis urbem terroribus implet :
cum subito dextrum offulsit conatibus omen.

Cerva fuit, raro terris spectata colore,
quae candore nivem, candore anteiret olores.
hanc agreste Capys donum, cum moenia sulco
signaret, grato parvae mollitus amore,
nutrierat sensusque hominis donarat alendo.
inde exuta feram docilisque accedere mensis
atque ultro blanda attactu gaudebat erili.

---

[a] Rome.

[b] Much of the detail about this animal is taken from Virgil (*Aen.* vii. 483 foll.); but the hind of Capua differs in sex, colour, and longevity. Perhaps Dryden took from Silius the idea of his "milk-white Hind, immortal, and unchanged."

[c] The founder of Capua.

shore near Rhegium, victorious Fulvius, having driven away the invader from his native city,[a] brought news of disaster to the blockaded people of Capua, and prepared to put the finishing touch to their misery. He grasped the hand of every man famous in arms, and said: "Fight, to repel this disgrace. Why is treacherous Capua, a second Carthage to our state, still standing, after breaking her treaty and sending Hannibal against Rome, and after her claim to hold one of the consulships? Why does she, at ease behind her lofty towers, look out for the arrival of Hannibal and his Libyan host?" His words he backed up with deeds. He made his men rear high wooden towers, to rise above the top of the walls; or again he made haste to bind together beams with clamps of iron, that he might break the tall gate-posts and batter down the barriers of defence. Here rose a mound of earth whose sides were formed of planks arranged lattice-wise; and there high mantlets, teeming with arms, showed their protected roofs. When all the devices suggested by experience were complete, he gave the word at once and bade them scale the walls by the ladders. Thus he filled the citizens' hearts with dreadful panic; and suddenly a favourable omen smiled upon his enterprise.

There was there a hind[b] of a colour seldom seen by mortal eyes—whiter than snow and whiter than swansdown. When Capys[c] was tracing out the walls of his city with the plough, his heart was touched by the grateful affection of this little creature which the forest had given him; he had reared it and tamed it by his kindness. Soon it lost its wild nature, coming readily to its master's table, and even fawning with pleasure when he stroked it. The

aurato matres assuetae pectine mitem
comere et umenti fluvio revocare colorem.
numen erat iam cerva loci ; famulamque Dianae[a]
credebant, ac tura deum de more dabantur.
haec, aevi vitaeque tenax felixque senectam
mille indefessos viridem duxisse per annos,
saeclorum numero Troianis condita tecta
aequabat ; sed iam longo nox venerat aevo.
nam, subito incursu saevorum agitata luporum,
qui noctis tenebris urbem—miserabile bello
prodigium—intrarant, primos ad luminis ortus
extulerat sese portis pavidaque petebat
consternata fuga positos ad moenia campos.
exceptam laeto iuvenum certamine ductor
mactat, diva, tibi—tibi enim haec gratissima sacra—
Fulvius atque " adsis," orat, " Latonia, coeptis."

Inde alacer fidensque dea circumdata clausis
arma movet, quaque obliquo curvantur in orbem
moenia flexa sinu, spissa vallata corona
alligat et telis in morem indaginis ambit.
dum pavitant, spumantis equi fera corda fatigans,
evehitur porta sublimis Taurea cristis
bellator, cui Sidonius superare lacerto
ductor et Autololas dabat et Maurusia tela.
is trepido ac lituum tinnitu stare neganti
imperitat violenter equo, postquam auribus hostis
vicinum sese videt, et clamare propinquum :

[a] Diana.

matrons were accustomed to comb the gentle creature's flanks with a golden comb, and to renew its whiteness by bathing it in the river. The hind had become the deity of the city; the people believed that it had Diana for its mistress, and offered incense to it as to other deities. This animal was long-lived: it was fortunate enough to prolong a green old age through a thousand years of activity, and numbered as many centuries as the city founded by the Trojan exiles; but now death came to it at last. For a fierce pack of wolves had entered the city in the darkness of night—an evil omen in time of war—and the hind, startled by their sudden onset, had sallied forth from the gates at early dawn, and sought, in wild alarm, the fields that lay near the walls. The soldiers, delighting in the chase, caught it, and their general, Fulvius, slaughtered it as an acceptable offering to Leto's daughter,[a] and prayed that the goddess might assist his enterprise.

Then, trusting in the goddess, Fulvius quickly moved forward the troops that surrounded the besieged city; and, at a point where the walls diverged from the straight line to make a curve, he invested them with a dense ring of assailants and penned them in like a beast in the toils. While the citizens trembled, Taurea rode forth from the gate; his helmet-plume rose high as he controlled the hot temper of his foaming steed: Hannibal himself admitted that none of his Autololes or Moors could hurl the spear in battle with as much force as Taurea. His horse was restive and refused to stand still amid the blare of the trumpets; but the rider schooled him by force, and when he saw himself within earshot of the enemy, shouted at close quarters: "Let

"Claudius huc," inquit—praestabat Claudius arte
bellandi et merita mille inter proelia fama—
"huc," inquit, "solum, si qua est fiducia dextrae,
det sese campo atque ineat certamina mecum."
Una mora Aeneadae, postquam vox attigit aures,
dum daret auspicium iusque in certamina ductor:
praevetitum namque et capital, committere Martem
sponte viris. erumpit ovans, ut Fulvius arma
imperio solvit, patulumque invectus in aequor
erigit undantem glomerato pulvere nubem.
indignatus opem ammenti socioque iuvare
expulsum nodo iaculum atque accersere vires
Taurea vibrabat nudis conatibus hastam.
inde furens ira telum contorquet in auras.
at non idem animus Rutulo; speculatur et omni
corpore perlustrat, qua sit certissima ferro
in vulnus via. nunc vibrat, nunc comprimit hastam
mentiturque minas; mediam tunc transiit ictu
parmam, sed grato fraudata est sanguine cuspis.
tum strictum propere vagina detegit ensem.
et iam ferrata rapiebat calce volantem
Taurea cornipedem, fugiens minitantia fata.
at Rutulus levior cedentis prendere terga
iam profugo rapidus fusis instabat habenis.
utque metus victum, sic ira et gloria portis
victorem immisit meritique cupido cruoris.
ac dum vix oculis, vix credunt mentibus hostem
confisum nullo comitante irrumpere tectis,

---

[a] This single combat is described by Livy (xxiii. 46. 12): the champions were Claudius Asellus, a Roman, and Cerrinus Vibellius Taurea, a Campanian.

[b] See note to i. 318.

Claudius," he cried—this Claudius was a famous swordsman who had gained glory in a thousand battles—" let Claudius, if he has confidence in his right arm, come forth alone hither to the field, and meet me here in single combat."[a]

The Roman, when he heard the challenge, only waited till the general's sanction gave him leave to begin; for the soldiers were forbidden, on pain of death, to fight for their own hand. When the command of Fulvius made him free to accept the challenge, he rushed forth jubilant, and rode over the open plain, sending up a billowy cloud of gathering dust. Disdaining the help of a thong or the use of a knotted strap to add force to his weapon,[b] Taurea brandished his spear with the strength of his unaided arm. Then in furious rage he hurled his spear into the air. Far different was the purpose of the Roman: he scanned closely every part of the other's body, seeking the surest place for his point to penetrate. Now he brandished his spear, and again he checked it, and made a feint of striking; at last he pierced Taurea's shield through the centre, but the point was cheated of the blood it coveted. Then he drew his sword quickly from the sheath. And now Taurea, fleeing from imminent death, urged on his flying steed with the iron upon his heel. But the Roman was more nimble in pursuit of his retreating foe and pressed hard at full gallop upon the fugitive. Both entered the gate, the vanquished driven on by fear, and the conqueror by rage and love of glory and by thirst for the blood that was his due. The citizens could hardly believe their eyes and doubted their own senses, when they saw a single foeman gallop boldly into the town; but, while they trembled, he rode on

per mediam propere trepidantum interritus urbem
egit equum adversaque evasit ad agmina porta.
Hinc ardore pari nisuque incurrere muris
ignescunt animi penetrataque tecta subire.
tela simul flammaeque micant. tunc saxeus imber
ingruit, et summis ascendunt turribus hastae.
nec pronum audendi virtute excellere cuiquam ;
aequarunt irae dextras. Dictaea per auras
tranat et in medium perlabitur urbis harundo.
laetatur non hortandi, non plura monendi
Fulvius esse locum : rapiunt sibi quisque laborem.
quos ubi tam erectos animi videt, et super esse
factorum sibi quemque ducem, ruit impete vasto
ad portam magnaeque optat discrimina famae.
Tres claustra aequaevo servabant corpore fratres,
quis delecta manus centeni cuique ferebant
excubias unaque locum statione tenebant.
forma ex his Numitor, cursu plantaque volucri
praestabat Laurens, membrorum mole Taburnus.
sed non una viris tela : hic mirabilis arcu,
ille hastam quatere ac medicatae cuspidis ictu
proelia moliri et nudo non credere ferro,
tertius aptabat flammis ac sulphure taedas.
qualis Atlantiaco memoratur litore quondam
monstrum Geryones immane tricorporis irae,
cui tres in pugna dextrae varia arma gerebant :
una ignes saevos, ast altera pone sagittas
fundebat, validam torquebat tertia cornum ;
atque uno diversa dabat tria vulnera nisu.
hos ubi non aequis variantes proelia consul

---

[a] Livy evidently disbelieved this detail of the duel.
[b] *Cf.* i. 278 foll.

unterrified right through the city and returned safe to his own army by the gate on the opposite side.[a]

Then all hearts burned with equal zeal and effort to attack the walls and force their way into the town. Weapons and fire-brands flashed together. Stones were hurled in showers, and spears rose to the height of the bastions. Nor was it easy for any man to distinguish himself by valour: rage lent equal strength to every arm. Cretan arrows darted through the sky and flew on to the centre of the city. Fulvius rejoiced that there was no further need for encouragement or appeal; for one and all were eager for the fray. When he saw their high spirit, and also that each man was his own leader in action, he rushed with mighty force against the gate and sought out glorious hazards.

Three brothers of equal age guarded the gate, and each had a chosen band of a hundred men who kept watch and were stationed together. Among the brothers Numitor excelled in beauty, Laurens in speed of foot, and Taburnus in size and stature. Nor were they armed alike: one was a marvellous archer; another brandished the spear and fought with an envenomed point, distrustful of the naked steel; while the third was skilled in hurling fire-brands and lighted torches. They were like Geryon,[b] that dread monster with triple body who is said to have lived long ago on the beach of Atlas: when he fought, his three hands plied different weapons: one hurled fierce fire, and a second, behind the first, shot arrows, while the third brandished a stout spear; and so with a single effort he inflicted three separate wounds. When the consul saw the brothers, each fighting with his different weapon, and the heap of

conspexit telis et portae limina circum
stragem ac perfusos subeuntum sanguine postes,
concitat intortam furiatis viribus hastam.
letum triste ferens auras secat Itala taxus
et, qua nudarat, dum fundit spicula ab alto,
arcum protendens, Numitor latus, ilia transit.
at, non obsaepto contentus limine Martem
exercere, levis bello sed turbidus ausi,
Virrius incauto fervore eruperat amens
reclusa in campum porta miseramque furori
vincentum obtulerat pubem. ruit obvia in arma
Scipio et oblatum metit insatiabilis agmen.
  Tifata umbrifero generatum monte Calenum
nutrierant audere trucem ; nec corpore magno
mens erat inferior. subsidere saepe leonem,
nudus inire caput pugnas, certare iuvenco
atque obliqua trucis deducere cornua tauri
assuerat crudoque aliquo se attollere facto.
is, dum praecipites expellit Virrius urbe,
seu spreto, seu ne fieret mora, nudus in aequor
thorace exierat leviorque premebat anhelos
pondere loricae et palantes victor agebat.
iamque Veliternum media transegerat alvo,
iam solitum aequali ludo committere equestres
Scipiadae pugnas Marium tellure revulso
perculerat saxo. miser implorabat amicum
cum gemitu expirans, scopulusque premebat hiantem.
sed, validas saevo vires duplicante dolore,
effudit lacrimas pariter cornumque sonantem
Scipio, solamen properans optabile in armis

[a] See xi. 65 foll.

corpses round the gate, and the gate-posts red with the blood of the attackers, he brandished his spear with furious strength and threw it. The spear, made of Italian yew, clove the air and bore with it cruel death; it pierced the body of Numitor in the side, which he had exposed while holding out his bow and raining arrows with lifted arms. But Virrius,[a] hot-headed but of little account in battle, was not content to fight within the confinement of the walls: in his headstrong folly he opened a gate, sallied out into the plain, and exposed his hapless followers to the rage of the victorious Romans. For Scipio rushed to meet their onset and mowed down the opposing ranks, insatiable in his fury.

The shady hill of Tifata had given birth and nurture to Calenus, a fierce warrior; great was his body, and his fiery spirit as great. Often did he surprise a lion in its lair, or go to battle with head uncovered, or wrestle with a steer and force down to earth the horns of an angry bull; and often he gained glory by some desperate deed. When Virrius made his precipitate sally from the town, Calenus followed; but he wore no corslet, either because he despised its protection or to gain time; and, carrying less weight, he harassed the Romans who panted under their heavy armour, and drove them before him in defeat and disorder. Already he had run Veliternus through the belly; already he had overthrown Marius with a stone torn from the earth—Marius who was wont to tilt with Scipio, his equal in age, in mimic warfare. In his death-agony he cried to his friend for help, and the stone crushed in his open mouth. Grief doubled Scipio's strength. Even as he wept, he hurled his whizzing spear, eager that his friend

hostem prostrato morientem ostendere amico.
tranavit, volucris liquidas ceu scinderet auras,
hasta viri pectus rupitque immania membra:
quanta est vis agili per caerula summa Liburnae,
quae, pariter quotiens revocatae ad pectora tonsae
percussere fretum, ventis fugit ocior et se,
quam longa est, uno remorum praeterit ictu.
Ascanium Volesus, proiectis ocius armis,
quo levior peteret muros, per aperta volantem
assequitur planta. deiectum protinus ense
ante pedes domini iacuit caput; ipse secutus
corruit ulterior procursus impete truncus.
nec spes obsessis ultra reserata tueri
moenia: convertunt gressus recipique precantes
infandum! excludunt socios, dum cardine verso
obnixi torquent obices, munimina sera.
acrius hoc instant Itali clausosque fatigant.
et, ni caeca sinu terras nox conderet atro,
perfractae rapido patuissent milite portae.
Sed non in requiem pariter cessere tenebrae.
hinc sopor impavidus, qualem victoria novit;
at Capua, aut maestis ululantum flebile matrum
questibus, aut gemitu trepidantum exterrita patrum,
tormentis finem metamque laboribus orat.
mussat perfidiae ductor coetuque[1] senatus
Virrius a Poeno nullam docet esse salutem,

[1] ductor coetuque *Summers*: ductorque caputque *edd.*

should find consolation for his fall by seeing his enemy dying. Like a bird cleaving the clear sky, the spear pierced the breast of Calenus and shattered his huge frame. With such force the light Liburnian galley skims over the surface of the deep; when the oars, drawn back to the rowers' chests, strike the water in unison, she flies swifter than the winds, and a single stroke of their blades carries her further than her own length.

Volesus had quickly thrown down his shield, that he might reach the city with more speed; he overtook Ascanius who was rushing over the open plain, and cut off his head with the sword; the head lay in front of the man's feet, and then the headless body fell further on; so fast was he running. The besieged could no longer hope to defend walls already unbarred. They beat a retreat to the town, and (horrible to tell) shut out their comrades as they begged to be admitted: the hinges turned and the bolts were forcibly thrust home, when such precautions were too late. This made the Romans press their attack more fiercely against the beleaguered city. And, if black night had not thrown her robe of darkness over the earth, the eager soldiers would have broken down the gates and passed through them.

But the darkness did not bring the same rest to both armies. On one side there was untroubled sleep, such as the conqueror knows. But Capua, terrified either by piteous complaints and shrieks of the weeping women or by the laments of the troubled senators, prayed for an end to her sufferings and a limit to her hardships. Virrius, the arch-traitor, was discomfited. Expelling from his heart all desire of

vociferans, pulsis vivendi e pectore curis :
" speravi sceptra Ausoniae pepigique, sub armis
si dexter Poenis deus et Fortuna fuisset,
ut Capuam Iliaci migrarent regna Quirini.
qui quaterent muros Tarpeiaque moenia, misi ;
nec mihi poscendi vigor afuit, alter ut aequos
portaret fasces nostro de nomine consul.
hactenus est vixisse satis. dum copia noctis,
cui cordi comes aeterna est Acherontis ad undam
libertas, petat ille meas mensasque dapesque ;
et, victus mentem fuso per membra Lyaeo
sopitoque necis morsu, medicamina cladis
hauriat ac placidis exarmet fata venenis."
haec ait et turba repetit comitante penates.
aedibus in mediis consurgens ilice multa
extruitur rogus, hospitium commune peremptis.
  Nec vulgum cessat furiare dolorque pavorque.
nunc menti Decius serae redit, et bona virtus
exilio punita truci. despectat ab alto
sacra Fides agitatque virum fallacia corda.
vox occulta subit, passim diffusa per auras :
" foedera, mortales, ne saevo rumpite ferro,
sed castam servate Fidem. fulgentibus ostro
haec potior regnis. dubio qui frangere rerum
gaudebit pacta ac tenues spes linquet amici,
non illi domus, aut coniux, aut vita manebit
umquam expers luctus lacrimaeque : aget, aequore semper

---

[a] Hannibal's army is meant: see line 101.
[b] In Hades.
[c] Twenty-seven senators accepted his invitation (Livy).
[d] See xi. 158. [e] See ii. 480 foll.

kings by war. Many an effort they made without success, and the foreign king pressed hard upon Janiculum.[a] At last peace was decided on: they ended hostilities, stopped the war, and agreed to a treaty; and hostages were given in pledge of its fulfilment. But Roman hearts could not be tamed —witness heaven!—but were ready to face any danger for the sake of glory. With other Roman maidens Cloelia was sent across the river to the king as a pledge for peace—young Cloelia who was not twelve years old. Of brave deeds done by men I say nothing; but this maiden, in spite of the king and the treaty, in spite of her youth and the river, swam fearlessly across the astonished Tiber, stemming the stream with childish arms. If nature had changed her sex, perhaps Porsena would never have been able to return to the Tyrrhene[b] land. But, not to detain you longer, from her this young Cloelius is descended, and owes his glorious name to that famous maiden."

While Cinna told this tale, a sudden shout was heard not far away on their left hand. From a disordered heap of weapons and mangled corpses they had drawn forth the body of Paulus in the centre of the pile. How changed, alas! how unlike the Paulus whose prowess lately disordered the ranks of Carthage, or the Paulus who overthrew the kingdom of the Taulantes[c] and bound the king of Illyricum in chains! His grey hairs were black with dust, and his beard defiled with clotted gore; his teeth were shattered by the impact of the great stone; and his whole body was one wound.

Hannibal's joy was redoubled by the sight. "Fly, Varro, fly!" he cried, "and save your life—I care not, so long as Paulus is dead. You are a consul:

et populo consul totas edissere Cannas !
concedam hanc iterum, si lucis tanta cupido est,
concedam tibi, Varro, fugam. at, cui fortia et hoste
me digna haud parvo caluerunt corda vigore,
funere supremo et tumuli decoretur honore.
quantus, Paule, iaces ! qui tot mihi milibus unus
maior laetitiae causa es. cum fata vocabunt,
tale precor nobis, salva Carthagine, letum."
haec ait et socium mandari corpora terrae,
postera cum thalamis Aurora rubebit apertis,
imperat armorumque iubet consurgere acervos,
arsuros, Gradive, tibi. tum munera iussa,
defessi quamquam, accelerant sparsoque propinquos
agmine prosternunt lucos : sonat acta bipenni
frondosis silva alta iugis. hinc ornus et altae
populus alba comae, validis accisa lacertis,
scinditur, hinc ilex, proavorum consita saeclo.
devolvunt quercus et amantem litora pinum
ac, ferale decus, maestas ad busta cupressos.
funereas tum deinde pyras certamine texunt,
officium infelix et munus inane peremptis,
donec anhelantes stagna in Tartessia Phoebus
mersit equos, fugiensque polo Titania caecam
orbita nigranti traxit caligine noctem.
post, ubi fulserunt primis Phaëthontia frena
ignibus, atque sui terris rediere colores,
supponunt flammam et manantia corpora tabo
hostili tellure cremant. subit horrida mentem
formido incerti casus, tacitusque pererrat
intima corda pavor, si fors ita Martis iniqui

[a] See note to vi. 1.

life, he told the assembled senate that they must not rely on Hannibal to save them. "I hoped"—so he cried aloud—"that we should rule Italy; and I promised that, if Fortune and Heaven favoured the Carthaginian armies, the empire of Trojan Quirinus should be transferred to Capua. I sent a force [a] to batter down the walls of Rome and the Tarpeian citadel; and I had the boldness to demand that one of the two consuls should be of our nation, carrying the rods of office and ranking with his colleague. I am content to have lived till now. To-night is ours: if any man would fain go down to the river of Acheron[b] with Freedom as his companion for ever, let him come to my table and sup with me. There the wine shall spread through his frame and overpower his senses; death shall lose its sting, and he shall swallow the antidote for defeat, and disarm Fate by means of merciful poison." Thus he spoke and went back to his house, and many [c] went with him. In the centre of the house a great pyre of oak-wood was raised, to receive them all alike after death.

The populace meanwhile were still maddened by rage and fear. Now, too late, they remember Decius[d] and the harsh sentence of exile passed upon his noble courage. The goddess Loyalty [e] looked down from heaven and troubled their traitorous hearts. A mysterious voice was heard and filled all the air: "Ye mortals, break not your oaths with the sword, but keep faith unstained. Loyalty outshines the purple sheen of monarchs. If a man rejoices to break his plighted word in the hour of danger, and betrays the dwindling hopes of his friend, neither his household, nor his wife, nor his life, shall ever be free from mourning and tears. Loyalty, whom he despised and

ac tellure premens, aget aegrum nocte dieque
despecta ac violata Fides." adit omnia iamque
concilia ac mensas contingit et, abdita nube,
accumbitque toris epulaturque improba Erinys.
ipsa etiam Stygio spumantia pocula tabo
porrigit et large poenas letumque ministrat.
Virrius interea, dum dat penetrare medullas
exitio, ascenditque pyram atque amplexibus haeret
iungentum fata et subici iubet ocius ignes.

Stringebant tenebrae metas, victorque ruebat.
iamque superstantem muro sociosque Milonem
voce attollentem pubes Campana videbat.
pandunt attoniti portas trepidoque capessunt
castra inimica gradu, quis leto avertere poenas
defuerant animi. patet urbs, confessa furorem,
et reserat Tyrio maculatas hospite sedes.
matronae puerique ruunt maestumque senatus
concilium nullique hominum lacrimabile vulgus.
stabant innixi pilis exercitus omnis
spectabantque viros, et laeta et tristia ferre
indociles, nunc propexis in pectora barbis
verrere humum, nunc foedantes in pulvere crinem
canentem et turpi lacrima precibusque pudendis
femineum tenues ululatum fundere in auras.

Atque ea dum miles miratur inertia facta
expectatque ferox sternendi moenia signum,
ecce repens tacito percurrit pectora sensu
religio et saevas componit numine mentes,

wronged, shall hound him ever over land and sea, and persecute her victim day and night." Hidden in a cloud, a Fury was present now at every meeting and every meal, lying on the couches and boldly sharing the feast. In person she hands to the guests the foaming cup of deadly poison, and offers them with lavish hand the penalty of death. Meanwhile Virrius gave time to the deadly drink to reach his inmost parts ; then he ascended the pyre, embraced the friends who were dying together with him, and bade the fire to be kindled at once.

Darkness was near its ending, and the conquerors came rushing on. And now the people of Capua saw Milo standing on the wall and calling to his comrades to follow. Then the gates were thrown open by the terrified citizens ; and those who had lacked courage to escape punishment by death made their way with faltering steps to the hostile camp. The city stood open ; the people confessed their mad folly and unbarred their houses polluted by hospitality to the Carthaginians. Women and children came flocking, and sorrowing senators, and the rabble whom none could pity. There stood the Roman soldiers, leaning on their javelins, and gazed at those men, unable to bear either prosperity or adversity, who now swept the ground with beards that covered their breasts, and now defiled their grey hairs in the dust, while, shedding unmanly tears and putting up shameful prayers for mercy, they filled the air with womanish wailings.

While the soldiers looked with wonder at such weakness, and waited eagerly for the command to raze the walls, a sudden awe, felt but not expressed, came over them, and some divine power tamed their

ne flammam taedasque velint, ne templa sub uno
in cinerem traxisse rogo. subit intima corda,
perlabens sensim, mitis deus ; ille superbae
fundamenta Capyn posuisse antiquitus urbi,
non cuiquam visus, passim monet ; ille refusis
in spatium immensum campis habitanda relinqui
utile tecta docet. paulatim atrocibus irae
languescunt animis, et vis mollita senescit.

Pan Iove missus erat, servari tecta volente
Troïa, pendenti similis Pan semper et imo
vix ulla inscribens terrae vestigia cornu.
dextera lascivit caesa Tegeatide capra
verbera laeta movens festo per compita coetu.
cingit acuta comas et opacat tempora pinus,
ac parva erumpunt rubicunda cornua fronte ;
stant aures, imoque cadit barba hispida mento.
pastorale deo baculum, pellisque sinistrum
velat grata latus tenerae de corpore dammae.
nulla in praeruptum tam prona et inhospita cautes,
in qua non, librans corpus similisque volanti,
cornipedem tulerit praecisa per avia plantam.
interdum inflexus medio nascentia tergo
respicit arridens hirtae ludibria caudae.
obtendensque manum solem infervescere fronti
arcet et umbrato perlustrat pascua visu.
hic, postquam mandata dei perfecta malamque
sedavit rabiem et permulsit corda furentum,

---

[a] Capys.

[b] Tegea is a town of Arcadia, and Arcadia is the home of Pan.

[c] The reference is to the Lupercalia, a feast in honour of Pan celebrated every year on February 15, when the priests, called Luperci, ran about the city, striking persons whom they met with strips of goat-skin.

ferocity, making them loath to hurl their fire-brands and reduce all the temples of Capua to ashes in a single conflagration. A merciful god made his way by slow degrees into their inmost hearts. Unseen by any eye, he taught them all that Capys had laid the foundations of that proud city in ancient times, and showed that it was expedient to leave human habitations for that vast extent of plain. By degrees their angry passions died down, and their violence was softened and weakened.

It was Pan whom Jupiter had sent, in his desire to save the city founded by the Trojan [a]—Pan, who seems ever to stand on tiptoe, and whose horny hoof leaves scarce any print upon the ground. His right hand plays with a lash of Tegean [b] goat-skin and deals sportive blows among the holiday crowd at the cross-ways.[c] Pine-needles wreathe his locks and shade his temples, and a pair of little horns sprout from his ruddy brow. He has pointed ears, and a rough beard hangs down from his chin. He carries a shepherd's crook, and the soft skin of a roe-deer gives a welcome covering to his left side. There is no cliff so steep and dangerous, but he can keep his balance on it like a winged thing, and move his horny hoofs down the untrodden precipice. Sometimes he turns round and laughs at the antics of the shaggy tail that grows behind him; or he puts up a hand to keep the sun from scorching his brow and surveys the pasture-lands with shaded eyes.[d] Now, when he had duly done the bidding of Jupiter, calming the angry passions of the soldiers and softening their hearts, he went swiftly back to the glades

[d] Silius seems to be describing one of the works of art in which Pan is thus represented.

Arcadiae volucris saltus et amata revisit
Maenala ; ubi, argutis longe de vertice sacro
dulce sonans calamis, ducit stabula omnia cantu.
At legio Ausonidum, flammas ductore iubente
arceri portis stantesque relinquere muros,
—mite decus mentis—condunt ensesque facesque.
multa deum templis domibusque nitentibus auro
egeritur praeda, et victus alimenta superbi,
quisque bonis periere, virum de corpore vestes
femineae, mensaeque alia tellure petitae,
poculaque Eoa luxum irritantia gemma.
nec modus argento, caelataque pondera facti
tantum epulis auri, tum passim corpora longo
ordine captiva, et domibus deprompta talenta,
pascere longinquum non deficientia bellum,
immensique greges famulae ad convivia turbae.
Fulvius, ut finem spoliandis aedibus, aere
belligero revocante, dedit, sublimis ab alto
suggestu, magnis fautor non futilis ausis,
" Lanuvio generate," inquit, " quem Sospita Iuno
dat nobis, Milo, Gradivi cape victor honorem,
tempora murali cinctus turrita corona."
tum sontes procerum meritosque piacula prima
acciet et iusta punit commissa securi.

---

[a] A town and mountain in Arcadia. [b] See xi. 41.

[c] Tables, made from round sections of the *citrus*-tree, a kind of cypress which grew in Mauretania, were a favourite article of luxury among the ancients.

[d] Juno was worshipped under this title at Lanuvium. The Milo whom Cicero defended in 52 B.C. was a native of Lanuvium : Silius implies that the hero of Capua was an ancestor.

[e] This was decorated with the turrets of a battlement and

of Arcadia and to Maenalus,[a] the mountain that he loves; on that sacred height he makes sweet music far and wide with his melodious pipe, and all the flocks from far away follow it.

Then, when the Roman general ordered that the gates should not be fired and the walls should be left standing—such moderation did him honour—the soldiers put away swords and fire-brands. From the temples of the gods and from houses glittering with gold, booty was brought forth in abundance, and all the appliances of luxurious living, and the delights that had brought ruin to their possessors—womanish garments stripped from the backs of men,[b] tables imported from foreign lands,[c] and cups whose orient pearls whetted the taste for extravagance. Of silver plate there was no end, and there was heavy gold plate also, embossed with carving and intended only for feasts. There were long processions of slaves everywhere; and money enough to carry on a protracted war was taken from private houses; and the hordes of menials who had waited at the banquets of the rich were past counting.

When Fulvius sounded the recall and stopped the plundering of the houses, he spoke from his lofty seat, a zealous rewarder of brave deeds: "Milo, son of Lanuvium, whom Juno the Preserver [d] gave to us, receive now the decoration which Mars confers on the conqueror, and bind your brows with the turrets of the mural crown." [e] Then he summoned those of the nobles whose guilt marked them out as the first victims, and punished their crime as it deserved by the headsman's axe.

was given to the soldier who was first to scale the walls of a besieged city.

Hic atrox virtus—nec enim occuluisse probarim
spectatum vel in hoste decus—clamore feroci
Taurea " tune," inquit, " ferro spoliabis inultus
te maiorem anima ? et iusso lictore recisa
ignavos cadet ante pedes fortissima cervix ?
haud umquam hoc vobis dederit deus." inde, minaci
obtutu torvum contra et furiale renidens,
bellatorem alacer per pectora transigit ensem.
cui ductor : " patriam moriens comitare cadentem.
qui nobis animus, quae dextera cuique viritim,
decernet Mavors. tibi, si rebare pudendum
iusta pati, licuit pugnanti occumbere letum."
Dum Capua infaustam luit haud sine sanguine culpam,
interea geminos terra crudelis Hibera
Fortuna abstulerat, permiscens tristia laetis,
Scipiadas, magnumque decus magnumque dolorem.
forte Dicarchea iuvenis dum sedit in urbe
Scipio, post belli repetens extrema penates,
huc tristes lacrimas et funera acerba suorum
fama tulit. duris quamquam non cedere suetus,
pulsato lacerat violenter pectore amictus.
non comites tenuisse valent, non ullus honorum
militiaeve pudor : pietas irata sinistris
caelicolis furit atque odit solacia luctus.
iamque dies iterumque dies absumpta querelis.
versatur species ante ora oculosque parentum.
ergo excire parat manes animasque suorum
alloquioque virum tantos mulcere dolores.

---

[a] See ll. 142 foll.

[b] Scipio's father and his uncle were defeated and killed in Spain, both within one month, in 212 B.C.

[c] Puteoli.

But here Taurea,[a] brave in defiance—I cannot think it right to conceal a noble deed, even if done by an enemy—shouted out in anger: "Will you take with the steel the life of one greater than yourself, and take it with impunity? Shall the lictor do your bidding and lay the severed head of a hero before the feet of cowards? Never shall Heaven give this power to the Romans." Then, fronting his judge with a fierce stare and a frenzied laugh, he drove his trusty sword instantly through his own breast. Fulvius answered him thus: "Die with your country and share her fall! Mars will judge each of us, for courage and for bravery in battle. You, if you thought it beneath you to submit to just punishment, might have met death in battle."

While Capua thus atoned with blood for her fatal error, meanwhile cruel Fortune, who deals out sorrow and joy together, had slain the two Scipios [b] on Spanish territory—once the boast of their country and now her grief. It chanced that young Scipio was then resting in the city of Dicaearchus.[c] Fighting was over, and he was revisiting his home, when rumour brought him bitter tears to shed for the untimely death of his kinsmen. Though it was not his wont to yield to misfortune, he beat his breast now and rent his garments in the violence of his grief. No efforts of his friends, no regard for his high station and military command, could restrain him: his love raged against the cruelty of Heaven and refused all consolation. Day followed day, and was spent by him in lamenting. The faces of his lost kinsmen were ever present before his eyes. Therefore he determined to call up the dead, the spirits of his dear ones, and to soothe his great grief

hortatur vicina palus, ubi signat Averni
squalentem introitum stagnans Acherusius umor.
noscere venturos agitat mens protinus annos.
  Sic ad Cymaeam, quae tum sub nomine Phoebi
Autonoë tripodas sacros antrumque tenebat,
fert gressus iuvenis consultaque pectoris aegri
pandit et aspectus orat contingere patrum.
nec cunctata diu vates : " mactare repostis
mos umbris," inquit, " consueta piacula nigras
sub lucem pecudes reclusaeque abdere terrae
manantem iugulis spirantum caede cruorem.
tunc populos tibi regna suos pallentia mittent.
cetera, quae poscis, maiori vate canentur.
namque tibi Elysio repetita oracula campo
eliciam veterisque dabo inter sacra Sibyllae
cernere fatidicam Phoebei pectoris umbram.
vade, age et, a medio cum se nox umida cursu
flexerit, ad fauces vicini castus Averni
duc praedicta sacris duro placamina Diti.
mella simul tecum et puri fer dona Lyaei."
  Hoc alacer monitu et promissae nomine vatis,
apparat occulto monstrata piacula coepto.
inde, ubi nox iussam procedens contigit horam
et spatia aequarunt tenebras transacta futuras,
consurgit stratis pergitque ad turbida portae
ostia Tartareae ; penitus quis abdita vates
promissa implerat Stygioque sedebat in antro.

---

[a] See xii. 121. [b] A Sibyl.

by speech with them. He was encouraged by the nearness of that swamp, where the stagnant water of Acheron marks the unsightly descent to Avernus.[a] He was eager to learn at once the secrets of the future.

Thus young Scipio bent his steps to Cumae, where Autonoë [b] then ruled, as Apollo's priestess, the sacred tripods and grotto; and to her he revealed the purpose of his sad heart, and asked to see his kinsmen face to face. The priestess did not tarry long: "It is customary," she said, "to slay black-fleeced sheep before the dawn, as offerings to the dead in their graves, and then to bury in an open trench the blood that flows from the throats of the still living victims. Then the pale kingdoms will render up their inhabitants to your view. As to your further demands, a greater priestess than I shall answer you. For I will summon up a response all the way from the Elysian Fields, and will permit you to see at your sacrifice the shade of that ancient Sibyl who declares the mind of Apollo. Up, then! and when dewy night has moved past her middle point, then purify yourself and go to the neighbouring gorge of Avernus and take with you the animals I have named, as a sacrifice to soften the stony heart of Pluto. Take honey also with you and an offering of unmixed wine."

Encouraged by this advice and by the name of the priestess whose aid was promised him, Scipio made ready in secret the prescribed victims. Then, when night in her course had reached the hour appointed and the darkness past was equal to the darkness yet to come, he rose from his bed and went to the stormy entrance of the gate to Tartarus, where the priestess, faithful to her word, was sitting in the deep recess of the Stygian grotto. Then, where

tum, qua se primum rupta tellure recludit
invisus caelo specus atque eructat acerbam
Cocyti laxo suspirans ore paludem,
inducit iuvenem ferroque cavare refossam
ocius urget humum atque, arcanum murmur anhelans,
ordine mactari pecudes iubet. ater operto
ante omnes taurus regi, tum proxima divae
caeditur Hennaeae casta cervice iuvenca.
inde tibi, Alecto, tibi, numquam laeta Megaera,
corpora lanigerum procumbunt lecta bidentum.
fundunt mella super Bacchique et lactis honorem.
"sta, iuvenis, faciemque, Erebo quae surgit ab omni,"
exclamat vates, " patere : accedentia cerno
Tartara et ante oculos assistere tertia regna.
ecce ruunt variae species, et quicquid ab imo
natum hominum exstinctumque chao est; iam cuncta videbis,
Cyclopas Scyllamque et pastos membra virorum
Odrysiae telluris equos. contende tueri
eductumque tene vagina interritus ensem.
quaecumque ante animae tendent potare cruorem,
dissice, dum castae procedat imago Sibyllae.
interea cerne ut gressus inhumata citatos
fert umbra et properat tecum coniungere dicta ;
cui datur ante atros absumpti corporis ignes,
sanguine non tacto, solitas effundere voces."
aspicit et subito turbatus Scipio visu
" quinam te, qui casus," ait, " dux maxime, fessae

[a] One of the infernal rivers : it seems to stand here for Acheron.
[b] Pluto.
[c] Proserpina, who was carried off from Henna to the nether world.
[d] See note to ii. 530.
[e] The sky and earth form the First Kingdom, the sea is the Second, and Hades the Third : see note to viii. 116.

the earth begins to part and the hollow hateful to heaven opens up, while its wide mouth pants and belches forth acrid air from the marsh of Cocytus,[a] she led him on and bade him hasten to dig a trench in the earth with his sword and slay the victims in due order; and with quick-drawn breath she muttered mystic words. First of all, a black bull was offered to the Invisible King,[b] and next an unmated heifer to the goddess of Henna.[c] Lastly, chosen sheep with woolly fleeces were slain in honour of Alecto[d] and of Megaera, the Fury who never smiles. And over them honey was poured, with an offering of wine and milk. "Stand firm, young man," she cried, "and endure the sight of those who are rising from all Erebus. I see all Tartarus approaching, and the Third[e] Kingdom of the world presents itself to our sight. Lo, shapes of all kinds come flocking, and all mankind who have been born and have died since the primal chaos; soon you shall see everything—Cyclopes and Scylla, and the Thracian horses that fed on human flesh.[f] Fix your gaze firmly upon them all, and grasp your drawn sword undaunted. If any spirits press forward to drink of the blood before the form of the chaste Sibyl advances, hew them in pieces. But meantime look at yonder unburied ghost[g] which comes quickly hither and desires to have speech with you. Until the funeral fire has consumed his body, he is permitted to speak as he was wont, without tasting of the blood." Scipio looked at him, and was appalled by the sudden sight: "Great leader," he said, "what mishap has robbed

[f] The horses of Diomede the Thracian: see note to iii. 38.

[g] The ghost of Appius Claudius who was mortally wounded at Capua.

eripuit patriae, cum tales horrida poscunt
bella viros ? nec enim dextra concesserit ulli
Appius, aut astu. decimum lux rettulit ortum,
ut te, cum Capua remearem, vulnera vidi
mulcentem, hoc uno maestum, quod adire nequires
saucius ad muros et Martis honore careres."
contra quae ductor : " fesso mihi proxima tandem
lux gratos Phaëthontis equos avertit et atris
aeternum demisit aquis. sed lenta meorum
dum vanos ritus cura et sollemnia vulgi
exsequitur, cessat flammis imponere corpus,
ut portet tumulis per longum membra paternis.
quod te per nostri Martis precor aemula facta,
arce quae putres artus medicamina servant,
daque vago portas quamprimum Acherontis adire."
Tunc iuvenis : " gens o veteris pulcherrima Clausi,
haud ulla ante tuam, quamquam non parva fatigent,
curarum prior exstiterit. namque ista per omnes
discrimen servat populos variatque iacentum
exsequias tumuli et cinerum sententia discors.
tellure, ut perhibent, (is mos antiquus) Hibera
exanima obscenus consumit corpora vultur.
regia cum lucem posuerunt membra, probatum est
Hyrcanis adhibere canes. Aegyptia tellus
claudit adorato[1] post funus stantia saxo
corpora et a mensis exsanguem haud separat umbram.
exhausto instituit Pontus vacuare cerebro

[1] adorato *Bothe* : odorato *edd.*

[a] Hades.
[b] See note to viii. 412.
[c] The digression about funeral customs that follows (ll. 468-487) is so out of place here and so unworthy of the writer that some editors have expelled it from the text.
[d] This is the famous "skeleton at the feast," which reminded the Egyptian feasters that they too were mortal.

your suffering country of your aid, at a time when cruel war calls for such men as you? For Appius need yield to no man either in valour or in craft. Ten times has the dawn returned since I came back from Capua and saw you under cure for your wounds; and you regretted nothing, except that your wounds prevented you from approaching the walls of the city and sharing the glory of victory." The general answered: "It was only one day later that the pleasant sight of the sun's coursers was taken from me on my sick-bed, and I sank for ever in the dark stream of death. But the piety of my friends is slow to act, and seeks to observe the meaningless rites and customs of the people; hence they delay to burn my body, meaning to carry it far away to the tomb of my fathers. Therefore I entreat you by our rivalry in feats of arms, keep away from me those drugs which preserve the body from corruption, and suffer my wandering spirit to enter Acheron[a] without delay."

And Scipio replied: "Noblest scion of ancient Clausus,[b] no business of my own (and I have heavy tasks to perform) shall take precedence of your request. [c]All over the world the practice is different in this matter, and unlikeness of opinion produces various ways of burying the dead and disposing of their ashes. In the land of Spain, we are told (it is an ancient custom) the bodies of the dead are devoured by loathly vultures. When a king dies in Hyrcania, it is the rule to let dogs have access to the corpse. The Egyptians enclose their dead, standing in an upright position, in a coffin of stone, and worship it; and they admit a bloodless spectre to their banquets.[d] With the peoples of the Black Sea it is the custom to empty the skull by extracting the

ora virum et longum medicata reponit in aevum.
quid, qui reclusa nudos Garamantes harena
infodiunt? quid, qui saevo sepelire profundo
exanimos mandant Libycis Nasamones in oris?
at Celtae vacui capitis circumdare gaudent
ossa, nefas, auro ac mensis ea pocula servant.
Cecropidae ob patriam Mavortis sorte peremptos
decrevere simul communibus urere flammis.
at gente in Scythica suffixa cadavera truncis
lenta dies sepelit, putri liquentia tabo."

Talia dum memorant, umbra veniente Sibyllae,
Autonoë "finem hic," inquit, "sermonibus adde
alternis. haec, haec veri fecunda sacerdos,
cui tantum patuit rerum quantum ipse negarit
plus novisse deus. me iam comitante tuorum
tempus abire globo et pecudes imponere flammis."

At gravida arcanis Cymes anus attigit ore
postquam sacrificum delibavitque cruorem,
in decus egregiae vultus intenta iuventae
"aetherea fruerer cum luce, haud segniter," inquit,
"Cymaeo populis vox nostra sonabat in antro.
tum te permixtum saeclis rebusque futuris
Aeneadum cecini. sed non sat digna mearum
cura tuis vocum: nec enim conquirere dicta
aut servare fuit proavis sollertia vestris.
verum age, disce, puer, quando cognoscere cordi est,
iam tua deque tuis pendentia Dardana fatis.
namque tibi cerno properatum oracula vitae

---

[a] The superior Sibyl who comes up from the Elysian Fields.
[b] Cumae.
[c] An allusion to the refusal of Tarquinius Superbus to buy the books of the Sibyl.

brain and to preserve the embalmed body for centuries. The Garamantes, again, dig a hole in the sand and bury the corpse naked, while the Nasamones in Libya commit their dead to the cruel sea for burial. Then the Celts have a horrid practice: they frame the bones of the empty skull in gold, and keep it for a drinking-cup. The Athenians passed a law, that the bodies of all who had fallen in battle in defence of their country should be burnt together on a single pyre. Again, among the Scythians the dead are fastened to tree-trunks and left to rot, and time at last is the burier of their bodies."

While thus they spoke, the ghost of the Sibyl[a] approached, and Autonoë bade them stop their discourse: "Here," she said, "here is the priestess, the fountain of truth; to her so much is revealed that Apollo himself would not claim to know more. The time has come for me to depart in company with your band of followers, and place the victims upon the fire."

But when the ancient dame of Cyme, that depository of hidden things, had tasted with her lips the blood of the victims, she gazed on the goodly face of the young hero: "While yet I enjoyed the light of heaven," she said, "my voice was not silent but rang out to the nations from the cave of Cyme.[b] And then I prophesied of you and your part in the future fortunes of the Roman people. But your nation did not give due heed to my sayings.[c] For your ancestors lacked the wit to collect or preserve my oracles. But mark me now, my son, and you shall learn, since you would fain know it, your own destiny and the destiny of Rome that depends on yours. For I see that you are eager to learn from

hinc petere et patrios visu contingere manes.
armifero victor patrem ulcisceris Hibero,
creditus ante annos Martem, ferroque resolves
gaudia Poenorum et missum laetabere bello
omen, Hiberiacis victa Carthagine terris.
maius ad imperium posthac capiere, nec ante
Iupiter absistet cura quam cuncta fugarit
in Libyam bella et vincendum duxerit ipse
Sidonium tibi rectorem. pudet urbis iniquae,
quod post haec decus hoc patriaque domoque carebit."
sic vates gressumque lacus vertebat ad atros.
Tum iuvenis : " quaecumque datur sors durior aevi,
obnitemur," ait, " culpa modo pectora cessent.
sed, te oro, quando vitae tibi causa labores
humanos iuvisse fuit, siste, inclita virgo,
paulisper gressum et nobis manesque silentum
enumera Stygiaeque aperi formidinis aulam."
Annuit illa quidem, sed " non optanda recludis
regna," ait. " hic tenebras habitant volitantque per umbras
innumeri quondam populi. domus omnibus una.
in medio vastum late se tendit inane ;
huc, quicquid terrae, quicquid freta et igneus aër
nutrivit primo mundi genitalis ab aevo,
Mors communis agit : descendunt cuncta, capitque
campus iners, quantum interiit restatque futurum.
cingunt regna decem portae : quarum una receptat

---

[a] Scipio was twenty-four years old when he accepted the chief command in Spain in 211 B.C.

[b] New Carthage (now Cartagena), taken by Scipio in 210 B.C.

[c] The consulship, which he held in 205 B.C.

[d] He was brought to trial for malversation in 187 B.C. and retired to Liternum, where he died soon afterwards.

me a forecast of your life, and to have sight of your kinsmen's ghosts. Trusted with command before the proper age,[a] you shall be victorious in battle on the Ebro, and shall avenge your sire ; with the sword you shall put an end to the rejoicing of the Carthaginians; and, when you have conquered the Carthage in Spain,[b] you will welcome the conquest as an omen for the war. Then you will be chosen for a higher office[c]; and Jupiter will continue to watch over you until he has driven all the invaders back to Africa and himself brought Hannibal to be conquered by you. Shame on the unjust citizens, who will deprive of home and country a hero who has done such things!"[d] Thus spoke the prophetess and was turning her steps to the dark pools of Hades.

Then Scipio said : " However hard the lot in life assigned me, I shall struggle to overcome it ; the consciousness of innocence is all I ask. But, famous Maiden, since the purpose of your life was ever to help mankind in their troubles, I entreat you to stay your steps a while, that you may name the spirits of the speechless dead and reveal to me the dreadful abode of Hades."

She consented, but said : " The realm you seek to see is not one to be desired. The countless generations of past ages dwell here in darkness and flit through the shadows. For all alike there is but one habitation. In the midst there is a vast extent of empty space ; and down hither, driven by one common doom, come all things—whatever has been born of earth or sea or the fiery air since the beginning of the world ; and the barren plain has room for all the dead and for those who have yet to be born. Round this realm there are ten gates. One of these admits

belligeros, dura Gradivi sorte creatos,
altera, qui leges posuere atque inclita iura
gentibus et primas fundarunt moenibus urbes;
tertia ruricolas, Cereris iustissima turba
quae venit ad manes et fraudum illaesa veneno.
exin, qui laetas artes vitaeque colendae
invenere viam nec dedignanda parenti
carmina fuderunt Phoebo, sua limina servant.
proxima, quos venti saevaeque hausere procellae,
naufraga porta rapit; sic illam nomine dicunt.
finitima huic noxa gravido et peccasse fatenti
vasta patet populo: poenas Rhadamanthus in ipso
expetit introitu mortemque exercet inanem.
septima femineis reseratur porta catervis,
umentes ubi casta fovet Proserpina lucos.
infantum hinc gregibus versasque ad funera taedas
passis virginibus turbaeque in limine lucis
est iter extinctae, et vagitu ianua nota.
tum, seducta loco et laxata lucida nocte,
claustra nitent, quae secreti per limitis umbram
Elysios ducunt campos; hic turba piorum,
nec Stygio in regno, caeli nec posta sub axe,
verum, ultra Oceanum sacro contermina fonti,
Lethaeos potat latices, oblivia mentis.
extrema hinc, auro fulgens, iam lucis honorem
sentit et admoto splendet ceu sidere lunae.
hac animae caelum repetunt ac mille peractis,
oblitae Ditem, redeunt in corpora lustris.
has passim nigrum pandens Mors lurida rictum
itque reditque vias et portis omnibus errat.

---

[a] One of the judges of the dead.

[b] He inflicts on the dead punishments which they cannot feel.

warriors, men born to endure war's hardships; the second opens to those who made laws and famous statutes for their nations, and were the first to found walled cities; the third admits honest country-folk dear to Ceres, who come down to Hades untouched by the poison of unfair dealings. The next gate is reserved for those who discovered fine arts and a civilized way of life, and uttered poems which their father, Phoebus, need not despise. The next, called the gate of shipwreck, lets in those whom winds and fierce storms destroyed. The sixth gate opens wide for the multitude who are oppressed by sin and confess their guilt; close by the entrance sits Rhadamanthus [a] and demands penalties and punishes unsubstantial death.[b] The seventh gate is unbarred for the companies of women, and here chaste Proserpina tends her dewy groves. The next gate is known for the crying of infants; and hither come a multitude of babes who died on the threshold of life, and maidens whose wedding-torches lighted their funerals instead. Next, in a place apart and radiant with gloom dispersed, stands a shining portal which leads to the Elysian Fields by a secret shady path; and here dwell the righteous, not in the realm of Hades nor under the cope of heaven, but, beyond the Ocean stream and hard by a sacred spring, they drink the water of Lethe and forget their past. Last is the tenth gate; glittering with gold, it enjoys the privilege of light and shines as if the moon's disk were close beside it. By this gate souls rise again to heaven and, after the lapse of five thousand years, enter new bodies and forget Pluto. Here pale Death, with her hideous jaws agape, paces to and fro continually and wanders from gate to gate.

"Tum iacet in spatium sine corpore pigra vorago
limosique lacus ; large exundantibus urit
ripas saevus aquis Phlegethon et, turbine anhelo
flammarum resonans, saxosa incendia torquet.
parte alia torrens Cocytos sanguinis atri
vorticibus furit et spumanti gurgite fertur.
at, magnis semper divis regique deorum
iurari dignata palus, picis horrida rivo,
fumiferum volvit Styx inter sulphura limum.
tristior his Acheron sanie crassoque veneno
aestuat et, gelidam eructans cum murmure harenam,
descendit nigra lentus per stagna palude.
hanc potat saniem non uno Cerberus ore,
haec et Tisiphones sunt pocula, et atra Megaera
hanc sitit, at nullo rabies restinguitur haustu.
ultimus erumpit lacrimarum fontibus amnis
ante aulam atque aditus et inexorabile limen.

"Quanta cohors, omni stabulante per atria monstro,
excubat et manes permixto murmure terret !
Luctus edax Maciesque, malis comes addita morbis,
et Maeror pastus fletu et sine sanguine Pallor
Curaeque Insidiaeque atque hinc queribunda Senectus,
hinc angens utraque manu sua guttura Livor,
et, deforme malum ac sceleri proclivis, Egestas
Errorque infido gressu et Discordia gaudens
permiscere fretum caelo. sedet ostia Ditis
centenis suetus Briareus recludere palmis
et Sphinx, virgineos rictus infecta cruore,

---

[a] He had three heads.

[b] Tisiphone and Megaera are two of the Furies : see note to ii. 530 : the third is Alecto.

[c] To the four rivers usually placed in Hades Silius adds a fifth not mentioned by other writers.

[d] When she sees the prosperity of others.

"Then there lies stretching far and wide a lifeless morass, with no creature to be seen, and muddy pools. Here fierce Phlegethon burns its banks with overflowing stream and rolls along fiery rocks, resounding with a roaring blast of flame. Elsewhere Cocytus rushes down, raving with eddies of black blood and foaming as it flows. Next is the Styx, by which the high gods and even the king of the gods deign to swear; dreadful with its stream of pitch, it carries down sulphur and steaming mud together. Acheron, more terrible than these, seethes with venom and clotted poison, and spouts up icy sand with a rumbling noise, as its black current goes slowly down through the stagnant pools. From this foul stream Cerberus drinks with more than one mouth [a]; this is the drink of Tisiphone also, and black Megaera [b] thirsts for it, though no draught can slake her fury. Last of all, a river of tears [c] takes its rise before the entrance to the ruler's palace and the threshold that no prayers can soften.

"How great a company of terrible shapes keep watch and have their abode in the courtyard, terrifying the dead with the noise of their mingled voices! Consuming Grief is there, and Leanness which waits upon sore disease; and Sorrow that feeds on tears, and bloodless Pallor; Remorse and Treachery are there; here is querulous Old Age, and there Jealousy which strangles herself with both hands [d]; and Poverty, an unsightly plague that leads men to crime; Error, with staggering gait, and Discord that delights to confound sea with sky.[e] There sits Briareus, ever accustomed to open the gates of Pluto with his hundred hands; and the Sphinx whose maiden mouth is stained with human blood; and

[e] *i.e.* to cause general confusion.

Scyllaque Centaurique truces umbraeque Gigantum.
Cerberus hic ruptis peragrat cum Tartara vinclis,
non ipsa Alecto, non feta furore Megaera
audet adire ferum, dum fractis mille catenis
viperea latrans circumligat ilia cauda.
"Dextra vasta comas nemorosaque brachia fundit
taxus, Cocyti rigua frondosior unda.
hic dirae volucres pastusque cadavere vultur
et multus bubo ac sparsis strix sanguine pennis
Harpyiaeque fovent nidos atque omnibus haerent
condensae foliis ; saevit stridoribus arbor.
Has inter formas coniux Iunonis Avernae,
suggestu residens, cognoscit crimina regum.
stant vincti, seroque piget sub iudice culpae ;
circum errant Furiae Poenarumque omnis imago.
quam vellent numquam sceptris fulsisse superbis !
insultant duro imperio non digna nec aequa
ad superos passi manes ; quaeque ante profari
non licitum vivis, tandem permissa queruntur.
tunc alius saevis religatur rupe catenis,
ast alius subigit saxum contra ardua montis,
vipereo domat hunc aeterna Megaera flagello.
talia letiferis restant patienda tyrannis.
sed te maternos tempus cognoscere vultus,
cuius prima venit non tardis passibus umbra."
Adstabat fecunda Iovis Pomponia furto.

---

[a] The Harpies were rapacious monsters, with the face and body of a woman and the wings of a bird.

[b] Avernian Juno is Proserpina, and her husband is Pluto.

[c] The legend here set forth, that Jupiter, in the form of a serpent, was the father of Scipio, seems to have been believed by the vulgar at Rome ; and Scipio himself was perhaps not unwilling that it should be believed.

Scylla and the fierce Centaurs, and the ghosts of the Giants. Cerberus is here ; when he bursts his bonds and moves through Tartarus, not even Alecto or Megaera, the mother of madness, dares to face the savage hound, when, after snapping a thousand chains, he bays and twines round his loins his snake-like tail.

"On the right hand, a great yew-tree spreads its foliage and leafy arms ; and the running water of Cocytus refreshes its growth. Here birds of ill omen dwell—vultures who feed on carrion, troops of owls, and screech-owls with blood-spotted plumage ; and Harpies [a] have their nests here and cling in clusters to every leaf : the tree resounds with their harsh cries.

"Surrounded by these shapes and sitting on a lofty throne, the husband of Avernian Juno [b] tries guilty kings. They stand before him in chains and repent of their crimes too late before their judge : Furies and Penalties in every shape hover round. How great now their regret that they ever held the glittering sceptre of tyranny ! Those who in life suffered undeserved and unjust punishment from them now mock their harsh rulers ; and the complaints they could not utter in life they have leave at last to express. Then one of them is bound upon a rock with fetters of iron, and another pushes a stone up a steep mountain, and a third is for ever lashed by Megaera with her scourge of snakes. Such are the penalties in store for death-dealing tyrants. But it is time for you to look on your mother's face ; her ghost is the first to come, and comes with speed."

Pomponia now stood near. The secret love of Jupiter had made her Scipio's mother.[c] For, when

namque ubi cognovit Latio surgentia bella
Poenorum Venus, insidias anteire laborans
Iunonis, fusa sensim per pectora patrem
implicuit flamma ; quae ni provisa fuissent,
Sidonia Iliacas nunc virgo accenderet aras.
ergo ubi gustatus cruor, admonuitque Sibylla
et dedit alternos ambobus noscere vultus,
sic iuvenis prior : " o magni mihi numinis instar,
cara parens, quam, te ut nobis vidisse liceret,
optassem Stygias vel leto intrare tenebras !
quae sors nostra fuit, cui te, cum prima subiret,
eripuit sine honore dies et funere carpsit ! "
excipit his mater : " nullos, o nate, labores
mors habuit nostra ; aetherii dum pondere partus
exsolvor, miti dextra Cyllenia proles
imperio Iovis Elysias deduxit ad oras
attribuitque pares sedes, ubi magna moratur
Alcidae genetrix, ubi sacro munere Leda.
verum age, nate, tuos ortus, ne bella pavescas
ulla, nec in caelum dubites te attollere factis,
quando aperire datur nobis, nunc denique disce.
sola die caperem medio cum forte petitos
ad requiem somnos, subitus mihi membra ligavit
amplexus, non ille, meo veniente marito,
assuetus facilisque mihi. tum luce corusca,
implebat quamquam languentia lumina somnus,
vidi, crede, Iovem. nec me mutata fefellit
forma dei, quod, squalentem conversus in anguem,
ingenti traxit curvata volumina gyro.
sed mihi post partum non ultra ducere vitam
concessum. heu, quantum gemui, quod spiritus ante

[a] The fire of Vesta.
[b] Pomponia died in childbirth.
[c] Mercury : see note to iii. 168.

Venus learnt that the arms of Carthage were rising against Rome, she strove to anticipate the wiles of Juno, and entrapped her father's heart with a slow-spreading flame. But for this foresight, a Carthaginian virgin would now be kindling the altars of Ilium.[a] So, when the ghost had tasted of the blood and the Sibyl had informed her and suffered the pair to recognize one another, Scipio thus began: "Dear mother, as sacred to me as a mighty god, how gladly would I even have died and so entered the Stygian darkness, for a sight of you! What a lot was mine! The first day of my life was a day of disaster that snatched you from me and laid you in the grave." His mother replied: "My son, no suffering attended my death[b]: when I was delivered of the divine burden I carried, the god born on Cyllene[c] conducted me with gentle hand by the command of Jupiter and gave me a place of equal honour in Elysium, where Leda and the great mother of Alcides are permitted by the god to dwell. But mark me, my son, and at last you shall learn what I am permitted to disclose—the secret of your birth; then no wars will affright you, and you may be confident of rising to heaven by your achievements. It chanced that I was alone at midday, enjoying the sleep that my weariness required, when suddenly I was clasped in an embrace—no common and familiar union, as when my husband came to me; and then in radiant light, though my half-closed eyes were full of sleep, I saw—doubt me not—I saw Jupiter! Nor was I deceived by the god's disguise; for he had changed himself into a serpent covered with scales and drew his coils after him in huge curves. But I was not permitted to live on after my delivery. What grief was mine, that my

haec tibi quam noscenda darem discessit in auras ! "
his alacer colla amplexu materna petebat ;
umbraque ter frustra per inane petita fefellit.
  Succedunt simulacra virum concordia, patris
unanimique simul patrui. ruit ipse per umbram,
oscula vana petens, iuvenis fumoque volucri
et nebulis similes animas apprendere certat.
" quis te, care pater, quo stabant Itala regna,
exosus Latium deus abstulit ? hei mihi ! nam cur
ulla fuere adeo, quibus a te saevus abessem,
momenta ? opposito mutassem pectore mortem.
quantos funeribus vestris gens Itala passim
dat gemitus ! tumulus vobis, censente senatu,
Mavortis geminus surgit per gramina campo."
nec passi plura, in medio sermone loquentis
sic adeo incipiunt. prior haec genitoris imago :
" ipsa quidem virtus sibimet pulcherrima merces ;
dulce tamen venit ad manes, cum gloria vitae
durat apud superos, nec edunt oblivia laudem.
verum age, fare, decus nostrum, te quanta fatiget
militia. heu, quotiens intrat mea pectora terror,
cum repeto, quam saevus eas, ubi magna pericla
contingunt tibi ! per nostri, fortissime, leti
obtestor causas, Martis moderare furori.
sat tibi sint documenta domus ! octava terebat
arentem culmis messem crepitantibus aestas,
ex quo cuncta mihi calcata meoque subibat
germano devicta iugum Tartessia tellus.
nos miserae muros et tecta renata Sagunto,

spirit departed before I could tell you these things!" Hearing this, Scipio strove eagerly to embrace his mother; but thrice the unsubstantial ghost eluded his grasp.

Her place was taken by the spirits of his father and his uncle—a pair of loving brothers. Scipio rushed through the gloom, seeking to embrace them; in vain, for the spirits he was fain to clasp were like mist or drifting smoke. "Beloved father, what god so hated Latium that he carried off you, the pillar of Roman rule? Alas! why was I ever unfeeling enough to be absent one moment from your side? I might have thrown myself in front of you and died in your stead. How sorely all Italy mourns for your deaths! By decree of the Senate, a double tomb is now rising in your honour on the grassy Field of Mars." They suffered him to say no more: even while he spoke, thus they began reply. His father's ghost spoke first: "Virtue is indeed its own noblest reward; yet the dead find it sweet, when the fame of their lives is remembered among the living and oblivion does not swallow up their praises. But make haste, glorious scion of our house, and tell how great is the burden of war you are now bearing. Alas, how often dread comes over me, when I remember your fiery onset in the face of great peril! I entreat you, my hero, bear in mind what brought us two to our deaths, and control your ardour in battle. Be warned by the experience of your kinsmen. The eighth summer was thrashing the rattling ears of ripe corn; eight years had passed since I had set my foot on the neck of all Spain and my brother had conquered the land and made it pass beneath the yoke. We rebuilt hapless Saguntum and gave her new walls;

nos dedimus Baetin nullo potare sub hoste ;
nobis indomitus convertit terque quaterque
germanus terga Hannibalis. pro barbara numquam
impolluta fides ! peterem cum victor adesum
cladibus Hasdrubalem, subito venale, cohortes
Hispanae, vulgus, Libyci quas fecerat auri
Hasdrubal, abrupto liquerunt agmine signa.
tunc hostis socio desertos milite, multum
ditior ipse viris, spisso circumdedit orbe.
non segnis nobis nec inultis, nate, peracta est
illa suprema dies, et laude inclusimus aevum."
  Excipit inde suos frater coniungere casus :
" excelsae turris post ultima rebus in artis
subsidium optaram supremaque bella ciebam.
fumantes taedas ac lata incendia passim
et mille iniecere faces. nil nomine leti
de superis queror : haud parvo data membra sepulcro
nostra cremaverunt in morte haerentibus armis.
sed me luctus habet, geminae ne clade ruinae
cesserit affusis oppressa Hispania Poenis."
  Contra quae iuvenis turbato fletibus ore :
" Di, quaeso, ut merita est, dignas pro talibus ausis
Carthago expendat poenas. sed continet acres
Pyrenes populos, qui, vestro Marte probatus,
excepit fessos et notis Marcius armis
successit bello. fusos quoque fama ferebat
victores acie, atque exacta piacula caedis."

---

[a] The Guadalquivir.

[b] There were three Carthaginian armies then in Spain, and three commanders : (1) Hasdrubal, brother of Hannibal, who fell at the battle of the Metaurus ; (2) Hasdrubal, son of Gisco ; and (3) Mago.

[c] This was Gnaeus Scipio who only survived his brother by a month.

[d] L. Marcius Septimus is highly praised by Livy (xxv. 37).

we made it possible to drink the water of the Baetis [a] and fear no foe ; again and again we forced the invincible brother of Hannibal [b] to retreat. But, alas, barbarians are ever foul traitors. Hasdrubal was crippled by defeat, and I was in victorious pursuit of him, when suddenly the Spanish cohorts, a mercenary rabble whom Hasdrubal had enslaved to Libyan gold, broke their ranks and deserted our standards. Thus left in the lurch by our allies, we were far inferior in number to the enemy ; and they formed a dense ring round us. We died not unavenged, my son : we played the man on that last day and ended our lives in glory."

Then his brother [c] added the story of his own death : " When all was over and I was hard beset, I sought the protection of a lofty tower and fought my last battle there. Smoking torches and a thousand fire-brands were hurled at the building, and the conflagration spread far. I have no grudge against the gods on the score of my death : by them my limbs were consigned for burning to no humble sepulchre, and I kept my armour in death. But I grieve to think that, after the disaster that brought me and my brother low, Spain may have yielded under pressure to the attacks of Carthage."

The young man answered, and his face was marred with weeping : " Ye Gods, I pray that Carthage may be punished as she deserves for such doings. But the fierce tribes of the Pyrenees are now held in check by Marcius,[d] a famous warrior who proved his worth in your army ; he protected our defeated forces and carried on the war ; report even said that the Carthaginians had been routed in a battle and paid the penalty for your death." Cheered by these tidings,

his laeti rediere duces loca amoena piorum,
prosequiturque oculis puer adveneratus euntes.
 Iamque aderat multa vix agnoscendus in umbra
Paulus et epoto fundebat sanguine verba :
" lux Italum, cuius spectavi Martia facta,
multum uno maiora viro, descendere nocti
atque habitanda semel subigit quis visere regna ? "
cui contra tales effundit Scipio voces :
" armipotens ductor, quam sunt tua fata per urbem
lamentata diu ! quam paene ruentia tecum
traxisti ad Stygias Oenotria tecta tenebras !
tum tibi defuncto tumulum Sidonius hostis
constituit laudemque tuo quaesivit honore."
dumque audit lacrimans hostilia funera Paulus,
ante oculos iam Flaminius, iam Gracchus et aegro
absumptus Cannis stabat Servilius ore.
appellare viros erat ardor et addere verba,
sed raptabat amor priscos cognoscere manes.
 Nunc meritum saeva Brutum immortale securi
nomen, nunc superos aequantem laude Camillum,
nunc auro Curium non umquam cernit amicum.
ora Sibylla docet venientum et nomina pandit.
" hic fraudes pacis Pyrrhumque a limine portae
reiecit, visus orbus ; tulit ille ruentem
Thybridis in ripas regem solusque revulso
pone ferox ponte exclusit redeuntia regna.
si tibi dulce virum, primo qui foedera bello

---

[a] On the field of Cannae, where Scipio was in command of a legion.

[b] See x. 518 foll.

[c] He caused his own sons to be beheaded for conspiring to restore the Tarquins.

[d] See note to i. 626.

[e] Manius Curius Dentatus, consul in 290 B.C., who refused bribes from the Samnites and from Pyrrhus.

[f] Appius Claudius Caecus, who refused to make peace with Pyrrhus.

the generals went back to the pleasant places of the blest, while the young man gazed after them as they went, and worshipped them.

Next Paulus came, hard to recognize in the dim light, and drank of the blood, and spoke thus: "Bright star of Italy, whose martial feats, too great by far for a single arm, these eyes beheld,[a] who forces you to descend into darkness and to visit this realm where those who enter must dwell for ever?" Scipio spoke thus in answer: "O mighty captain, how long did all Rome mourn your death! How nearly you carried down the Roman city in your fall to Stygian darkness! Also the Carthaginian, our foe, built a tomb for your dead body and sought to gain glory by honouring you."[b] While Paulus shed tears to hear of his burial by the enemy, Flaminius came in sight, and Gracchus, and the sad face of Servilius who fell at Cannae. Scipio was eager to call them by name and converse with them; but his strong desire to look on the heroes of the past carried him away.

He saw Brutus who gained eternal fame by the merciless axe,[c] and then Camillus,[d] peer of the gods in glory, and Curius[e] next who never welcomed gold. The Sibyl revealed to him their faces and names as they came up. "This blind man[f] drove Pyrrhus from his door and spurned the king's dishonest overtures for peace; that other[g] withstood the king who attacked the Tiber banks, and, when the bridge was broken down behind him, kept out the returning tyrants by his valour, single-handed. If you desire to see the man who concluded the peace after the

[g] Horatius Cocles, who kept the bridge against Lars Porsena.

Phoenicum pepigit, vidisse, hic inclitus ille
aequoreis victor cum classe Lutatius armis.
si studium et saevam cognoscere Hamilcaris umbram,
ille est (cerne procul) cui frons nec morte remissa
irarum servat rabiem. si iungere cordi est
colloquium, sine gustato det sanguine vocem."
atque ubi permissum, et sitiens se implevit imago,
sic prior increpitat non miti Scipio vultu:
" taliane, o fraudum genitor, sunt foedera vobis?
aut haec Sicania pepigisti captus in ora?
bella tuus toto natus contra omnia pacta
exercet Latio et, perruptis molibus, Alpes
eluctatus adest, fervet gens Itala Marte
barbarico, et refluunt obstructi stragibus amnes."
post quae Poenus ait: " decimum modo coeperat annum
excessisse puer, nostro cum bella Latinis
concepit iussu, licitum nec fallere divos
iuratos patri. quod si Laurentia vastat
nunc igni regna et Phrygias res vertere tentat,
o pietas, o sancta fides, o vera propago!
atque utinam amissum reparet decus!" inde citato
celsus abit gressu, maiorque recessit imago.
Exin designat vates, qui iura sub armis
poscenti dederint populo primique petitas
miscuerint Italis Piraeo litore leges.
laetatur spectatque virum insatiabilis ora
Scipio et appellet cunctos, ni magna sacerdos

---

[a] See note to vi. 687. [b] Hannibal. [c] See i. 98 foll.

[d] The decemvirs who were supreme at Rome from 451 to 449 B.C.: they drew up the Twelve Tables, the first Roman code of laws, which was based upon Athenian law.

[e] The harbour of Athens.

first war with Carthage, here Lutatius [a] stands, the famous conqueror whose fleet won the great sea-battle. If you wish to look also on the ghost of fierce Hamilcar, yonder he moves—you can see him in the distance—and his frown is not relaxed even by death but still retains its fierce resentment. If you would fain converse with him, suffer him to taste the blood and speak." When leave was given and the thirsty ghost had drunk his fill, Scipio thus began to reproach him, frowning upon him: "Is this the way, O father of lies, that Carthage keeps her treaties? Is this the compact you made when a prisoner in Sicily? Your son,[b] breaking all covenants, is waging war all over Italy; he has burst all barriers and fought his way over the Alps, and is upon us; all the land is ablaze with barbarous warfare, and our rivers run backwards, choked with corpses." The Carthaginian answered: "Hannibal had hardly completed his tenth year when he vowed at my bidding to make war against Rome [c]; and he may not deceive the gods by whom his father swore. But if he is now laying Italy waste with fire and striving to destroy her power, then I hail him as my true son, dutiful to me and faithful to his oath; and I pray that he may regain the glory that we lost." Then, with head held high, Hamilcar departed in haste; and his ghost seemed taller as it went away.

Next the priestess pointed out the men who held the sword and, in answer to their demand, gave laws to the people [d]; they were the first to borrow statutes from the shore of the Piraeus [e] and blend them with the laws of Italy. Scipio saw the decemvirs with gladness and could not gaze long enough at them; he would have addressed them all, but the great

admoneat turbae innumerae: " quot milia toto
credis in orbe, puer, lustras dum singula visu,
descendisse Erebo ? nullo non tempore abundans
umbrarum huc agitur torrens, vectatque capaci
agmina mole Charon, nec sufficit improba puppis."
post haec, ostendens iuvenem, sic virgo profatur :
" hic ille est, tellure vagus qui victor in omni
cursu signa tulit, cui pervia Bactra Dahaeque,
qui Gangen bibit et Pellaeo ponte Niphaten
astrinxit, cui stant sacro sua moenia Nilo."
incipit Aeneades : " Libyci certissima proles
Hammonis, quando exsuperat tua gloria cunctos
indubitata duces, similique cupidine rerum
pectora nostra calent, quae te via, fare, superbum
ad decus et summas laudum perduxerit arces."
ille sub haec : " turpis lenti sollertia Martis.
audendo bella expedias. pigra extulit artis
haud umquam sese virtus. tu magna gerendi
praecipita tempus ; mors atra impendet agenti."
haec effatus abit. Croesi mox advolat umbra,
dives apud superos, sed mors aequarat egenis.

Atque hic, Elysio tendentem limite cernens
effigiem iuvenis, caste cui vitta ligabat
purpurea effusos per colla nitentia crines,
" dic," ait, " hic quinam, virgo ? nam luce refulget
praecipua frons sacra viro, multaeque secuntur
mirantes animae et laeto clamore frequentant.

---

[a] Alexander the Great. [b] A river in Armenia. [c] Alexandria. [d] Homer.

priestess reminded him that the number of ghosts was infinite. "How many thousands, my son, do you suppose have come down to Erebus from all the world, while you look at this and that? Every moment an overflowing torrent of the dead is driven hither, and Charon ferries the host across in the roomy bark that cannot hold them all, despite its size." Then the priestess pointed to a young man [a] and spoke thus: "That is he, who ranged in arms over every land, who found a way through Bactra and the Dahae, and drank of the Ganges—the Macedonian who threw a bridge over the Niphates,[b] and whose city,[c] named after himself, stands on the sacred Nile." The Roman addressed him thus: "O true-born son of Libyan Ammon, since your undisputed fame eclipses that of all other commanders, and my heart is fired with the same thirst for glory, tell me the path by which you rose to your proud eminence and the topmost pinnacle of achievement." Alexander made answer: "Cunning and caution disgrace a general. Boldness is the way to win a war. Valour without speed has never risen triumphant over danger. When there is great work to be done, do it instantly; dark death hovers over your head while you are acting." Thus he spoke, and departed. Next the ghost of Croesus flitted up; in the upper world he was rich, but death had set him on a level with beggars.

And now Scipio saw a figure [d] moving along the Elysian path, whose hair rippled over his shining shoulders and was duly confined by a purple fillet. "Say who is this, Maiden," he asked; "for his sacred brow shines with a light beyond compare, and many souls follow him and escort him with cries of wonder

qui vultus! quam, si Stygia non esset in umbra,
dixissem facile esse deum!" "non falleris," inquit
docta comes Triviae, "meruit deus esse videri,
et fuit in tanto non parvum pectore numen.
carmine complexus terram, mare, sidera, manes
et cantu Musas et Phoebum aequavit honore.
atque haec cuncta, prius quam cerneret, ordine terris
prodidit ac vestram tulit usque ad sidera Troiam."
Scipio, perlustrans oculis laetantibus umbram,
"si nunc fata darent, ut Romula facta per orbem
hic caneret vates, quanto maiora futuros
facta eadem intrarent hoc," inquit, "teste nepotes!
felix Aeacide, cui tali contigit ore
gentibus ostendi! crevit tua carmine virtus."
Sed, quae tanta adeo grassantum turba, requirens,
heroum effigies maioresque accipit umbras.
invicto stupet Aeacide, stupet Hectore magno
Aiacisque gradum venerandaque Nestoris ora
miratur, geminos aspectat laetus Atridas
iamque Ithacum, corde aequantem Peleia facta.
victuram hinc cernit Ledaei Castoris umbram;
alternam lucem peragebat in aethere Pollux.
Sed subito vultus monstrata Lavinia traxit.
nam virgo admonuit, tempus cognoscere manes
femineos, ne cunctantem lux alma vocaret.

---

[a] Hecate or Diana: see note to viii. 362.

[b] This refers to the Eleventh Book of the *Odyssey*, where there is a description of Hades and its inhabitants.

[c] The Homeric heroes are meant.

[d] Ulysses.

[e] See note to ix. 295.

[f] The wife of Aeneas and daughter of King Latinus.

and delight. What a countenance is his! Were he not in the darkness of Hades, I should have said confidently that he was a god." "You are right," answered the wise handmaid of Trivia [a]; "he deserved to seem divine; a great genius dwelt in his mighty mind. His poetry embraced earth and sea, the sky and the nether world; he rivalled the Muses in song and Apollo in glory. All this region also, before he ever saw it, he revealed to mortals [b]; and he raised the fame of Troy to heaven —Troy the mother of Rome." Scipio gazed with joyful eyes at the ghost of Homer and said: "If Fate would suffer this poet now to sing of Roman achievements, for all the world to hear, how much deeper an impression the same deeds would make upon posterity, if Homer testified to them! How fortunate was Achilles, when such a poet displayed him to the world! The hero was made greater by the poet's verse."

When Scipio asked who pressed forward in such crowded ranks, he was told that they were the spirits of heroes [c] and the mighty among the dead. He marvelled at Achilles the invincible and gigantic Hector; the vast stride of Ajax and the reverend face of Nestor moved his wonder; he looked with delight at the two Atridae and the Ithacan,[d] as great in counsel as Achilles in battle. And next he saw the shade of Castor, Leda's son; he would soon return to life; and Pollux now was spending his turn of life [e] in the upper world.

But suddenly Lavinia [f] was pointed out to him and attracted his gaze. For the Sibyl warned him that it was time to review the ghosts of women; for, if he delayed, dawn might summon him to depart.

" felix haec," inquit, " Veneris nurus ordine longo
Troiugenas iunxit sociata prole Latinis.
vis et Martigenae thalamos spectare Quirini ?
Hersiliam cerne ; hirsutos cum sperneret olim
gens vicina procos, pastori rapta marito
intravitque casae culmique e stramine fultum
pressit laeta torum et soceros revocavit ab armis.
aspice Carmentis gressus. Evandria mater
haec fuit et vestros tetigit praesaga labores.
vis et, quos Tanaquil vultus gerat ? haec quoque castae
augurio valuit mentis venturaque dixit
regna viro et dextros agnovit in alite divos.
ecce pudicitiae Latium decus, inclita leti
fert frontem atque oculos terrae Lucretia fixos.
non datur, heu tibi, Roma, nec est, quod malle deceret,
hanc laudem retinere diu. Verginia iuxta,
cerne, cruentato vulnus sub pectore servat,
tristia defensi ferro monumenta pudoris,
et patriam laudat miserando in vulnere dextram.
illa est, quae Thybrim, quae fregit Lydia bella,
nondum passa marem, quales optabat habere
quondam Roma viros, contemptrix Cloelia sexus."
cum, subito aspectu turbatus, Scipio poscit,
quae poenae causa, et qui sint in crimine manes,
tum virgo : " patrios fregit quae curribus artus
et stetit adductis super ora trementia frenis,
Tullia, non ullos satis exhaustura labores,

[a] Hersilia, wife of Romulus, acted as peace-maker in the war caused by the rape of the Sabine women.

[b] The Sabines.

[c] See note to vii. 18.

[d] The wife of the elder Tarquin.

[e] She was stabbed by her father, to save her from the lust of Appius Claudius.

[f] See x. 492 foll.

[g] The daughter of Servius Tullius and queen of L. Tarquinius.

"She was happy as the daughter-in-law of Venus, and the offspring of her marriage bound Trojans and Latins together for all time to come. Would you see also the consort of Quirinus, the son of Mars? Yonder is Hersilia.[a] When the neighbour nation[b] despised such unkempt suitors in days gone by, she was carried off by a shepherd-bridegroom and entered his hut, and lay well pleased upon his bed of straw, and forced her kinsmen to throw down their arms. See where Carmentis[c] moves; she was the mother of Evander, and her prophecies hinted at this present war. Would you look also on the face of Tanaquil[d]? Chaste of heart, she too had the gift of prophecy, and foretold the kingly rule of her husband, recognizing the favour of heaven in the flight of a bird. Next see Lucretia, famous for her death, the glory of Roman chastity; her face and eyes are fixed upon the ground. Not long, alas, was Rome permitted to enjoy this boast which ought to be preferred to any other. Beside her see Virginia[e]; her bleeding breast still shows the wound—the sad record of maidenhood defended by the sword—and she still approves of her father's hand that struck the piteous blow. Yonder is Cloelia,[f] the maiden who stemmed the Tiber and stopped the Etruscan army, triumphing over her sex; ancient Rome prayed to have sons as brave as she." Then a sudden sight appalled Scipio, and he asked who was the guilty shade and why she was punished. The priestess answered: "This is Tullia[g]; she crushed her father's body beneath her chariot-wheels, and pulled the reins till she halted above his quivering features; therefore she floats on the burning stream of Phlegethon and will never

ardenti Phlegethonte natat : fornacibus atris
fons rapidus furit atque ustas sub gurgite cautes
egerit et scopulis pulsat flagrantibus ora.
illa autem, quae tondetur praecordia rostro
alitis—en quantum resonat plangentibus alis
armiger ad pastus rediens Iovis !—hostibus arcem
virgo, immane nefas, adamato prodidit auro
Tarpeia et pactis reseravit claustra Sabinis.
iuxta—nonne vides ? neque enim leviora domantur
delicta—illatrat ieiunis faucibus Orthrus,
armenti quondam custos immanis Hiberi,
et morsu petit et polluto eviscerat ungue.
nec par poena tamen sceleri ; sacraria Vestae
polluit, exuta sibi virginitate, sacerdos.
sed satis haec vidisse, satis."
Mox deinde : " videnti
nunc animas tibi, quae potant oblivia, paucas
in fine enumerasse paro, et remeare tenebris.
hic Marius : nec multa dies iam restat ituro
aetheriam in lucem. veniet tibi origine parva
in longum imperium consul ; nec Sulla morari
iussa potest, aut amne diu potare soporo.
lux vocat et nulli divum mutabile fatum.
imperium hic primus rapiet, sed gloria culpae,
quod reddet solus, nec tanto in nomine quisquam
exsistet, Sullae qui se velit esse secundum.
ille, hirta cui subrigitur coma fronte, decorum
et gratum terris Magnus caput ; ille deum gens,

---

[a] On the Capitol at Rome : the Tarpeian rock afterwards bore her name.

[b] The two-headed dog of Geryon, a brother of Cerberus.

[c] This probably refers to Cornelia, the Senior Vestal Virgin, who was condemned by Domitian to be buried alive for unchastity.

come to an end of her suffering: the water rushes madly forth from dark furnaces, bringing up calcined rocks to the surface and lashing her face with burning stones. That other, whose heart-strings are gnawed by an eagle's beak,—hark to the sound of flapping wings with which the armour-bearer of Jove returns to its meal,—is Tarpeia, a maiden guilty of a monstrous crime. She loved gold, and for its sake betrayed the citadel [a] to the enemy, and opened the gates to the Sabines who had promised to reward her. Near her—do you not see? no venial crimes are punished here—Orthrus,[b] who once guarded the cattle of the Spanish monster, is barking at a victim with famished throat, biting and tearing out her inward parts with his filthy claws. Yet her punishment is not equal to her crime: a priestess of Vesta,[c] she profaned the shrine by losing her maidenhood. But enough, enough, of all these sights."

Soon she added: "I purpose now to end by pointing out to your view a few of the spirits who are drinking forgetfulness here, and then I shall go back to the darkness. Here is Marius, soon to ascend to the upper world; from small beginnings he will rise to hold power for long as consul. Nor can Sulla put off compliance with the summons, or drink long of the river of oblivion. Life calls for him, and the destiny which no god may alter. He will be the first to seize supreme power; but, criminal as he is, he can boast that he alone will surrender it [d]; and no man who rises to such greatness will ever be willing to follow the example of Sulla. That comely head which the world loved is the head of Magnus,[e] with its fleece of hair rising from the forehead; the

[d] Sulla resigned the dictatorship. [e] Pompey.

stelligerum attollens apicem, Troianus Iulo
Caesar avo. quantas moles, cum sede reclusa
hinc tandem erumpent, terraque marique movebunt!
heu miseri, quotiens toto pugnabitis orbe !
nec leviora lues, quam victus, crimina victor."
  Tum iuvenis lacrimans : " restare haec ordine duro
lamentor rebus Latiis. sed luce remota
si nulla est venia, et merito mors ipsa laborat,
perfidiae Poenus quibus aut Phlegethontis in undis
exuret ductor scelus, aut quae digna renatos
ales in aeternum laniabit morsibus artus ? "
" ne metue," exclamat vates. " non vita sequetur
inviolata virum : patria non ossa quiescent.
namque ubi fractus opum magnae certamine pugnae
pertulerit vinci turpemque orare salutem,
rursus bella volet Macetum instaurare sub armis.
damnatusque doli, desertis coniuge fida
et dulci nato, linquet Carthaginis arces
atque una profugus lustrabit caerula puppe.
hinc Cilicis Tauri saxosa cacumina viset.
pro ! quanto levius mortalibus aegra subire
servitia atque hiemes aestusque fugamque fretumque
atque famem, quam posse mori ! post Itala bella
Assyrio famulus regi falsusque cupiti
Ausoniae motus, dubio petet aequora velo,
donec, Prusiacas delatus segniter oras,
altera servitia imbelli patietur in aevo
et latebram munus regni. perstantibus inde

---

[a] Caesar, no less than Pompey, will die a violent death.

[b] The battle of Zama in 202 B.C., where Hannibal was defeated by Scipio.

[c] Antiochus III., king of Syria.

[d] Prusias was king of Bithynia. When the Romans demanded his surrender, Hannibal swallowed poison. He was seventy years old.

other, whose high head is crowned with a star, is Caesar, the offspring of gods and the descendant of Trojan Iulus. When these two at last break forth from their seclusion in Hades, what fearful disorder they will stir up on land and sea! Alas, unhappy men, how often will you wage war over the whole earth! And the victor will pay no less dearly for his crimes than the vanquished." [a]

Scipio answered weeping: "I grieve at the harsh destiny in store for the Roman state. But, if there is no forgiveness in the land of darkness and death itself is justly punished, how shall Hannibal suffer enough for his treachery? Will the waters of Phlegethon serve to burn away his sin, or will some bird tear with its beak for ever his body for ever renewed?" "Fear not," cried the priestess: "no life of untroubled prosperity shall be his; his bones shall not rest in his native land. For all his strength will be broken in a great battle [b]; he will suffer defeat and stoop to beg for his life; and then he will try to wage a fresh war with the armies of Macedon. Condemned as a traitor, he will leave his faithful wife and darling son behind him, abandon Carthage, and flee across the sea with a single ship. Next he will visit the rocky heights of Mount Taurus in Cilicia. Ah, how much easier men find it to bear cold and heat and hunger, bitter slavery and exile, and the perils of the sea, rather than face death! After the war in Italy he will serve a Syrian king,[c] and, cheated of his hope to make war against Rome, he will put to sea with no certain destination, and at last drift idly to the land of Prusias,[d] where, too old to fight any more, he will suffer a second slavery and find a hiding-place by the king's favour. At last, when

Aeneadis reddique sibi poscentibus hostem,
pocula furtivo rapiet properata veneno
ac tandem terras longa formidine solvet."
  Haec vates Erebique cavis se reddidit umbris.
tum laetus socios iuvenis portumque revisit.

---

[a] Puteoli or Cumae: see ll. 385, 400.

Rome persists in demanding the surrender of her foe, in hasty stealth he will swallow a draught of poison, and free the world at last from a long-enduring dread."

Thus the priestess spake, and returned to her dark cavern in Erebus ; and Scipio went back joyfully to his comrades in the harbour.[a]

LIBER QUARTUS DECIMUS

ARGUMENT

The campaign of Marcellus in Sicily: a description of the island (1-78). *Causes of the war. Death of Hiero, king of Syracuse: succession of Hieronymus* (79-95). *Hieronymus is murdered, and general confusion follows* (96-109). *Marcellus prepares for action* (110-124). *He takes Leontini by storm* (125-177). *He blockades Syracuse by land and sea*

Flectite nunc vestros, Heliconis numina, cantus
Ortygiae pelagus Siculique ad litoris urbes.
muneris hic vestri labor est, modo Daunia regna
Aeneadum, modo Sicanios accedere portus,
aut Macetum lustrare domos et Achaica rura,
aut vaga Sardoo vestigia tingere fluctu,
vel Tyriae quondam regnata mapalia genti,
extremumve diem et terrarum invisere metas.
sic poscit sparsis Mavors agitatus in oris.
ergo age, qua litui, qua ducunt bella, sequamur.
Ausoniae pars magna iacet Trinacria tellus,
ut semel expugnante Noto et vastantibus undis
accepit freta, caeruleo propulsa tridente.

---

[a] A small island which formed part of Syracuse.
[b] Italy.
[c] Spain: see note to i. 270.
[d] Sicily, which has three promontories, Pelorus, Pachynus, and Lilybaeum.

BOOK XIV

ARGUMENT (*continued*)

(178-191). *Allies of Syracuse* (192-247). *Allies of Rome* (248-257). *Sicilian allies of Carthage* (258-276). *Confidence of the Syracusans* (277-291). *The genius of Archimedes foils all the attempts of the Romans* (292-352). *A sea-fight* (353-579). *An outbreak of plague delays operations* (580-617). *At last the city is taken* (618-684).

TURN your song now, ye goddesses of Helicon, to the sea of Ortygia [a] and the cities of the Sicilian coast. Such is your toilsome task—to visit now the Daunian realm [b] of the Aeneadae and now the harbours of Sicily, or to traverse the land of the Macedonians and the country of Greece, or to dip your wandering feet in the sea of Sardinia, and to behold either the reed-huts once ruled by Carthage, or the World's End [c] where the sun goes down. War waged in many separate lands requires this of us. Come, then, let us follow whither the trumpets and the wars summon us!

The Isle of Three Capes [d] is a large fragment of Italy. It has lain there ever since, battered by the fury of winds and waves, and pushed forth by Neptune's trident,[e] it let in the sea. For long ago the

[e] Earthquakes were supposed to be the work of Neptune: Silius implies that Sicily was separated from the mainland by an earthquake followed by an inundation.

namque per occultum caeca vi turbinis olim
impactum pelagus laceratae viscera terrae
discidit et, medio perrumpens arva profundo,
cum populis pariter convulsis transtulit urbes.
ex illo servans rapidus divortia Nereus
saevo dividuos coniungi pernegat aestu.
sed spatium, quod dissociat consortia terrae,
latratus fama est (sic arta intervenit unda)
et matutinos volucrum tramittere cantus.
multa solo virtus : iam reddere foenus aratris,
iam montes umbrare olea, dare nomina Baccho
cornipedemque citum lituis generasse ferendis,
nectare Cecropias Hyblaeo accedere ceras.
hic et Paeonios arcano sulphure fontes,
hic Phoebo digna et Musis venerabere vatum
ora excellentum, sacras qui carmine silvas,
quique Syracosia resonant Helicona camena.
promptae gens linguae ; ast eadem, cum bella cieret,
portus aequoreis sueta insignire tropaeis.

Post dirum Antiphatae sceptrum et Cyclopia regna
vomere verterunt primum nova rura Sicano :
Pyrene misit populos, qui nomen ab amne
ascitum patrio terrae imposuere vacanti.
mox Ligurum pubes Siculo ductore novavit
possessis bello mutata vocabula regnis.
nec Cres dedecori fuit accola : duxerat actos
moenibus e centum non fausta ad proelia Minos,

[a] The honey of Mount Hymettus at Athens was famous.

[b] The famous poets of Sicily were Stesichorus, Empedocles, Epicharmus, and Theocritus.

[c] King of the Laestrygonians : see viii. 530.

main, with the invisible force of a tornado, dashed itself unseen against the bowels of the land and tore it apart; then rushing over the fields in full flood, it uprooted whole cities with their inhabitants and carried them to a distance. From that time the fast-running tide maintains the separation, and its fierceness forbids those thus parted to come together again. But the space between the severed lands is so small that, as the story goes, the barking of dogs and early crowing of cocks can be heard across the water; so narrow is the strait. The soil of the island has many virtues. Here it gives a rich return to the plough, and there the hills are shady with olive-trees; its vines are famous, and it breeds swift horses, fit to endure the sound of the war-trumpet; nor is the nectar of Hybla inferior to the honeycombs of Athens.[a] Here you will admire healing springs, whose sulphur waters have secret virtue; and here you will marvel at the utterance of mighty poets,[b] bards worthy of Apollo and the Muses, who make the sacred groves re-echo with song and Helicon resound with the Muse of Syracuse. The Sicilians are ready of tongue; but also, when they made war, they often adorned their harbours with trophies won by victories at sea.

The first rulers of the island were the Cyclopes and cruel Antiphates[c]; and next the virgin soil was ploughed by the Sicani, who came from the Pyrenees and named the uninhabited country after a river of their native land. Then Siculus led a band of Ligurians into the island, and conquered it, and once more changed its name.[d] Nor was the land disgraced by settlers from Crete, whom Minos, when he sought

[d] From Sicania to Sicilia.

Daedaleam repetens poenam. qui fraude nefanda
postquam perpetuas iudex concessit ad umbras
Cocalidum insidiis, fesso Minoia turba
bellandi studio Siculis subsedit in oris.
miscuerunt Phrygiam prolem Troianus Acestes
Troianusque Helymus, structis qui pube secuta
in longum ex sese donarunt nomina muris.
nec Zanclaea gerunt obscuram moenia famam,
dextera quam tribuit posito Saturnia telo.
sed decus Hennaeis haud ullum pulchrius oris,
quam quae Sisyphio fundavit nomen ab Isthmo
et multum ante alias Ephyraeis fulget alumnis.
hic Arethusa suum piscoso fonte receptat
Alpheon, sacrae portantem signa coronae.

At non aequus amat Trinacria Mulciber antra.
nam Lipare, vastis subter depasta caminis,
sulphureum vomit exeso de vertice fumum.
ast Aetna eructat tremefactis cautibus ignis
inclusi gemitus, pelagique imitata furorem
murmure per caecos tonat irrequieta fragores
nocte dieque simul. fonte e Phlegethontis ut atro
flammarum exundat torrens piceaque procella
semiambusta rotat liquefactis saxa cavernis.
sed quamquam largo flammarum exaestuet intus
turbine, et assidue subnascens profluat ignis,

---

[a] See note to xii. 89.

[b] They killed Minos by pouring hot water over him when he was in his bath.

[c] Trojan. Egesta and Elyma are the two cities.

[d] Zancle, "sickle," was the ancient Greek name of Messana, derived from its shape. [e] Sicily.

[f] Syracuse: a colony from Corinth whose ancient name was Ephyra. Sisyphus was the mythical founder of Ephyra.

[g] A fountain in Syracuse: it was supposed that the Alpheus, a river of Elis, flowed under the sea to meet Are-

to punish Daedalus,[a] brought forth from his hundred cities to suffer defeat. For, when Minos, slain by the horrid treachery of the daughters of Cocalus,[b] went down to everlasting darkness to sit in judgement there, his war-wearied army settled in Sicily. Then two Trojans, Acestes and Helymus, brought in a Phrygian[c] stock; they had followers with them and gave their own names to the cities they built—names that were to last for ages. The walls of Zancle[d] too are not unknown to fame; for Saturn made it famous when he laid down his sickle there. But the land of Henna[e] can boast nothing more beautiful than the city[f] which has built herself a name from the Isthmus of Sisyphus, and outshines all the other cities by reason of its Corinthian inhabitants. Here Arethusa[g] welcomes her loved Alpheüs to her waters abounding in fish, when he comes bearing trophies from the sacred games.

But the Fire-god, no friend to Sicily, loves to dwell in her hollow caverns. Thus Lipare,[h] whose interior is devoured by huge furnaces, vomits forth sulphurous smoke from its hollow summit. Then Etna belches forth the noise of her pent-up fire from her tottering cliffs; night and day alike she rages like an angry sea with unceasing thunder-roll and muffled roaring. A torrent of flame wells forth, as if from the fatal stream of Phlegethon, and hurls out a pitchy shower of red-hot stones from its molten depths. But, though the interior of Etna boils over with an inexhaustible storm of flame, and though fresh fire is constantly generated below and streams

thusa, and brought with it the crowns that Olympian victors had cast into the stream.

[h] The Lipari islands, north of Sicily.

summo cana iugo cohibet, mirabile dictu,
vicinam flammis glaciem, aeternoque rigore
ardentes horrent scopuli ; stat vertice celsi
collis hiems, calidamque nivem tegit atra favilla.
Quid referam Aeolio regnatas nomine terras
ventorumque domos atque addita claustra procellis ?
hic versi penitus Pelopea ad regna Pachyni
pulsata Ionio respondent saxa profundo.
hic, contra Libyamque situm Caurosque furentes,
cernit devexas Lilybaeon nobile chelas.
at, qua diversi lateris frons tertia terrae
vergit in Italiam prolato ad litora dorso,
celsus harenosa tollit se mole Pelorus.
His longo mitis placide dominator in aevo
praefuerat terris Hieron, tractare sereno
imperio vulgum pollens et pectora nullo
parentum exagitare metu, pactamque per aras
haud facilis temerare fidem, socialia iura
Ausoniis multos servarat casta per annos.
verum, ubi fata virum fragili solvere senecta,
primaevo cessit sceptrum exitiale nepoti,
et placida indomitos accepit regia mores.
namque bis octonis nondum rex praeditus annis
caligare alto in solio nec pondera regni
posse pati et nimium fluxis confidere rebus.
iamque brevi nullum, delicta tuentibus armis,
fas notum ignotumque nefas ; vilissima regi
cura pudor. tam praecipiti materna furori

---

[a] Another name for the Lipari islands. For Aeolus as the jailer of the winds see ix. 491.

[b] The constellation so called.

[c] Hicro III., king of Syracuse, a faithful and valuable ally of Rome, died in 215 B.C. when he was more than ninety

forth, yet—marvellous to tell—the mountain-top is white and harbours ice and flame side by side. The burning peaks are stiff with perpetual frost, eternal winter lies on the lofty summit, and hot snow is hidden beneath black ashes.

I need not mention the realm of Aeolus,[a] where the winds are at home and the storms are kept in prison. On the South coast Pachynus stretches far towards the Peloponnese, and its rocks reply to the Ionian waves that dash against them. On the West famous Lilybaeum faces Libya and its fierce West-winds, and sees the Scorpion[b] sink down. And lastly Pelorus, the third headland of Sicily, the North-east coast, turns toward Italy, prolonging its stony ridge to the sea, and raising high its mountain of sand.

During a long life a kindly ruler[c] had governed the island with gentle sway. Hiero had power to rule his people in peace, and harassed his subjects with no terrors; he was slow to violate a pledge sanctioned by oath, and had for many years kept unstained the tie of alliance with Rome. But when the Fates laid him low with old age and decrepitude, the sceptre passed in a fatal hour to his youthful grandson, and the peaceful palace admitted a prince of unbridled passions. The young man's head—he was not yet sixteen—was turned by his elevation to the throne; he could not support the burden of his crown and trusted overmuch to transient prosperity. Thus in a short time, while his crimes were protected by the sword, right disappeared and wrong in every form was rife; decency was the last thing that the monarch thought of; and his headlong passions were

years old, and was succeeded by his grandson, Hieronymus, a boy of fifteen.

Pyrrhus origo dabat stimulos proavique superbum
Aeacidae genus atque aeternus carmine Achilles.
ergo ardor subitus Poenorum incepta fovendi;
nec sceleri mora: iam iungit nova foedera, pacto,
cederet ut Siculis victor Sidonius oris.
sed stabant Poenae, tumulumque negabat Erinnys,
qua modo pactus erat socium non cernere, terra.
saevos namque pati fastus iuvenemque cruento
flagrantem luxu et miscentem turpia diris
haud ultra faciles, quos ira metusque coquebat,
iurati obtruncant. nec iam modus ensibus: addunt
femineam caedem atque insontum rapta sororum
corpora prosternunt ferro. nova saevit in armis
libertas iactatque iugum: pars Punica castra,
pars Italos et nota volunt; nec turba furentum
defit, quae neutro sociari foedere malit.
  Tali Trinacriae motu rebusque Sicanis
exitio regis trepidis, sublimis honore
(tertia nam Latios renovarat purpura fasces)
Marcellus classem Zanclaeis appulit oris.
atque ubi cuncta viro caedesque exposta tyranni
ambiguaeque hominum mentes, Carthaginis arma
quos teneant et quanta locos, quod vulgus amicum
duret Troiugenis, quantos Arethusa tumores
concipiat perstetque suas non pandere portas,
incumbit bello ac totam per proxima raptim
armorum effundit flammato pectore pestem.
non aliter Boreas, Rhodopes a vertice praeceps

[a] His mother, Nereis, was the daughter of Pyrrhus, king of Epirus; and Pyrrhus claimed descent from Achilles.
[b] In favour of the king of Syracuse.
[c] His body was left unburied.
[d] The ancient name of Messana: see note to l. 48.

heated by his mother's descent [a] from Pyrrhus, and by his noble ancestry, the Aeacidae and Achilles immortalized in poetry. Therefore he was in eager haste to further the designs of Carthage ; nor did he postpone his crime but made a new treaty at once, stipulating that Hannibal, having conquered Rome, should withdraw from Sicily.[b] But retribution was at hand, and the Fury denied him a grave [c] in that very soil from which he had just bargained that his ally should be excluded. For a band of conspirators could not endure the young man's ferocity and pride, his extravagance and thirst for blood, his contempt for decency together with his inhuman cruelty, and were so wrought up by fear and anger that they murdered him. Nor did the sword stop there : they went on to kill women also, and his innocent sisters were seized and slain. New-found freedom brandished the sword and threw off the yoke. Some favoured the army of Carthage, and others the Romans, their ancient allies ; nor were there wanting wild spirits who preferred to join neither alliance.

Such was the disturbance and excitement which the king's death had aroused in Sicily, when Marcellus brought his fleet to anchor at Zancle [d] ; he held high office ; for the purple had brought him the consular rods for the third time. And when he had heard all—the murder of the tyrant, the division of opinion among the people, the number of the Carthaginian troops and the points occupied by them, what cities remained friendly to the Romans, and how Syracuse, puffed up with pride, obstinately refused to open her gates—then Marcellus took the field in indignation and speedily poured forth all the horrors of war upon the surrounding country. So the North-wind, when it has rushed down headlong from Rhodope's height

cum sese immisit decimoque volumine pontum
expulit in terras, sequitur cum murmure molem
eiecti maris et stridentibus affremit alis.
prima Leontinos vastarunt proelia campos,
regnatam diro quondam Laestrygone terram.
instabat ductor, cui tarde vincere Graias
par erat ac vinci turmas. ruit aequore toto
(femineum credas maribus concurrere vulgum)
et Cereri placitos fecundat sanguine campos.
sternuntur passim ; pedibusque evadere letum
eripuit rapidus Mavors ; nam ut cuique salutem
promisit fuga, praeveniens dux occupat ense.
" ite, gregem metite imbellem ac succidite ferro,"
clamat, cunctantes urgens umbone catervas.
" pigro luctandi studio certamen in umbra
molle pati docta et gaudens splendescere olivo,
stat, mediocre decus vincentum, ignava iuventus.
haec laus sola datur, si viso vincitis hoste."
ingruit, audito ductore, exercitus omnis ;
solaque, quod superest, secum certamina norunt,
quis dextra antistet spoliisque excellat opimis.
Euboici non per scopulos illisa Caphareo
Euripi magis unda furit, pontumve sonantem
eicit angusto violentius ore Propontis ;
nec fervet maiore fretum rapiturque tumultu,
quod ferit Herculeas extremo sole columnas.
Mite tamen dextrae decus inter proelia tanta
enituit fama. miles Tyrrhenus, Asilo

---

[a] It was anciently believed that in a storm at sea every tenth wave was especially formidable.

[b] Antiphates : see viii. 530.

[c] A rocky promontory on the south coast of Euboea.

[d] The Sea of Marmora.

[e] The Straits of Gibraltar.

and hurled the tenth [a] rolling wave upon the shore, follows with a roar the flood of water it has thrown up and rages with boisterous wings. The army first laid waste the plains of Leontini—the land once ruled by the savage Laestrygonian king.[b] The general pressed on fast: in his eyes, delay in defeating Greek troops was as shameful as defeat. He flew all over the field—it seemed like a contest of men against women—and enriched with blood the fields that Ceres loves. The enemy fell in heaps, and the speed of battle made it impossible for any to escape death by flight. For whenever a fugitive hoped to save his life, Marcellus was before him and barred the way with his sword. "On, on!" he cried; "mow down this feeble folk and lay them low with the steel"; and he pushed the laggards on with the boss of his shield. "Cowards stand before you, men who have learnt to endure easy bouts of wrestling in the shade, and who delight to oil their limbs till they glisten; and those who conquer them in battle get little glory. To beat them at sight is the only credit you can gain." Thus addressed by their general, the whole army advanced to the attack; their only rivalry now was with one another, as they contended who should excel in deeds of valour and take the choicest spoil. The current of the Euripus by Euboea does not rage more fiercely when it dashes through its rocky channel upon Caphareus,[c] nor the Propontis [d] when it drives out the sounding waves from its narrow mouth; nor does the narrow sea that beats upon the Pillars of Hercules [e] near the setting sun boil and rush on with louder uproar.

So fierce was the battle, and yet a noble deed of mercy that was done there became famous. A Tuscan

nomen erat, captus quondam ad Thrasymenna fluenta,
servitium facile et dominantis mollia iussa
expertus Beryae, patrias remearat ad oras
sponte faventis eri ; repetitisque impiger armis
tum veteres Siculo casus Mavorte piabat.
atque is, dum medios inter fera proelia miscet,
illatus Beryae, cui, pacta ad regia misso
Poenorum a populis sociataque bella gerenti,
aerato cassis munimine clauserat ora,
invadit ferro iuvenem trepideque ferentem
instabiles retro gressus prosternit harena.
at miser, audita victoris voce, trementem
cunctantemque animam Stygia ceu sede reducens,
cassidis a mento malefidae vincula rumpit
iungebatque preces atque addere verba parabat.
sed, subito aspectu et noto conterritus ore,
Tyrrhenus ferrumque manu revocavit et ultro
talia cum gemitu lacrimis effudit obortis :
" ne, quaeso, supplex lucem dubiusque precare ;
fas hostem servare mihi. multo optimus ille
militiae, cui postremum est primumque, tueri
inter bella fidem : tu letum evadere nobis
das prior et servas nondum servatus ab hoste.
haud equidem dignum memet, quae tristia vidi,
abnuerim dignumque iterum in peiora revolvi,
si tibi per medios ignes mediosque per enses
non dederit mea dextra viam." sic fatur et ultro
attollit vitaque exaequat munera vitae.

At, compos Sicula primum certaminis ora
coepti, Marcellus victricia signa, quieto

soldier, named Asilus, taken prisoner earlier at Lake Trasimene, had found easy service and a kind master in Beryas, his captor, and had returned to his native land with the consent and aid of his owner. Now he had gone back to active service and was making good his former mishap by fighting in Sicily. And now, while fighting in the centre of the fray, he came upon Beryas, who had been sent by the Carthaginians to make a treaty with the king of Syracuse and was fighting side by side with the Syracusans; but his face was concealed by the brazen helmet that he wore. Asilus attacked him with the steel, and, as he tottered feebly backwards, hurled him to the ground. Then, when he heard his conqueror's voice, the poor wretch, recalling his life as it were from Hades in fear and trembling, tore from his chin the straps that bound his useless helmet, and asked for mercy at the same time. He was about to say more, when the Tuscan, startled by the sudden sight of that familiar face, withdrew his sword and thus addressed his antagonist, ere he could speak, with sighs and tears: "Sue not, I pray, to me for life with doubts and entreaties. For me it is right to save my enemy. The noble warrior is he, whose first and last thought is to keep faith even in time of war. You began it and saved me from death before I saved you. I should deserve the troubles I have met, and should deserve to meet again with worse troubles, if my right hand failed to clear a path for you through fire and sword." With these words he raised Beryas willingly from the ground and granted a life in exchange for the life he had received.

Then Marcellus, having won his first battle on Sicilian soil, moved forward with his army unmolested

agmine progrediens, Ephyraea[a] ad moenia vertit.
inde Syracosias castris circumdedit arces.
sed ferri languebat amor : sedare monendo
pectora caeca virum atque iras evellere avebat.
nec, renuant si forte sibi et si mitia malle
credant esse metum, laxis servatur omissa
obsidio claustris ; quin contra intentior ipse
invigilat cautis, frontem imperterritus, armis
et struit arcana necopina pericula cura.
haud secus Eridani stagnis ripave Caÿstri[b]
innatat albus olor pronoque immobile corpus
dat fluvio et pedibus tacitas eremigat undas.[c]
Interea, dum incerta labat sententia clausis,
exciti populi atque urbes socia arma ferebant :
incumbens Messana freto minimumque revulsa
discreta Italia atque Osco memorabilis ortu[d] ;
tum Catane, nimium ardenti vicina Typhoeo[e]
et generasse pios quondam celeberrima fratres,
et, cui non licitum fatis, Camarina, moveri.
tum, quae nectareis vocat ad certamen Hymetton,
audax Hybla, favis, palmaque arbusta Selinus
et, iusti quondam portus, nunc litore solo
subsidium infidum fugientibus aequora, Mylae.
necnon altus Eryx, necnon e vertice celso
Centuripae largoque virens Entella Lyaeo,

---

[a] Ephyrean = Corinthian = Syracusan.

[b] A river of Lydia, famous for its swans.

[c] The concealed operations of Marcellus are amusingly illustrated by the hidden activity of the swan's feet while its body remains motionless.

[d] So called, because the Mamertine mercenaries who seized Catana came from Campania, once inhabited by Oscans.

[e] Typhoeus, a giant, was imprisoned under Etna. Two

and turned his victorious standards against the walls of Syracuse,[a] surrounding the fortifications with his troops. But he felt less eagerness for battle: he hoped to calm the blind passion of the citizens by his warnings and to expel the anger from their hearts. Yet, in case they defied him and ascribed to cowardice his choice of forbearance, the siege was strictly carried on, and his grasp was not loosened: on the contrary, he kept a closer watch than ever, with fearless brow and wary strategy, and in secrecy contrived surprises for the enemy. So a white swan floats on the still waters of the Eridanus or by the bank of Caÿster,[b] and lets the current carry its motionless body, while its feet row on beneath the unruffled stream.[c]

Meantime, while the besieged Syracusans were divided in their minds, Marcellus summoned forth the peoples and cities; and they brought their forces to aid him. Such were—Messana, famous for its Oscan founders,[d] a coast-town that lies nearest to Italy of all Sicilian towns; and Catana, too close to the fire of Typhoeus, and famous for the pair of dutiful sons[e] whom she bore long ago; and Camarina, which the Fates would not suffer to be moved[f]; and Hybla, whose honeycombs boldly challenge Hymettus for sweetness[g]; and Selinus, planted with palm-trees; and Mylae, once a sufficient harbour, though now the bare beach offers but a doubtful refuge to shipwrecked mariners. Lofty Eryx too was loyal, and Centuripae from her high peak, and Entella, where the green vine-plant grows abundantly

brothers, Amphinomus and Anapias, once carried their parents out of danger when there was an eruption of Etna.

[f] The people of Camarina were warned by an oracle not to change the site of their city.

[g] See line 26.

Entella, Hectoreo dilectum nomen Acestae.
non Thapsos, non e tumulis glacialibus Acrae
defuerunt ; Agyrina manus geminoque Lacone
Tyndaris attollens sese affluit. altus equorum
mille rapit turmam atque hinnitibus aera flammat,
pulveream volvens Acragas ad inania nubem.
ductor Grosphus erat, cuius caelata gerebat
taurum parma trucem, poenae monimenta vetustae.
ille, ubi torreret subiectis corpora flammis,
mutabat gemitus mugitibus ; actaque veras
credere erat stabulis armenta effundere voces.
haud impune quidem ; nam dirae conditor artis
ipse suo moriens immugit flebile tauro.
venit, ab amne trahens nomen, Gela ; venit Halaesa
et qui praesenti domitant periura Palici
pectora supplicio ; Troianaque venit Acesta ;
quique per Aetnaeos Acis petit aequora fines
et dulci gratam Nereida perluit unda.
aemulus ille tuo quondam, Polypheme, calori,
dum fugit agrestem violenti pectoris iram,
in tenues liquefactus aquas evasit et hostem
et tibi victricem, Galatea, immiscuit undam.
necnon qui potant Hypsamque Alabimque sonoros
et perlucentem splendenti gurgite Achaten ;
qui fontes, vage Chrysa, tuos et pauperis alvei
Hipparin ac facilem superari gurgite parco
Pantagian rapidique colunt vada flava Symaethi.

---

[a] Entellus and Acestes were Trojans, who founded cities in Sicily.

[b] Castor and Pollux, sons of Tyndarus.

[c] The brazen bull in which Phalaris, tyrant of Agrigentum (Acragas), used to roast his enemies.

[d] The sulphur springs there were believed to punish perjury with instant death.

—Entella, a name dear to Trojan Acestes.[a] Nor was Thapsus backward, nor the men of Acrae, descending from their icy heights. From Agyrium men came flocking, and from Tyndaris that boasts of the Spartan Twins.[b] Hilly Acragas sent a troop of a thousand horse, whose neighings made the air hot and rolled a cloud of dust to the sky. Their leader was Grosphus, upon whose shield a fierce bull was engraved, in memory of an ancient punishment.[c] When men's bodies were roasted over a fire in the bull, their cries took the sound of a bull bellowing; and one might believe that the sounds were produced by real cattle driven from their stalls. But punishment followed; for the inventor of this inhuman contrivance died in the bull he had made, lowing pitifully. Gela, named after a river, came; Halaesa came, and Palaeca that punishes perjured men with sudden death[d]; and Trojan Acesta; and the Acis which flows to the sea through the territory of Etna and bathes the grateful sea-nymph[e] with its sweet waters. (Acis was once a lover and a rival of Polyphemus; and, while fleeing from the clownish rage of the furious giant, was turned into a stream of water; thus he escaped his enemy, and mixed his stream in triumph with Galatea's flood.) There came too those who drink of Hypsa and Alabis, loud-sounding rivers, and the transparent waters of shining Achates; men came from winding Chrysa and scanty Hipparis and the Pantagias whose slender stream is easily crossed, and from the yellow waters of fast-flowing Symaethus.

[e] Galatea, who had two rival suitors, Acis and Polyphemus, turned the former into a river, to save his life.

litora Thermarum, prisca dotata camena,
armavere suos, qua mergitur Himera ponto
Aeolio. nam dividuas se scindit in oras,
nec minus occasus petit incita quam petit ortus ;
Nebrodes gemini nutrit divortia fontis,
quo mons Sicania non surgit ditior umbrae.
Henna deum lucis sacras dedit ardua dextras.
hic specus, ingentem laxans telluris hiatum,
caecum iter ad manes tenebroso limite pandit,
qua novus ignotas Hymenaeus venit in oras :
hac Stygius quondam, stimulante Cupidine, rector
ausus adire diem, maestoque Acheronte relicto,
egit in illicitas currum per inania terras.
tum rapta praeceps Hennaea virgine flexit
attonitos caeli visu lucemque paventes
in Styga rursus equos et praedam condidit umbris.
Romanos Petraea duces, Romana petivit
foedera Callipolis lapidosique Engyon arvi,
Hadranum Ergetiumque simul telaque superba
lanigera Melite et litus piscosa Calacte,
quaeque procelloso Cephaloedias ora profundo
caeruleis horret campis pascentia cete,
et qui correptas sorbentem verticis haustu
atque iterum e fundo iaculantem ad sidera puppes
Tauromenitana cernunt de sede Charybdim.
haec Latium manus et Laurentia signa fovebat.
  Cetera Elissaeis aderat gens Sicana votis.
mille Agathyrna dedit perflataque Trogilos Austris,

---

[a] Thermae was close to Himera, which was the birthplace of Stesichorus, a famous lyric poet.
[b] There was a famous temple of Ceres at Henna.
[c] Pluto : see note to i. 93.
[d] Proserpina.
[e] Malta, which had a reputation for textile products.

On the shore where the Himera falls into the Aeolian sea, Thermae armed her men—Thermae rich in the possession of a bygone poet.[a] The river splits up into two channels, and its swift waters flow both east and west; and the Nebrodes, as rich in shade as any mountain in Sicily, feeds both divided streams. From her sacred groves[b] Henna on the height sent forth holy men to battle. (At Henna a cave, opening up a vast fissure in the earth, reveals a hidden way and dark passage to Hades, by which a strange bridal procession once came up to a land unknown. For by it the Stygian king,[c] stung by Cupid's arrow, dared to approach the light of day and, leaving doleful Acheron, drove his chariot through empty space to the forbidden earth. There he seized in haste the maiden of Henna[d] and then turned back towards the Styx his horses, terrified by the sight of heaven and the sunlight, and buried his prize in the darkness.) Staunch to the Roman generals and the Roman alliance were Petraea and Callipolis and Engyon of the stony fields; Hadranum and Ergetium too; Melita,[e] proud of her woollen fabrics, and Calacte whose strand abounds with fish; and Cephaloedium, whose beach dreads in time of storms the sea monsters that feed in the blue fields of ocean; and the men of Tauromenium, who see Charybdis[f] catching ships and swallowing them in her whirlpool, and then again shooting them up from the depths to the stars. All these supported Rome and the standards of Italy.

The other cities of Sicily took the side of Carthage. Agathyrna sent a thousand men; and so did Trogilus, blown on by the South-winds, and Phacelina, where

[f] The famous whirlpool in the Straits of Messina.

mille Thoanteae sedes Phacelina Dianae.
tergemino venit numero fecunda Panhormos,
seu silvis sectere feras, seu retibus aequor
verrere, seu caelo libeat traxisse volucrem.
non Herbesos iners, non Naulocha pigra pericli
sederunt, non frondosis Morgentia campis
abstinuit Marte infido ; comitata Menaeis
venit Amastra viris et parvo nomine Tisse
et Netum et Mutyce pubesque liquentis Achaeti.
Sidonios Drepane atque undae clamosus Helorus
et mox servili vastata Triocala bello,
Sidonios Arbela ferox et celsus Ietas
et bellare Tabas docilis Cossyraque parva
nec maior Megara iunctae concordibus ausis
iuvere et strato Gaulum spectabile ponto,
cum sonat alcyones cantu nidosque natantes
immota gestat, sopitis fluctibus, unda.
ipsa Syracusae patulos urbs inclita muros
milite collecto variisque impleverat armis.
ductores facilem impelli laetamque tumultus
vaniloquo plebem furiabant insuper ore :
numquam hoste intratos muros et quattuor arces ;
et Salaminiacis quantam Eoisque tropaeis
ingenio portus urbs invia fecerit umbram,
spectatum proavis : ter centum ante ora triremes
unum naufragium, mersasque impune profundo
clade pharetrigeri subnixas regis Athenas.

---

[a] See note to iv. 769.

[b] Triocala was fortified and held by slaves in a servile war from 103–100 B.C.

[c] It was believed that the sea was calm for fourteen days in midwinter when the fabulous birds called "halcyons" were breeding.

[d] Achadrina, Tyche, Neapolis, and Nasos (*i.e.* the island of Ortygia).

stands a shrine of Taurian Diana.[a] Thrice that number came from Panhormos, rich in game, whether you follow the wild beasts in the woods, or sweep the sea with nets, or prefer to bring down birds from the sky. Neither Herbesos nor Naulocha sat idle, indifferent to the crisis ; nor did Morgentia of the leafy plains abstain from traitorous war ; Amastra came forward, together with Menae and Tisse unknown to fame ; Netum and Mutyce and the soldiers of the river Achaetus. Aid came to the Carthaginians from Drepane, from the Helorus whose stream is heard afar, and from Triocala, laid waste later in the Servile War.[b] On the same side was bold Arbela, and hilly Ietas ; Tabas skilled in arms, and little Cossyra, no larger than Megara, fought side by side ; also the island of Gaulum, a fair sight when it resounds with the halcyon's song and her floating nest rides on the smooth surface of the unruffled sea.[c] Syracuse herself, that famous city, had filled her spacious walls with mustered troops and arms of every kind. The boastful speeches of the leaders roused to hotter rage a people easily swayed and fond of disturbance : " Never," said they, " has an enemy set foot within the walls of Syracuse and her four fortresses [d] ; our ancestors saw how the city, made impregnable by the nature of her harbour, eclipsed the laurels that Salamis won from the Eastern king [e] ; three hundred triremes sank in one common shipwreck before their eyes ; and Athens, proud as she was to have defeated the bow-bearing king, sank down unavenged to destruction in the sea." Thus

[e] In 413 B.C. Syracuse defeated the Athenian fleet which had itself defeated Xerxes, the Persian king, at Salamis in 480 B.C.

flammabant vulgum geniti Carthagine fratres,
Poeni matre genus ; sed quos, sub crimine pulsus
urbe Syracosia, Libycis eduxerat oris
Trinacrius genitor, geminaque a stirpe parentum
astus miscebant Tyrios levitate Sicana.
  Quae cernens ductor, postquam immedicabile visa
seditio, atque ultro bellum surgebat ab hoste,
testatus divos Siculorum amnesque lacusque
et fontes, Arethusa, tuos, ad bella vocari
invitum ; quae sponte diu non sumpserit, hostem
induere arma sibi : telorum turbine vasto
aggreditur muros atque armis intonat urbi.
par omnes simul ira rapit ; certantque ruuntque.
turris, multiplici surgens ad sidera tecto,
exibat, tabulata decem cui crescere Graius
fecerat et multas nemorum consumpserat umbras.
armatam hinc igni pinum et devolvere saxa
certabant calidaeque picis diffundere pestem.
huic procul ardentem iaculatus lampada Cimber
conicit et lateri telum exitiabile figit.
pascitur adiutus Vulcanus turbine venti,
gliscentemque trahens turris per viscera labem
perque altam molem et totiens nascentia tecta,
scandit ovans rapidusque vorat crepitantia flammis
robora et, ingenti simul exundante vapore
ad caelum, victor nutantia culmina lambit.
implentur fumo et nebula caliginis atrae,
nec cuiquam evasisse datur ; ceu fulminis ictu
correptae rapido in cineres abiere ruinae.

---

[a] Hippocrates and Epicydes.

[b] Archimedes, the greatest mathematician and engineer of antiquity. His name, not admissible in dactylic metre, is not mentioned. See ll. 341, 676.

[c] A Roman soldier.

the populace was set on fire by two brothers,[a] born at Carthage of a Carthaginian mother; but their father was a Sicilian who had been expelled from Syracuse on a criminal charge. Brought up in Africa, they showed their mixed origin, combining Carthaginian cunning with the frivolity of Sicilians.

Marcellus saw all this; and, now that the rebellion seemed a thing past mending and the enemy were beginning war unprovoked, he called the gods of Sicily to witness, with the rivers and lakes and Arethusa's spring, that he was challenged to war against his will, and forced by the enemy to don those arms that he had long refused to put on. Then he assailed the walls with a tornado of missiles and thundered in arms against the city. The same ardour carried all his men along; they vied with one another in activity. There was a tower, a building of many floors that rose up to the sky; the genius of a Greek[b] had given it ten stories and had used up many a shady tree for the work. From it the besieged busily launched lighted torches and stones, and filled the air with the menace of burning pitch. Then Cimber[c] aimed from a distance and threw a fire-brand, and the fatal weapon stuck fast in the side of the tower. The fire, fed and strengthened by the wind, spread the growing peril through the interior of the tower; climbing triumphant up the lofty structure and its ten successive stories, it quickly devoured the crackling timbers, till the victorious flames licked the tottering summit, while a huge cloud of smoke spouted up to the sky. Wreaths of smoke filled all the interior with black darkness, and not a single man escaped; as if struck by sudden lightning, the building crumbled down into ashes.

Par contra pelago miseris fortuna carinis.
namque ubi se propius tectis urbique tulere,
qua portus muris pacatas applicat undas,
improvisa novo pestis conterruit astu.
trabs fabre teres atque, erasis undique nodis,
navali similis malo, praefixa gerebat
uncae tela manus ; ea celso ex aggere muri
bellantes curvi rapiebat in aera ferri
unguibus et mediam revocata ferebat in urbem.
nec solos vis illa viros, quin saepe triremem
belligerae rapuere trabes, cum desuper actum
incuterent puppi chalybem morsusque tenaces.
qui, simul affixo vicina in robora ferro
sustulerant sublime ratem, miserabile visu,
per subitum rursus laxatis arte catenis
tanta praecipitem reddebant mole profundo,
ut totam haurirent undae cum milite puppem.
his super insidiis angusta foramina murus
arte cavata dabat, per quae clam fundere tela
tutum erat, opposito mittentibus aggere valli.
nec sine fraude labos, arta ne rursus eodem
spicula ab hoste via vicibus contorta redirent.
calliditas Graia atque astus pollentior armis
Marcellum tantasque minas terraque marique
arcebat ; stabatque ingens ad moenia bellum.

Vir fuit Isthmiacis decus immortale colonis,
ingenio facile ante alios telluris alumnos,
nudus opum, sed cui caelum terraeque paterent.

---

[a] Archimedes.

On the other hand the Roman ships met with equal misfortune at sea. For when they came close to the buildings of the city, at a point where the harbour-water laps gently against the walls, they were discomfited by the cunning device of an unexpected weapon. A spar like a ship's mast, skilfully rounded and with all its knots planed away, carried an iron-clawed grapnel at its extremity; and this spar, when let down from the height of the wall, caught up the attackers with its iron claws, and, when it was hauled back, landed them within the city. Nor did this engine of war catch up men only: it often hoisted up a war-ship, when it struck the vessel from above with the descending steel of its unyielding jaws. As soon as it had fixed its iron point in the nearest ship and raised the vessel up into the air, then a piteous sight was seen: the cables were suddenly let go by machinery, and lowered their prey with such force and speed that the ship and her company were swallowed up whole by the sea. In addition to these devices, small loopholes were skilfully bored in the wall, through which weapons could be shot secretly and safely; for the high wall protected the marksmen. But their task was not free from danger; for weapons thrown by the enemy might come back in revenge by the same narrow openings. Thus the ingenuity of a Greek [a] and cunning more powerful than force kept Marcellus and all his threats at bay by sea and land, and the mighty armament stood helpless before the walls.

There was living then in Syracuse a man [a] who sheds immortal glory on his city, a man whose genius far surpassed that of other sons of earth. He was poor in this world's goods, but to him the secrets of

ille, novus pluvias Titan ut proderet ortu
fuscatis tristis radiis ; ille, haereat anne
pendeat instabilis tellus ; cur foedere certo
hunc affusa globum Tethys circumliget undis,
noverat atque una pelagi lunaeque labores,
et pater Oceanus qua lege effunderet aestus.
non illum mundi numerasse capacis harenas
vana fides. puppes etiam constructaque saxa
feminea traxisse ferunt contra ardua dextra.

Hic dum Italum ductorem astu Teucrosque fatigat,
adnabat centum late Sidonia velis
classis subsidio et scindebat caerula rostris.
erigitur subitas in spes Arethusia proles
adiungitque suas, portu progressa, carinas.
nec contra Ausonius tonsis aptare lacertos
addubitat mersisque celer fodit aequora remis.
verberibus torsere fretum ; salis icta frequenti
albescit pulsu facies, perque aequora late
spumat canenti sulcatus gurgite limes.
insultant pariter pelago, ac Neptunia regna
tempestate nova trepidant. tum vocibus aequor
personat, et clamat scopulis clamoris imago.
ac iam diffusus vacua bellator in unda
cornibus ambierat patulos ad proelia fluctus,
navali claudens umentem indagine campum.
ac simili curvata sinu diversa ruebat

[a] The ebb and flow of the tides are meant.

[b] This may refer to some religious ceremony in which men might not take part: cp. xvii. 16 foll.

[c] For *Arethusia* see note on l. 53.

heaven and earth were revealed. He knew how the rising sun portended rain when its rays were dull and gloomy; he knew whether the earth is fixed where it hangs in space or shifts its position; he knew the unalterable law by which Ocean surrounds the world with the girdle of its waters; he understood the contest between the moon and the tides,[a] and the ordinance that governs the flow of Father Ocean. Not without reason men believed that Archimedes had counted the sands of this great globe; they say too that he had moved ships and carried great buildings of stone, though drawn by women only,[b] up a height.

While Archimedes thus wore out by his devices the Roman general and his men, a great Carthaginian fleet of a hundred sail was speeding to the aid of Syracuse and cleaving the blue sea with their beaks. The hopes of the citizens[c] at once rose high: they sailed forth from the harbour and added their vessels to the fleet. The Romans on their side were not slow to suit their arms to the oar, and speedily ploughed the water with their blades. Their oars churned up the sea, the surface of the water was whitened by their repeated strokes, and a wake of foam spread wide over the hoary deep. Both fleets rode proudly on the wave, and a new kind of storm disquieted Neptune's realm. The sea rang with the sound of voices, and the shouting was re-echoed by the cliffs. And now the Roman fleet, disposed over the empty space of sea, had enclosed the wide waters with its two wings, in preparation for battle; and their vessels, like a ring of hunters, shut in the watery plain. And then the enemy's fleet came on, also drawn up in the form of a crescent, and cramping

classis et artabat lunato caerula gyro.
nec mora : terrificis saevae stridoribus aeris,
per vacuum late cantu resonante profundum,
increpuere tubae, quis excitus aequore Triton
expavit tortae certantia murmura conchae.
vix meminere maris ; tam vasto ad proelia nisu
incumbunt proni positisque in margine puppis
extremae plantis nutantes spicula torquent.
sternitur effusis pelagi media area telis,
celsaque anhelatis exsurgens ictibus alnus
caerula migranti findit spumantia sulco.
  Ast aliae latera atque incussi roboris ictu
detergent remos ; aliae per viscera pinus
tramissis ipso retinentur vulnere rostris,
quo retinent. medias inter sublimior ibat
terribilis visu puppis, qua nulla per omne
egressa est Libycis maior navalibus aevum.
sed quater haec centum numeroso remige pontum
pulsabat tonsis, veloque superba capaci
cum rapidum hauriret Borean et cornibus omnes
colligeret flatus, lento se robore agebat,
intraret fluctus solis quasi pulsa lacertis.
procurrunt levitate agili docilesque regentis
audivisse manum Latio cum milite puppes.
  Has ut per laevum venientes aequor Himilco
in latus obliquas iussamque incurrere proram
conspexit, propere divis in vota vocatis
aequoris, intento volucrem de more sagittam

---

[a] A sea deity and son of Neptune.

[b] The flag-ship of Himilco, who commanded the Carthaginian troops carried by the fleet.

[c] The ship, even under press of sail, moved so slowly, because of its enormous size, that you would have thought it was only propelled by oars.

the sea with its wings. Quickly the trumpets sounded, and the cruel braying of the brass struck terror as it echoed far over the empty space of sea; and the noise brought Triton [a] up from the depths, alarmed by a din that drowned his twisted shell. The combatants almost forgot the sea beneath them: with so mighty an effort they bend forward to fight, planting their feet on the very gunwale of their vessels, and leaning over as they shoot their missiles. The space of sea between the fleets was strewn with spent weapons; and the ships, raised high in the water by the strokes of the panting oarsmen, ploughed the foaming sea with an ever-shifting furrow.

Some ships had the oars on their broadside swept away by the impact of a hostile craft; others, after ramming an enemy with their beaks, were held fast themselves by the injury they had inflicted. In the middle of the fleet, one formidable vessel [b] towered above the rest; no huger ship was ever launched from the arsenals of Carthage. She struck the water with four hundred oars; and when she proudly caught the force of the wind with her spread of sail, and gathered in every breeze with the ends of her yards, her great bulk moved forward as slowly as if she were propelled over the water by oars alone.[c] The ships that carried the Roman soldiers were light and handy in their advance, and answered readily to the hand of the steersman.

When Himilco saw them coming up to take him on his left flank, with orders to use their rams, he quickly put up a prayer to the gods of the sea and took a feathered arrow and laid it duly against

assignat nervo ; utque oculis libravit in hostem
et calamo monstravit iter, diversa relaxans
bracchia, deduxit vultu comitante per auras
in vulnus telum ac residentis puppe magistri
affixit plectro dextram ; nec deinde regenda
puppe manus valuit, flectenti immortua clavo.
dumque ad opem accurrit ceu capta navita puppe,
ecce iterum fatoque pari nervoque sagitta,
in medium perlapsa globum, transverberat ictu
orba gubernacli subeuntem munera Taurum.
Irrumpit Cumana ratis, quam Corbulo ductor
lectaque complebat Stabiarum litore pubes.
numen erat celsae puppis Lucrina Dione.
sed superingestis propior quia subdita telis
bella capessebat, media subsedit in unda
divisitque fretum. clamantum spumeus ora
Nereus implet aquis, palmaeque, trahente profundo,
luctantum frustra summis in fluctibus exstant.
hic, audax ira, magno per caerula saltu
Corbulo transgressus (nam textam robore turrim
appulerant nexae ferri compage triremes)
evadit tabulata super flammaque comantem
multifida pinum celso de culmine quassat.
inde atros alacer pastosque bitumine torquet,
amentante Noto, Poenorum aplustribus ignes.
Intrat diffusos pestis Vulcania passim
atque implet dispersa foros ; trepidatur omisso
summis remigio ; sed enim tam rebus in artis

[a] A town near Pompeii, which perished together with Pompeii in the eruption of Vesuvius in August A.D. 79.

[b] Venus.

[c] It seems that this tower was manned by Romans, and that Corbulo climbed up it in order to throw fire-brands from it upon the Carthaginian flag-ship.

the taut string. Then he measured with the eye the distance of the enemy and showed its path to the arrow, and, relaxing his extended arms, stood watching its flight through the sky till it struck its mark. A steersman was sitting by the stern, and the arrow pinned his hand to the helm ; and the hand could no longer steer the ship but stuck lifeless to the guiding tiller. The crew ran up to help him, thinking their vessel already taken, when, lo, a second arrow, shot from the same string with the same success, passed between the crowd of sailors and pierced Taurus, when he was about to take charge of the masterless helm.

On there came a ship of Cumae, with Corbulo for captain, and manned by a chosen crew from the strand of Stabiae [a] ; Dione [b] of the Lucrine lake stood on the high poop as guardian-goddess. But the ship, fighting at too close quarters beneath a shower of missiles from above, settled down in mid-sea, parting the waves asunder. The foaming sea stifled the cries of the sailors, and their helpless hands, drawn down by the deep, stuck up on the surface, as they struggled to swim. Then, emboldened by wrath, Corbulo, with one great leap, covered the distance and boarded a wooden tower,[c] which two triremes, bound together with iron clamps, had brought alongside. He climbed up the stages of the tower, and from the top brandished a blazing torch of split pine-wood. From there he rained down on the stern-ornaments of the Carthaginian ship fatal fires fed with pitch ; and the wind added strength to his missiles.

The plague of fire made its way in at every point and spread till it filled all the decks. In the confusion the upper banks of oarsmen ceased to row ; but in

fama mali nondum tanti penetrarat ad imos.
at rapidus fervor, per pingues unguine taedas
illapsus, flammis victricibus insonat alveo.
qua nondum tamen intulerat vim Dardana lampas,
parcebatque vapor, saxorum grandine dirus
arcebat fatumque ratis retinebat Himilco.
hic miser, igniferam dum ventilat aëre pinum,
murali saxo per lubrica sanguine transtra
volvitur in fluctus, Lycchaei vulnere, Cydnus.
fax nidore gravi foedavit comminus auras,
ambusto instridens pelago. ferus inde citatum
missile adorata contorquet Sabratha puppe—
Hammon numen erat Libycae gentile carinae
cornigeraque sedens spectabat caerula fronte :
" fer, pater, afflictis, fer," ait, " Garamantice vates,
rebus opem inque Italos da certa effundere tela."
has inter voces tremulo venit agmine cornus
et Neptunicolae transverberat ora Telonis.

Urgebant nihilo levius iam in limine mortis,
quos fuga praecipites partem glomerarat in unam
puppis, adhuc vacuam taedae ; sed, proxima cursu
fulmineo populatus, inevitabilis ardor
correptam flammis involvit ovantibus alnum.
primus, ope aequorei funis delapsus in undas,
qua nondum Stygios glomerabat Mulciber aestus,
ambustus socium remis aufertur Himilco.
proxima nudarunt miserandi fata Batonis

[a] See notes to iii. 10 ; ix. 298.

that emergency the news of their danger had not yet reached the lower benches. Soon the spreading blaze, moving on by means of fire-brands oozing resin, crackled with victorious flames in the hold. Still, where the heat was less fierce and the Roman fire-brands had not yet penetrated, Himilco stood, keeping off the foe with a dreadful hail of stones and delaying the doom of his ship. Here the hapless Cydnus, while swinging a fire-brand, was struck by a huge stone from the hand of Lycchaeus; his body rolled over the benches slippery with blood and fell into the water; the fire-brand hissed in the glowing sea, and the stench of it poisoned the air around. Then Sabratha, in rage, hurled his swift spear; but first he prayed to the gods on the stern; Ammon, the native god of Libya, was the guardian of the vessel, and sat there looking over the sea, wearing the horns on his brow.[a] "O Father, O Prophet of the Garamantes," he cried: "help us in the hour of disaster, and grant that my weapon may find its mark in a Roman!" While he spoke thus, the spear-shaft sped on with quivering flight and pierced the head of Telon, a dweller by the sea.

But none the less fiercely fought those who, at death's door, had squeezed themselves in headlong flight into that part of the ship which alone was untouched by the fire; but there was no escape from it. It devoured every obstacle with lightning speed and caught the whole ship and wrapt it in triumphant flames. Himilco was the first to leave the vessel: at a point where the fire-god's hellish heat was not yet at its height, he slipped down, half burnt, to the water by help of a cable, and was rowed away by friendly oars. Next, the pitiful death of Bato

desertam ductore ratem. bonus ille per artem
crudo luctari pelago atque exire procellas.
idem, quid Boreas, quid vellet crastinus Auster,
anteibat ; nec pervigilem tu fallere vultum,
obscuro quamvis cursu, Cynosura, valeres.
is, postquam adversis nullus modus : " accipe nostrum,
Hammon, sanguinem," ait, " spectator cladis iniquae."
atque, acto in pectus gladio, dextra inde cruorem
excipit et large sacra inter cornua fundit.
  Hos inter Daphnis, deductum ab origine nomen
antiqua, fuit infelix, cui linquere saltus
et mutare casas infido marmore visum.
at princeps generis quanto maiora paravit
intra pastorem sibi nomina ! Daphnin amarunt
Sicelides Musae ; dexter donavit avena
Phoebus Castalia et iussit, proiectus in herba
si quando caneret, laetos per prata, per arva
ad Daphnin properare greges rivosque silere.
ille ubi, septena modulatus harundine carmen,
mulcebat silvas, non umquam tempore eodem
Siren assuetos effudit in aequore cantus ;
Scyllaei tacuere canes ; stetit atra Charybdis ;
et laetus scopulis audivit iubila Cyclops.
progeniem hauserunt et nomen amabile flammae.
  Innatat ecce super transtris fumantibus asper
Ornytos ac longam sibimet facit aequore mortem,
qualis Oïliades, fulmen iaculante Minerva,

---

[a] See note to iii. 665.

[b] Daphnis, the Sicilian shepherd, was the inventor of pastoral poetry ; and this Daphnis was his descendant.

[c] Ajax of Locris, the son of Oïleus, was punished by Pallas for ill-treatment of Cassandra : on his voyage home from Troy, she killed him by a flash of lightning.

deprived the deserted ship of her navigator. Great skill had he to battle with the angry sea and outsail the tempest. He also knew beforehand what the North-wind and the South portended for the morrow; nor could the Little Bear,[a] however obscured its movements, escape his sleepless eyes. When he saw there was no limit to disaster, he cried out to his god: "Ammon, who lookest idly on at our cruel defeat, to thee I offer my blood." Then he drove his sword into his own breast, and, catching in his hand the blood that flowed from it, poured it in abundance between the horns of the deity.

Among the crew was Daphnis, ill-fated Daphnis, a name famous in ancient times[b]; he had thought fit to leave his woodland glades and give up his country home for the treacherous sea. But how much greater the fame gained by his ancestor who was content with a shepherd's life! The Sicilian Muses loved Daphnis; Apollo favoured him and gave him the shepherd's pipe from Castalia, and bade the brooks keep silence and the happy flocks to hasten over meadow and field to hear Daphnis, whenever he lay on the grass and sang. When he played on his pipe of seven reeds and charmed the trees, the Siren never sent forth her wonted song over the sea at the same time; Scylla's dogs were silent, black Charybdis was motionless, and the Cyclops on his rocky heights loved to hear the joyful strain. Now his descendant, bearing a name so dear, was swallowed up by the flames.

Behold hardy Ornytus, who swims on above the smoking benches and by swimming inflicts on himself a lingering death; even so the son of Oïleus,[c] when struck by Minerva's lightning, stemmed the rising

surgentes domuit fluctus ardentibus ulnis.
transigitur valida medius, dum se allevat, alni
cuspide Marmarides Sciron : pars subnatat unda
membrorum, pars extat aquis totumque per aequor
portatur, rigido, miserandum, immortua rostro.
accelerant puppes utrimque atque ora ruentum
sanguinei feriunt remorum aspergine rores.
ipse adeo senis ductor Rhoeteius ibat
pulsibus et valido superabat remige ventos.
quam rapidis puppem manibus frenare Lilaeus
dum tentat, saeva truncatur membra bipenni,
ac fert haerentes trabibus ratis incita palmas.
  Sicania Aeoliden portabant transtra Podaetum.
hic, aevo quamquam nondum excessisset ephebos,
nec sat maturus laudum, seu fervida corda
seu laevi traxere dei, bellique cupido,
arma puer niveis aptarat picta lacertis
et freta gaudebat celsa turbare Chimaera.
iamque super Rutula, super et Garamantide pinu
ibat ovans, melior remo meliorque sagitta ;
et iam turrigerum demerserat aequore Nessum ;
heu puero malesuada rudi nova gloria pugnae !
dum cristam galeae trucis exuviasque precatur
de duce Marcello superos temerarius, hasta
excepit raptim vulnus letale remissa.
pro qualis ! seu splendentem sub sidera nisu
exigeret discum, iaculo seu nubila supra
surgeret, aligeras ferret seu pulvere plantas
vix tacto, vel dimensi spatia improba campi

---

[a] Marmarica was a region of Africa, bordering on Egypt.
[b] For *Rhoeteius* see note on ii. 51.
[c] The Aeolian Islands.

waves with arms on fire. Sciron, a Marmarid,[a] while rising on a wave, was run through the body by the powerful beak of a ship. Half his body was under water, and half above it; and this was carried all over the sea—a piteous sight—fastened in death upon the metal beak. Both fleets now increased their speed, and the rowers' faces, as they sped on, were spattered with a bloody dew from the splashing oars. The Roman[b] commander's ship itself was propelled by six banks of oars, and its stalwart rowers made it move faster than the wind. When Lilaeus quickly caught hold of it and tried to stop it, his wrists were severed by a merciless axe, and the ship flew on, with his hands still sticking to the gunwale.

Podaetus, a native of Aeolia,[c] was borne on a Sicilian vessel. He had not yet attained the years of manhood and was still unripe for glory in arms; but he was led on, either by his eager spirit and passion for war, or by evil fortune; and, still a boy, he wielded a painted shield with his snow-white arm, and rejoiced to ruffle the sea with his tall ship, the *Chimaera*. On he went triumphant, outstripping Roman ships and Carthaginian alike, having better oarsmen and better archers. Already he had sunk the turret-ship, *Nessus*; but, alas, the tiro was tempted to ruin by his first taste of glory. While he prayed to Heaven in his rash folly that he might strip the general, Marcellus, of his armour and menacing helmet-plume, an answering spear-cast dealt him a deadly wound. Alas for so splendid a youth! Whether he hurled on high the shining discus, or threw the javelin above the clouds, or ran with flying feet that skimmed over the course, or covered with one swift leap a vast stretch of measured

transiret velox saltu, decuere labores.
sat prorsus, sat erat decoris discrimine tuto,
sat laudis : cur facta, puer, maiora petebas ?
illum, ubi labentem pepulerunt tela sub undas,
ossa Syracosio fraudatum naufraga busto,
fleverunt freta, fleverunt Cyclopia saxa
et Cyane et Anapus et Ortygie Arethusa.
Parte alia Perseus—puppem hanc Tiberinus agebat—
quaque vehebatur Crantor Sidonius, Io
concurrunt. iniecta ligant hinc vincula ferri
atque illinc, steteruntque rates ad proelia nexae.
nec iaculo aut longe certatur harundine fusa,
comminus et gladio terrestria proelia miscent.
perrumpunt Itali, qua caedes prima reclusit
monstravitque viam ; vasta sed mole catenas
hortatur socios et vincla abrumpere ferri
ac parat hostili resoluta puppe receptos
avehere et paribus pelago diducere ab armis :
Aetnaeo Polyphemus erat nutritus in antro
atque inde antiquae nomen feritatis amabat ;
ubera praebuerat parvo lupa ; corporis alti
terribilis moles, mens aspera, vultus in ira
semper et ad caedes Cyclopia corde libido.
isque relaxatis membrorum pondere vinclis
impulerat puppim et mergebat gurgite tonsas
duxissetque ratem, pressa Laronius hasta
ni propere duro nitentem exsurgere velox
affixet transtro. vix morte incepta remittit ;

---

[a] The Cyclopes inhabited the rocky slopes by Etna : Cyane was a spring and Anapus a river near Syracuse : for Arethusa see note to l. 53.

[b] Silius is referring to Polyphemus in the *Odyssey*, a cannibal giant.

ground—each competition became him. There was enough, quite enough, of glory and praise to be won in bloodless strife: why was the lad ambitious of greater deeds? When he fell, and the fatal weapon sank him beneath the wave and cheated his sea-tossed bones of a grave in Syracuse, he was mourned by the straits and the rocks of the Cyclopes; Cyane and the river Anapus and Ortygian Arethusa wept for him.[a]

Elsewhere the *Perseus*, commanded by Tiberinus, and the *Io* which carried the Carthaginian Crantor, met in conflict. The two ships stood motionless for battle, bound together by iron clamps launched from both decks. Their weapons were not javelins or arrows shot from a distance; they fought, as if on land, with the sword and at close quarters. The Romans burst their way in, at a point where a passage was opened and made clear by the first slaughter; but one man urged his comrades to burst the heavy chains and fetters of iron; and, when the ship was set free, he intended to carry off those who had boarded the hostile craft and to put the sea between them and their fellows. This was Polyphemus; he had been reared in a cave of Mount Etna, and hence he loved a name that recalled the ferocity of ancient times[b]; a she-wolf had suckled him in infancy; his great stature and huge frame inspired awe; his heart was cruel, and his eyes flashed anger continually; and a blood-lust worthy of the Cyclopes filled his breast. By strength of limb he had burst the chains and started the ship; he dipped his oars and would have pulled the vessel along, had not the spear of Laronius, hastily hurled, pinned him fast to the wooden thwart, as he rose with effort to his oar. His purpose was

namque manus servat dum suetos languida ductus,
ignavum summo traxit super aequore remum.
  Perculsi cuneo Poeni densentur in unum,
quod caret hoste, latus, subito cum pondere victus,
insiliente mari, submergitur alveus undis.
scuta virum cristaeque et inerti spicula ferro
tutelaeque deum fluitant. hic robore fracto
pugnat inops chalybis seseque in proelia rursus
armat naufragio ; remis male fervidus ille
festinat spoliare ratem, discrimine nullo
nautarum interdum convulsa sedilia torquens.
non plectro ratis aut frangendae in vulnera prorae
parcitur, et pelago repetuntur nantia tela.
vulneribus patulis intrat mare ; mox sua ponto
singultante anima propulsa refunditur unda.
nec desunt, qui correptos complexibus artis
immergant pelago et, iaculis cessantibus, hostem
morte sua perimant. remeantum gurgite mentes
crudescunt, ac pro ferro stat fluctibus uti.
haurit sanguineus contorta cadavera vortex.
hinc clamor, gemitus illinc mortesque fugaeque
remorumque fragor flictuque sonantia rostra.
perfusum bello fervet mare ; fessus acerbis
terga fuga celeri Libyae convertit ad oras
exigua sese furatus Himilco carina.
  Concessere mari tandem Graiusque Libysque,

hardly arrested by death; for his dying hand still went through the familiar motions and pulled the useless oar over the surface of the water.

The discomfited Carthaginians crowded together, in wedge-shaped formation, into that side of their ship that was free from the enemy; but she gave way under the sudden weight, the sea rushed in, and the *Io* sank beneath the wave. Shields and helmets float on the water, images of tutelary gods and javelins with useless points. One man, having no steel, uses a broken piece of wood for a weapon and arms himself afresh with fragments of shipwreck; another, with misguided zeal, hastens to rob his vessel of its oars; and some tear up indiscriminately the rowers' benches and hurl them at the enemy. Neither helm nor prow was spared: each was broken up to use as a weapon; and floating missiles were picked up, to use again. The water found its way into gaping wounds, and soon, expelled by the sobbing breath of the wounded men, poured back into the sea. Some grappled with a foe in close embrace and drowned him; lacking weapons, they died themselves that they might kill their enemies. Those who emerged from the water grew more savage, and were resolved to use the sea as their weapon; and at last the sea-tossed corpses were swallowed up by the blood-stained eddies. There was shouting on one side, and, on the other, groaning and death and flight, and the snapping of oars mingled with the noise of clashing beaks. The sea boiled beneath the storm of battle; and Himilco, worn out by disaster, stole away in a little boat and fled in haste towards the coast of Africa.

At last the Greeks and Carthaginians retreated to

et iam captivae vinclis ad litora longo
ordine ducuntur puppes. flagrantibus alto
stant aliae taedis : splendet lucente profundo
Mulciber, et tremula vibratur imagine pontus.
ardet nota fretis Cyane pennataque Siren.
ardet et Europe, nivei sub imagine tauri
vecta Iovi ac prenso tramittens aequora cornu ;
et quae, fusa comas, curvum per caerula piscem
Nereis umenti moderatur roscida freno.
uritur undivagus Python et corniger Hammon
et, quae Sidonios vultus portabat Elissae,
bis ternis ratis ordinibus grassata per undas.
at vinclis trahitur cognata in litora Anapus
Gorgoneasque ferens ad sidera Pegasus alas.
ducitur et Libyae puppis signata figuram
et Triton captivus et ardua rupibus Aetne,
spirantis rogus Enceladi, Cadmeaque Sidon.
  Nec mora tum trepidos hac clade irrumpere muros
signaque ferre deum templis iam iamque fuisset,
ni subito importuna lues inimicaque pestis,
invidia divum pelagique labore parata,
polluto miseris rapuisset gaudia caelo.
criniger aestiferis Titan fervoribus auras
et patulam Cyanen lateque palustribus undis
stagnantem Stygio Cocyti opplevit odore
temporaque autumni, laetis florentia donis,
foedavit rapidoque accendit fulminis igni.

---

[a] This is not consistent with l. 196, where it was said that Typhoeus was buried under Etna: two giants were not imprisoned under a single volcano.

[b] This may refer to the corpses floating in the harbour, or to the exhaustion following a great effort.

the land; and soon their captive ships were towed ashore in long procession, while others, lit up with flames, still kept the sea. The fire blazed over the shining water, and the sea rippled with the quivering reflection. Among the burning ships was the *Cyane*, well known to those waters, and the winged *Siren*; *Europa* too, who rode on the back of Jove disguised as a snow-white bull, and grasped one horn as she moved over the water; and the watery *Nereid* with floating hair, who drove a curving dolphin over the deep with dripping rein; the sea-traversing *Python* was burnt, and horn-crowned *Ammon*, and the vessel that bore the likeness of Tyrian *Dido* and was propelled by six banks of oars. The *Anapus*, on the other hand, was towed to her native shore, and the *Pegasus* who raised to heaven his wings born of the Gorgon; and other ships were carried captive—that which bore the likeness of *Libya*, and the *Triton*, and *Etna* of the rocky peaks, the pyre that covers living Enceladus,[a] and *Sidon*, the city of Cadmus.

The citizens were terrified by this defeat, and Marcellus would have been able at once to burst through the walls and lead his eagles against the temples of the gods, had not a sore pestilence and cruel plague, caused by the ill-will of heaven and the fight at sea,[b] suddenly infected the air and robbed the wretched Romans of this triumph. The golden-haired Sun filled the air with fervent heat, and infected with the deadly stench of Cocytus the water of Cyane which spreads far and wide into a stagnant fen; he marred the kindly gifts of autumn [c] and burnt them up with swift lightning-flames. The air was thick and

[c] The yield of the vines and fruit-trees: the corn harvest was over.

fumabat crassus nebulis caliginis aër ;
squalebat tellus, vitiato fervida dorso,
nec victum dabat aut ullas languentibus umbras.
atque ater picea vapor expirabat in aethra.
vim primi sensere canes ; mox nubibus atris
fluxit deficiens penna labente volucris ;
inde ferae silvis sterni ; tum serpere labes
Tartarea atque haustis populari castra maniplis.
arebat lingua, et gelidus per viscera sudor
corpore manabat tremulo ; descendere fauces
abnuerant siccae iussorum alimenta ciborum.
aspera pulmonem tussis quatit, et per anhela
igneus efflatur sitientum spiritus ora.
lumina, ferre gravem vix sufficientia lucem,
unca nare iacent, saniesque immixta cruore
expuitur, membrisque cutis tegit ossa peresis.
heu dolor ! insignis notis bellator in armis
ignavo rapitur leto. iactantur in ignem
dona superba virum, multo Mavorte parata.
succubuit medicina malis. cumulantur acervo
labentum et magno cineres sese aggere tollunt.
passim etiam deserta iacent inhumataque late
corpora, pestiferos tetigisse timentibus artus.
serpit pascendo crescens Acherusia pestis
nec leviore quatit Trinacria moenia luctu
Poenorumque parem castris fert atra laborem.
aequato par exitio et communis ubique
ira deum atque eadem leti versatur imago.
  Nulla tamen Latios fregit vis dura malorum,
incolumi ductore, viros, cladeque repemdit

smoky and dark with vapours ; the earth was hot and dry, and its surface was marred by the heat ; it yielded no food, and no shade for the sick ; and a gloomy mist hung in the pitch-black sky. The dogs were first to feel the mischief ; next the birds flagged in their flight and dropped down from the black clouds ; and then the beasts of the forest were laid low. Soon the infernal plague spread further, depopulating the camp and devouring the soldiers. Their tongues were parched ; a cold sweat issued from the vital parts and poured down from the shivering frame ; and the dry throat refused a passage to the nourishment prescribed. The lungs were shaken by a hard cough, and the breath of the thirsting sufferers came forth from their panting mouths as hot as fire. The sunken eyes could hardly endure the burden of light ; the nose fell in ; matter mixed with blood was vomited, and the wasted body was mere skin and bone. Alas for the warrior famous for feats of war and now carried off by an ignoble death ! Noble trophies earned in many a fight were cast upon the funeral-pyre. The healing art was baffled by the disease. The ashes of the dead were heaped up till they formed a great pile. And all round lay corpses, unattended and unburied ; for men feared to touch the infectious limbs. The deadly plague, growing by what it fed on, spread further and shook the walls of Syracuse with mourning as grievous and made the Carthaginians suffer no less than the Roman army. The wrath of heaven fell with equal destruction upon both sides, and the same image of death was present everywhere.

Yet, so long as Marcellus lived, no cruel visitation of calamity could break the spirit of the Romans, and the safety of that single life among such heaps of dead

unum inter strages tutum caput. ut gravis ergo
primum letiferos repressit Sirius aestus,
et minuere avidae mortis contagia pestes,
ceu, sidente Noto cum se maria alta reponunt,
propulsa invadit piscator caerula cumba,
sic tandem ereptam morbis grassantibus armat
Marcellus pubem, lustratis rite maniplis.
circumstant alacres signa auditisque tubarum
respirant laeti clangoribus. itur in hostem ;
et, si fata ferant, iuvat inter proelia ferro
posse mori ; socium miseret, qui sorte pudenda
in morem pecudum effudere cubilibus atris
illaudatam animam. tumulos inhonoraque busta
respiciunt, et vel nullo iacuisse sepulcro
quam debellari morbis placet. ardua primus
ad muros dux signa rapit. tenuata iacendo
et macie in galeis abscondunt ora, malusque,
ne sit spes hosti, velatur casside pallor.
infundunt rapidum convulsis moenibus agmen
condensique ruunt : tot bellis invia tecta
totque uno introitu capiuntur militis arces.

Totum, qua vehitur Titan, non ulla per orbem
tum sese Isthmiacis aequassent oppida tectis.
tot delubra deum totque intra moenia portus,
adde fora et celsis suggesta theatra columnis
certantesque mari moles, adde ordine longo
innumeras spatioque domos aequare superbas
rura. quid, inclusos porrecto limite longis
porticibus sacros iuvenum certamine lucos ?

---

[a] The common fate of a defeated army in ancient times.

[b] The Gymnasia, always so dear to the Greeks and so much despised by the Romans.

atoned for their sufferings. Therefore, as soon as the fierce Dog-star cooled its pestilential heat and the devouring plague became less infectious, then, even as the fisherman rows his boat out to sea, when the wind is still and the deep at rest, so at last Marcellus armed his men, snatched from the clutch of disease, and purified the ranks with due sacrifices. Eagerly they gathered round the standards, and breathed freely when they heard the blare of the trumpets. They march to the attack; and, if fate so ordain it, they are glad that the chance of dying by the sword in battle is not denied them; and they pity their comrades who died like sheep and met an ignoble death, drawing their last breath on their dark barrack-beds. Looking back at the grave-mounds of the unhonoured dead, they feel that even to lie unburied [a] is better than to be conquered by disease. Marcellus went first and hurried the lofty standards forward against the walls. Behind their helmets they hid faces emaciated by sickness, and concealed their unhealthy colour, that the enemy might conceive no hopes from it. With speed they pour a host over the shattered walls, and rush on in close order; all those impregnable buildings and all those forts were taken by a single armed assault.

In all the earth round which the Sun drives his chariot no city at that time could rival Syracuse. So many temples had she, so many harbours within the walls; market-places also, and theatres raised up on lofty pillars, and piers that strove with the sea, and an endless succession of palaces whose spaciousness defied the competition of country-houses. Then there were spaces devoted to athletic contests of youth,[b] enclosed by a long vista of far-stretching

quid tot captivis fulgentia culmina rostris ?
armaque fixa deis ? aut quae Marathonius hostis
perdidit, aut Libya quae sunt advecta subacta ?
hic Agathocleis sedes ornata tropaeis ;
hic mites Hieronis opes ; hic sancta vetustas
artificum manibus. non usquam clarior illo
gloria picturae saeclo ; non aera iuvabat
ascire ex Ephyre ; fulvo certaverit auro
vestis, spirantes referens subtemine vultus,
quae radio caelat Babylon, vel murice picto
laeta Tyros, quaeque Attalicis variata per artem
aulaeis scribuntur acu aut Memphitide tela.
iam simul argento fulgentia pocula, mixta
quis gemma quaesitus honos, simulacra deorum
numen ab arte datum servantia ; munera rubri
praeterea ponti depexaque vellera ramis,
femineus labor.
His tectis opibusque potitus
Ausonius ductor, postquam sublimis ab alto
aggere despexit trepidam clangoribus urbem,
inque suo positum nutu, stent moenia regum,
an nullos oriens videat lux crastina muros,
ingemuit nimio iuris tantumque licere
horruit et, propere revocata militis ira,
iussit stare domos, indulgens templa vetustis
incolere atque habitare deis. sic parcere victis

[a] See ll. 282 foll.

[b] Agathocles, who died at an uncertain age in 289 B.C., rose from a private and obscure station to be tyrant of Syracuse and king of Sicily. He defeated the Carthaginians in many great battles in Africa.

[c] See ll. 79 foll.

[d] Corinthian bronzes were greatly prized by the ancients.

[e] Gold embroidery was invented by Attalus III., king of Pergamus in Asia.

[f] Pearls.

[g] See note to vi. 4.

colonnades; and many lofty buildings adorned with the beaks of captured ships; and armour fixed on temple-walls, either taken from the Athenian enemy [a] or brought across the sea from conquered Libya. Here stood a building adorned with the trophies won by Agathocles,[b] and there was displayed the peaceful wealth of Hiero [c]; and here the handiwork of famous artists was consecrated by antiquity. Nowhere in that age was the art of the painter more splendid; Syracuse had no desire to import bronzes from Corinth [d]; and her tapestry, wrought with ruddy gold and reproducing in the woof living likenesses of men, might rival the fabrics wrought by the shuttles of Babylon or by Tyre that prides herself on her embroidered purple; it might match the intricate patterns worked by the needle on the hangings of Attalus [e] or the woven stuffs of Egypt. There were cups also of shining silver, made more beautiful by inserted jewels, and images of the gods, in which the divinity was preserved by the artist's genius, and the spoils of the Red Sea [f] also, and wool combed from the branches of trees [g] by the hands of women.

Such was the city and such the wealth, of which the Roman general was now master. He stood on a lofty eminence and looked down on the city where the noise of the trumpets spread terror. A sign from him would determine whether those royal walls should remain standing or vanish utterly before the morrow dawned. He groaned aloud because of his excess of power, and shrank back from what he might have done. Quickly restraining the violence of the soldiers, he ordered that the houses should be left standing, and granted their temples to the gods to inhabit as of old. Thus mercy to the conquered took the

pro praeda fuit, et sese contenta nec ullo
sanguine pollutis plausit Victoria pennis.
tu quoque ductoris lacrimas, memorande, tulisti,
defensor patriae, meditantem in pulvere formas
nec turbatum animi tanta feriente ruina.
  Ast reliquum vulgus, resoluta in gaudia mente,
certarunt victi victoribus. aemulus ipse
ingenii superum, servando condidit urbem.
ergo exstat saeclis stabitque insigne tropaeum
et dabit antiquos ductorum noscere mores.
  Felices populi, si, quondam ut bella solebant,
nunc quoque inexhaustas pax nostra relinqueret urbes!
at, ni cura viri, qui nunc dedit otia mundo,
effrenum arceret populandi cuncta furorem,
nudassent avidae terrasque fretumque rapinae.

---

[a] Archimedes was studying a mathematical problem, when a Roman soldier killed him in ignorance: Marcellus buried his body and provided for his family.

[b] The emperor Domitian: he did something to check the rapacity of provincial governors. Some editors suppose that Nerva, who succeeded Domitian A.D. 96, is meant here.

place of plunder; and the goddess of victory, asking no more than victory, waved her wings unspotted by blood, in approval of herself. Thou too, O famous man,[a] defender of thy native city, didst win tears from the conqueror. Archimedes was calmly poring over a figure traced in the sand, when the great disaster came down upon him.

But the people generally gave themselves up to rejoicing; and the vanquished were as happy as the victors. Marcellus matched the gods in merciful temper and, by saving the city, was its second founder. Therefore it remains and will remain for ages as a splendid trophy, and will throw light on the character of our generals in former times.

Happy would the nations be, if our peaceful governors would imitate our former generals and spare the cities from rapine. As it is, if that prince[b] who has now given peace to the world had not checked the unbridled passion for universal spoliation, land and sea would have been stripped bare by greedy robbers.

LIBER QUINTUS DECIMUS

ARGUMENT

The Senate cannot decide what general to send to Spain. P. Cornelius Scipio is eager to go, but his kinsmen dissuade him (1-17). *He is visited by Virtue and Pleasure who contend for his allegiance* (18-128). *Encouraged by Virtue's arguments, he asks for the command and receives it : an omen of success* (129-151). *His fleet lands at Tarraco* (152-179). *His father's ghost exhorts him in a dream to take New Carthage : he does so* (180-250). *He sacrifices to the gods, rewards his soldiers, and distributes the spoil : he restores a Spanish maiden to her lover and is praised by Laelius for this action* (251-285). *War against Philip, king of Macedon*

At nova Romuleum carpebat cura senatum,
quis trepidas gentes Martemque subiret Hiberum,
attritis rebus. geminus iacet hoste superbo
Scipio, belligeri Mavortia pectora fratres.
hinc metus, in Tyrias ne iam Tartessia leges
concedat tellus propioraque bella pavescat.
anxia turba patrum quasso medicamina maesti
imperio circumspectant divosque precantur,
qui laceris ausit ductor succedere castris.
  Absterret iuvenem, patrios patruique piare
optantem manes, tristi conterrita luctu

[a] The father and uncle of Africanus : see xiii. 671 foll.

[b] Spain.

[c] Rome was further from Spain than Carthage was.

BOOK XV

ARGUMENT (*continued*)

(286-319). *Fabius takes Tarentum by a trick* (320-333). *The consuls, Marcellus and Crispinus, are beaten by Hannibal and Marcellus is killed* (334-398). *In Spain Hasdrubal is put to flight by Scipio: praise of Laelius* (399-492). *Hasdrubal crosses the Alps, to join his brother in Italy* (493-514). *Great alarm at Rome. The consul, C. Claudius Nero, is warned in a dream by a personification of Italy to march northwards against Hasdrubal* (515-559). *Nero joins the other consul, M. Livius* (560-600). *The battle of the Metaurus* (601-807). *Nero returns to Lucania and displays to Hannibal his brother's head fixed on a pike* (807-823).

But now the Roman Senate was harassed by a fresh anxiety. Who was to undertake the war in Spain and protect the natives discouraged by defeat? Both the Scipios,[a] both the brothers who had waged war with martial spirit, had been slain by the triumphant enemy. Thus there was a risk that the land of Tartessus [b] would now yield to the supremacy of Carthage, through dread of an enemy nearer home.[c] Meeting in anxiety and sorrow, the Senate sought for some remedy to heal the tottering state, and prayed to Heaven for a general who would dare to take over the decimated army.

The young Scipio was eager to appease the spirits of his father and uncle; but all his kinsmen, dismayed

et reputans annos cognato sanguine turba.
si gentem petat infaustam, inter busta suorum
decertandum hosti, qui fregerit arma duorum,
qui consulta ducum ac flagret meliore Gradivo.
nec promptum teneris immania bella lacertis
moliri regimenque rudi deposcere in aevo.

Has, lauri residens iuvenis viridante sub umbra,
aedibus extremis volvebat pectore curas,
cum subito assistunt, dextra laevaque per auras
allapsae, haud paulum mortali maior imago,
hinc Virtus, illinc virtuti inimica Voluptas.
altera Achaemenium spirabat vertice odorem,
ambrosias diffusa comas et veste refulgens,
ostrum qua fulvo Tyrium suffuderat auro;
fronte decor quaesitus acu, lascivaque crebras
ancipiti motu iaciebant lumina flammas.
alterius dispar habitus: frons hirta nec umquam
composita mutata coma; stans vultus, et ore
incessuque viro propior laetique pudoris,
celsa humeros niveae fulgebat stamine pallae.

Occupat inde prior, promissis fisa, Voluptas:
"quis furor hic, non digne puer, consumere bello
florem aevi? Cannaene tibi graviorque palude
Maeonius Stygia lacus excessere Padusque?
quem tandem ad finem bellando fata lacesses?
tune etiam tentare paras Atlantica regna

---

[a] The choice of Hercules between Virtue and Pleasure was the subject of a famous apologue by the sophist Prodicus: it is preserved in the *Memorabilia* of Xenophon (ii. 1 foll.), and Silius follows this version closely.

[b] Lake Trasimene.

[c] Spain, which is bordered by the Atlantic.

by their grievous loss and mindful of his youth, sought to dissuade him. If he went to that land of ill omen, he must stand on the graves of his dear ones to fight against a foe who had baffled the dispositions and beaten the armies of them both, and was now flushed with victory. Nor was it a simple task to take the burden of a mighty war on young shoulders, nor easy for a beardless youth to ask the command of an army.

These anxious thoughts filled the young man's mind, as he sat beneath the green shadow of a bay-tree that grew behind the dwelling; and suddenly two figures, far exceeding mortal stature, flew down from the sky and stood to right and left of him: Virtue was on one side, and Pleasure, the enemy of Virtue, on the other.[a] Pleasure's head breathed Persian odours, and her ambrosial tresses flowed free; in her shining robe Tyrian purple was embroidered with ruddy gold; the pin in her hair gave studied beauty to her brow; and her roving wanton eyes shot forth flame upon flame. The appearance of the other was far different: her hair, seeking no borrowed charm from ordered locks, grew freely above her forehead; her eyes were steady; in face and gait she was more like a man; she showed a cheerful modesty; and her tall stature was set off by the snow-white robe she wore.

Then Pleasure spoke first, confident in what she could promise: "This is madness, my son, to use up all the flower of your age in war. You deserve better things. Have you forgotten Cannae and the river Po, and the Lydian lake,[b] more terrible than the Stygian swamp? How long will you persist in defying fortune on the battle-field? Do you intend to attack the realm of Atlas[c] also and the city of

Sidoniasque domos? moneo, certare periclis
desine et armisonae caput obiectare procellae.
ni fugis hos ritus, Virtus te saeva iubebit
per medias volitare acies mediosque per ignes.
haec patrem patruumque tuos, haec prodiga Paulum,
haec Decios Stygias Erebi detrusit ad undas,
dum cineri titulum memorandaque nomina bustis
praetendit nec sensurae, quod gesserit, umbrae.
at si me comitere, puer, non limite duro
iam tibi decurrat concessi temporis aetas.
haud umquam trepidos abrumpet bucina somnos;
non glaciem Arctoam, non experiere furentis
ardorem Cancri nec mensas saepe cruento
gramine compositas; aberunt sitis aspera et haustus
sub galea pulvis plenique timore labores;
sed current albusque dies horaeque serenae,
et molli dabitur victu sperare senectam.
quantas ipse deus laetos generavit in usus
res homini plenaque dedit bona gaudia dextra!
atque idem, exemplar lenis mortalibus aevi,
imperturbata placidus tenet otia mente.
illa ego sum, Anchisae Venerem Simoëntos ad undas
quae iunxi, generis vobis unde editus auctor.
illa ego sum, verti superum quae saepe parentem
nunc avis in formam, nunc torvi in cornua tauri.
huc adverte aures. currit mortalibus aevum,
nec nasci bis posse datur; fugit hora, rapitque
Tartareus torrens ac secum ferre sub umbras,

[a] For the death of Paulus see x. 232 foll.

[b] P. Decius Mus gave up his life to save the Roman army in battle against the Latins, 340 B.C.; his son, of the same name, repeated the act of heroism in the battle of Sentinum against the Samnites, 295 B.C.

[c] A river of Troy.

[d] Aeneas.

[e] A swan, when he courted Leda.

Carthage? Take my advice, and cease to fight against danger and expose your life to the storm of clashing weapons. Unless you abandon the worship of her, stern Virtue will bid you dash right through battle and flame. She it was who sent your father and uncle down to the Stygian waters of Erebus, she who threw away the lives of Paulus[a] and the Decii,[b] while holding out a glorious epitaph on the tomb that covers his ashes to the ghost that cannot even be conscious of the great deeds he did on earth. But if you follow me, my son, then your allotted term of life will move along no rugged path. Never will the trumpet break your troubled sleep; you will not feel the northern cold nor the fierce heat of Cancer nor the pangs of thirst, nor take your meal many a time on the blood-stained turf, nor gulp down the dust behind your helmet, suffering fearful hardship. No: you will pass happy days and unclouded hours, and a life of ease will warrant you in hoping for length of days. What great things the gods themselves have created for the use and enjoyment of man! How many harmless pleasures they have supplied with bountiful hand! And they themselves set an example of peaceful existence to men; for they live at ease, and their peace of mind is never broken. I am she who wedded Venus to Anchises by the waters of Simoïs,[c] and from them was born the founder of your nation.[d] I am she who turned the Father of the gods into many different shapes: at one time he became a bird,[e] at another a bull with threatening horns. Attend to me. The life of man fleets fast away, and no man can be born a second time; time flies, and the stream of death carries us away and forbids us to carry to the lower world the things that

si qua animo placuere, negat. quis luce suprema
dimisisse meas sero non ingemit horas ? "
Postquam conticuit finisque est addita dictis,
tum Virtus : " quasnam iuvenem florentibus," inquit,
" pellicis in fraudes annis vitaeque tenebras,
cui ratio et magnae caelestia semina mentis
munere sunt concessa deum ? mortalibus alti
quantum caelicolae, tantumdem animalibus isti
praecellunt cunctis. tribuit namque ipsa minores
hos terris Natura deos ; sed foedere certo
degeneres tenebris animas damnavit Avernis.
at, quis aetherii servatur seminis ortus,
caeli porta patet. referam quid cuncta domantem
Amphitryoniaden ? quid, cui, post Seras et Indos
captivo Liber cum signa referret ab Euro,
Caucaseae currum duxere per oppida tigres ?
quid suspiratos magno in discrimine nautis
Ledaeos referam fratres vestrumque Quirinum ?
nonne vides, hominum ut celsos ad sidera vultus
sustulerit deus ac sublimia finxerit ora,
cum pecudes volucrumque genus formasque ferarum
segnem atque obscenam passim stravisset in alvum ?
ad laudes genitum, capiat si munera divum,
felix ad laudes hominum genus. huc, age, paulum
aspice—nec longe repetam—modo Roma minanti
impar Fidenae contentaque crescere asylo,
quo sese extulerit dextris ; idem aspice, late
florentes quondam luxus quas verterit urbes.

---

[a] Hercules. [b] Bacchus. [c] Castor and Pollux.

[d] A town in the Sabine country and a formidable neighbour to Rome in her infancy.

[e] The earliest settlement of Romulus was a Sanctuary for criminals.

gave us pleasure in life. Who, when his last hour comes, does not regret too late that he let slip the seasons of Pleasure ? "

When Pleasure had ceased speaking and was silent, Virtue began : " How," she asked, " can you mislead this young man in the flower of his age and tempt him to a life of obscurity ? The goodness of the gods has granted him reason and germs of the divine intelligence from heaven. Man stands as high above all other animals as the gods above mortals. For Nature herself assigned man to earth as a lesser god ; but her fixed law has condemned degenerate souls to dwell in the darkness of Avernus. On the other hand the gate of heaven stands open to those who have preserved the divine element born with them. Need I speak of Amphitryon's son [a] who destroyed all monsters ? or of Liber,[b] whose chariot was drawn through the cities by Caucasian tigers when he came back in triumph from the conquered East, after subduing the Chinese and the Indians ? or of Quirinus, the hero of Rome, or the Brethren [c] whom Leda bore, to whom sailors cry in their sore distress ? See you not, how the Creator raised the faces of mankind towards heaven and gave them countenances that look upwards, though he had caused all herds and flocks, all birds and beasts, to creep on their belly, inactive and unsightly ? But man is born for glory, if he can appreciate heaven's gift, and in pursuit of glory he is happy. Listen to me for a moment—I shall not go far for an example. Rome was once no match for the attacks of Fidena [d] and was content with the growth that the Asylum [e] gave her : but see to what a height she has been raised by the valour of her citizens. Consider too the cities which once spread and

quippe nec ira deum tantum nec tela nec hostes,
quantum sola noces animis illapsa, Voluptas.
Ebrietas tibi foeda comes, tibi Luxus et atris
circa te semper volitans Infamia pennis;
mecum Honor ac Laudes et laeto Gloria vultu
et Decus ac niveis Victoria concolor alis.
me cinctus lauro producit ad astra Triumphus.
casta mihi domus et celso stant colle penates,
ardua saxoso perducit semita clivo.
asper principio—neque enim mihi fallere mos est—
prosequitur labor: annitendum intrare volenti,
nec bona censendum, quae Fors infida dedisse
atque eadem rapuisse valet. mox celsus ab alto
infra te cernes hominum genus. omnia contra
experienda manent quam spondet blanda Voluptas.
stramine proiectus duro patiere sub astris
insomnes noctes frigusque famemque domabis.
idem iustitiae cultor, quaecumque capesses,
testes factorum stare arbitrabere divos.
tunc, quotiens patriae rerumque pericula poscent,
arma feres primus; primus te in moenia tolles
hostica; nec ferro mentem vincere nec auro.
hinc tibi non Tyrio vitiatas murice vestes,
nec donum deforme viro fragrantis amomi,
sed dabo, qui vestrum saevo nunc Marte fatigat
imperium, superare manu laurumque superbam
in gremio Iovis excisis deponere Poenis."

[a] The image of Jupiter in the Capitoline temple was a seated figure, and the triumphing general laid his laurels on the lap of the god.

flourished but were overthrown by luxury. For neither the wrath of heaven nor the attacks of foemen are as fatal as Pleasure alone when she infects the mind. She brings with her an ugly train, Drunkenness and Luxury; and dark-winged Disgrace ever hovers round her. My attendants are Honour and Praise, Renown and Glory with joyful countenance, and Victory with snow-white wings like mine. And Triumph, crowned with laurel, raises me at last to heaven. My household is pure; my dwelling is set on a lofty hill, and a steep track leads there by a rocky ascent. Hard at first—it is not my way to hold out false hopes—is the toil you must endure. If you seek to enter, you must exert yourself; and you must not reckon as good those things which fickle Fortune can give and can also take away. Soon you will gain the height and look down upon mankind below you. Pleasure makes you smooth promises; from me you will experience the opposite in all respects. Lying on a hard bed of straw, you will endure sleepless nights under the stars, and you will master cold and hunger. Also you will worship justice in all your doings and believe that the gods stand and witness your every action. Then, whenever your country and the danger of the state demand it, you will be the first to take up arms and the first to enter the breach in the enemy's walls; neither steel nor gold will ever master your mind. Therefore I will give you, not garments stained with Tyrian purple nor fragrant perfumes that a man should blush to use, but victory—victory over the fierce foe who is now harassing the empire of Rome; you shall destroy the Carthaginians and place your proud laurel upon the knees [a] of Jove."

Quae postquam cecinit sacrato pectore Virtus,
exemplis laetum vultuque audita probantem
convertit iuvenem. sed enim indignata Voluptas
non tenuit voces. " nil vos iam demoror ultra,"
exclamat. " venient, venient mea tempora quondam,
cum docilis nostris magno certamine Roma
serviet imperiis, et honos mihi habebitur uni."
sic quassans caput in nubes se sustulit atras.
At iuvenis, plenus monitis, ingentia corde
molitur iussaeque calet virtutis amore.
ardua rostra petit, nullo fera bella volente,
et gravia ancipitis deposcit munera Martis.
arrecti cunctorum animi ; pars lumina patris,
pars credunt torvos patrui revirescere vultus.
sed quamquam instinctis tacitus tamen aegra pericli
pectora subrepit terror, molemque paventes
expendunt belli, et numerat favor anxius annos.
Dumque ea confuso percenset murmure vulgus,
ecce, per obliquum caeli squalentibus auro
effulgens maculis, ferri inter nubila visus
anguis et ardenti radiare per aëra sulco,
quaque ad caeliferi tendit plaga litus Atlantis,
perlabi resonante polo. bis terque coruscum
addidit augurio fulmen pater, et vaga late
per subitum moto strepuere tonitrua mundo.
tum vero capere arma iubent genibusque salutant

---

[a] Her heart is compared here to an oracle.

[b] The orator's platform in the Forum. Scipio was now only twenty-four : he was a military tribune who had held no office higher than that of aedile ; yet he was now (211 B.C.) raised by a vote of the Assembly to the position of a proconsul commanding an army.

[c] The West, *i.e.* Spain : see note to i. 201.

When Virtue had uttered these prophecies from the shrine of her heart,[a] she gained Scipio to her side; he rejoiced in the examples set before him, and his face showed his approval. But Pleasure was wroth and could not refrain from speech. "I will detain the pair of you no longer," she cried; "but my time will yet come, when Rome will learn my lessons and be eager to obey my commands; and then I alone shall be honoured." Then, shaking her head with anger, she soared into the dark clouds.

Now Scipio, with a heart full of Virtue's counsel, conceived mighty designs and was fired with love for the high task imposed upon him. Though all men shrank from war, he climbed the high Rostrum[b] and claimed for himself the heavy burden of a doubtful contest. There was universal excitement: some thought they saw his father's face, and others that the stern features of his uncle had grown young again. But, though men were encouraged, yet an unspoken fear of the hazard crept into their doubting hearts; they measured with fear the huge burden of the war; and Scipio's supporters were uneasy when they reckoned up his years.

But while the people were considering these things, speaking low in their uncertainty, lo, a serpent, glittering with rough spots of gold, was seen to glide athwart the sky between the clouds, tracing a furrow of fire in the heavens, and it moved on towards the quarter where the sky ends in the shore of Atlas,[c] the supporter of the firmament. Nor was the sky silent; for Jupiter twice and three times confirmed the portent with his thunder, and his far-flung bolts crashed suddenly, and the heavens were shaken. Then indeed men fell on their knees to hail the portent;

summissi augurium: hac iret, qua ducere divos
perspicuum, et patrio monstraret semita signo.
Certatim comites rerum bellique ministros
agglomerant sese atque acres sociare labores
exposcunt; laudumque loco est isdem esse sub armis.
tum nova caeruleum descendit classis in aequor.
it comes Ausonia atque in terras transit Hiberas.
ut, cum saeva fretis immisit proelia, Caurus
Isthmon curvata sublime superiacit unda
et, spumante ruens per saxa gementia fluctu,
Ionium Aegaeo miscet mare. celsus in arma
emicat ac prima stans Scipio puppe profatur:
"dive tridentipotens, cuius maria ire per alta
ordimur, si iusta paro, decurrere classi
da, pater, ac nostros ne sperne iuvare labores.
per pontum pia bella veho." levis inde secunda
aspirans aura propellit carbasa flatus;
iamque agiles, Tyrrhena sonant qua caerula, puppes
Ausonium evasere latus Ligurumque citatis
litora tramittunt proris. hinc gurgite ab alto
tellurem procul irrumpentem in sidera cernunt,
aërias Alpes. occurrunt moenia Graiis
condita Massiliae: populis haec cincta superbis,
barbarus immani cum territet accola ritu,
antiquae morem patriae cultumque habitumque
Phocaïs armiferas inter tenet hospita gentes.
hinc legit Ausonius sinuatos gurgite ductor
anfractus pelagi. nemoroso vertice celsus

---

[a] Scipio was begotten by Jupiter in the form of a serpent: see xiii. 634 foll.; and the appearance of a serpent at this crisis was therefore invented by Silius.

[b] Not in person, but their hearts went with him.

[c] Neptune.

[d] What we call the Riviera.

[e] Emigrants from Phocaea in Asia Minor.

they urged Scipio to take arms and go whither the gods so clearly summoned him, and where his path was marked out by the image of his father.[a]

Men flocked eagerly to join him as comrades in war and helpers in the campaign, and begged to share his arduous labours : to serve in the same army with him was glory enough. Then a new fleet was launched on the blue sea. All Italy went with him[b] and crossed over to the land of Spain. So the North-west wind, when it has launched fierce battle on the deep, hurls the arching waves high over the Isthmus of Corinth, and, rushing over the bellowing rocks with foaming flood, mingles the waters of the Ionian sea with the Aegean. Then Scipio sprang up in arms and standing forth on the stern of his ship prayed thus : " Divine Lord of the trident,[c] whose deep seas we are in act to cross, if my design is just, suffer my fleet to complete her voyage, and deign, O Father, to assist our efforts. The war I carry across the sea is a just war." Then a light breeze blew, and drove the sails on with favouring breath. Quickly the vessels slipped past the coast of Italy, where the Tyrrhene sea splashes, and then their prows sped along the strand of the Ligurians.[d] And now from the deep they sighted far away the soaring Alps where earth invades the sky. Next came the city of Massilia founded by Greeks.[e] The settlers from Phocaea, though girt about by warlike tribes and horrified by the savage rites of their uncivilized neighbours,[f] still retain, among unpeaceful surroundings, the customs and manners and dress of their ancient home. Then the Roman general threaded his course along the curving coastline, till lofty hills with tree-clad tops were

[f] The Gauls, who sacrificed human victims to their gods.

apparet collis, fugiuntque in nubila silvae
Pyrenes ; tunc Emporiae veteresque per ortus
Graiorum vulgus, tunc hospita Tarraco Baccho.
considunt portu. securae gurgite clauso
stant puppes, positusque labor terrorque profundi.
  Nox similes morti dederat placidissima somnos :
visa viro stare effigies ante ora parentis
atque hac aspectu turbatum voce monere :
" nate, salus quondam genitoris, nate, parentis
et post fata decus, bellorum dira creatrix
evastanda tibi tellus, et caede superbi
ductores Libyae cauta virtute domandi,
qui sua nunc trinis diducunt agmina castris.
si conferre manum libeat coëantque vocatae
hinc atque hinc acies, valeat quis ferre ruentes
tergemina cum mole viros ? absiste labore
ancipiti, sed nec segnis potiora capesse.
urbs colitur, Teucro quondam fundata vetusto,
nomine Carthago ; Tyrius tenet incola muros.
ut Libyae sua, sic terris memorabile Hiberis
haec caput est : non ulla opibus certaverit auri,
non portu celsove situ, non dotibus arvi
uberis aut agili fabricanda ad tela vigore.
invade aversis, nate, hanc ductoribus urbem.
nulla acies famae tantum praedaeve pararit."
  Talia monstrabat genitor propiusque monebat,
cum iuvenem sopor et dilapsa reliquit imago.
surgit et infernis habitantia numina lucis

[a] At the battle of the Ticinus : see iv. 454 foll.

[b] There were three : Hasdrubal, son of Gisgo ; Mago ; and Hasdrubal, son of Hamilcar and brother of Hannibal.

[c] New Carthage, the chief arsenal and military base of the Carthaginians in Spain.

sighted and the forests of the Pyrenees were lost in the clouds; then came Emporiae, an ancient settlement of Greeks, and Tarraco next, where the grapevine is at home. There they found rest in harbour; the ships rode in safety behind the breakwater, and the fatigues and dangers of the sea were forgotten.

The profound stillness of night had brought slumber deep as death to Scipio, until he dreamed that the ghost of his father stood before him and warned him thus, while he was dismayed by the apparition: "Son who once saved your father's life,[a] son who bring me honour even in my grave, this land, the accursed mother of war, you must utterly lay waste; and the Libyan generals,[b] flushed with slaughter, you must conquer by valour and prudence. At present they keep their armies apart in three separate camps. If you chose to join battle, and they summoned their forces to meet from the different points, who could withstand the onset of three united armies? Abandon that dangerous enterprise; but bestir yourself and adopt a better plan. There is a city [c] here, founded by Teucer long ago; Carthage is its name, and the population is Punic. Like the Carthage in Libya, this Carthage in Spain is a famous capital. No other city can rival its stores of gold, or its harbour and lofty site, or its wealth of fertile land, or its skill and activity in forging weapons of war. Attack this city, my son, while the generals' backs are turned. No victory in the field could bring you as much glory and as much booty."

Thus his father advised him and was coming closer to warn him, when the young man awoke from sleep and the vision faded away. He rose up and prayed to the gods who dwell in the nether world, and

ac supplex patrios compellat nomine manes :
" este duces bello et monstratam ducite ad urbem ;
vobis ultor ego et Sarrano murice fulgens
inferias mittam fusis insignis Hiberis
et tumulis addam sacros certamine ludos."
praegreditur celeratque vias et corripit agmen
pernici rapidum cursu camposque fatigat.
sic, ubi prosiluit Pisaeo carcere praeceps,
non solum ante alios, sed enim, mirabile dictu,
ante suos it victor equus, currumque per auras
haud ulli durant visus aequare volantem.

Iamque Hyperionia lux septima lampade surgens
sensim attollebat propius subeuntibus arces
urbis, et admoto crescebant culmina gressu.
at pelago vectus servata Laelius hora,
quam dederat ductor subigendae ad moenia classi,
a tergo affusis cingebat tecta carinis.
Carthago, impenso naturae adiuta favore,
excelsos tollit pelago circumflua muros.
artatas ponti fauces modica insula claudit,
qua Titan ortu terras aspergit Eoo.
at, qua prospectat Phoebi iuga sera cadentis,
pigram in planiciem stagnantes egerit undas,
quas auget veniens refluusque reciprocat aestus.
sed gelidas a fronte sedet sublimis ad Arctos
urbs imposta iugo pronumque excurrit in aequor
et tuta aeterno defendit moenia fluctu.

Audax, ceu plano gradiens victricia campo

[a] Pisa is the place in Elis where the Olympian games were held : the race referred to is that in which four-horse chariots competed.

accosted the ghosts of his kinsmen by name with supplication: "Take the command yourselves and lead me to the city you have told of. You shall be avenged by me; and, when the Spaniards are routed, I shall stand conspicuous in gleaming Tyrian purple and offer sacrifice at your graves; and I shall honour your tombs further by sacred games and competitions." Marching in front, he quickened the pace and carried his army along at high speed, and scoured the plains. So at Pisa,[a] when the unbeaten race-horse has sprung forward from the starting-place, he moves in front of his rivals and also, wonderful to relate, in front of the horses harnessed to the same chariot; and no eye can follow the car in its flight through the air.

And now, as they drew near, sunrise on the seventh day of their march revealed the citadel of Carthage growing higher hour by hour; and the towers rose in height, the nearer the army came. Then, at the hour appointed by the general, Laelius came up by sea with the fleet and blockaded the city in the rear with a line of ships. Carthage is highly favoured by nature: its high walls are compassed by the sea; and a small island confines the narrow entrance of the bay, on the side where the morning sun showers his rays on the earth. But where the chariot of the setting sun is seen at evening, there is a barren expanse covered with standing water which the ebb and flow of the tide diminish and increase. In front of this lagoon stands the city facing the frozen North; it stands high on an eminence and runs out towards the sea beneath, and protects its walls by means of the eternal sea.

The Roman soldiers made haste to scale the

ferret signa, iugum certabat scandere miles.
Aris ductor erat. qui contra, amplexus in artis
auxilium atque excelsa loci, praesepserat arcem.
pugnabat natura soli ; parvoque superne
bellantum nisu passim per prona voluti
truncato instabiles fundebant corpore vitam.
verum ubi concessit pelagi revolubilis unda,
et fluctus rapido fugiebat in aequora lapsu,
quaque modo excelsae sulcarant caerula puppes,
hac impune dabat Nereus transcurrere planta :
hinc tacite nitens informidatus adire
ductor Dardanius, subitam trahit aequore pubem,
perque undas muris pedes advolat. inde citati
a tergo accelerant, qua fisus fluctibus Aris
incustoditam sine milite liquerat urbem.
tum prostratus humi, miserandum, victa catenis
Poenus colla dedit populumque addixit inermem.
hanc oriens vidit Titan, cum surgeret, urbem
vallari castris captamque aspexit eandem,
ocius Hesperio quam gurgite tingueret axem.
  Aurora ingrediens terris exegerat umbras ;
principio statuunt aras : cadit ardua taurus
victima Neptuno pariter pariterque Tonanti.
tum merita aequantur donis, ac praemia virtus
sanguine parta capit : phaleris hic pectora fulget ;
hic torque aurato circumdat bellica colla ;
ille nitet celsus muralis honore coronae.
Laelius ante omnes, cui dextera clara domusque,

[a] These were decorations awarded by the commander for good service ; they were of some precious metal and worn on the breast, like our medals. The *torquis* was a circular ornament worn as a collar. For the " mural crown " see note to xiii. 366.

height, as boldly as if they were carrying victorious standards over level ground. The leader of the defence was Aris. In his evil plight he trusted to the high ground for protection and had fortified the citadel beforehand. The nature of the ground fought for him: a slight effort of the defenders hurled many of the Romans from their footing; and rolling down the steep with mangled limbs, many breathed their last. But when the tide turned and the water of the lagoon flowed back fast into the sea, then it was possible to pass safely on foot over the place where tall ships had lately ploughed their furrows; and from this point, where none feared him, Scipio made his silent effort to approach the walls, bringing up the crews in haste from the ships and wading forward at speed. Thence they ran with all haste to the rear of the city, which Aris, relying on the sea, had left unguarded. Then the defeated Carthaginian prostrated himself—a pitiable object—and yielded his neck to the fetters, surrendering the disarmed inhabitants to slavery. Thus the sun, which at his rising saw this city surrounded by an army, also saw it taken, before he dipped his chariot in the western waters.

Dawn came on and expelled darkness from the earth. First of all, altars were reared. A tall bull was slain as an offering to Neptune, and another was sacrificed to the Thunderer. Then good service gained its due reward, and valour received the prizes earned by wounds. On one man's breast glittered bosses [a] of metal; another warrior put a circlet of gold round his neck; and a third displayed with pride the decoration of a "mural crown." Laelius, above all, famous for his exploits and his lineage,

ter dena bove et aequorei certaminis alto
donatur titulo Poenique recentibus armis
rectoris. tunc hasta viris, tunc Martia cuique
vexilla, ut meritum, et praedae libamina dantur.
Postquam perfectae laudes hominumque deumque,
captivae spectantur opes digestaque praeda :
hoc aurum patribus, bello haec Martique talenta,
hoc regum donis, divum hoc ante omnia templis,
cetera bellantum dextrae pulchroque labori.
quin etiam accitus populi regnator Hiberi,
cui sponsa et sponsae defixus in ossibus ardor ;
hanc notam formae concessit laetus ovansque
indelibata gaudenti virgine donum.
tum vacui curis vicino litore mensas
instituunt festoque agitant convivia ludo.
Laelius effatur : " macte, o venerande, pudici,
ductor, macte animi. cedat tibi gloria lausque
magnorum heroum celebrataque carmine virtus.
mille Mycenaeus qui traxit in aequora proras
rector, et Inachiis qui Thessala miscuit arma,
femineo socium violarunt foedus amore,
nullaque tum Phrygio steterunt tentoria campo
captivis non plena toris ; tibi barbara soli
sanctius Iliaca servata est Phoebade virgo."
haec atque his paria alterno sermone serebant,
donec Nox, atro circumdata corpus amictu,
nigrantes invexit equos suasitque quietem.
Emathio interea tellus Aetola tumultu
fervebat, Macetum subitis perculsa carinis.

---

[a] The " continence of Scipio " became a stock theme of later moralists.

[b] Agamemnon. [c] Achilles. [d] Cassandra.

received thirty kine, and a glorious decoration for his victory at sea, and the arms just stripped from the Punic general. Spears and martial banners were then awarded to each according to his deserts, and part of the booty was picked out for them.

When the services of men and gods were duly rewarded, the captured treasure was reviewed and the booty divided up. This gold was for the Senate, these talents for the purposes of war; the allied kings received presents, and the temples of the gods were enriched first of all; the remainder fell to the soldiers who had fought so nobly. Moreover, Scipio summoned the ruler of a Spanish tribe; this man had a promised bride, a maiden famous for her beauty, whom he loved passionately; and Scipio, joyful and triumphant, gave her back freely to her bridegroom who rejoiced in an unpolluted bride.[a] Then, with minds at ease, they set tables on the shore hard by and feasted and made merry. Laelius spoke thus: "A blessing upon your chaste heart, O noble leader! The praise and glory of mighty heroes, and their achievements famed in song, must hide their heads before you. The ruler of Mycenae[b] who launched a thousand ships, and he[c] who brought Thessalians to join the Argive ranks, were led by the love of women to violate the bond of alliance; and every tent then pitched on the plains of Troy was full of captive paramours; but you alone had more regard for the honour of a foreign maiden than was shown to Apollo's Trojan priestess.'[d] Thus and in this style they held converse together, until black-robed Night drove her dark steeds into the sky and wooed men to slumber.

Meanwhile the land of Aetolia, dismayed by a sudden invasion of the Macedonian fleet, was involved

proximus hinc hosti dextras iungebat Acarnan.
causa novi motus Poenis regique Philippo
in bellum Ausonium sociatae foedere vires.
hic, gente egregius veterisque ab origine regni,
Aeacidum sceptris proavoque tumebat Achille.
ille et nocturnis conterruit Oricon armis ;
quaque per Illyricum Taulantius incola litus
exiguos habitat non ullo nomine muros,
turbidus incessit telis. ille aequore vectus,
nunc et Phaeacum Thesprotiaque arva lacessens,
Epirum cassis lustrabat futilis ausis.
nunc et Anactoria signa ostentavit in ora
Ambraciosque sinus Olpaeaque litora bello
perfudit rapido. pepulit vada fervida remis
Leucatae et Phoebi vidit citus Actia templa.
nec portus Ithacae, Laërtia regna, Samenque
liquit inaccessam fluctuque sonantia cano
saxa Cephallenum et scopulosis Neriton arvis.
ille etiam, Pelopis sedes et Achaica adire
moenia praegaudens, tristem Calydona Dianae
Oeneasque domos, Curetica tecta, subibat,
promittens contra Hesperiam sua proelia Grais.
tum lustrata Ephyre Patraeque et regia Pleuron
Parnasusque biceps Phoeboque loquentia saxa.
ac saepe ad patrios bello revocante penates,

---

[a] Philip V., king of Macedonia, an ally of Carthage since 215 B.C., took sides with the Acarnanians against the Aetolians, who were Roman allies. For *Emathio* see note to iii. 400.

[b] Philip's mother was a daughter of Pyrrhus, king of Epirus, who traced his descent to Achilles.

[c] A seaport town in Epirus, near the Illyrian frontier. For the many places mentioned below an ancient atlas may be consulted.

[d] The Peloponnese.

in a fierce struggle with Philip [a]; and the Acarnanians, their next neighbours, made common cause with the foe. This new disturbance was due to an alliance formed between the Carthaginians and King Philip against the Romans. Philip had a splendid pedigree [b] and an ancient monarchy; he was proud to wield the sceptre of the Aeacids and proud of his descent from Achilles. He terrified Oricon [c] by a night-attack; and where the people of Taulas dwell in small and nameless villages along the Illyrian coast, he made a fierce assault in arms. He put to sea and fell upon the lands of the Phaeacians and Thesprotians, and rushed through Epirus with a campaign that led to nothing. At another time he displayed his standards on the coast of Anactorium, and overran with his arms the bays of Ambracia and the shore of Olpae. His oars stirred to fury the waters of Leucate, and he saw, as he rushed along, the temple of Apollo at Actium. Nor did he leave unvisited the harbours of Ithaca where Laërtes once reigned, or remote Same, or the rocks of Cephallenia against which the hoary waves bellow, or the stony fields of Neritus. He went further: he visited with special joy the land of Pelops [d] and the cities of Achaia, and approached the city of Oeneus that suffered from Diana's vengeance [e] and was once inhabited by the Curetes; he promised the Greeks that he would fight for them against Rome. Next he swept through Ephyre [f] and Patrae and the royal city of Pleuron, and Parnassus with its two peaks, and the cliffs that have a voice for Apollo.[g] Often too he was recalled to his own country by war,

[e] She sent the Calydonian boar to punish Oeneus for not sacrificing to her.

[f] Corinth.

[g] The oracle of Delphi is meant.

cum modo Sarmaticus regna infestaret Orestes,
aspera nunc Dolopum vis exundasset in agros,
incepto tamen haud facilis desistere vano,
belli per Graias umbram circumtulit oras :
donec, nunc pelago, nunc terra exutus, omisit
spem positam in Tyriis et supplex foedera sanxit
Dardana nec legem regno accepisse refugit.
Tunc et Tyndarei Latias fortuna Tarenti
auxit opes laudemque simul. nam perfida tandem
urbs Fabio devicta seni, postremus in armis
ductoris titulus cauti. sollertia tutum
tum quoque adepta decus, captis sine sanguine muris.
namque ut compertum, qui Punica signa regebat
feminea exuri flamma, tacitusque quietae
exin virtuti placuit dolus, ire sorori
(nam castris erat in Rutulis) germanus amatae
cogitur et magnis muliebria vincere corda
pollicitis, si reclusas tramittere portas
concedat Libycus rector. votique potitus
evicto Fabius Poeno circumdata telis
incustodita penetravit moenia nocte.
Sed quisnam aversos Phoebum tunc iungere ab urbe
Romulea dubitaret equos, qui tempore eodem
Marcellum acciperet letum oppetiisse sub armis ?
moles illa viri calidoque habitata Gradivo
pectora et haud ullis umquam tremefacta periclis—
heu quanta Hannibalem clarum factura ruina !—

[a] In 197 B.C. Philip was completely defeated by the Romans at Cynoscephalae, a range of hills in Thessaly, and had to accept harsh conditions of peace.

[b] A fearful crime or tragedy was supposed to cause the sun to turn back in the sky.

[c] The consuls for 208 B.C., Marcellus and T. Quinctius Crispinus, were entrapped by Hannibal in Apulia: the former was killed, and the latter soon died of wounds.

when the kingdom was attacked by the Orestae from Sarmatia or a fierce swarm of Dolopes invaded his country. Yet he was loath to abandon his useless designs, and carried on a pretence of warfare round all the coasts of Greece. But at last, stripped of his power by sea and land, he ceased to rely on Carthage and begged for an alliance with Rome and was forced to endure limitations of his kingly power.[a]

And now the fate of Tarentum, the Spartan city, increased both the power and glory of Rome. For that disloyal city was at length conquered by old Fabius, and this was the last exploit of that ever-cautious commander. Here also cunning won a victory without running risks, and the city was taken with no blood spilt. When he learnt that the commander of the Punic garrison was passionately in love with a woman, Fabius, a brave man but a lover of peace, adopted a stratagem. The woman's brother was present in the Roman camp; and he was compelled to go to his sister and promise a rich reward, irresistible to a woman's heart, if the Punic commander would open the gates and suffer an entrance to be made. The Carthaginian gave way, and Fabius gained his object: he surrounded the town with his army and entered it in the night when no guard was kept.

But when the news came at the same time that Marcellus had met his death in battle, who could doubt that the sun was then driving his steeds backwards [b] and away from Rome? That giant frame lay low; that heart, where the fierce god of war made his home and which never quailed before any danger, was cold; the terror of Carthage lay dead on the field.[c] How great, alas, that fall, that was to bring

procubuere : iacet campis Carthaginis horror,
forsan Scipiadae confecti nomina belli
rapturus, si quis paulum deus adderet aevo.
Collis Agenoreum dirimebat ab aggere vallum
Ausonio—Dauni Mavors consederat arvis.
curarum comes et summi Crispinus honoris
Marcello socius communia bella ciebat.
ad quem Marcellus : " gestit lustrare propinquas
mens silvas medioque viros imponere monti,
ne Libys occultis tumulum prior occupet ausis
si cordi est, te participem, Crispine, laboris
esse velim. numquam desunt consulta duobus."
haec ubi sedere, ardentes attollere sese
iam dudum certant in equos. Marcellus, ut arma
aptantem natum aspexit laetumque tumultu,
" vincis," ait, " nostros mirando ardore vigores.
sit praematurus felix labor. urbe Sicana
qualem te vidi, nondum permitteret aetas
cum tibi bella, meo tractantem proelia vultu !
huc, decus, huc, nostrum, lateri te iunge paterno
et me disce novum Martem tentare magistro."
tum, pueri colla amplectens, sic pauca precatur :
" summe deum, Libyco, faxis, de praeside nunc his,
his humeris tibi opima feram." nec plura, sereno
sanguineos fudit cum Iupiter aethere rores
atque atris arma aspersit non prospera guttis.
vixdum finitis intrarant vocibus artas
letiferi collis fauces, cum turba volucris
invadunt Nomades iaculis nimboque feruntur
aetherio similes, caeca fundente latebra
armatos in bella globos. circumdata postquam

[a] Apulia. [b] The consulship.
[c] Syracuse. [d] See note to i. 133.

fame to Hannibal! Perhaps, if some god had permitted Marcellus to live a little longer, he would have taken from Scipio the glory of ending the war.

The land of Daunus [a] was then the theatre of war, and a hill rose between the camps of the two armies. Crispinus shared the burden of command with Marcellus and held the same high office [b]; and they carried on the war together. To him Marcellus said: "I would fain search the neighbouring woods and station troops upon the hill that divides us; or Hannibal may steal a march on us and seize it before we do. If you approve, I should wish you, Crispinus, to take part in the affair. Two heads are better than one." When this was settled, all were eager to mount at once their mettled steeds. Marcellus saw his son fitting on his armour and enjoying the excitement, and said: "Your wondrous enthusiasm outstrips your father's exertions. May your youthful arm meet with success! How I admired you in the Sicilian capital,[c] when, too young to fight, you watched the battle with a countenance like mine! Come hither, pride of my heart, stay by your father's side, and let me teach the art of war to you, the tiro." Then he embraced the boy with this brief prayer: "Grant, O greatest of the gods, that I may offer to you choice spoils,[d] taken from the Libyan general, and borne on my son's shoulders!" Ere he could say more, Jupiter rained down a bloody dew from a clear sky, and dark drops fell on their ill-fated armour. Scarcely had Marcellus ceased speaking, scarcely had they entered the gorge of the fatal hill, when a swift troop of Numidians attacked them with the javelin, rushing on like a stormy cloud; and armed masses swarmed forth to battle from their ambush. When the brave

nil restare videt virtus, quod debeat ultra
iam superis, magnum secum portare sub umbras
nomen mortis avet. tortae nunc eminus hastae
altius insurgit, nunc saevit comminus ense.
forsan et enasset rapidi freta saeva pericli,
ni telum adversos nati venisset in artus.
tum patriae tremuere manus, laxataque luctu
fluxerunt rigidis arma infelicia palmis.
obvia nudatum tramittit lancea pectus,
labensque impresso signavit gramina mento.
  At postquam Tyrius saeva inter proelia ductor
infixum adverso vidit sub pectore telum,
immane exclamat : " Latias, Carthago, timere
desine iam leges ; iacet exitiabile nomen,
Ausonii columen regni. sed dextera nostrae
tam similis non obscurus mittatur ad umbras.
magnanima invidia virtus caret." alta sepulchri
protinus extruitur caeloque educitur ara.
convectant silvis ingentia robora ; credas
Sidonium cecidisse ducem. tum tura dapesque
et fasces clipeusque viri, pompa ultima, fertur.
ipse facem subdens : " laus," inquit, " parta perennis.
Marcellum abstulimus Latio. deponere forsan
gens Italum tandem arma velit. vos ite superbae
exsequias animae et cinerem donate supremi
muneris officio ; numquam hoc tibi, Roma, negabo."
alterius par atque eadem fortuna laborum
consulis : exanimem sonipes ad signa revexit.
  Talia in Ausonia. sed non et talis Hiberis

---

[a] The living have duties towards the gods ; but the dead, and those whose death is imminent, have no longer such duties: see Virg. *Aen.* xi. 51.

man, thus surrounded, saw that he owed no dues to the gods any more,[a] he was fain to carry with him to the world below the glory of a noble death. At one time he rose in the saddle to hurl his spear to a distance, at another he plied his fierce sword at close quarters. Perhaps he might have survived that dreadful pass of instant danger, had not a weapon struck his son's body in front. Then the father's hands shook, and his ill-starred shield, loosened by his grief, fell from his nerveless grasp. A lance came and pierced his undefended breast; he fell and marked the turf with the imprint of his chin.

But when Hannibal amid the rage of battle saw the weapon still sticking in the consul's manly heart, he gave a mighty shout: "Carthage, you need dread no longer the dominion of Rome! That name of terror, that pillar of the Roman state, lies low. Yet one who was my peer in battle must not go down unhonoured to the shades. In heroic breasts there is no room for jealousy." At once a sepulchral altar was raised on high. Great trees were brought from the forest; one might suppose that Hannibal himself had fallen. Then incense and meat-offerings, the consul's rods and his shield, were borne along in funeral procession. Hannibal himself lighted the pyre: "We have gained immortal glory," he said, "by robbing Rome of Marcellus. It may be that Italy will at last consent to lay down her arms. You, my men, march in the funeral train of that proud spirit, and give to his ashes the last tribute; never will I refuse to Rome this concession." The other consul fared no whit better in the battle: his horse bore him back to the camp, a dying man.

So things went in Italy. But far different was the

armorum eventus campis. Carthaginis omnes
per subitum raptae pernix victoria late
terruerat gentes. ducibus spes una salutis,
si socias iungant vires. ingentibus orsum
auspiciis iuvenem, ceu patria gestet in armis
fulmina, sublimi vallatam vertice montis
et scopulis urbem, cumulatam strage virorum,
non toto rapuisse die, qua Martius ille
Hannibal in terra consumpto verterit anno
nec pube aequandam nec opum ubertate Saguntum.
  Proximus, applicito saxosis aggere silvis,
tendebat, fratris spirans ingentia facta,
Hasdrubal. hic robur mixtusque rebellibus Afris
Cantaber, hic volucri Mauro pernicior Astur;
tantaque maiestas terra rectoris Hibera,
Hannibalis quantus Laurenti terror in ora.
forte dies priscum Tyriis sollemnis honorem
rettulerat, quo, primum orsi Carthaginis altae
fundamenta, novam coepere mapalibus urbem.
et laetus, repetens gentis primordia, ductor
festa coronatis agitabat gaudia signis,
pacificans divos. fraternum laena nitebat
demissa ex humeris donum, quam foederis arti
Trinacrius Libyco rex inter munera pignus
miserat, Aeoliis gestatum insigne tyrannis.
aurata puerum rapiebat ad aethera penna

[a] See note to l. 148.
[b] The brother of Hannibal, who fell in the battle of the Metaurus.
[c] Carthage.
[d] Hieronymus: see xiv. 97.

issue of warfare on the fields of Spain. The conquest of Carthage, made with such lightning speed, had terrified all the surrounding tribes. The Carthaginian generals were in a desperate plight unless they could unite their forces. They saw that the young commander had begun his career with a prodigious success, as if he wielded in battle the thunderbolts of his sire[a]; that within twenty-four hours he had taken a city defended by its site upon a lofty hill and its steep approach, and had heaped it with the corpses of the slain, whereas it had taken Hannibal, that great commander, fighting in the same country, a full year to overthrow Saguntum, so inferior to Carthage in population and wealth.

Nearest to Scipio lay Hasdrubal,[b] filled with pride in his brother's great deeds; his camp was pitched close to a tree-clad height. His main strength was in Cantabrians together with revolted Africans and Asturians, swifter than the nimble Moors; and Hasdrubal was as much revered in Spain as Hannibal was dreaded in Italy. It so happened that time had brought round an ancient Punic festival—the day on which the first foundations of the great city[c] were laid and a beginning of the new settlement was made with native huts. And Hasdrubal, recalling the early history of his country, made merry and kept high holiday, wreathing his standards with flowers, and seeking the favour of Heaven. Down from his shoulders fell a splendid mantle, a gift from Hannibal. Sicilian tyrants had worn this garment in state, and the king of Syracuse[d] had given it with other presents to Hannibal as a pledge of their close alliance. Two scenes were embroidered upon it. An eagle with golden plumage and outspread wings was carrying

per nubes aquila, intexto librata volatu.
antrum ingens iuxta, quod acus simulavit in ostro,
Cyclopum domus. hic recubans manantia tabo
corpora letifero sorbet Polyphemus hiatu.
circa fracta iacent excussaque morsibus ossa.
ipse manu extenta Laërtia pocula poscit
permiscetque mero ructatos ore cruores.

Conspicuus Siculi Tyrius subteminis arte
gramineas pacem superum poscebat ad aras:
ecce inter medios hostilia nuntius arma,
quadrupedante invectus equo, adventare ferebat.
turbatae mentes, imperfectusque deorum
cessat honos. ruptis linquunt altaria sacris;
clauduntur vallo, tenuemque ut roscida misit
lucem Aurora polo, rapiunt certamina Martis.
audax Scipiadae stridentem Sabura cornum
excepit, geminaeque acies velut omine motae.
exclamat Latius ductor: "prima hostia vobis,
sacrati manes, campo iacet. en age, miles,
in pugnam et caedes, qualis spirantibus ire
assueras ducibus, talis rue." dumque ea fatur,
incumbunt. Myconum Laenas Cirtamque Latinus
et Thysdrum Maro et incestum Catilina Nealcen
germanae thalamo obtruncat. cadit obvius acri
Kartalo Nasidio, Libycae regnator harenae.
te quoque Pyrenes vidit conterrita tellus
permixtum Poenis et vix credenda furentem,

Ganymede through the clouds to heaven.[a] And beside him was the likeness of a great cave where the Cyclopes dwelt, wrought by the needle on purple. Here Polyphemus lay, swallowing down with his death-dealing jaws the bleeding bodies of men; around him lay the broken bones ejected from his maw. He himself held out his hand to demand the wine-cup from Ulysses, and vomited forth blood mixed with wine.

Every eye rested on this garment, a triumph of Sicilian embroidery, while Hasdrubal, standing before altars of turf, prayed for the favour of the gods. But suddenly a mounted messenger brought news to the assembly that a hostile force was approaching. There was general dismay, and the worship of the gods was stopped in the middle. The rites were broken off and the altars abandoned. The Carthaginians sought the shelter of their camp, and, when dewy dawn kindled a faint light in the sky, they hastened to battle. When bold Sabura was struck by Scipio's whizzing spear, both armies took it for an omen and were moved by it. "Ye sacred ghosts," cried Scipio, "your first victim has bit the dust. On, ye soldiers! fight and slay! Rush on even as ye used to rush, when your generals[b] were still living!" Even while he spoke, they began the work. Myconus was killed by Laenas, Cirta by Latinus, Thysdrus by Maro, and Nealces, the incestuous lover of his sister, by Catilina. Kartalo, the ruler of African sands, was met and slain by fierce Nasidius. And the land of the Pyrenees[c] was afraid when she saw Laelius raging in the midst of the enemy with a fury beyond

[a] To serve Jupiter as cup-bearer.
[b] The dead Scipios. [c] Spain.

magnum Dardaniae, Laeli, decus, omnia felix
cui natura dedit, nullo renuente deorum.
ille foro auditus, cum dulcia solverat ora,
aequabat Pyliae Neleia mella senectae.
ille, ubi suspensi patres et curia vocem
posceret, ut cantu, ducebat corda senatus.
idem, cum subitum campo perstrinxerat aures
murmur triste tubae, tanto fervore ruebat
in pugnam atque acies, ut natum ad sola liqueret
bella : nihil vitae peragi sine laude placebat.
tunc et furtiva tractantem proelia luce
deiecit Galam ; sacris Carthaginis illum
supposito mater partu subduxerat olim,
sed stant nulla diu deceptis gaudia divis.
tunc Alabim, Murrum atque Dracen demisit ad umbras,
femineo clamore Dracen extrema rogantem ;
huius cervicem gladio inter verba precesque
amputat : absciso durabant murmura collo.
At non ductori Libyco par ardor in armis.
frondosi collis latebras ac saxa capessit
avia, nec caedes extremave damna movebant
agminis. Italiam profugus spectabat et Alpes,
praemia magna fugae. tacitum dat tessera signum :
dimissa in colles pugna silvasque ferantur
dispersi et summam, quicumque evaserit, arcem
Pyrenes culmenque petat. tum primus, honore

[a] C. Laelius, friend and companion of Africanus, played a conspicuous part in this war. His son, C. Laelius Sapiens, was the friend of the younger Africanus ; and this description by Silius is more applicable to him than to his father : he was known as Sapiens, and Cicero used his name as a title for his treatise " On Friendship."

[b] Homer compares the eloquence of old Nestor, son of Neleus, to honey. [c] See iv. 765 foll.

belief. Laelius[a] was the pride and glory of Rome, a man to whom bountiful Nature gave every gift and on whom every god smiled. When he spoke in the market-place and opened his eloquent lips, his words were as sweet as the honey that fell from the mouth of Nestor,[b] the ancient king of Pylos. When the Senate was doubting what to do and desired that an orator should address them, Laelius swayed all their hearts as if by magic. Yet Laelius too, when the fierce note of the trumpet had struck upon men's ears on the battle-field, rushed into the fray with such ardour that he seemed to have been intended by Nature for war only; no scene in life but he was determined to win honour from it. Now he overthrew Gala, a soldier who owed his life to a trick: his mother had saved him from the sacrificial fire of Carthage,[c] and had put another infant in his place; but no rejoicing lasts that is got by cheating the gods. Next he sent down to the shades Alabis, Murrus, and Draces; the last of these cried out in his extremity with womanish shrieking; but the sword severed his neck in the midst of his entreaties, and the lips still babbled when the head was off.

But Hasdrubal was by no means equally eager to fight. He sought concealment in forest-clad hills and pathless rocks, unmoved by the slaughter of his men and his terrible losses. He fled with his eye upon Italy and the Alps[d]—rich rewards for flight. The word of command went round in secret: the soldiers were to stop fighting and disperse among the woods and hills, and all who got off safely were to make for the highest peak of the Pyrenees. Hasdrubal set

[d] His purpose, which he carried out, was to make his way to Italy over the Alps.

armorum exuto et parma celatus Hibera,
in montes abit atque volens palantia linquit
agmina. desertis Latius victricia signa
immittit miles castris. non urbe recepta
plus ulla partum praedae tenuitque moratas
a caede, ut Libycus ductor providerat, iras.
fluminei veluti deprensus gurgitis undis,
avulsa parte inguinibus causaque pericli,
enatat intento praedae fiber avius hoste.
impiger occultis Poenus postquam abditur umbris,
saxosae fidens silvae, maiora petuntur
rursus bella retro et superari certior hostis.
Pyrenes tumulo clipeum cum carmine figunt:
HASDRUBALIS SPOLIUM GRADIVO SCIPIO VICTOR.

Terrore interea posito trans ardua montis
Bebrycia populos armabat Poenus in aula,
mercandi dextras largus belloque parata
prodigere in bellum facilis. praemissa feroces
augebant animos argenti pondera et auri,
parta metalliferis longo discrimine terris.
hinc nova complerunt haud tardo milite castra
venales animae, Rhodani qui gurgite gaudent,
quorum serpit Arar per rura pigerrimus undae.
iamque, hieme affecta, mitescere coeperat annus.
inde, iter ingrediens rapidum per Celtica rura,
miratur domitas Alpes ac pervia montis

---

[a] The gland, for the sake of which the beaver was pursued. This fable is mentioned by many writers of antiquity.

[b] The Pyrenees.

[c] See iii. 443: this phrase seems to stand for "Gaul" in general.

the example: putting off his splendid armour and carrying a Spanish shield for disguise, he fled to the mountains and deliberately left his army scattered in disorder. The Roman soldiers carried their victorious standards into the empty camp. Never did a captured city offer more plunder; and this, as Hasdrubal had foreseen, delayed the swords in their work of slaughter. So the beaver, when caught in the stream of a river, bites off the part of his body that brought him into danger, and swims away, while his captors are busy with their prize.[a] When the Carthaginians, trusting to the rocks and forests, had hastily concealed themselves in the woods, Scipio turned round, in search of more serious warfare and a foe whom he was more confident of defeating. They nailed up a shield on a peak of the Pyrenees with this inscription: "This trophy taken from Hasdrubal is offered to Mars by his conqueror, Scipio."

Meanwhile Hasdrubal, free from alarm, had crossed the mountain-range[b] and was arming the tribes in the kingdom of Bebryx.[c] He paid highly for soldiers and spent lavishly on war the wealth he had gained by war. The zeal of that spirited people was quickened by masses of gold and silver which he had got from mines far away and sent on ahead of his march. Thus the new camp was soon filled with a mercenary army—men who rejoice in the waters of the Rhone, and those through whose fields the Arar, most sluggish of rivers, creeps on. By now winter was wearing through and the season became milder. Thence Hasdrubal marched quickly through Gaul, and saw with wonder the conquered Alps and the passage over the heights; he looked for the print of

ardua et Herculeae quaerit vestigia plantae
germanique vias divinis comparat ausis.
  Ut vero ventum in culmen, castrisque resedit
Hannibalis, " quos Roma," inquit, " quos altius, oro,
attollit muros, qui post haec moenia fratri
victa meo stent incolumes ? sit gloria dextrae
felix tanta precor ; neve usque ad sidera adisse
invideat laevus nobis deus." agmine celso
inde alacer, qua munitum declivis ab alto
agger monstrat iter, properatis devolat armis.
non tanto strepuere metu primordia belli ;
nunc geminum Hannibalem, nunc iactant bina coire
hinc atque hinc castra, et pastos per prospera bella
sanguine ductores Italo coniungere Martem
et duplicare acies ; venturum ad moenia cursu
hostem praecipiti et visurum haerentia porta
spicula, Elissaeis nuper contorta lacertis.
  His super infrendens sic secum Oenotria Tellus :
" tantone, heu superi ! spernor contempta furore
Sidoniae gentis, quae quondam sceptra timentem
nati Saturnum nostris considere in oris
et regnare dedi ? decima haec iam vertitur aestas,
ex quo proterimur ; iuvenis, cui sola supersunt
in superos bella, extremo de litore rapta
intulit arma mihi temeratisque Alpibus ardens
in nostros descendit agros. quot corpora texi
caesorum, stratis totiens deformis alumnis !
nulla mihi floret bacis felicibus arbor ;
immatura seges rapido succiditur ense ;

---

[a] When Hannibal came close to Rome : see xii. 558 foll.

[b] Saturn, when driven out by his son Jupiter, fled to Italy, where King Janus received him kindly and made him a partner of his throne.

Hercules' foot, and ranked his brother's crossing with the exploit of that divine hero.

But, when he reached the summit and rested in Hannibal's camp, "How can Rome," he cried, "build walls high enough to withstand my brother, when even these barriers could not keep him out? I pray that his noble achievement may be crowned with success, and that no unfriendly god may resent our approach to the sky." Thence he hastened on his lofty line of march by a pass where the heights sloped down and showed a regular highway; and he flew down it with forced marches. Not even the first invasion caused as much terror and confusion in Italy. Men said that here was a second Hannibal; that the two armies were joining hands, and the two generals, gorged with Italian blood and with victory, were combining their forces and doubling their strength; the enemy would come in headlong haste to Rome, and there they would see still sticking in the gate the javelins which Carthaginian arms had lately hurled.[a]

In fierce anger at these things the Land of Italy spoke thus to herself: "Ye gods, am I so utterly despised by the madness of Carthage—I, who when Saturn feared the sceptre of his son, suffered him to settle within my borders and to reign there?[b] The tenth year is passing since Hannibal began to tread me under foot; that youth, who has only the gods still to defy, hurried an army against me from the ends of the earth; he made light of the Alps and came down in fury upon my fields. How many corpses of the slain have I covered! How often has my face been marred by the bodies of my own children! No olive-tree of mine is covered with a fair crop of berries; the corn in the fields is cut down

culmina villarum nostrum delapsa feruntur
in gremium foedantque suis mea regna ruinis.
hunc etiam, vastis qui nunc sese intulit oris,
perpetiar, miseras quaerentem exurere belli
reliquias ? tum me scindat vagus Afer aratro,
et Libys Ausoniis commendet semina sulcis,
ni cuncta, exultant quae latis agmina campis,
uno condiderim tumulo." dum talia versat,
et thalamos claudit Nox atra deumque hominumque,
tendit Amyclaei praeceps ad castra nepotis.
is tum Lucanis cohibentem finibus arma
Poenum vicini servabat caespite valli.
hic iuvenem aggreditur Latiae telluris imago :
" Clausorum decus atque erepto maxima Romae
spes Nero Marcello, rumpe atque expelle quietem.
magnum aliquid tibi, si patriae vis addere fata,
audendum est, quod, depulso quoque moenibus hoste,
victores fecisse tremant. fulgentibus armis
Poenus inundavit campos, qua Sena relictum
Gallorum a populis servat per saecula nomen.
ni propere alipedes rapis ad certamina turmas,
serus deletae post auxiliabere Romae.
surge, age, fer gressus. patulos regione Metauri
damnavi tumulis Poenorum atque ossibus agros."
his dictis abit atque abscedens visa paventem
attrahere et fractis turmas propellere portis.
Rumpit flammato turbatus corde soporem

[a] C. Claudius Nero, consul in 207 B.C. : for his Spartan descent see note to viii. 412.

[b] The name of a town and a little river in Umbria : it was supposed that the Senones, the invaders of 390 B.C., had given it its name.

[c] The river in Umbria, where the great battle was fought.

unripe by the swift sword; the roofs of houses in the country fall down into my lap, and make my realm hideous with their ruins. Must I endure Hasdrubal too who has invaded my devastated land and seeks to consume with fire the little that war has left? Then the African nomad will plough my fields, and the Libyan will commit seed to the furrows of Italy, unless I bury in one grave all those armies that tread so proudly on my wide plains." Thus she reflected; and while black Night shut in the slumbers of gods and men, she hastened to the camp where the scion of Sparta [a] lay. Behind his rampart of turf he was watching Hannibal, who was close at hand and kept his army within the limits of the Lucanian country. Here Italy in visible form accosted the general: "Glory of the Clausi and chief hope of Rome now that Marcellus is lost, awake instantly from slumber! If you desire to prolong the life of your country, you must strike a blow so bold that, even after the foe has been driven from our walls, the conquerors will shudder at the thought of what they have done. The glittering arms of Hasdrubal have covered the plains where the Sena [b] has kept for centuries the name given it by the Gallic tribe. Unless you lead your squadrons to battle with utmost speed, Rome will be destroyed and you will come to her aid too late. Up then at once and march! I have condemned the open fields by the Metaurus [c] to be the grave where the bones of the Carthaginians shall lie." Thus she spoke and departed; and, even as she went, she seemed to draw after her the hesitating general, and to break down the gates of the camp for the horsemen to rush out.

With a heart on fire Claudius sprang up in disorder

ac, supplex geminas tendens ad sidera palmas,
Tellurem Noctemque et caelo sparsa precatur
astra ducemque viae tacito sub lumine Phoeben.
inde legit dignas tanta ad conamina dextras.
quaque iacet superi Larinas accola ponti,
qua duri bello gens Marrucina fidemque
exuere indocilis sociis Frentanus in armis,
tum, qua vitiferos domitat Praetutia pubes,
laeta laboris, agros, et penna et fulmine et undis
hibernis et Achaemenio velocior arcu
evolat. hortator sibi quisque: "age, perge, salutem
Ausoniae ancipites superi et, stet Roma cadatve,
in pedibus posuere tuis," clamantque ruuntque.
hortandi genus—acer avet praecedere ductor.
illum augent cursus annisi aequare sequendo
atque indefessi noctemque diemque feruntur.

At Roma, adversi tantum mala gliscere belli
accipiens, trepidare metu nimiumque Neronem
speravisse queri, atque uno sibi vulnere posse
auferri restantem animam. non arma nec aurum
nec pubem nec, quem fundat, superesse cruorem.
scilicet Hasdrubalem invadat, qui ad proelia soli
Hannibali satis esse nequit? iam rursus, ubi arma
avertisse suo cognorit devia vallo,
haesurum portis Poenum; venisse, superbo
qui fratri certet, cui maxima gloria cedat
urbis deletae. fremit amens corde sub imo
ordo patrum ac magno interea meditatur amore
servandi decoris, quonam se fine minanti

[a] The Adriatic.

from his slumber. Then he raised both hands to heaven and prayed devoutly to Earth and Night, to the Stars that strewed the sky, and the Moon whose silent light was to lead them on their way. Next he chose out warriors fit for the mighty enterprise. His march lay through the country where the men of Larinum live hard by the Upper Sea,[a] where the warlike Marrucini dwell, and the Frentani, ever faithful allies in time of war, and where the men of Praetutia till the vine-clad hills and rejoice in their toil. On he flew, faster than wings and thunderbolts, than winter floods and Parthian shafts. Each man urged himself to speed: "Haste! haste! Upon your speed depends the safety of your country and the preservation or fall of Rome; so the doubting gods have decreed"; thus they cried as they rushed on. Instead of addressing them, their general was eager to lead the van, and in the struggle to keep up with him they went still faster; night and day they sped on and never tired.

But at Rome men trembled with fear, when they heard that the dangers of defeat were growing apace. They complained that Nero was too sanguine, and that a single disaster might rob them of all remaining life. "We have neither weapons nor gold nor men, nor any blood left to shed. Is he, forsooth, who cannot match Hannibal alone to attack Hasdrubal? Hannibal will come again and beset our gates, when he learns that our army has left its camp and gone far away. The new-comer and his haughty brother will contend for that highest prize—the destruction of Rome." Thus the senators protested in utter distraction; yet they were fain to maintain their dignity, and considered any expedient by which they

servitio eripiat divosque evadat iniquos.
hos inter gemitus obscuro noctis opacae
succedit castris Nero, quae coniuncta feroci
Livius Hasdrubali vallo custode tenebat.
belliger is quondam scitusque accendere Martem
floruerat primo clarus pugnator in aevo.
mox falso laesus non aequi crimine vulgi,
secretis ruris tristes absconderat annos.
sed, postquam gravior moles terrorque periclo
poscebat propiore virum, revocatus ad arma
tot caesis ducibus, patriae donaverat iram.

At non Hasdrubalem fraudes latuere recentum
armorum, quamquam tenebris Nox texerat astus.
pulveris in clipeis vestigia visa movebant
et, properi signum accursus, sonipesque virique
substricti corpus. bis claro bucina signo
praeterea gemino prodebat iuncta magistro
castra regi. verum, fratri si vita supersit,
qui tandem licitum socias coniungere vires
consulibus? sed enim solum, dum vera patescant,
cunctandi restare dolum Martemque trahendi.
nec consulta fugae segni formidine differt.

Nox, somni genetrix, mortalia pectora curis
purgarat, tenebraeque horrenda silentia alebant:
erepit, suspensa ferens vestigia, castris
et muta elabi tacito iubet agmina passu.
illunem nacti per rura tacentia noctem
accelerant vitantque sonos; sed percita falli

[a] M. Livius Salinator, Nero's colleague in the consulship: he had been condemned and fined for embezzlement after the Illyrian war of 219 B.C., and had retired from public life.

might escape impending slavery and the wrath of angry gods. While they lamented thus, Nero under cover of night entered the camp occupied by Livius [a] and defended by its ramparts against proud Hasdrubal who lay close beside it. Livius, once a soldier and a skilful commander in the field, had won great glory as a fighter in his youth; but afterwards he was condemned on a false charge by the unjust populace and had buried himself in dudgeon in the solitude of the country. But when a dangerous crisis and the fear of imminent danger demanded his help, he came forward again to serve, when so many generals had fallen, forgoing his resentment for the sake of his country.

But the secret arrival of a fresh army, though hidden from view by the darkness of night, did not escape Hasdrubal. He was struck by the traces of dust upon the shields, and by the emaciation of men and horses which proved the speed of their march; also the repetition of the trumpet-call revealed that two armies were here combined under two generals. But, if his brother were still living, how had he suffered the consuls to unite their forces? The only policy for him was to keep still until the truth was revealed, and to decline immediate battle. He resolved to flee, and his flight was not delayed by any sluggish fear.

Night, the mother of sleep, had eased the hearts of men of their troubles, and darkness deepened the dreadful silence of the hour. Hasdrubal crept out of his camp on tiptoe and ordered his army to slip out without speech or noise. The night was moonless, and they increased their speed over the sleeping country; they tried to make no sound, but the Earth,

sub tanto motu Tellus nequit. implicat actas
caeco errore vias umbrisque faventibus arto
circumagit spatio sua per vestigia ductos.
nam, qua curvatas sinuosis flexibus amnis
obliquat ripas refluoque per aspera lapsu
in sese redit, hac, casso ducente labore,
exiguum involvunt frustratis gressibus orbem,
inque errore viae tenebrarum munus ademptum.
  Lux surgit panditque fugam. ruit acer apertis
turbo equitum portis, atque omnes ferrea late
tempestas operit campos. nondum arma manusque
permixtae, iam tela bibunt praemissa cruorem.
hinc, iussae Poenum fugientem sistere, pennae
Dictaeae volitant ; hinc lancea turbine nigro
fert letum cuicumque viro, quem prenderit ictus.
deponunt abitus curam trepidique coactas
constituunt acies et spes ad proelia vertunt.
  Ipse inter medios (nam rerum dura videbat)
Sidonius ductor, tergo sublimis ab alto
quadrupedantis equi, tendens vocemque manusque :
" per decora, extremo vobis quaesita sub axe,
per fratris laudes oro, venisse probemus
germanum Hannibalis. Latio Fortuna laborat
adversis documenta dare atque ostendere, quantus
verterit in Rutulos domitor telluris Hiberae,
suetus ad Herculeas miles bellare columnas.
forsitan et pugnas veniat germanus in ipsas.

---

[a] Silius represents the soil of Italy as actively hostile to the invaders.

[b] Hasdrubal intended to retreat across the river at dawn.

[c] See note to i. 270.

[d] The Straits of Gibraltar.

trampled by so many moving feet, could not be deceived. She confused their tracks and made them lose their way in the dark [a]; and, favoured by the darkness, she made them go round and round without advancing and retrace their steps. For, where the river runs its winding course with curving banks and flows back over a stony bottom to meet its own channel higher up, there with fruitless effort the men went round and round in short circles, and made no headway; and the darkness ceased to help them when they had lost their way.[b]

Dawn rose and revealed the fugitives. The gates of the Roman camp were opened, an eager swarm of cavalry galloped out, and a storm of steel hid all the plains far and wide. There was no hand-to-hand fighting as yet; but already the missiles shot in advance drank blood. At one point, Cretan arrows, bidden to arrest the flight of the enemy, flew through the air; at another, the fatal force of the javelins brought death to every man whom they struck. Giving up all thought of flight, the enemy were forced to draw up their line in haste, and rested their hopes on battle.

In their midst was Hasdrubal, who saw the difficulty of their situation. High on the back of his tall charger, he stretched out his hands and raised his voice: "By the glory you have gained at the World's End,[c] and by my brother's achievements, I conjure you to show that Hannibal's brother is here. Fortune is fain to teach Rome a lesson by defeat, and to prove the might of an army which conquered Spain and fought many a time by the Pillars of Hercules,[d] and has now turned its attention to the Romans. It is possible that Hannibal may arrive just in time for

digna viro, digna, obtestor, spectacula pleno
corporibus properate solo. quicumque timeri
dux bello poterat, fratri iacet; unica nunc spes,
et poena et latebris infracto Livius aevo
damnatum offertur vobis caput. ite, agite, oro,
sternite ductorem, cum quo concurrere fratri
sit pudor, et turpi finem donate senectae."

At contra Nero: "quid cessas clusisse labores
ingentis belli? pedibus tibi gloria, miles,
parta ingens: nunc accumula coepta ardua dextra.
heu temere abducto liquisti robore castra,
ni factum absolvit victoria. praecipe laudem:
adventu cecidisse tuo memorabitur hostis."

Parte alia, insignis nudatis casside canis,
Livius: "huc, iuvenes, huc me spectate ruentem
in pugnas; quantumque meus patefecerit ensis,
tantum intrate loci: et tandem praecludite ferro
iam nimium patulas Poenis grassantibus Alpes.
quod ni veloci prosternimus agmina Marte,
et fulmen subitum Carthaginis Hannibal adsit,
qui deus infernis quemquam nostrum eximat umbris?"
hinc, galea capite accepta, dicta horrida ferro
sancit et, obtectus senium, fera proelia miscet.
illum, per cuneos et per densissima campi
corpora tot dantem leto, quot spicula torsit,

the battle. Make haste, I implore you, to prepare a scene fit for him to behold, by covering the field with corpses. All the Roman generals who could inspire fear[a] have been overthrown by my brother; their only hope now is Livius, and he, aged by his condemnation and seclusion,[b] is now at your mercy, a doomed victim. Go forward manfully, I entreat you! Lay low the general against whom Hannibal would be ashamed to fight, and put a merciful end to his dishonoured old age."

Nero on his side spoke thus: "Soldiers, why hesitate to end the struggle of this tremendous war? You have gained great glory by your march; now complete your enterprise by valour in the field. You left your camp and robbed it of its strength for no sufficient reason, unless victory justifies the deed. Be first to reap the glory; men will always tell how the enemy was defeated by your arrival."

At another point Livius addressed his men; he had taken off his helmet, and his white hair made him conspicuous. "Look hither, soldiers," he said; "look at me as I rush into battle. Fill with your bodies the passage opened up by my sword, and close once for all with the steel the Alps that offer too easy a passage to Punic invaders. If we fail to overthrow their ranks with a speedy victory, and if Hannibal, the thunderbolt of Carthage, comes up suddenly, what god can save a single one of us from the shades below?" Then he put his helmet on, and made good his threats with his sword, and fought amain with his grey head covered. Where the ranks of the foe stood thickest on the field, he slew a man for every javelin he cast;

[a] Flaminius, Servilius, Paulus, Marcellus.
[b] See note to l. 596.

turbati fugere Macae, fugere feroces
Autololes Rhodanique comas intonsa iuventus.
  Fatidicis Nabis veniens Hammonis harenis
improba miscebat securus proelia fati,
ceu tutante deo ; ac patriis spolia Itala templis
fixurum vano tumidus promiserat ore.
ardebat gemma Garamantide caerula vestis,
ut cum sparsa micant stellarum lumina caelo,
et gemmis galeam clipeumque accenderat auro.
casside cornigera dependens infula sacros
prae se terrores divumque ferebat honorem.
arcus erat pharetraeque viro atque incocta cerastis
spicula, et armatus peragebat bella veneno.
necnon, cornipedis tergo de more repostus,
sustentata genu per campum pondera conti
Sarmatici prona adversos urgebat in hostes.
tum quoque transfixum telo per membra, per arma
consulis ante oculos magno clamore Sabellum
asportabat ovans et ovans Hammona canebat.
non tulit hanc iram tantosque in corde tumores
barbarico senior telumque intorsit et una
praedam animamque simul victori victor ademit.
  Adsilit, audito tristis clamore ruinae,
Hasdrubal, et coeptantem Arabum raptare perempto
gemmiferi spolium cultus auroque rigentes
exuvias iaculum a tergo perlibrat ad ossa.
iam correpta miser geminis velamina palmis

---

[a] The Gauls whom Hasdrubal had brought with him.
[b] See note to i. 415. [c] The poison mentioned below.
[d] In imitation of his god.
[e] This was worn by priests, and might therefore inspire awe.
[f] A favourite weapon with Sarmatian and Scythian horsemen.

and before him fled in disorder Macae and warlike Autololes and the long-haired warriors from the Rhone.[a]

Nabis who came from the prophetic sands of Ammon[b] fought there with foul weapons.[c] He had no fear of death, thinking that his god protected him; and he had vowed, in his pride and folly, to fasten upon the temple of his nation trophies taken from Italy. His blue mantle was bright with Garamantian gems which twinkled like the stars scattered through the sky; his helmet blazed with jewels and his shield with gold. There were horns[d] on his helmet, and from it hung down a fillet[e] that displayed the wrath of heaven and the honour due to the gods. His arms were a bow and quiver and javelins steeped in the venom of asps; for he used poison for his weapon of war. Further, sitting back on his horse in the customary position, he supported on his knee a heavy Sarmatian pike[f] and drove it downwards upon the foes in front. Now too he had driven his weapon with a great shout through the shield and body of Sabellus, and was carrying off his victim in triumph and calling in triumph on the name of Ammon. But the aged consul saw it and resented such fierceness and such arrogance in the heart of the barbarian: hurling his javelin, he robbed Nabis of his victim and his life at one blow, and proved victorious over the victor.

Hasdrubal heard with grief the cry with which Nabis fell, and hastened up. Standing behind him, he drove a javelin through Arabus, piercing him to the bone, as he was beginning to strip the dead man of his jewelled garments and his armour stiff with gold. The hapless man had clutched the garments

carpebat propere et trepidos nudaverat artus.
concidit ac sacras vestes atque aurea fila
reddidit exanimo, spoliatum lapsus in hostem.
at Canthus Rutilum, Canthus possessor harenae,
qua celebre invicti nomen posuere Philaeni,
ditem ovium Rutilum obtruncat, cui mille sub altis
lanigerae balant stabulis. ipse, otia molli
exercens cura, gelido nunc flumine soles
frangebat nimios pecori, nunc laetus in herba
tondebat niveae splendentia vellera lanae,
aut, pecus e pastu cum sese ad tecta referret,
noscentes matres spectabat ovilibus agnos.
occubuit clipei transfixo proditus aere
et sero ingemuit stabulis exire paternis.

Acrius hoc Italum pubes incurrit et urget,
ut torrens, ut tempestas, ut flamma corusci
fulminis, ut Borean pontus fugit, ut cava currunt
nubila, cum pelago caelum permiscuit Eurus.
procerae stabant, Celtarum signa, cohortes,
prima acies ; hos impulsu cuneoque feroci
laxat vis subita ; et fessos errore viarum
nec soli faciles longique laboris anhelos
avertit patrius genti pavor. addere tergo
hastas Ausonius teloque instare sequaci
nec donare fugam. cadit uno vulnere Thyrmis,
non uno Rhodanus ; profligatumque sagitta
lancea deturbat Morinum et iam iamque cadentem.

---

[a] The Philaeni were two Carthaginian brothers who consented to be buried alive, in order to give Carthage the advantage in a boundary dispute with Cyrene. Their place of burial, near the Greater Syrtis, bore their name.

[b] Cp. iv. 311.

with both hands, tearing them off in haste, and had uncovered the quivering limbs. Now he fell over the body of the foe he had robbed, and gave back to the dead man the gold embroidery of his priestly robes. Then Rutilus was slain by Canthus, the lord of the coast to which the unconquered Philaeni gave a famous name.[a] Rutilus was rich in flocks: a thousand sheep bleated in his upland pens; and he himself, living at ease an unlaborious life, was wont now to temper the excessive heat for his flock by dipping them in the coolness of a river, and now, sitting well pleased upon the sward, to shear their shining snow-white fleeces; or, when the ewes came home from pasture, he would watch how the lambs in the pens recognized their dams. The treacherous metal of his shield was pierced through, and he died, lamenting too late that he had ever left his home and his sheep-folds.

All the more fiercely the Romans assailed the foe and pressed their attack, like a flood or a tempest, like the fire of a flashing thunderbolt, like the sea driven by the North-wind, like the hollow clouds that speed overhead when the East-wind has mingled sea and sky. In the front line under their standards the Gauls were stationed, men of great stature. Their ranks were broken by a sudden and violent attack in wedge-like formation; tired out by their straggling march, breathless after prolonged exertion, and distressed by the heat, they turned and fled with the unsteadiness characteristic of their nation.[b] The Romans speared their backs; and the arrows flew close behind them and cut off their retreat. Thyrmis was slain by a single wound, Rhodanus by more than one; and, when Morinus was struck by an arrow and in the act of falling, a javelin threw him from the saddle. Livius,

cedentes urget, totas largitus habenas,
Livius acer equo et turmis abeuntibus infert
cornipedem. tunc aversi turgentia colla
disicit ense Mosae. percussit pondere terram
cum galea ex alto lapsum caput, at residentem
turbatus rapuit sonipes in proelia truncum.
hic Cato—nam medio vibrabat et ipse tumultu—:
" si, primas," inquit, " bello cum amisimus Alpes,
hic iuveni oppositus Tyrio foret, hei mihi quanta
cessavit Latio dextra, et quot funera Poenis
donarunt pravi suffragia tristia Campi ! "
Iamque inclinabant acies, cunctisque pavorem
Gallorum induerat pavor, et Fortuna ruebat
Sidonia ; ad Rutulos Victoria verterat alas.
celsus, ceu prima reflorescente iuventa,
ibat consul, ovans maior maiorque videri.
ecce, trahens secum canentem pulvere turmam,
ductor Agenoreus subit, intorquensque lacertis
tela, sonat : " cohibete fugam. cui cedimus hosti ?
nonne pudet ? conversa senex marcentibus annis
agmina agit ; nunc, quaeso, mihi nunc dextera in armis
degenerat, nostrique piget ? mihi Belus avorum
principium, mihi cognatum Sidonia Dido
nomen, et ante omnes bello numerandus Hamilcar
est genitor ; mihi, cui cedunt montesque lacusque
et campi atque amnes, frater ; me magna secundum
Carthago putat Hannibali ; me Baetis in oris
aequant germano passae mea proelia gentes."

---

[a] This probably refers to the goitre or swelling of the throat by which inhabitants of the Alps were and are often disfigured.

[b] See l. 594 foll.

[c] The Guadalquivir.

with reins cast loose, pressed eagerly on the fugitives, and dashed his steed against the retreating squadrons. Then from behind he severed with his sword the swollen neck [a] of Mosa. The head and the helmet fell heavily upon the ground, while his frightened horse carried off the sitting body into the battle. Then Cato, who himself also was rushing to and fro in the centre of the fight, spoke thus: "Would that Livius had stood in Hannibal's path, when we lost the Alps at the beginning of the war! Alas! how mighty an arm Rome left unused! how many lives have been saved to Carthage by the harsh verdict of a misguided assembly!" [b]

By now the line was giving way; the cowardice of the Gauls had made cowards of all the army. The Fortune of Carthage was collapsing, and Victory had flown over to the side of Rome. Erect on his horse the consul moved triumphant, and seemed to have renewed his youth and added to his stature. But suddenly Hasdrubal came up, and a squadron white with dust followed him. Brandishing his weapons, he cried to his men: "Cease your flight! Who is the enemy before whom we are retreating? For shame! A feeble old man is putting our army to flight. Has my arm, I ask, waxed feeble for the first time in this battle, and are you discontented with me? Belus is the author of my line, and I am akin to Dido, the Tyrian queen; Hamilcar, most famous among warriors, was my sire; my brother is he whom neither mountains nor lakes, neither plains nor rivers, can withstand; mighty Carthage reckons me as second to Hannibal, and in the country of the Baetis [c] the tribes who have felt my arm in battle put me on a

talia dum memorat, medios ablatus in hostes,
ut nova conspecti fulserunt consulis arma,
hastam praepropero nisu iacit. illa per oras
aerati clipei et loricae tegmina summo
incidit haud felix umero parceque petitum
perstrinxit corpus nec multo tincta cruore,
vana sed optanti promisit gaudia Poeno.
Turbati Rutuli, confusaque pectora visu
terrifico. tunc increpitans conamina consul:
" femineis laesum vana inter cornua corpus
unguibus, aut palmis credas puerilibus ictum.
ite, docete, viri, Romanae vulnera suerint
quanta afferre manus." tum vero effunditur ingens
telorum vis, et densa sol vincitur umbra.
iamque per extentos alterna strage virorum
corpora fusa iacent campos, demersaque in undam
iunxerunt cumulo crescente cadavera ripas.
ut, cum venatu saltus exercet opacos
Dictynna et laetae praebet spectacula matri,
aut Cynthi nemora excutiens aut Maenala lustrans,
omnis Naiadum plenis comitata pharetris
turba ruit, striduntque sagittiferi goryti.
tum per saxa ferae perque ipsa cubilia fusae,
per valles fluviosque atque antra virentia musco
multa strage iacent. exultat vertice montis
gratam perlustrans oculis Latonia praedam.
Audito ante alios senioris vulnere, rumpit
per medios Nero saevus iter, visaque virorum

[a] This is supposed to refer to horns blown by women at the festivals of Bacchus; a raving Bacchant might be quite capable of scratching a censorious bystander. But the phrase is strange, and the text may be corrupt.

[b] Diana: see note to ii. 71.

[c] Latona.

[d] A mountain in Delos.

level with my brother." While speaking thus he rushed into the centre of the enemy, and, when the bright shield of the consul flashed full in his sight, swung his spear and threw it. His too great haste failed of success: passing through the border of the brazen shield and through the breastplate, it grazed the point of the shoulder; but it drew little blood, and the wound was slight. The triumph which it promised to Hasdrubal's prayer was not granted.

The Romans were dismayed, and their spirits fell at the fearsome sight. But Livius made light of the assault: "Believe that a woman's hand, amid the idle din of horns,[a] has scratched my skin, or that a child has struck me with its open palm. On, on, my men! and show what sort of wounds are dealt by a Roman arm." Immediately a huge cloud of weapons was discharged and veiled the sun with its thick shade. And soon by mutual slaughter the wide-spreading fields were covered with dead men's bodies, and the corpses that fell into the river were heaped up till they made a bridge across it. So, when Dictynna[b] goes a-hunting in the shady uplands, her mother[c] watches with joy and pride, while she beats the coverts of Cynthus[d] or traverses Mount Maenalus; and all her train of Naiads attend her, speeding on with full quivers and rattling bow-cases. Then the wild creatures, stricken among the rocks and even in their lairs, lie dead in heaps through valleys and streams and caverns green with moss. From a mountain height the daughter of Latona reviews her spoil with pride.

Nero heard sooner than the rest that the elder consul was wounded, and fiercely burst a passage through the midst of the fight. When he saw that

aequali pugna: "quid enim, quid deinde relictum est
Italiae fatis? hunc si non vincitis hostem,
Hannibalem vincetis?" ait. Ruit ocius amens
in medios; Tyriumque ducem inter prima frementem
agmina ut aspexit, rabidi ceu belua ponti,
per longum sterili ad pastus iactata profundo,
cum procul in fluctu piscem male saucia vidit,
aestuat et, lustrans nantem sub gurgite praedam,
absorbet late permixtum piscibus aequor.
non telo mora, non dictis. "haud amplius," inquit,
"elabere mihi. non hic nemora avia fallent
Pyrenes, nec promissis frustrabere vanis,
ut quondam terra fallax deprensus Hibera
evasti nostram mentito foedere dextram."

Haec Nero et intorquet iaculum; nec futilis ictus.
nam latere extremo cuspis librata resedit.
invadit stricto super haec interritus ense
collapsique premens umbone trementia membra:
"si qua sub extremo casu mandata referri
germano vis forte tuo, portabimus," inquit.
contra Sidonius: "leto non terreor ullo.
utere Marte tuo, dum nostris manibus adsit
actutum vindex. mea si suprema referre
fratri verba paras, mando: Capitolia victor
exurat cinerique Iovis permisceat ossa
et cineres nostros." cupientem annectere plura
ferventemque ira mortis transverberat ense

[a] Livy (xxvi. 17) relates that in 211 B.C. Claudius Nero, then a praetor, landed in Spain with 6000 men and caught Hasdrubal in a trap; but Hasdrubal was able to delude the

the battle was indecisive, he cried: "What still remains for Italy to suffer? If you cannot conquer Hasdrubal, how will you conquer Hannibal?" Then he rushed with wild speed into the centre of the foe and there saw Hasdrubal raging in their van. So a monster of the angry deep tosses long over the sea and finds no food; but, when the suffering creature sights a fish far off in the waves, in fury he marks his prey as it swims near the surface, and swallows down a wide tract of sea and the fishes within it. Nero was swift to strike and swift to speak: "No longer," he cried, "shall you slip out of my grasp. The pathless forests of the Pyrenees will not conceal you here, nor shall you cheat me again with empty promises, as you did once, when you were trapped in Spain and escaped my vengeance by the trick of a sham treaty." [a]

Thus Nero spoke and hurled his javelin; nor did he miss his mark. For the well-aimed point just lodged in the other's side, and he fell. Nero next attacked him fearlessly with his sword drawn, and forced down the trembling limbs with the boss of his shield. "If haply there is any dying message," he said, "which you wish carried to your brother, I will bear it." Hasdrubal answered: "No death affrights me. Take what battle gives you: it is enough for me that the avenger of my death will come quickly. If you wish to report my last words to my brother, this is my message: let him burn the conquered Capitol with fire and mingle my bones and ashes with the ashes of Jupiter." In the fierce anger of death he was fain to say more; but his conqueror's sword smote him and

Roman general by a pretended negotiation, under cover of which he drew off his forces.

et rapit infidum victor caput. agmina fuso
sternuntur duce, non ultra fidentia Marti.
Iamque diem solisque vias nox abstulit atra,
cum vires parco victu somnoque reducunt;
ac, nondum remeante die, victricia signa,
qua ventum, referunt clausis formidine castris.
tum Nero, procera sublimia cuspide portans
ora ducis caesi: "Cannas pensavimus," inquit,
"Hannibal, et Trebiam et Thrasymenni litora tecum
fraterno capite. i, duplica nunc perfida bella
et geminas accerse acies. haec praemia restant,
qui tua tramissis optarint Alpibus arma."
compressit lacrimas Poenus minuitque ferendo
constanter mala et inferias in tempore dignas
missurum fratri clauso commurmurat ore.
tum, castris procul amotis, adversa quiete
dissimulans, dubia exclusit certamina Martis.

[a] See l. 516.

struck off his traitorous head. When their leader had fallen, his troops, having lost all hope of victory, were mowed down.

And now dark night stole away the light and ended the sun's journey. During the night the Roman soldiers refreshed themselves with a frugal meal and brief slumber. Then, before the light returned, they bore their victorious standards back by the same route to the camp which fear kept closed. And Nero, carrying the head of the slain general aloft on a spear-point, spoke thus : " By your brother's head, Hannibal, we have repaid you in full for Cannae and the Trebia and the shore of Lake Trasimene. I defy you now to fight two treacherous wars at once and summon two armies to your side.[a] Such is the reward that remains for any who desire to cross the Alps and fight by your side." Hannibal suppressed his tears, and made the disaster less by bearing it bravely. He vowed under his breath that in due time he would yet sacrifice fit victims to his brother's shade. Meanwhile he concealed his reverse by inaction, removing his camp to a distance, and avoiding the risks of a battle.

LIBER SEXTUS DECIMUS

ARGUMENT

Hannibal moves about in the Bruttian country (1-22). *The Carthaginians are driven out of Spain: Mago is defeated and flees to Carthage* (25, 26). *Hanno is taken prisoner by Scipio* (28-77). *The army of Hasdrubal, son of Gisgo, is destroyed* (78-114). *Masinissa, a Numidian prince, joins Scipio* (115-167). *Scipio and Hasdrubal at the court of*

Bruttia maerentem casus patriaeque suosque
Hannibalem accepit tellus. hic aggere saeptus
in tempus posita ad renovandum bella coquebat:
abditus ut silva, stabulis cum cessit ademptis,
amisso taurus regno gregis avia clauso
molitur saltu certamina, iamque feroci
mugitu nemora exterret perque ardua cursu
saxa ruit; sternit silvas rupesque lacessit
irato rabidus cornu; tremit omnis ab alto
prospectans scopulo pastor nova bella parantem.
sed vigor, hausurus Latium, si cetera Marti
adiumenta forent, prava obtrectante suorum
invidia, revocare animos ac stare negata
cogebatur ope et senio torpescere rerum.
parta tamen formido manu et tot caedibus olim
quaesitus terror velut inviolabile telis

BOOK XVI

ARGUMENT (*continued*)

Syphax, a Numidian king: Syphax makes a treaty with the Romans; but evil omens follow (168-274). *Scipio returns to Spain and holds games in honour of his father and uncle* (275-591). *He returns to Rome and is elected consul: in spite of the opposition of Fabius, he gets permission to cross over to Africa* (592-700).

MOURNING over the disaster that had befallen his country and himself, Hannibal retired to the land of the Bruttii. Here, behind his ramparts, he nursed plans for renewing the war which for the time he had abandoned. So a bull, when driven from his stall and deprived of his mastery over the herd, hides in the forest and prepares for conflict in a secret distant glade: his fierce bellowing terrifies the woods; he rushes on over steep hills; he knocks down trees and assaults the rocks with the fury of his angry horns; and every herdsman trembles, when from some high cliff he sees him preparing to renew the strife. Hannibal's fiery spirit might have destroyed Rome, if the other requirements of war had been forthcoming; but he was thwarted by the perverse jealousy of his own countrymen. Supplies were refused to him, and he was forced to tame his proud spirit and let it rust in idleness. Yet his valour had gained him respect, and the dread inspired by repeated bloody victories in

servabant sacrumque caput ; proque omnibus armis
et castrorum opibus dextrisque recentibus unum
Hannibalis sat nomen erat. tot dissona lingua
agmina, barbarico tot discordantia ritu
corda virum mansere gradu, rebusque retusis
fidas ductoris tenuit reverentia mentes.
  Nec vero Ausonia tantum se laetus agebat
Dardanidis Mavors ; iam terra cedit Hibera
auriferis tandem Phoenix depulsus ab arvis ;
iam Mago, exutus castris, agitante pavore
in Libyam propero tramisit caerula velo.
  Ecce aliud decus, haud uno contenta favore,
nutribat Fortuna duci. nam concitus Hannon
adventabat, agens crepitantibus agmina caetris
barbara, et indigenas serus raptabat Hiberos.
non ars aut astus belli vel dextera deerat,
si non Scipiadae concurreret. omnia ductor
magna adeo Ausonius maiori mole premebat :
ut Phoebe stellas, ut fratris lumina Phoeben
exsuperant montesque Atlas et flumina Nilus,
ut pater Oceanus Neptunia caerula vincit.
vallantem castra—obscuro nam vesper Olympo
fundere non aequam trepidanti coeperat umbram—
aggreditur Latius rector, subitoque tumultu
caeduntur passim coepti munimina valli
imperfecta : supercontexere herbida lapsos
pondera, et in tumuli concessit caespes honorem.
  Vix uni mens digna viro, novisse minores

---

[a] The narrative now returns to Spain.

[b] Hannibal's brother and one of his chief officers : in the summer of 203 B.C. he was defeated in Cisalpine Gaul and died of his wounds on board ship, while returning to Carthage.

the past kept him safe from all attacks, like a sacred thing. The name of Hannibal was enough: it took the place of all weapons and camp-equipment and fresh recruits. That great army, of men with no common language and divided by so many differences of barbaric custom, stood firm; and respect for their leader kept them loyal in defeat.

Nor was it only in Italy that the god of war smiled upon the Romans.[a] The Carthaginians were driven at last from the land of gold and departed from Spanish territory; Mago [b] too, deprived of his camp and driven by fear, sailed swiftly across the sea to Libya.

Now once again Fortune, not content with what she had done for him already, was preparing another triumph for Scipio. For Hanno was hastening up at the head of a horde of barbarians with clashing targets, and was hurrying forward, when it was too late, the native Iberians. He had skill and cunning and valour enough, had his opponent been any other than Scipio. But the Roman general dwarfed all these great qualities by his greater force, as the stars are excelled by the moon and the moon by her brother's light; as Atlas is the monarch of mountains and the Nile of rivers; as Father Ocean is superior to all the seas. Hanno was fortifying his camp in haste—for evening had begun to throw an unfriendly darkness over him from the dusky heavens—when Scipio attacked him, and with sudden uproar the palisade they had begun to erect was knocked down uncompleted. The heavy sods were heaped on the top of the fallen men, and the turf became a soldier's sepulchre.

Scarce one of these men showed courage that

quam deceat pretiumque operis sit tradere famae.
Cantaber ingenti membrorum mole timeri
vel nudus telis poterat Larus. hic fera gentis
more securigera miscebat proelia dextra.
et, quamquam fundi se circum pulsa videret
agmina, deleta gentilis pube catervae,
caesorum implebat solus loca ; seu foret hostis
comminus, expleri gaudebat vulnere frontis
adversae ; seu laeva acies in bella vocaret,
obliquo telum reflexum Marte rotabat.
at, cum pone ferox aversi in terga veniret
victor, nil trepidans retro iactare bipennem
callebat, nulla belli non parte timendus.
huic ducis invicti germanus turbine vasto
Scipio contorquens hastam, cudone comantes
disiecit crines ; namque altius acta cucurrit
cuspis, et elata procul est eiecta securi.
at iuvenis, cui telum ingens accesserat ira,
barbaricam assiliens magno clamore bipennem
incutit. intremuere acies, sonuitque per auras
pondere belligero pulsati tegminis umbo.
haud impune quidem ; remeans nam dextera ab ictu
decisa est gladio ac dilecto immortua telo.
qui postquam murus miseris ruit, agmina concors
avertit fuga confestim dispersa per agros.
nec pugnae species sed poenae tristis imago
illa erat, hinc tantum caedentum atque inde ruentum.
per medios Hannon, palmas post terga revinctus,
ecce trahebatur lucemque (heu dulcia caeli

deserves to be known by posterity; only one is worthy of record. This was a Cantabrian, Larus by name, who could have inspired fear even unarmed; so gigantic was his frame. After the fashion of his nation he fought with a battle-axe; and, though he saw the ranks around him defeated and overthrown, yet, when all his countrymen were destroyed, he filled single-handed the places of the slain. If his foe stood face to face, Larus rejoiced to glut his rage by smiting him on the forehead; or, if he was forced to meet an enemy on his left hand, he whirled his weapon round and struck a sidelong blow. Or, when a victorious foe attacked him from behind, he was not dismayed but could ply his axe in that direction, a formidable fighter all round. But Scipio, the brother of the invincible general, hurled a spear with mighty force at Larus, which cut off the plume that fluttered on his leathern cap; for the weapon was aimed too high, and the lifted axe diverted it to a distance. Then the Spaniard, made more formidable by his furious anger, sprang up with a loud cry and struck with his barbarous weapon. Both armies trembled, and loud rang the boss of Scipio's shield when the heavy battle-axe came down upon it. But he paid dear for the blow: his right hand as it recovered from the stroke was lopped off by Scipio's sword and clung in death to its favourite weapon. When this bulwark had fallen, the ill-fated army turned at once and fled as one man and were scattered over the land. It was less like a battle than a scene of ruthless execution—slayers on one side and slaughtered on the other. Now see Hanno dragged through the midst of the throng, his hands bound behind his back; though a captive in bonds, he begged for life. Ah,

lumina !) captivus lucem inter vincla petebat.
cui rector Latius : " tanta, en, qui regna reposcant,
quis cedat toga et armiferi gens sacra Quirini !
servitio si tam faciles, cur bella refertis ? "
  Haec inter celerare gradum, coniungat ut arma,
Hasdrubalem ignarum cladis praenuntius affert
explorator eques. raptat dux obvia signa
ac, postquam optatam laetus contingere pugnam
vidit et ad letum magno venientia cursu
agmina, suspiciens caelum : " nil amplius," inquit,
" vos hodie posco, superi. protraxtis ad arma
quod profugos, satis est. in dextra cetera nobis
vota, viri ; rapite, ite, precor. vocat ecce furentes
hinc pater, hinc patruus. gemina o mihi numina belli,
ducite, adeste ; sequor. dignas spectabitis, aut me
praescia mens fallit, vestro iam nomine caedes.
nam quis erit tandem campis telluris Hiberae
bellandi modus ? en umquam lucebit in orbe
ille dies, quo te armorum, Carthago, meorum
aspiciam sonitus admotaque bella trementem ? "
  Dixerat, et raucus stridenti murmure clangor
increpuit ; tonuere feris clamoribus astra.
concurrunt ; quantumque rapit violentia ponti
et Notus et Boreas et inexorabilis Auster,
cum mergunt plenas tumefacta sub aequora classes ;
aut cum letiferos accendens Sirius ignes
torret anhelantem saevis ardoribus orbem ;
tantum acies hominumque ferox discordia ferro

---

[a] The son of Gisco.

[b] The dog-star, whose appearance in summer the ancients connected with epidemics and plagues.

how sweet to see the light of heaven! The Roman general answered thus: "These are the men who claim to rule the world, before whom the Roman gown and the sacred nation of warlike Quirinus must bow! If you are so ready to be slaves, why do you make war afresh?"

Meanwhile a mounted scout brought tidings that Hasdrubal,[a] unaware of the defeat, was coming up in haste to join the other army. Scipio rushed his men to meet him; and when he saw the battle he longed for within his grasp and the foe marching at full speed to death, he looked up to heaven and said: "Ye gods, I ask no more of you to-day. Ye have brought the fugitives forth to battle, and I am content. The rest depends upon your valour, my men: hasten forward, I pray you! My father here, my uncle there, stir your rage. Go ye before me and help me—I follow you, my twin gods of war. Unless my prophetic soul deceives me, ye shall see to-day a slaughter worthy of your fame. Will there ever come an end of fighting on these Spanish plains? Will that day ever dawn on earth, when I shall see Carthage trembling before the clash of my weapons and the near approach of my army?"

He ended; and the hoarse note and loud blare of the trumpets broke out, and the sky thundered with cries of battle. Then the armies met. Many are the victims claimed by the fury of the sea, when the North-wind and pitiless South-winds whelm fleets with their crews beneath the swollen waves; and many by Sirius,[b] when he kindles his deadly fires and burns up the panting earth with his fierce heat; and no less havoc was wrought by the sword in this battle and by the furious strife of men. No upheaval of

demetit. haud ullus terrarum aequarit hiatus
pugnarum damna ; aut strages per inhospita lustra
umquam tot dederit rabies horrenda ferarum.
iam campi vallesque madent, hebetataque tela.
et Libys occubuere et amantes Martis Hiberi.
stat tamen una loco perfossis debilis armis
luctaturque acies, qua concutit Hasdrubal hastam.
nec finem daret ille dies animosaque virtus,
ni perlapsa viro loricae tegmine harundo
et parco summum violasset vulnere corpus
suasissetque fugam. rapido certamina linquit
in latebras evectus equo noctisque per umbram
ad Tartessiacos tendit per litora portus.
  Proximus in pugna ductori Marte manuque
regnator Nomadum fuerat, mox foedere longo
cultuque Aeneadum nomen Masinissa superbum.
huic fesso, quos dura fuga et nox suaserat atra,
carpenti somnos subitus rutilante coruscum
vertice fulsit apex, crispamque involvere visa est
mitis flamma comam atque hirta se spargere fronte.
concurrunt famuli et serpentes tempora circum
festinant gelidis restinguere fontibus ignes.
at grandaeva, deum praenoscens omina, mater :
" sic sit, caelicolae ; portentaque vestra secundi
condite," ait. " duret capiti per saecula lumen.
ne vero, ne, nate, deum tam laeta pavesce
prodigia aut sacras metue inter tempora flammas.
hic tibi Dardaniae promittit foedera gentis,
hic tibi regna dabit regnis maiora paternis,

---

[a] Masinissa, now sixteen years old, had commanded Hasdrubal's cavalry. The prophetic fire is an invention of the poet's, who remembered that the elevation of Servius Tullius and of Ascanius was thus presaged. But is it likely that Masinissa should take his aged mother upon a foreign campaign ?

the earth could cost as many lives; and no fearful rage of wild beasts could ever work such carnage in their savage haunts. Plains and valleys soon were soaked, and weapons lost their edge. Africans and warlike Spaniards fell alike, Yet, where Hasdrubal brandished his spear, one body of men still held its ground and fought on, though their shields were pierced and their resistance was feeble. Nor would that day have ended the struggle, nor that courage have failed, had not an arrow pierced Hasdrubal's corslet, inflicting a slight surface wound. Thus tempted to flight, he galloped away from the battle-field to a hiding-place, and then under cover of night rode on along the coast to the harbour at Tartessus.

Masinissa,[a] a Numidian prince, had been Hasdrubal's right-hand man in the battle; and his name became famous later for his long alliance with Rome and his devotion to her. The darkness of night and the hardships of retreat had made sleep welcome; and he was sleeping, tired out, when suddenly a ruddy tongue of fire was seen to burn bright on the crown of his head; the harmless flame caught his curling locks and spread over his shaggy brow. His servants came round in haste and strove to quench with cold water the flames that were creeping round his temples. But his aged mother recognized a divine omen and said: "Be it so, ye gods! Be propitious and ratify your portent. May the light shine on his head for centuries to come! And you, my son, fear not such a favourable sign from heaven, and let not the sacred flame on your brow alarm you. This fire assures you of an alliance with the Roman people; this fire will bring you a kingdom wider than your fathers ever ruled, and shall add your name to the

ignis, et adiunget Latiis tua nomina fastis."
sic vates, iuvenisque animum tam clara movebant
monstra, nec a Poenis ulli virtutis honores,
Hannibal ipse etiam iam iamque modestior armis.
  Aurora obscuri tergebat nubila caeli
vixque Atlantiadum rubefecerat ora sororum:
tendit in Ausonios et adhuc hostilia castra.
atque, ubi se vallo intulerat, ductorque benigno
accepit Latius vultu, rex talibus infit:
"caelestum monita et sacrae responsa parentis
disque tua, o Rutulum rector, gratissima virtus
avulsum Tyriis huc me duxere volentem.
si tibi non segnes tua contra fulmina saepe
visi stare sumus, dignam te, nate Tonantis,
afferimus dextram. nec nos aut vana subegit
incertae mentis levitas et mobile pectus,
aut spes et laeti sectamur praemia Martis;
perfidiam fugio et periuram ab origine gentem.
tu, quando Herculeis finisti proelia metis,
nunc ipsam belli nobiscum invade parentem.
ille tibi, qui iam gemino Laurentia lustro
possedit regna et scalas ad moenia Romae
admovet, in Libyam flammis ferroque trahendus.
  Sic Nomadum ductor. tunc dextra Scipio dextram
amplexus: "si pulchra tibi Mavorte videtur,
pulchrior est gens nostra fide. dimitte bilingues
ex animo socios. magna hinc te praemia clarae
virtutis, Masinissa, manent; citiusque vel armis

[a] This sentence gives two additional reasons for Masinissa's change of sides.
[b] The Pleiades, which set in autumn about sunrise.
[c] See note to xiii. 637.
[d] Carthage.
[e] *i.e.* deceitful.

history of Rome." Thus spoke the prophetess; and the young man's heart was moved by a miracle so unmistakable. Also, his valour had received no recognition from Carthage; and even Hannibal bore himself less proudly day by day in the field.[a]

Dawn was clearing away the dark clouds from the sky and had hardly tinged with red the faces of Atlas's daughters,[b] when Masinissa made his way to the camp of the Romans, still his foes. When he had passed the rampart and was received by the Roman general with friendly looks, the king thus began: "The warning of the gods and the prophecy of my revered mother, together with your great deeds so blest of Heaven, have torn me away from the Carthaginians and brought me hither unreluctant to you, the leader of the Roman army. If you saw me many a time resisting your thunderbolts, then, O son of the Thunder-god,[c] I offer you an arm worthy your acceptance. I have not acted thus from foolish fickleness of mind or instability of purpose, nor is my heart set on the rewards of victorious warfare; but treachery I cannot bear and a nation that has ever been false. Your campaign as far as the Pillars of Hercules is completed; let us now together attack the mother of war[d] herself. With fire and sword you must force back to Libya the man who for twice five years has been the master of Italy and is now planting his ladders against the walls of Rome."

Thus spoke the king of Numidia. Then Scipio grasped his hand and said: "If our nation seems to you noble in war, she is nobler still in keeping of her word. Banish from your mind those double-tongued[e] allies. We offer you splendid rewards, Masinissa, for noble service; and Scipio will sooner be overcome

quam gratae studio vincetur Scipio mentis.
cetera quae Libyam portari incendia suades,
expediet tempus ; nec enim sunt talia rerum
non meditata mihi, et mentem Carthago fatigat."
hinc iuveni dona insignem velamine picto
dat chlamydem stratumque ostro, quem ceperat ipse
deiecto victor Magone animique probarat,
cornipedem ; tum, qua divum libabat ad aras
Hasdrubal, ex auro pateram galeamque comantem.
exin, firmato sociali foedere regis,
vertendas agitat iam nunc Carthaginis arces.

Massylis regnator erat ditissimus oris
nec nudus virtute Syphax ; quo iura petebant
innumerae gentes extremaque litore Tethys.
multa viro terra ac sonipes et belua, terror
bellorum, nec non Marti delecta iuventus.
nec foret, aut ebore aut solido qui vinceret auro
Gaetulisve magis fucaret vellus aënis.
has adiungere opes avidus reputansque laborem,
si vertat rex ad Poenos, dare vela per altum
imperat atque animo iam tum Africa bella capessit.
verum ubi perventum, et portus tenuere carinae,
iam, trepida fugiens per proxima litora puppe,
Hasdrubal afflictis aderat nova foedera quaerens
rebus et ad Tyrios Massylia signa trahebat.

---

[a] Syphax was in fact king of the Masaesyli, who occupied the western part of the extensive country called loosely by the Romans Numidia: he was a ruling sovereign, while Masinissa's father, Gala, was still king of the Massyli or eastern Numidians. [b] Elephants.

[c] Gaetulia was a district of Africa where the natives made a purple dye from shell-fish: cp. l. 569.

in battle than in gratitude for benefits received. Further, you bid me carry fire-brands to Libya. Time will clear the way. For I have not failed to ponder such matters, and the thought of Carthage gives me no rest." Then he gave presents to the prince—a richly embroidered mantle and a steed with purple housings which Scipio himself had taken when he unhorsed Mago, and had approved for its mettle; also a golden bowl from which Hasdrubal was wont to pour libation to the gods, and a crested helmet. When the treaty of alliance with Masinissa was concluded, forthwith Scipio laid his plans for overthrowing at once the towers of Carthage.

In the Massylian country Syphax [a] was the richest prince; nor was he lacking in noble qualities. His sway was owned by countless tribes, and his power extended as far as the Ocean. He was rich in territory and in horses, and in those huge beasts [b] that spread terror on the battle-field; he had also an army of picked soldiers. Nor was there any man richer than he in ivory and solid gold, and none who dyed more fleeces in vats of Gaetulia.[c] Scipio, eager to annex these resources and conscious of the danger if the king were to side with Carthage, ordered ships to put to sea and, in fancy, was already making war in Africa. But when the voyage was over and the ships made the harbour, Hasdrubal,[d] who was sailing in hasty retreat along the neighbouring coast, made his appearance, seeking new allies for his distressed country, and tried to gain the Massylian army for Carthage.

[d] Son of Gisco. This meeting of Scipio and Hasdrubal at the court of Syphax is historical; Livy mentions it.

Audito pariter populorum in regna duorum
advenisse duces, qui tota mole laborent
disceptentque armis, terrarum uter imperet orbi,
celsus mente Syphax acciri in tecta benigne
imperat et tanto regni se tollit honore.
tum laetos volvens oculos adversa per ora,
sic Latium affatur iuvenem ac prior incipit ultro :
" quam te, Dardanide pulcherrime, mente serena
accipio intueorque libens ! quamque ora recordor
laetus Scipiadae ! revocat tua forma parentem.
nam repeto, Herculeas Erythia ad litora Gades
cum studio pelagi et spectandis aestibus undae
venissem, magnos vicina ad flumina Baetis
ductores miro quodam me cernere amore.
tum mihi dona viri praeda delecta tulere,
arma simul regnoque meo tum cognita primum
cornipedum frena atque arcus, qui cedere nostris
non norunt iaculis, et veteres tribuere magistros
militiae, qui dispersas sine lege catervas
vestro formarent ritu ad certamina Martis.
ast ego, cum contra, nostris quae copia regnis,
nunc auri ferrem, nivei nunc munera dentis,
nil valui precibus : solos sibi cepit uterque,
quos cohibebat ebur vaginae sectilis, enses.
quare, age, laetus ave nostros intrare penates.
ac, mea quando affert Libycum fortuna per undas
ductorem, facili, quae dicam, percipe mente.
et vos, qui Tyriae regitis Carthaginis arces,
Hasdrubal, huc aures, huc quaeso advertite sensus.
quanta per Ausonios populos torrentibus armis

[a] An ancient name of the island on which the city of Gades was built. For the tides see note to iii. 46.

[b] The two Scipios. [c] The Guadalquivir.

When Syphax heard that the generals of two great nations had come at the same time to his capital—nations which were at war and striving with might and main to decide which of them should rule the world—his heart was lifted up. He ordered that the strangers should be welcomed to his palace; and the respect shown to his power made him swell with pride. Then with cheerful looks he scanned the faces before him, and thus addressed the Roman general before Scipio could speak: "Goodliest of the sons of Rome, I welcome you with unclouded brow and rejoice to look upon you. I recall with pleasure the face of Scipio, your father; you remind me of him. For I remember that, when I visited Gades, the city of Hercules, and the shore of Erythia,[a] attracted by the Ocean and desirous to observe its tides, I was strangely moved when I beheld the great Roman generals,[b] encamped hard by on the river Baetis.[c] Then they gave me presents chosen from the spoil, and weapons also, and bridles for horses, which my realm had never known till then, and bows, not inferior to our javelins; and they gave me veteran soldiers to train my irregular hordes in the Roman manner of warfare. But when I offered in return such things as my country is rich in—gifts of gold or snow-white ivory—my entreaties were of no avail. Each of the generals accepted one thing only—a sword enclosed in a scabbard of carved ivory. Up then with joy and be glad to come under my roof! Further, since fortune has brought the Punic general hither across the sea, hear with indulgent ear what I shall say. Ye also who rule the city of Tyrian Carthage, I pray you, Hasdrubal, to turn your ears and thoughts to my words. None can help knowing what a storm of

tempestas ruat et Latio suprema minetur,
utque bibant Tyrium bis quinos saeva per annos
Sicana nunc tellus, nunc litora Hibera cruorem,
cui nescire licet ? quin ergo tristia tandem
considunt bella, et deponitis arma volentes ?
tu Libya, tu te Ausonia cohibere memento.
haud deformis erit vobis ad foedera versis
pacator mediusque Syphax." subiungere plura
non passus, gentis morem arbitriumque senatus
Scipio demonstrat, vanique absistere coepti
spe iubet et patres docet haec expendere solos.
suadendi modus hic ; quodque est de parte diei
exacti super, ad mensas et pocula vertunt.
atque, epulis postquam finis, dant corpora somno
et dura in noctem curarum vincula solvunt.

Iamque novum terris pariebat limine primo
egrediens Aurora diem, stabulisque subibant
ad iuga solis equi, necdum ipse ascenderat axem,
sed prorupturis rutilabant aequora flammis :
exigit e stratis corpus vultuque sereno
Scipio contendit Massyli ad limina regis.
illi mos patrius fetus nutrire leonum
et catulis rabiem atque iras expellere alendo.
tum quoque fulva manu mulcebat colla iubasque
et fera tractabat ludentum interritus ora.
Dardanium postquam ductorem accepit adesse,
induitur chlamydem, regnique insigne vetusti
gestat laeva decus ; cinguntur tempora vitta
albente, ac lateri de more astringitur ensis.

furious warfare rages through Italy and threatens Rome with destruction; and how, for twice five years, first the cruel soil of Sicily and then the coasts of Spain have drunk Punic blood. Why should not the horrors of war cease at last? Why should you not agree to lay down your arms? Let each of you, Roman and African, be content to remain within his own country. If you incline to peace, Syphax will not disgrace you as peacemaker and mediator." But Scipio suffered him to say no more; he explained the temper of his people and the supreme power of the Senate, and bade the king abandon his fruitless design: the Senate alone had power to discuss such matters. This hint was enough; and the remaining part of the day was given up to feasting and wine. Then, when the feast was over, they laid them down to sleep, and were free, for the night, from the galling fetters of state affairs.

And now Dawn came forth from her threshold, bringing a new day for mortal men; and the coursers of the Sun left their stables for the yoke. The Sun himself had not yet mounted his car, but the sea was ruddy with flame that would soon burst forth. Scipio rose from his bed and went with unclouded brow to the king's palace. After the fashion of his country, Syphax used to keep lion-cubs and tame their ferocity by kindness; and now he was stroking their tawny necks and manes while they played, and handling their dreadful muzzles without fear. When he heard that Scipio had come, he put on his mantle, and his left hand bore the sceptre of his ancient kingdom; his temples were bound with a white fillet, and his sword was duly fastened by his side. Then he

hinc in tecta vocat, secretisque aedibus hospes
sceptrifero cum rege pari sub honore residunt.
Tum prior his infit terrae pacator Hiberae :
" prima mihi, domitis Pyrenes gentibus, ire
ad tua regna fuit properantem et maxima cura,
o sceptri venerande Syphax ; nec me aequore saevus
tardavit medio pontus. non ardua regnis
quaesumus aut inhonora tuis : coniunge Latinis
unanimum pectus sociusque accede secundis.
non tibi Massylae gentes extentaque tellus
Syrtibus et latis proavita potentia campis
amplius attulerint decoris, quam Romula virtus
certa iuncta fide et populi Laurentis honores.
cetera quid referam ? non ullus scilicet ulli
aequus caelicolum, qui Dardana laeserit arma."
Audivit laeto Massylus et annuit ore
complexusque virum, " firmemus prospera," dixit,
" omina, nec votis superi concordibus absint,
cornigerumque Iovem Tarpeiumque ore vocemus."
et simul exstructis caespes surrexerat aris ;
victimaque admotae stabat subiecta bipenni,
cum subito abruptis fugiens altaria taurus
exsiluit vinclis mugituque excita late
implevit tecta et, fremitu suspiria rauco
congeminans, trepida terrorem sparsit in aula.
vittaque, maiorum decoramen, fronte sine ullo
delapsa attactu, nudavit tempora regis.
talia caelicolae casuro tristia regno
signa dabant, saevique aderant gravia omina fati.

---

[a] See note to i. 408.

[b] Jupiter Ammon, the god most widely worshipped in Africa : see note to i. 415.

summoned Scipio to enter, and the pair—the sceptred king and his guest—took their seats, equally honoured, in an inner chamber.

Then the conqueror of Spain spoke first in these words: "Syphax, august sovereign, when I had conquered the tribes of the Pyrenees, my first and most important business was to hasten to your kingdom; nor was I kept back by the dangers of the sea between us. I ask nought difficult or dishonourable to your realm: unite heart and soul with the Romans, and take a share in their success. The Massylian tribes, your territory that stretches to the Syrtes,[a] your hereditary sway over broad lands—none of these things can bring you more glory than Roman valour faithfully allied to you, and honours paid you by the Roman people. Need I say more? None of the gods, be sure, looks with favour on any man who injures the armies of Rome."

The king heard him and consented with joyful countenance. He embraced Scipio and said: "Let us confirm this favourable beginning and call upon the gods—Jupiter with the horned head [b] and Jupiter of the Capitol—to be present at our common supplication." At once an altar of turf was reared high, and a bull was standing beneath the descending axe, when suddenly the victim burst its bonds and sprang away in flight from the altar, filling all the startled palace with its bellowing, and spreading terror among the dismayed attendants by its constant panting and hoarse roaring. The fillet also, his ancestral ornament, fell of itself from the king's forehead and left his temples bare. Such were the evil omens sent by the gods to the doomed monarch, and the menacing portents of disaster were present. A time was

hunc fractum bello regem solioque revulsum,
tempus erit, cum ducet agens ad templa Tonantis,
qui tunc orabat socialia foedera supplex.
his actis repetit portum puppesque secundo
dat vento et notis reddit se Scipio terris.
  Concurrere avidae gentes, variosque subacta
Pyrene misit populos. mens omnibus una ;
concordes regem appellant regemque salutant ;
scilicet hunc summum norunt virtutis honorem.
sed, postquam miti reiecit munera vultu,
Ausonio non digna viro, patriosque vicissim
edocuit ritus et Romam nomina regum
monstravit nescire pati, tum versus in unam,
quae restat, curam, nullo super hoste relicto,
et Latios simul et vulgum Baetisque Tagique
convocat ac medio in coetu sic deinde profatur :
" quando ita caelicolum nobis propensa voluntas
annuit, extremo Libys ut deiectus ab orbe
aut his occideret campis, aut, axe relicto
Hesperio, patrias exul lustraret harenas :
iam vestra tumulos terra celebrare meorum
est animus pacemque dare exposcentibus umbris.
mente favete pari atque aures advertite vestras.
septima cum solis renovabitur orbita caelo,
quique armis ferroque valent, quique arte regendi
quadriiugos pollent currus, quis vincere planta
spes est, et studium iaculis impellere ventos,
adsint ac pulchrae certent de laude coronae.

---

[a] Scipio.

[b] On the occasion of Scipio's triumph after Zama in 201 B.C.

[c] Spain.

[d] They had lived so long in Spain that they regarded it as their native land.

coming when he[a] who now sued humbly for a treaty of alliance would utterly defeat this king and hurl him from his throne, and then go before him in procession to the temple of the Thunder-god.[b] When these things were done, Scipio, going back to the harbour, launched his ships before a favourable wind and returned to a familiar land.[c]

The natives came flocking eagerly to meet him; and the conquered Pyrenees sent their manifold tribes. All had the same purpose: with one accord they called Scipio king and hailed him as king; for they know no higher tribute to a great man than this. But when with friendly mien he had declined their offers as unfitting for a Roman, and explained on his side the custom of his country and the hatred felt by Rome for the name of king, then he turned to his one remaining object, now that all enemies were disposed of. He summoned the Romans and also the peoples of the Baetis and the Tagus, and then made this speech to the assembled meeting: "Since the favour of heaven has granted us to expel the Libyans from this World's End, and they either lie dead on these plains or, banished from the West, tread as exiles[d] the sands of their native country, I purpose now to do honour to the tombs of my kinsmen who fell in your land, and to give to their shades the rest which they demand. Be of one mind with me, and lend a favouring ear. When the sun shall renew his course through the sky for the seventh time, then let all come hither—those who are mighty in the use of arms or skilled in driving a four-horsed chariot, and those who hope to win the prize for speed or delight to hurl a javelin through the air of heaven. Let them all come and compete together for the glory

praemia digna dabo, e Tyria spolia incluta praeda,
nec quisquam nostri discedet muneris expers."
sic donis vulgum laudumque cupidine flammat.
  Iamque dies praedicta aderat, coetuque sonabat
innumero campus, simulatasque ordine iusto
exsequias rector lacrimis ducebat obortis.
omnis Hiber, omnis Latio sub nomine miles
dona ferunt tumulisque super flagrantibus addunt.
ipse, tenens nunc lacte, sacro nunc plena Lyaeo
pocula, odoriferis aspergit floribus aras.
tum manes vocat excitos laudesque virorum
cum fletu canit et veneratur facta iacentum.
inde refert sese circo et certamina prima
inchoat ac rapidos cursus proponit equorum.
fluctuat aequoreo fremitu rabieque faventum,
carceribus nondum reseratis, mobile vulgus
atque fores oculis et limina servat equorum.
  Iamque, ubi prolato sonuere repagula signo,
et toto prima emicuit vix ungula cornu,
tollitur in caelum furiali turbine clamor.
pronique ac similes certantibus ore secuntur
quisque suos currus magnaque volantibus idem
voce locuntur equis. quatitur certamine circus
spectantum, ac nulli mentem non abstulit ardor.
instant praecipites et equos clamore gubernant.
fulvus, harenosa surgens tellure, sub auras
erigitur globus atque operit caligine densa
cornipedumque vias aurigarumque labores.

---

[a] It was not an actual funeral, because the bodies of the dead generals were not there.

of a victor's crown. I shall give fitting prizes—glorious spoils from the Carthaginian booty, nor shall any man depart without a gift from me." Thus he fired the minds of all by his generosity and their ambition to excel.

Now the appointed day came, and the plain was filled with the noise of a crowd past numbering; and Scipio, with tears in his eyes, led the semblance[a] of a funeral procession with due rites of burial. Every Spaniard and every soldier of the Roman army brought gifts to throw upon the blazing pyres. Scipio himself held goblets, filled either with milk or with sacred wine, and sprinkled fragrant flowers over the altars. Then he summoned the ghosts to rise up, and rehearsed with tears the glories of the dead, and did honour to their noble deeds. Thence he went back to the race-course and started the first contest—that which was to test the speed of horses. Even before the starting-gate was unbarred, the excited crowd surged to and fro with a noise like the sound of the sea, and, with a fury of partisanship, fixed their eyes on the doors behind which the racers were standing.

And now the signal was given, and the bolts flew back with a noise. Scarcely had the first hoof flashed into full view, when a wild storm of shouting rose up to heaven. Bending forward like the drivers, each man gazed at the chariot he favoured, and at the same time shouted to the flying horses. The course was shaken by the enthusiasm of the spectators, and excitement robbed every man of his senses. They lean forward and direct the horses by their shouting. A cloud of yellow dust rose up from the sandy soil, concealing with its darkness the running of the horses and the exertions of the drivers. One man backs

hic studio furit acris equi, furit ille magistri.
hos patriae favor, hos accendit nobile nomen
antiqui stabuli ; sunt, quos spes grata fatiget
et nova ferre iugum cervix ; sunt, cruda senectus
quos iuvet et longo sonipes spectatus in aevo.
evolat ante omnes rapidoque per aëra curru
Callaicus Lampon fugit atque ingentia tranat
exultans spatia et ventos post terga relinquit.
conclamant plausuque fremunt votique peractam
maiorem credunt praerepto limite partem.
at, quis interior cura et prudentia circi
altior, effusas primo certamine vires
damnare et cassis longe increpitare querelis
indispensato lassantem corpora nisu :
" quo nimius, quo, Cyrne, ruis ? (nam Cyrnus agebat)
verbera dimitte et revoca moderatus habenas."
heu surdas aures ! fertur securus equorum
nec meminit, quantum campi decurrere restet.
  Proximus, a primo distans, quantum aequore currus
occupat ipse, loci tantum, sed proximus ibat
Astur Panchates ; patrium frons alba nitebat
insigne et patrio pes omnis concolor albo ;
ingentes animi, membra haud procera decusque
corporis exiguum, sed tum sibi fecerat alas
concitus atque ibat campo indignatus habenas.
crescere sublimem atque augeri membra putares.
Cinyphio rector cocco radiabat Hiberus.
  Tertius aequata currebat fronte Peloro

[a] Four chariots, each drawn by four horses, took part in this race. The four drivers were : (1) Cyrnus ; (2) Hiberus ; (3) Durius ; (4) Atlas. By an odd convention only one horse in each team is named : these are : (1) Lampon ; (2) Panchates ; (3) Pelorus ; (4) Caucasus. All were of Spanish breed. The names of the horses are italicized, for the convenience of the reader.

with fury the mettled steed, another the charioteer. Some are zealous for horses of their own country, others for the fame of some ancient stud. One man is filled with joyful hope for an animal that is racing for the first time, while another prefers the green old age of a well-tried veteran. At the start, *Lampon*,[a] bred in Gallicia, left the rest behind; he rushed through the air with the flying car, galloping over the course with huge strides and leaving the winds behind him. The crowd roared with applause, thinking that with such a start their favourite had as good as won. But those who looked deeper and had more experience of the race-course, blamed the driver for putting forth all his strength at the beginning: from a distance they uttered vain protests, that he was tiring out his team with his efforts and keeping no reserve of power. "Whither are you careering too eagerly, Cyrnus?"—Cyrnus was the charioteer—"Be prudent! Put down your whip and tighten your reins!" But alas, his ears were deaf: on he sped, unsparing of his horses, and forgetting how much ground had still to be covered.

Next came *Panchates*, a chariot-length and no more behind the leader. Bred in Asturia,[b] he was conspicuous for the white forehead and four white feet of his sires. Though high-mettled, he was low of stature and lacked comeliness; but now his fiery spirit lent him wings, and he sped over the plain, impatient of the reins; he seemed to grow in stature and size as he ran. His driver, Hiberus, was gay with scarlet of Cinyphian[c] dye.

Third in order, neck and neck with *Pelorus*, ran

[b] See note to iii. 334. [c] See note on v. 288.

Caucasus. ipse asper, nec qui cervicis amaret
applausae blandos sonitus clausumque cruento
spumeus admorsu gauderet mandere ferrum.
at docilis freni et melior parere Pelorus
non umquam effusum sinuabat devius axem ;
sed laevo interior stringebat tramite metam,
insignis multa cervice et plurimus idem
ludentis per colla iubae. mirabile dictu,
nullus erat pater : ad Zephyri nova flamina campis
Vettonum eductum genetrix effuderat Harpe.
nobilis hunc Durius stimulabat in aequore currum ;
Caucasus antiquo fidebat Atlante magistro.
ipsum Aetola, vago Diomedi condita, Tyde
miserat ; exceptum Troiana ab origine equorum
tradebant, quos Aeneae Simoëntos ad undas
victor Tydides magnis abduxerat ausis.
at postremus Atlas, sed non et segnior ibat
postremo Durio ; pacis de more putares
aequata fronte et concordi currere freno.[1]
Iamque, fere medium evecti certamine campum,
in spatia addebant ; nisusque apprendere primos
Panchates animosus equos, super altior ire
et praecedentem iam iamque ascendere currum
pone videbatur, curvatisque ungula prima
Callaicum quatiens pulsabat calcibus axem.
sensit ut exhaustas, qui proximus ibat, Hiberus
Callaicas Cyrni vires, nec, ut ante, salire

[1] ll. 378-380 *were transposed by Bothe.*

[a] The goal round which the chariots had to turn when half the race was run: the skilful driver kept as near as possible to the post, without touching it.

[b] For this fable, which is found in other writers, see note to iii. 381: it was one way of accounting for the horses' speed.

Caucasus, a fractious animal that loved not the caressing hand that patted his neck, but rejoiced to bite and champ the iron in his mouth till blood came with the foam. *Pelorus*, on the other hand, was more tractable and obedient to the rein; never did he swerve aside and drive the car in crooked lines, but kept to the inside and grazed the turning-post [a] with his near wheel. He was conspicuous for the size of his neck and the thick mane that rippled over it. Strange to say, he had no sire: his dam, Harpe, had conceived him from the Zephyr of spring [b] and foaled him in the plains of the Vettones. This chariot was driven along the course by the noble Durius, while *Caucasus* relied upon ancient Atlas as his driver. *Caucasus* came from Aetolian Tyde,[c] the city founded by the wandering hero, Diomede; and legend traced his descent to the Trojan horses which the son of Tydeus,[d] successful in his bold attempt, stole from Aeneas by the river Simoïs. Atlas came last, but Durius was last also and moved no faster: one might have thought the pair were running peaceably side by side and keeping level.

And now, when near half the distance was completed, they quickened over the course; and spirited *Panchates*, struggling to catch up the team ahead, seemed to rise higher and at each moment to mount upon the chariot in front, and the hoofs of his prancing forefeet struck and rattled on the car of the Gallician horse. When Hiberus, who came second, saw that the Gallician team of Cyrnus was tiring, that the chariot was no longer

[c] See note to iii. 367.

[d] Diomede: the story is told in the *Iliad*: the Simoïs was a river at Troy.

praecipitem currum, et fumantes verbere cogi
assiduo violenter equos, ceu monte procella
cum subita ex alto ruit, usque ad colla repente
cornipedum protentus et in capita ardua pendens,
concitat ardentem, quod ferret lora secundus,
Panchatem vocesque addit cum verbere mixtas :
“tene, Astur, certante feret quisquam aequore palmam
erepto ? consurge, vola, perlabere campum
assuetis velox pennis. decrescit anhelo
pectore consumptus Lampon ; nec restat hianti,
quem ferat ad metas, iam spiritus.” haec ubi dicta,
tollit se sonipes, ceu tunc e carcere primo
corriperet spatium, et nitentem opponere curvos
aut aequare gradus Cyrnum post terga relinquit.
confremit et caelum et percussus vocibus altis
spectantum circus. fertur sublime per auras
altius attollens cervicem victor ovantem
Panchates sociosque trahit prior ipse iugales.
At postremus Atlas, Durius postremus in orbem
exercent artes ; laevos nunc appetit ille
conatus, nunc ille premit certatque subire
dexter, et alterni nequiquam fallere tentant :
donec, confisus primaevae flore iuventae,
obliquum Durius conversis pronus habenis
opposuit currum atque eversum propulit axem
Atlantis senio invalidi, sed iusta querentis :
“quo ruis ? aut quinam hic rabidi certaminis est mos ?
et nobis et equis letum commune laboras.”
dumque ea proclamat, perfracto volvitur axe

[a] As the four horses were harnessed abreast, this action was less difficult than it sounds.

[b] The three nameless horses which made up the team.

bounding ahead, and that the smoking horses were driven on by severe and repeated flogging, then, as when a sudden storm rushes down from a mountain-top, he leaned forward quickly as far as the necks of his coursers and hung above their crests,[a] and stirred up *Panchates*, who was chafing at being second in the race, and plied his whip, even while he called to the horse: "Steed of Asturia, shall any other get in front and win the prize when you are competing? Rise up and fly and glide over the plain with all your wonted speed, as if on wings! *Lampon* is panting hard; his strength is gone and he grows smaller; he has no breath left to carry to the goal." At these words, *Panchates* rose higher, as if he were just starting in the race; and Cyrnus, though he strove to block his rival by swerving, or to keep up with him, was soon left behind. The sky and the race-course resounded, smitten by the shouts of the spectators. Victorious *Panchates* raised his triumphant crest still higher as he ran on; and he drew after him his three partners in the yoke.[b]

The two last drivers were Atlas and Durius; and now they swerved aside and resorted to tricks. First, one tried to pass his rival on the left; and then the other came up on the right and strove to get in front; but both failed in their attempted strategy. At last Durius, young and confident, leaning forward and jerking at his reins, placed his chariot athwart his rival's course and struck the other car and upset it. Atlas, no match for the other's youth and strength, protested with justice: "Whither are you careering? or what mad fashion is this of racing? You seek to kill me and my horses together." As he cried out thus, he fell head first from the broken chariot; and

cernuus, ac pariter fusi, miserabile, campo
discordes sternuntur equi. quatit aequore aperto
lora suis victor, mediaque Pelorus harena
surgere nitentem fugiens Atlanta reliquit.
nec longum Cyrni defessos prendere currus.
hunc quoque, cunctantem et sero moderamina equorum
discentem, rapido praetervolat incitus axe;
impellit currum clamor vocesque faventum.
iamque etiam dorso atque umeris trepidantis Hiberi
ora superposuit sonipes, flatusque vapore
terga premi et spumis auriga calescere sentit.
incubuit campo Durius misitque citatos
verbere quadrupedes, nec frustra: aequare videtur,
aut etiam aequavit iuga praecedentia dexter.
attonitus tum spe tanta: "genitore, Pelore,
te Zephyro eductum nunc nunc ostendere tempus.
discant, qui pecudum ducunt ab origine nomen,
quantum divini praecellat seminis ortus.
victor dona dabis statuesque altaria patri."
et, ni successu nimio laetoque pavore
proditus elapso foret inter verba flagello,
forsan sacrasset Zephyro, quas voverat, aras.
tum vero infelix, veluti delapsa corona
victoris capiti foret, in se versus ab ira,
auratam medio discindit pectore vestem,
ac lacrimae simul et questus ad sidera fusi.
nec iam subducto parebat verbere currus.
pro stimulis dorso quatiuntur inania lora.

Interea metis, certus iam laudis, agebat
sese Panchates et praemia prima petebat

the horses too, a sorry sight, fell down and sprawled in disorder on the ground, while the conqueror shook his reins on the open course, and *Pelorus* flew up the middle of the track, leaving Atlas struggling to rise. It did not take him long to catch up the weary team of Cyrnus : he flew past with speedy car, though Cyrnus was learning too late the wisdom of controlling his pace. A shout of applause from his supporters drove the chariot on. And now *Pelorus* thrust his head over the back and shoulders of terrified Hiberus, till the charioteer felt the horse's hot breath and foam upon his neck. Durius pressed on along the plain, and increased the pace of his team by the whip. Nor was the effort vain : coming up on the right, he seemed to be, or even was, running neck and neck with his rival. Then, amazed by the prospect of such glory, he cried out : " Now, *Pelorus*, now is the time to show that the West-wind was your sire ! Let steeds that spring from the loins of mere animals learn how far superior is the issue of an immortal parent. When victorious, you shall offer gifts to your sire and rear an altar in his honour." And indeed, had he not, even while he spoke, been beguiled, by too great success and by his fearful joy, into dropping his whip, Durius would perhaps have consecrated to the West-wind the altars he had vowed. But now, as wretched as if the victor's wreath had fallen from his head, he turned his rage against himself, tearing the gold-embroidered garment from his breast, and weeping, and pouring out complaints to heaven. When the lash was gone, the team no longer obeyed the driver : in vain he flogged their backs with the reins for a whip.

Meanwhile *Panchates*, sure now of victory, sped on to the goal, and claimed the first prize with head

arduus : effusas lenis per colla, per armos
ventilat aura iubas ; tum, mollia crura superbi
attollens gressus, magno clamore triumphat.
par donum solido argento caelata bipennis
omnibus, at vario distantia cetera honore.
primus equum volucrem, Massyli munera regis
haud spernenda, tulit ; tulit hinc virtute secundus
e Tyria, quae multa iacet, duo pocula, praeda,
aurifero perfusa Tago. villosa leonis
terga feri et cristis horrens Sidonia cassis
tertius inde honor est ; postremo munere Atlantem,
quamvis perfracto senior subsederat axe,
accitum donat ductor, miseratus et aevum
et sortem casus ; famulus florente iuventa
huic datur, adiuncto gentilis honore galeri.
His actis ductor laeta ad certamina plantae
invitat positisque accendit pectora donis :
" hanc primus galeam (hac acies terrebat Hiberas
Hasdrubal), hunc ensem, cui proxima gloria cursus,
accipiet ; caeso pater hunc detraxit Hyempsae.
tertius extremam tauro solabere palmam.
cetera contenti discedent turba duobus
quisque ferox iaculis, quae dat gentile metallum."
Fulgentes pueri Tartessos et Hesperos ora
ostendere simul vulgi clamore secundo.
hos Tyria misere domo patria inclita Gades.
mox subit, aspersus prima lanugine malas,

[a] Either Syphax or Masinissa may be meant : see note to l. 170.

[b] A Carthaginian officer, not mentioned elsewhere in the poem.

held high. A light breeze fanned the mane that rippled over his neck and shoulders; then with proud step he raised his nimble limbs, and a great shout greeted his victory. Each competitor received alike a battle-axe of solid silver with carven work; but the other prizes differed from one another and were of unequal value. To the winner was given a flying steed, a desirable present from the Massylian king [a]; the second in merit next received two cups overlaid with gold of the Tagus, taken from the great heap of Carthaginian spoil; the third prize was the shaggy hide of a fierce lion and a Carthaginian helmet with bristling plumes; and lastly Scipio summoned Atlas and gave him a prize also in pity for his age and ill-fortune, though the old man had fallen down when his chariot was wrecked. To him was given a beautiful youth, to attend on him, together with a skin cap of Spanish fashion.

When this was over, Scipio summoned competitors for the gladsome foot-race, and offered prizes to heighten their zeal. "The winner," he said, "shall receive this helmet in which Hasdrubal terrified the armies of Spain; and the second in the race shall carry off this sword which my father took from the dead body of Hyempsa [b]; and lastly a bull shall console the runner who comes in third. The other bold competitors shall each receive a pair of the javelins that the Spanish mines supply, and shall depart content."

Two splendid youths, Tartessus and Hesperus, presented themselves together amid the applause of the spectators. They came from Gades, that famous colony of the Phoenicians. Next to come forward was Baeticus, whose cheeks were sprinkled

Baeticus ; hoc dederat puero cognomen ab amne
Corduba et haud parvo certamina laeta fovebat.
inde, comam rutilus sed cum fulgore nivali
corporis, implevit caveam clamoribus omnem
Eurytus ; excelso nutritum colle crearat
Saetabis, atque aderant trepidi pietate parentes.
tum Lamus et Sicoris, proles bellacis Ilerdae,
et Theron, potator aquae, sub nomine Lethes
quae fluit, immemori perstringens gurgite ripas.

Qui postquam, arrecti plantis et pectora proni
pulsantesque aestu laudum exultantia corda,
accepere tuba spatium, exsiluere per auras
ocius effusis nervo exturbante sagittis.
diversa et studia et clamor, pendentque faventes
unguibus atque suos, ut cuique est gratia, anheli
nomine quemque cient. grex inclitus aequore fertur,
nullaque tramissa vestigia signat harena.
omnes primaevi flaventiaque ora decori,
omnes ire leves atque omnes vincere digni.

Extulit, incumbens medio iam limite, gressum
Eurytus et primus brevibus, sed primus, abibat
praecedens spatiis. instat non segnius acer
Hesperos ac prima stringit vestigia planta
praegressae calcis. satis est huic esse priori ;
huic sperare sat est fieri se posse priorem.
acrius hoc tendunt gressus animique vigore
corpora agunt. auget pueris labor ipse decorem.
ecce, levi nisu postremoque agmine currens,

---

[a] The Baetis (now Guadalquivir).

[b] The meaning is, that Corduba had been generous in furnishing him with requisites for his athletic career.

[c] See note to iii. 359. [d] See note to i. 236.

over with the first down of manhood; Corduba had named the lad thus after her river,[a] and the city backed her favourite's successes at no small cost.[b] Next, Eurytus made all the ring resound with shouting; red was his hair but his body white as snow; Saetabis had given him birth and reared him on her lofty hill, and his parents were present, in a flutter of love and anxiety. After him came Lamus and Sicoris, sons of warlike Ilerda[c]; and lastly Theron, who drank of the river called Lethe,[d] which, as it flows along, grazes its bank with the waters of forgetfulness.

There they stood on tiptoe, bending forwards, with hearts beating high in the passion for renown; and, when the trumpet gave the signal to start, they sprang forward through the air swifter than arrows launched from the string. The spectators shouted, each zealous for his own favourite; hanging on tiptoe, with hoarse cries they called by name to the runner of their choice. The band of noble youths swept over the plain, leaving no print of their feet on the sand as they passed. All alike were young and fair of face; all were fleet of foot, and all deserved to win.

When half the distance was reached, Eurytus shot to the front, and kept ahead of the rest, not by much, but still ahead. Hard behind him came bold Hesperus, no slower than the other, and planted his foremost foot in the heel-marks of the leader. Eurytus was content to be in front; for Hesperus the hope that he might yet get in front was sufficient. Therefore they increase their activity, and their bodies are driven forward by their spirit; even their exertions add to their youthful comeliness. But see, Theron, who was last of the seven and running with little effort, now

postquam sat visus sibi concepisse vigoris,
celsus inexhaustas effundit turbine vires
non expectato subitusque erumpit et auras
praevehitur Theron : credas Cyllenida plantam
aetherio nexis cursu talaribus ire.
iamque hos iamque illos, populo mirante, relinquit
et, modo postremus, nunc ordine tertia palma,
Hesperon infestat sua per vestigia pressum.
nec iam, quem sequitur tantum, sed prima coronae
spes trepidat tantis venientibus Eurytus alis.
quartus sorte loci, sed, si tres ordine servent
inceptos cursus, nequiquam vana laborans,
Tartessos fratrem medio Therone premebat.
nec patiens ultra tollit sese aequore Theron
igneus et plenum praetervolat Hesperon irae.
unus erat super, et metae propioribus aegros
urebat finis stimulis ; quascumque reliquit
hinc labor, hinc penetrans pavor in praecordia vires,
dum sperare licet, brevia ad conanima uterque
advocat. aequantur cursus, pariterque ruebant.
et forsan gemina meruissent praemia palma
pervecti simul ad metas, ni, terga secutus
Theronis, fusam late per lactea colla
Hesperos ingenti tenuisset saevus ab ira
traxissetque comam. tardato laetus ovansque
Eurytus evadit iuvene atque ad praemia victor
emicat et galeae fert donum insigne coruscae.
cetera promisso donata est munere pubes

[a] See note on iii. 168.

felt that he had gathered sufficient strength: rising to his full height, he took all by surprise, putting forth in a sudden burst all the power he had been husbanding, and leaving the winds behind him. It might have been Mercury[a] himself, flying through the sky with his winged sandals fastened to his feet. The onlookers marvelled, as he passed one and then another, till he who had just before been last became the third in the order of the runners and pressed fiercely upon the track of Hesperus. And not only the lad in front of him but Eurytus himself, first favourite for the prize, was dismayed by such a display of swiftness. Fourth in order came Tartessus; but all his efforts were vain, if the three others kept their respective distances; he followed his brother, but Theron came between them. Theron's patience was at an end: with one fiery burst he flew over the course and passed Hesperus, who was filled with rage. One rival yet remained; and the sight of the goal close at hand goaded on their weary limbs; while hope was still possible, each summoned up his remaining strength for one short struggle—Theron exhausted by his effort, and Eurytus by the fear that crept into his heart. They came abreast and rushed on side by side. And perhaps they would have reached the goal together and shared the first prize; but Hesperus, coming behind Theron, in his fierce anger grasped the hair that spread loosely over Theron's snow-white neck, and tugged at it. When his rival was hampered thus, Eurytus passed on in joy and triumph and flew to receive the prize of victory. He carried off the glittering helmet, a splendid gift. The other youths gained the promised reward:

intonsasque comas viridi redimita corona
bina tulit patrio quatiens hastilia ferro.
  Hinc graviora virum certamina, comminus ensis
destrictus bellique feri simulacra cientur.
nec, quos culpa tulit, quos crimine noxia vita,
sed virtus animusque ferox ad laudis amorem,
hi crevere pares ferro ; spectacula digna
Martigena vulgo suetique laboris imago.
hos inter gemini (quid iam non regibus ausum ?
aut quod iam regni restat scelus ?) impia circo
innumero fratres, cavea damnante furorem,
pro sceptro armatis inierunt proelia dextris.
is genti mos dirus erat ; patriumque petebant
orbati solium lucis discrimine fratres.
concurrere animis, quantis confligere par est
quos regni furor exagitat ; multoque cruore
exsatiata simul portantes corda sub umbras
occubuere. pari nisu per pectora adactus
intima descendit mucro ; superaddita saevis
ultima vulneribus verba ; et, convicia volvens,
dirus in invitas effugit spiritus auras.
nec manes pacem passi ; nam corpora iunctus
una cum raperet flamma rogus, impius ignis
dissiluit, cineresque simul iacuisse negarunt.
cetera distincto donata est munere turba,
ut virtus et dextra fuit. duxere iuvencos,
impressis dociles terram proscindere aratris ;
duxere assuetos lustra exagitare ferarum

---

[a] The Roman soldiers.

[b] Livy (xxviii. 21) describes this incident of Scipio's games, but says that the two men were cousins, and that the elder

a green garland crowned the unshorn locks of each, and each brandished a pair of javelins made of Spanish steel.

When the boys' race was over, men engaged in more serious strife: swords were unsheathed at close quarters, and a mimicry of fierce warfare was waged. The swordsmen thus matched in arms were not men whom guilt and a life of crime had brought to this: valour urged them on and their eager desire of glory. It was a sight befitting the soldier sons of Mars,[a] and an imitation of their accustomed task. Among these a pair of twin brothers met in unnatural warfare for a throne—what crime have kings, wading through slaughter to a throne, left yet uncommitted?—while the vast ring of spectators cursed such madness. But such was the horrid custom of their nation; and the brothers hazarded their lives in competition for the crown of their dead father.[b] They met with such fury as befits men maddened by the passion for a throne; and, falling dead together, they carried to the shades hearts glutted with abundant bloodshed. The swords, driven home with equal effort by both, pierced the vital parts, and the mortal wounds were followed by last words, till their ghastly spirits fled into the reluctant air, still uttering curses. Even in death their enmity persisted; for, when a common pyre was consuming their bodies together, the flame refused to unite and parted asunder; and their ashes refused to rest together. The other swordsmen received different gifts, according to their valour and skill. Some carried off oxen trained to plough the soil, and others took from among the Moorish captives

of the two had an easy victory. But Silius was led astray by the story of the Theban brothers, Eteocles and Polynices.

venatu iuvenes, quos dat Maurusia praeda.
necnon argenti necnon insignia vestis
captivae pretia et sonipes et crista nitenti
insurgens cono, spolia exuviaeque Libyssae.
  Tum iaculo petiere decus, spectacula circi
postrema, et metae certarunt vincere finem
Burnus avis pollens, quem misit ripa metalli,[1]
qua Tagus auriferis pallet turbatus harenis;
et Glagus, insignis ventos anteire lacerto;
et, cuius numquam fugisse hastilia cervi
praerapida potuere fuga, venator Aconteus,
Indibilisque, diu laetus bellare Latinis,
iam socius; volucresque vagas deprendere nube
assuetus iaculis, idem et bellator, Ilerdes.
laus Burni prima, infixit qui spicula metae;
est donum serva, albentes invertere lanas
murice Gaetulo docta. at, quem proxima honorant
praemia, vicinam metae qui propulit hastam,
accepto laetus puero discessit Ilerdes,
cui ludus, nullam cursu non tollere dammam.
tertia palma habuit geminos insignis Aconteus
nec timidos agitare canes latratibus aprum.
  Quos postquam clamor plaususque probavit honores,
germanus ducis atque effulgens Laelius ostro
nomina magna vocant laeti manesque iacentum
atque hastas simul effundunt. celebrare iuvabat
sacratos cineres atque hoc decus addere ludis.
ipse etiam, mentis testatus gaudia vultu,
ductor, ut aequavit meritis pia pectora donis,

[1] metalli *seems to be corrupt.*

---

[a] See note to l. 176. [b] The two Scipios.

hunters accustomed to track wild beasts in their lairs. Gifts of silver also were awarded, and splendid garments from the spoil, and war-horses, and plumes rising on glittering helmets—the spoils taken from conquered Libyans.

And now, to end the games, men sought to win glory by casting the javelin. Five competitors strove to hit the mark—Burnus of noble ancestry, who came from the banks where the Tagus runs thick and yellow with golden sands; and Glagus, whose famous arm could outstrip the winds; and Aconteus the hunter, whose lance the deer, at their utmost speed, could never escape; and Indibilis, who long had loved to fight against Rome but was now her ally; and Ilerdes, whose bolt often shot down the birds that flew among the clouds, and who was also brave in battle. Burnus lodged his weapon in the mark and won the first prize—a handmaid who had skill to dye white wool with the purple of Gaetulia.[a] Then Ilerdes, whose spear came close to the mark, gained the second prize; he went off well-pleased with a lad, to whom it was mere child's play to run down and slay every deer of the forest. Aconteus who came third had for his prize a pair of hounds that feared not to drive a wild boar before them with loud barking.

When these awards were approved by shouts of applause, then Scipio's brother and Laelius, clad in glittering purple, gladly pronounced the great names of the dead [b] and summoned their ghosts, and launched their spears as they spoke, rejoicing to honour the sacred ashes and thus to give additional glory to the games. Scipio also, whose face revealed the happiness of his heart, first rewarded his faithful friends with gifts

et frater thoraca tulit multiplicis auri,
Laelius Asturica rapidos de gente iugales,
contorquet magnis victricem viribus hastam
consurgens umbrisque dari testatur honorem.
hasta volans, mirum dictu, medio incita campo
substitit ante oculos et terrae infixa cohaesit :
tum subitae frondes celsoque cacumine rami
et latam spargens quercus, dum nascitur, umbram.
ad maiora iubent praesagi tendere vates :
id monstrare deos atque hoc portendere signis.

Quo super augurio, pulsis de litore cunctis
Hesperio Poenis, ultor patriaeque domusque
Ausoniam repetit, Fama ducente triumphum.
nec Latium curis ardet flagrantius ullis,
quam iuveni Libyam et summos permittere fasces.
sed non par animis nec bello prospera turba
ancipiti senior temeraria coepta vetabant
magnosque horrebant cauta formidine casus.

Ergo, ubi delato consul sublimis honore
ad patres consulta refert, deturque potestas
orat delendae Carthaginis, altius orsus
hoc grandaeva modo Fabius pater ora resolvit :
" haud equidem metuisse queam, satiatus et aevi
et decoris, cui tam superest et gloria et aetas,
ne credat nos invidiae certamine consul
laudibus obtrectare suis. satis inclita nomen
gestat fama meum, nec egent tam prospera laude
facta nova. verum et patriae, dum vita manebit,

---

[a] Scipio, not being formally qualified, was not granted a regular triumph on his return to Italy.

[b] The consulship. He was unanimously elected consul for 205 B.C.

[c] Scipio.

equal to their deserts—his brother received a corslet plated thick with gold, and Laelius a pair of swift Asturian horses for harness—and then rose up and hurled his victorious spear with mighty strength, declaring that this was a tribute to the dead. Marvellous to tell, the flying spear stopped in mid-course and rooted itself in the ground, plain for all to see; then leafage appeared in a moment and tall branches; and an oak-tree at the instant of its birth threw a spreading shade. The prophets, foretelling the future, bade Scipio hope for greater things to come; for the gods, said they, indicated this result and made it manifest by the miracle.

When this prediction was uttered, Scipio, after driving the last Carthaginian from the Western coast and avenging his country and his kinsmen, went back to Italy, and Fame made his march a triumphal procession.[a] And the country had no more ardent desire than to entrust the highest office[b] to the young general, with Libya for his province. But the older men, whose cooler heads were averse to a hazardous war, frowned on rash undertakings, and their cautious fear shrank from serious disasters.

Therefore, when the consul,[c] in the dignity of the great office conferred upon him, opened the debate in the Senate, and asked that the task of destroying Carthage might be his, old Fabius opened his aged lips and lifted up his voice, to speak thus: "I have had so much of life and glory—more than enough of both—that I need not fear lest Scipio should suspect me of opposing his great enterprise from motives of jealousy. The voice of Fame is busy enough with my name, and a life so spent needs no fresh praise. But while I live I cannot without guilt fail my country

deesse nefas animumque nefas scelerare silendo.
bella nova in Libyae moliris ducere terras ?
hostis enim deest Ausoniae ? nec vincere nobis
est satis Hannibalem ? petitur quae gloria maior
litore Elissaeo ? stimuli si laudis agunt nos,
hanc segetem mete. composuit propioribus ausis
dignum te Fortuna parem. vult Itala tellus
ductoris saevi, vult tandem, haurire cruorem.
quo Martem aut quo signa trahis ? restinguere primum est
ardentem Italiam. tu fessos avius hostes
deseris ac septem denudas proditor arces.
an, cum tu Syrtim ac steriles vastabis harenas,
non dira illa lues notis iam moenibus urbis
assiliet, vacuumque Iovem sine pube, sine armis
invadet ? quanti, ut cedas Romamque relinquas,
emerit ! et tanto percussi fulmine belli
sicine te, ut nuper Capua est accitus ab alta
Fulvius, aequoreis Libyae revocabimus oris ?
vince domi et trinis maerentem funera lustris
Ausoniam purga bello. tum tende remotos
in Garamantas iter Nasamoniacosque triumphos
molire ; angustae prohibent nunc talia coepta
res Italae. pater ille tuus, qui nomina vestrae
addidit haud segnis genti, cum consul Hiberi
tenderet ad ripas, revocato milite primus
descendenti avide superatis Alpibus ultro
opposuit sese Hannibali. tu consul abire

[a] The Capitoline Hill. [b] See xii. 570.

[c] A round number: thirteen years would be more exact—218–205 B.C. [d] See iv. 51 foll.

or stain my conscience by silence. Do you intend, Scipio, to carry a fresh campaign to Libya? Is Italy free from the enemy, and is it not enough for us to defeat Hannibal? What higher prize than that is offered by the Libyan shore? If glory is our motive, here is the field for you to reap. Nearer home, Fortune has pitted against you a foeman worthy of your steel. The soil of Italy would fain, would fain at last drink the blood of that merciless commander. Whither would you carry off your army and your standards? The first thing is to put out the conflagration of Italy. You run away and leave an exhausted foe behind you, and treacherously strip the Seven Hills of their defenders. While you are laying waste the barren sands of the Syrtis, will not that monster assault the walls of Rome which he knows already, and attack the seat of Jupiter [a] when it has neither men nor weapons to defend it? What a price would he not pay, to secure your departure from the city! And shall we, when we are stricken by such a thunderbolt of war, recall you from the shore of Africa, even as Fulvius was lately summoned from the towers of Capua [b]? Conquer at home and cleanse Italy from war—Italy that has been mourning her dead for thrice five years [c]! That done, then take your way to the distant Garamantes, and earn triumphs over Nasamonians. Such enterprises are barred at present by the sore straits of our country. Your famous father, whose activities brought fresh glory to your house, was on his way as consul to the banks of the Hiberus; but, when Hannibal had crossed the Alps and was coming down to devour us, your father recalled his army and was the first to throw himself boldly in Hannibal's path.[d]

a victore paras hoste atque avellere nobis
scilicet hoc astu Poenum? si deinde sedebit
impavidus nec te in Libyam tuaque arma sequetur,
capta damnabis consulta improvida Roma.
sed fac turbatum convertere signa tuaeque
classis vela sequi: nempe idem erit Hannibal, idem,
cuius tu vallum vidisti e moenibus urbis."
haec Fabius; seniorque manus paria ore fremebat.
  Tum contra consul: "caesis ductoribus olim
magnanimis gemino leto, cum tota subisset
Sidonium possessa iugum Tartessia tellus,
non Fabio, non, quis eadem est sententia cordi,
quoquam ad opem verso, fateor, primoribus annis
excepi nubem belli solusque ruenti
obieci caelo caput atque in me omnia verti.
tum grandaeva manus puero male credita bella,
atque idem hic vates temeraria coepta canebat.
dis grates laudemque fero, sub numine quorum
gens Troiana sumus. puer ille et futilis aetas
imbellesque anni necdum maturus ad arma
Scipio restituit terras illaesus Hiberas
Troiugenis; pepulit Poenos, solisque secutus
extremas ad Atlanta vias, exegit ab orbe
Hesperio nomen Libyae nec rettulit ora
signa prius quam fumantes circa aequora vidit
Romano Phoebum solventem litore currus.
ascivit reges idem. nunc ultimus actis
restat Carthago nostris labor. hoc sator aevi

---

[a] The meaning is: "you dared not face Hannibal then, and he is no less formidable now."

[b] The Romans.

[c] Territory made Roman by Scipio's conquests.

Do you, a consul, intend to leave behind a victorious foe and by this device, forsooth! to tear the Carthaginian from our throats? If he remains coolly where he is, refusing to follow you and your army to Africa, you will curse your short-sighted strategy when Rome is taken. But suppose that he does take fright and march his army away, and is willing to follow the sails of your fleet; even then he will surely be the same Hannibal, whose camp you saw from the walls of Rome.[a]" Thus Fabius spoke, and the older senators expressed loud approval of his speech.

Then Scipio answered him: "In the hour when two noble generals fell together and the whole of Spain was occupied by Carthage and had come under her yoke, neither Fabius nor any one of those who share his opinions came to the rescue then. I faced that war-cloud, young as I was—I admit it—and I alone exposed my life when heaven was falling, and drew all the danger upon myself. Then the old men declared that it was a mistake to trust a mere boy as general; and the same prophet of evil who warns you to-day spoke then of foolhardiness. I praise and thank the gods whose power protects the race of Troy.[b] That 'boy,' too young for service in the field and unripe for arms, that Scipio, recovered Spain for Rome and never suffered defeat; he routed the Carthaginians and followed the sun's course to its setting beside Atlas, and expelled the name of Libya from the western world; nor did he withdraw his army from the land, until he saw the Sun-god unharnessing his reeking coursers by the Ocean upon Roman territory.[c] Kings also he gained over as allies. Now Carthage alone remains, and the conquest of Carthage will crown my career; I know this

Iupiter aeterni monet. Hannibali ecce senectus
intremit, aut aegros simulat mentita timores,
ne finem longis tandem peperisse ruinis
sit noster titulus. certe iam dextera nobis
experta, et robur florentibus auximus annis.
ne vero fabricate moras ; sed currere sortem
hanc sinite ad veterum delenda opprobria cladum,
quam mihi servavere dei. sat gloria cauto
non vinci pulchra est Fabio, peperitque sedendo
omnia Cunctator ; nobis nec Mago nec Hannon
nec Gisgone satus nec Hamilcare terga dedisset,
si segnes clauso traheremus proelia vallo.
Sidoniusne puer, vix pubescente iuventa,
Laurentes potuit populos et Troia adire
moenia flaventemque sacro cum gurgite Thybrim
et potuit Latium longo depascere bello ?
nos Libyae terris tramittere signa pigebit
et Tyrias agitare domos ? secura pericli
litora lata patent, et opima pace quieta
stat tellus. timeat tandem Carthago, timeri
assueta, et nobis, quamvis Oenotria nondum
Hannibale arva vacent, superesse intellegat arma.
illum ego, quem vosmet cauti consultaque vestra
in Latio fecere senem, cui tertia large
fundenti nostrum ducuntur lustra cruorem,
illum ego ad incensas trepidantem et sera paventem
advertam patriae sedes. an Roma videbit
turpia Agenoreae muris vestigia dextrae,
Carthago immunis nostros secura labores
audiet interea et portis bellabit apertis ?

---

[a] See ix. 306.

[b] The two Hasdrubals : Scipio mentions all the four enemy commanders whom he defeated in Spain.

from Jupiter, the Father of eternal life.[a] But see! the old men tremble at the thought of Hannibal: unless their fear is a mere pretence, that the glory of ending at last our long train of disasters may not fall to me. Without doubt my arm has now proved itself in war, and the strength of my youth has grown. But do not contrive delays; suffer the destiny which heaven has reserved for me to run its free course, that the shame of our former defeats may be wiped out. For wary Fabius it was glory enough to avoid defeat, and the Delayer gained all things for us by inaction. But neither Mago nor Hanno, neither Gisgo's son nor Hamilcar's,[b] would have fled before me, if I had remained idle in the protection of my camp and refused battle. If that Carthaginian boy, scarce entered upon manhood, could attack the Roman people, the walls of Rome, and the sacred stream of yellow Tiber—if he could feed on Latium during years of warfare, shall *we* shrink from sending an army across the sea to Africa, to flutter the dovecotes of Carthage? Their wide shores dread no danger; their land is undisturbed, and enriched by peace. Let Carthage, feared so long, at last feel fear in her turn; and let her learn that, though Italy is not yet delivered from Hannibal, we still have weapons to spare. Your cautious policy has suffered him to grow old in Italy; for thrice five years he has gone on shedding our blood in rivers; but I will bring him back in fear and trembling, when it is too late, to see the capital of his country consumed with fire. If Rome sees upon her walls the shameful traces of Hannibal's handiwork, shall Carthage meanwhile, free from fear and danger, hear the report of our sufferings and make war with open gates? By all means let

tum vero pulset nostras iterum improbus hostis
ariete Sidonio turres, si templa suorum
non ante audierit Rutulis crepitantia flammis."

Talibus accensi patres, fatoque vocante,
consulis annuerunt dictis, faustumque precati
ut foret Ausoniae, tramittere bella dederunt.

our insolent foe assault our towers again with Punic battering-rams, if he does not, before that time, hear the temples of his own gods crackling in flames kindled by Romans."

By this speech the Senate was carried away. They followed the call of destiny and assented to Scipio's proposals. Praying that the result might be fortunate for Italy, they allowed him to take his army across the sea.

LIBER SEPTIMUS DECIMUS

ARGUMENT

The image of Cybele is brought from Phrygia to Rome and received at Ostia by P. Scipio Nasica: the chastity of Claudia is vindicated (1-45). *Scipio crosses to Africa* (46-58). *He warns Syphax not to break faith with Rome: the camp of Syphax is burnt, and he is taken prisoner* (59-145). *Hasdrubal retreats to Carthage: Hannibal is recalled from Italy* (146-157). *Hannibal's dream before the arrival of the*

Hostis ut Ausoniis decederet advena terris,
fatidicae fuerant oracula prisca Sibyllae,
caelicolum Phrygia genetricem sede petitam
Laomedonteae sacrandam moenibus urbis;
advectum exciperet numen, qui, lectus ab omni
concilio patrum, praesentis degeret aevi
optimus. en nomen melius maiusque triumphis!
iamque petita aderat Latia portante Cybele
puppe; atque ante omnes, magno cedente senatu,
obvius accitis properabat Scipio sacris,
qui, genitus patruo ductoris ad Africa bella
tunc lecti, multa fulgebat imagine avorum.

---

[a] Cybele, the Great Mother, was the chief deity of Asia Minor; and her image, a square block of stone that had fallen from heaven, was kept at Pessinus, an ancient city of Galatia. This stone the Romans now imported. The oracle of Delphi required that the goddess should be welcomed to Rome by the most virtuous Roman; and P. Cornelius Scipio

BOOK XVII

ARGUMENT (*continued*)

summons (158-169). *He leaves Italy in obedience to the summons* (170-217). *He decides to go back to Italy but is prevented by a fearful storm* (218-291). *After landing in Africa he encourages his soldiers* (292-337). *Jupiter and Juno converse about the fate of Hannibal* (338-384). *The battle of Zama* (385-617). *Scipio returns in triumph to Rome* (618-654).

In ancient times the Sibyl had foretold that, in order to dislodge an invader from Italian soil, the Romans must invite the Mother of the Gods [a] to leave her seat in Phrygia, and must set up her worship within the walls of their city; and the goddess must be received at her landing by that citizen whom the whole body of the Senate chose out as the most virtuous of men then living. That was a title more glorious and higher than any triumph. So Cybele was invited, and now she was nearing land, on board a Roman vessel, when Scipio, given precedence by all the noble senators, made haste to meet the foreign deity. His father was uncle of the Scipio just chosen to conduct the war in Africa; and his lineage was long and illustrious. When he had welcomed the

Nasica, a youthful son of Cn. Scipio who had fallen in Spain, was chosen by the Senate to perform this duty.

isque ubi longinquo venientia numina ponto
accepit supplex palmis Tuscique sonora
Thybridis adduxit sublimis ad ostia puppim,
femineae tum deinde manus subiere, per amnem
quae traherent celsam religatis funibus alnum.
circum arguta cavis tinnitibus aera, simulque
certabant rauco resonantia tympana pulsu,
semivirique chori, gemino qui Dindyma monte
casta colunt, qui Dictaeo bacchantur in antro,
quique Idaea iuga et lucos novere silentes.
hos inter fremitus ac laeto vota tumultu
substitit adductis renuens procedere vinclis
sacra ratis subitisque vadis immobilis haesit.
tum puppe e media magno clamore sacerdos:
" parcite pollutis contingere vincula palmis!
et procul hinc, moneo, procul hinc, quaecumque profanae,
ferte gradus nec vos casto miscete labori,
dum satis est monuisse deae! quod si qua pudica
mente valet, si qua illaesi sibi corporis adstat
conscia, vel sola subeat pia munera dextra."
Hic, prisca ducens Clausorum ab origine nomen,
Claudia, non aequa populi male credita fama,
in puppim versis palmisque oculisque profatur:
" caelicolum genetrix, numen, quod numina nobis
cuncta creas, cuius proles terramque fretumque
sideraque et manes regnorum sorte gubernant,
si nostrum nullo violatum est crimine corpus,

[a] Dindyma and Ida are mountains in Phrygia, sacred to this goddess: Dicte is a mountain in Crete, whence the Curetes, the guardians of the infant Jupiter, brought her worship to Phrygia.

[b] One of the foreign priests who had brought the goddess over the sea.

[c] The Claudii: see note to viii. 412.

goddess after her long voyage with hands held up in prayer and, standing high, had brought the vessel to the loud-sounding mouth of Tuscan Tiber, the hands of women were next employed, to draw the tall ship up the stream with ropes. The cymbals made a noise all round with their hollow tinklings, and the hoarse note of the drums vied with the cymbals. And her troop of unsexed votaries were there—those who haunt the twin peaks of chaste Mount Dindyma, and who hold revel in the cave of Dicte, and those who know the heights of Ida and its silent sacred groves.[a] Amid their wild cries and the prayers of the rejoicing multitude, the sacred ship refused to answer the pull of the ropes: she stopped suddenly and remained motionless on the river-bed. Then a priest[b] cried aloud from the centre of the ship: "Touch not the ropes with guilty hands! Away, away! far from hence, all ye unchaste, I warn you, and take no share in the sacred task; or the goddess may not be content with a mere warning. But if any woman is strong in her chastity, if any who stands here is conscious of a body unstained, let her, even single-handed, undertake the pious duty."

Then Claudia spoke out. She derived her name from the ancient stock of the Clausi,[c] but false report among the people had darkened her fame. Turning her eyes and open hands to the vessel, she spoke thus: "O Mother of the gods, divine parent of all whom we worship, whose children cast lots for kingdoms and rule the earth and sea, the stars and the nether world,[d] if I am free from all stain of un-

[d] According to the legend, the lot assigned heaven and earth to Jupiter, the sea to Neptune, and the nether world to Pluto: see note to viii. 116.

testis, diva, veni et facili me absolve carina."
tum secura capit funem ; fremitusque leonum
audiri visus subito, et graviora per aures
nulla pulsa manu sonuerunt tympana divae.
fertur prona ratis (ventos impellere credas)
contraque adversas ducentem praevenit undas.
extemplo maior cunctis spes pectora mulcet
finem armis tandem finemque venire periclis.

Ipse alacer Sicula discedens Scipio terra
abscondit late propulsis puppibus aequor,
cui numen pelagi placaverat hostia taurus,
iactaque caeruleis innabant fluctibus exta.
tunc a sede deum purumque per aethera lapsae
armigerae Iovis ante oculos coepere volucres
aequoreas monstrare vias ac ducere classem.
augurium clangor laetum dabat ; inde, secuti
tantum praegressos liquida sub nube volatus,
quantum non frustra speculantum lumina servant,
litora Agenoreae tenuerunt perfida terrae.

Nec segnis, tanta in semet veniente procella,
Africa terribilem magno sub nomine molem
regis opes contra et Massyla paraverat arma ;
spesque Syphax Libycis una et Laurentibus unus
terror erat. campos pariter vallesque refusas
litoraque implerat nullo decorare tapete
cornipedem Nomas assuetus, densaeque per auras
condebant iaculis stridentibus aethera nubes.

---

[a] Cybele was commonly represented in art and in poetry as sitting in a car drawn by a pair of lions.

[b] Sicily was the province assigned to Scipio by the Senate ; but he was also authorized to cross over to Africa, if it seemed advisable.

[c] Eagles.

[d] Syphax : see note to xvi. 171.

chastity, come thou and bear me witness, and prove my innocence by the ease with which the vessel moves." Then, full of confidence, she grasped a rope; and suddenly it seemed that the roaring of lions [a] was heard, and Cybele's drums, though no hand beat them, sounded louder in all ears. The ship moved forward as if driven by the wind and outstripped Claudia as she drew it along against the stream. At once all hearts were cheered by stronger hopes that an end of war and an end of disaster was coming at last.

Scipio himself made haste to depart from Sicily [b] and hid the sea far and wide with his advancing ships. He had appeased the god of the sea by the sacrifice of a bull, and its inward parts were cast upon the blue water, to float there. Then, coming from the home of the gods and flying through the clear sky, the birds that bear the bolts of Jupiter [c] came into view, pointing out a path over the sea for the fleet to follow. The sound of their cries was an omen of success. The eagles flew in front through the clear heaven, keeping such a distance that the watcher's eye could still perceive them, and the ships followed till they reached the coast of treacherous Carthage.

Nor did Africa stand idle, on the approach of so fierce a storm. To meet the dreaded army and their famous general, she had acquired the resources of a king [d] and the Massylian warriors; and Syphax was at the same time the one hope of Carthage and the one menace to the Romans. The Numidians, riding bare-backed according to their custom, had filled the plains and broad valleys and sea-shore alike, and their javelins hurtled in thick clouds through the air and concealed the sky. For Syphax, forgetting his

immemor hic dextraeque datae iunctique per aras
foederis, et mensas testes atque hospita iura
fasque fidemque simul, pravo mutatus amore,
ruperat atque toros regni mercede pararat.
virgo erat eximia specie claroque parente,
Hasdrubalis proles ; thalamis quam cepit ut altis,
ceu face succensus prima taedaque iugali,
vertit opes gener ad Poenos, Latiaeque soluto
foedere amicitiae, dotalia transtulit arma.

Sed non Ausonio curarum extrema Syphacem
ductori monuisse fuit ; missique minantur :
stet regno, reputet superos, pacta hospita servet ;
longe coniugia ac longe Tyrios Hymenaeos
inter Dardanias acies fore. sanguine quippe,
si renuat, blando nimium facilique marito
statura obsequia et thalami flagrantis amores.

Sic Latius permixta minis sed cassa monebat
ductor ; nam surdas coniux obstruxerat aures.
ergo, asper monitis frustra nitentibus, enses
advocat et, castas polluti foederis aras
testatus, varia Martem movet impiger arte.
castra levi calamo cannaque intecta palustri,
qualia Maurus amat dispersa mapalia pastor,
aggreditur, furtum armorum tutantibus umbris,
ac tacita spargit celata incendia nocte.

---

[a] The son of Gisco. The girl's name is Sophonisba in Livy: the Greek writers call her Sophoniba.

[b] Syphax was a widower : it is implied that such passionate ardour would have been more excusable, if he had not been a bridegroom already.

pledged word, the alliance to which he had sworn, and the ties of hospitality cemented by meals in common, had broken faith and divine law; an ill-judged passion had changed his mind, and he had bought his bride at the price of his throne. The maiden was beautiful; and her father Hasdrubal[a] was famous. As soon as Syphax received her in the lofty marriage-chamber, as if the flame of the marriage-torch had set him on fire for the first time,[b] he made over his resources to his Punic father-in-law and broke his treaty of friendship with Rome by presenting his forces as a bridal gift to Carthage.

Not the least of Scipio's cares was to warn Syphax; and envoys were sent and uttered threats. They advised him to abide in his own kingdom, to be mindful of the gods and keep his pledge of friendship; his bride and his Carthaginian alliance would help him little when the Roman swords were busy. For, if he refused their advice, the too fond and compliant husband would pay with his life for his subservience to a bride whom he loved with passion.

Thus Scipio warned him and threatened also. But his warning was vain; for the bridegroom's ears were stopped. Therefore the general, angered by the failure of his counsel, had recourse to the sword; he appealed to the solemn oaths of alliance which the king had broken, and then began active warfare, leaving no device untried. As the enemy's tents were wattled with light rushes and reeds from the marshes, like the lonely cabins dear to the Moorish herdsman, Scipio attacked the camp while darkness concealed his stratagem, and in the silence of night scattered fire-brands undetected. Then, when the fires began

inde, ubi collecti rapidam diffundere pestem
coeperunt ignes et se per pinguia magno
pabula ferre sono, clare exspatiantur in auras
et fumos volucri propellunt lumine flammae.
it totis inimica lues cum turbine castris,
atque alimenta vorat strepitu Vulcanus anhelo
arida, et ex omni manant incendia tecto.
sentitur plerisque prius quam cernitur ignis
excitis somno, multorumque ora vocantum
auxilium invadunt flammae. fluit undique victor
Mulciber et rapidis amplexibus arma virosque
corripit ; exundat pestis, semustaque castra
albenti volitant per nubila summa favilla.
ipsius ingenti regis tentoria saltu
lugubre increpitans late circumvolat ardor ;
hausissetque virum, trepidus ni clade satelles
e somno ac stratis rapuisset multa precantem.
  Verum ubi mox iuncto sociarant aggere vires
Massylus Tyriusque duces, accitaque regno
lenierat pubes infaustae vulnera noctis,
ira pudorque dabant et coniux, tertius ignis,
immanes animos ; afflataque barbarus ora
castrorum flammis et se velamine nullo
vix inter trepidas ereptum ex hoste catervas
frendebat minitans ; sed enim non luce Syphacem
nec claro potuisse die nec sole tuente
a quoquam vinci. iactarat talia vecors,
sed iam claudebat flatus nec plura sinebat
Atropos et tumidae properabat stamina linguae.

---

[a] The reeds of which the tents were made.

[b] Clotho, Lachesis, and Atropos are the three Fates who spin the thread of men's lives; and it was the special duty of Atropos to cut the thread and so end the life.

to unite and spread the danger quickly, and to rush with a great noise over the rich food [a] provided for them, the flames rose up blazing to the sky and drove clouds of smoke before them with their flying glare. The dread scourge sped like a whirlwind over the whole camp; the fire-god devoured his dry food with loud panting breath; and every tent spouted flame. Many, starting from their sleep, felt the fire before they saw it; and the flames stifled the cries of many for aid. The fire-god spread everywhere victorious, and seized men and arms in his fierce embrace. The plague broke all bounds, and the burnt-out camp flew up in white ash to the topmost clouds. The fire, crackling doom, made a great leap to surround the quarters of Syphax himself, and would have devoured him, had not an attendant, fearing disaster, dragged him, uttering many a curse, from the bed he slept on.

But presently, when the Massylian and Carthaginian generals had united their forces behind a common rampart, and fresh troops summoned from all the kingdom had mitigated the disaster of the night, anger and shame and love for his bride—a third incentive—filled the king's heart with inordinate passion: he breathed out savage threats and ground his teeth, to think that his face had been scorched by the fire in the camp, and that he had with difficulty been rescued from the foe, a naked man in the midst of his discomfited soldiers. No man on earth, he declared, could ever have conquered Syphax in bright daylight or in face of the sun. Such was his mad boasting; but Atropos [b] was already putting an end to his insolence and suffered him to say no more; and the thread of that proud talker was nearly spun.

namque, ubi prosiluit castris, ceu turbidus amnis,
qui, silvas ac saxa trahens, per devia praeceps
volvitur et ripas spumanti gurgite laxat,
ante omnes praevectus equo, trahit agmina voce.
contra nava manus Rutuli celsusque ruebat
viso rege procul raptis exercitus armis.
ac sibi quisque : " videsne ? videsne, ut in agmine primo
Massylus volitet, deposcens proelia, rector ?
fac nostrum hoc, mea dextra, decus. violavit et aras
caelicolum et casti ductoris foedera rupit.
sit satis huic castris semel effugisse crematis."
sic secum taciti et certatim spicula fundunt.
prima in cornipedis sedit spirantibus ignem
naribus hasta volans erexitque ore cruento
quadrupedem, elatis pulsantem calcibus auras.
corruit asper equus, confixaque cuspide membra
huc illuc iactans, rectorem prodidit hosti.
invadunt vanumque fugae atque attollere fessos
annitentem artus revocato a vulnere telo
corripiunt ; tum vincla viro manicaeque, pudendum,
addita, et (exemplum non umquam fidere laetis)
sceptriferas arta palmas vinxere catena.
ducitur ex alto deiectus culmine regni,
qui modo sub pedibus terras et sceptra patensque
litora ad Oceani sub nutu viderat aequor.
prostratis opibus regni Phoenissa metuntur

For, when he rushed forth from the camp, like a swollen river, which carries trees and rocks with it, rolling headlong down a new channel and widening its banks with its foaming flood, so he rode in the van and summoned the ranks to follow him. Against him stood the valiant Roman infantry; and the horsemen, when they saw the king far off, seized their arms and rushed forward. Each man said to himself: "See, see! how the Massylian king rides in front of his army and challenges us to battle! May mine be the arm to win this glory [a]! He has profaned the altars of the gods and broken his word pledged to our stainless general. Let him be content with having escaped once from his camp on fire!" Such were their thoughts, as they hurled their javelins with a will. The first flying spear lodged in the fiery nostrils of the king's charger. With blood dripping from his face, the animal reared up and beat the air with his forefeet; then he fell down, in rage and pain, and, tossing from side to side the part pierced by the spear-point, betrayed his rider into the hands of the enemy. They fell upon him; and, though he strove to draw the weapon from the wound and by it to raise his injured limbs from the ground, flight was impossible, and they seized him. Then chains and fetters were laid upon him—a sorry sight, and a warning never to trust prosperity—and the hands that had wielded the sceptre were tightly bound. So he was led away—a king hurled down from his lofty throne, who had lately seen at his feet whole countries and their rulers, and whose control of the sea had stretched to the shore of Ocean. When the power of Syphax was overthrown, the Carthaginian

[a] Of killing or capturing Syphax.

agmina, et invisus Marti notusque fugarum
vertit terga citus damnatis Hasdrubal ausis.
Stabat Carthago, truncatis undique membris,
uni nixa viro ; tantoque fragore ruentem
Hannibal absenti retinebat nomine molem.
id reliquum fessos opis auxiliique ciere
rerum extrema iubent ; huc confugere paventes,
postquam se superum desertos numine cernunt.
nec mora : propulsa sulcant vada salsa carina,
qui revocent patriaeque ferant mandata monentis,
ne lentus nullas videat Carthaginis arces.
Quarta Aurora ratem Dauni devexerat oras,
et fera ductoris turbabant somnia mentem.
namque gravis curis carpit dum nocte quietem,
cernere Flaminium Gracchumque et cernere Paulum
visus erat simul adversos mucronibus in se
destrictis ruere atque Itala depellere terra ;
omnisque a Cannis Thrasymennique omnis ab undis
in pontum impellens umbrarum exercitus ibat.
ipse, fugam cupiens, notas evadere ad Alpes
quaerebat terraeque ulnis amplexus utrisque
haerebat Latiae, donec vis saeva profundo
truderet et rapidis daret asportare procellis.
His aegrum visis adeunt mandata ferentes
legati patriaeque extrema pericula pandunt :
Massyla ut ruerint arma, ut cervice catenas
regnator tulerit Libyae, letoque negato

---

[a] Once in Spain (see xvi. 112) and twice in Africa this Hasdrubal had saved himself by running away.
[b] Italy.
[c] All three had fallen in battle.

ranks were mowed down ; and Hasdrubal, no favourite of Mars and famous for repeated flights,[a] fled once more and gave up the struggle.

Now that all her limbs were severed, Carthage depended entirely upon one man for support ; and the great name of Hannibal, even in his absence, kept the edifice of her greatness from falling in utter ruin. He alone remained ; and her desperate plight forced her to summon him in her need of succour and support. When men saw themselves deprived of heaven's protection, they fled to him for refuge in their fear. Without delay envoys sailed across the salt sea, to recall him and carry a message from his country : he was warned that, should he linger, he might find no city of Carthage standing.

Dawn of the fourth day brought the vessel to the shores of Daunus,[b] when Hannibal's sleep was disturbed by terrible dreams. For while resting at night from his burden of anxiety, he dreamed that Flaminius and Gracchus and Paulus [c] were all attacking him at once with drawn swords and driving him off the soil of Italy ; and the whole army of ghosts from Cannae and Lake Trasimene were marching against him and forcing him to the sea. Eager to escape, he was fain to flee by his familiar path across the Alps, and clutched the soil of Italy with both arms ; but the pressure of his enemies drove him at last to the sea and gave him to the stormy winds to carry off.

Still troubled by his dream, he was approached by the envoys bearing their message. They explained the desperate danger of their country—how the Massylian army was overthrown ; how the king of Libya now bore fetters on his neck and was not

servetur nova pompa Iovi ; Carthago laboret
ut trepidi Hasdrubalis, qui rerum agitarit habenas,
non una concussa fuga. se, triste profatu,
vidisse, arderent cum bina in nocte silenti
castra, et luceret sceleratis Africa flammis.
praerapidum iuvenem minitari, Bruttia servet
litora dum Poenus, detracturum ignibus atris,
in quam se referat, patriam suaque inclita facta.
haec postquam dicta, et casus patuere metusque,
effundunt lacrimas dextramque ut numen adorant.
  Audivit torvo obtutu defixus et aegra
expendit tacite cura secum ipse volutans,
an tanti Carthago foret ; sic deinde profatur :
" o dirum exitium mortalibus ! o nihil umquam
crescere nec magnas patiens exsurgere laudes,
invidia ! eversam iam pridem exscindere Romam
atque aequasse solo potui, traducere captam
servitum gentem Latioque imponere leges.
dum sumptus dumque arma duci fessosque secundis
summisso tirone negant recreare maniplos,
dumque etiam Cerere et victu fraudasse cohortes
Hannoni placet, induitur tota Africa flammis,
pulsat Agenoreas Rhoeteia lancea portas.
nunc patriae decus et patriae nunc Hannibal unus
subsidium ; nunc in nostra spes ultima dextra.
vertentur signa, ut patres statuere ; simulque
et patriae muros et te servabimus, Hannon."

---

[a] See xvi. 11 foll.

[b] This rhetorical point, that he will save his bitterest enemy, is more in the manner of Lucan than of Silius: see Vol. I. p. xiv.

permitted to die, but kept alive to grace the triumphal procession to Jupiter's temple; how Carthage was dismayed and shattered by the repeated retreats of the cowardly Hasdrubal, who was now master of the state. With sorrow they told how they had seen two camps burning in the silence of night, and all Africa lit up with evil flames. Scipio (they said) moved with lightning speed, and threatened that, while Hannibal lingered on the Bruttian coast, he would destroy Carthage with fatal fires, and Hannibal would have no country to return to, bringing his mighty deeds with him. When they had spoken thus and revealed their disasters and fears, they wept and kissed his hand as if it were a god's.

The general listened with a fixed and stern countenance. He kept silence and pondered anxiously in his heart, considering whether Carthage was worth so great a sacrifice. And then he spoke thus: "How dreadful the doom that waits on mortal men! how envy ever stunts the growth of great deeds and nips them in the bud! Long ago I might have overthrown Rome and sacked the city and levelled her with the ground; I might have carried her people away into slavery and dictated conditions of peace. But I was refused money and weapons and fresh recruits for my army which victories had worn out [a]; and Hanno thought fit to cheat my soldiers even of bread to eat; and now all Africa is wreathed with fire, and the Roman lance beats on the gates of Carthage. Hannibal is now the glory of his country and her only rock of refuge; their one remaining hope is in my right arm. I shall march away, as the senate has decreed; I shall save the walls of Carthage and at the same time save Hanno." [b]

Haec ubi detonuit, celsas e litore puppes
propellit multumque gemens movet aequore classem.
non terga est ausus cedentum invadere quisquam,
non revocare virum ; cunctis praestare videntur,
quod sponte abscedat, superi, tandemque resolvat
Ausoniam. ventos optant, et litora ab hoste
nuda videre sat est. ceu flamina comprimit Auster
cum fera et abscedens reddit mare, navita parco
interea voto non auras poscit amicas,
contentus caruisse Noto, pacemque quietam
pro facili cursu reputat satis. omnis in altum
Sidonius visus converterat undique miles ;
ductor defixos Itala tellure tenebat
intentus vultus, manantesque ora rigabant
per tacitum lacrimae, et suspiria crebra ciebat,
haud secus ac patriam pulsus dulcesque penates
linqueret et tristes exul traheretur in oras.
Ut vero affusis puppes procedere ventis,
et sensim coepere procul subsidere montes,
nullaque iam Hesperia et nusquam iam Daunia tellus,
haec secum infrendens : " mentisne ego compos et hoc nunc
indignus reditu, qui memet finibus umquam
amorim Ausoniae ? flagrasset subdita taedis
Carthago, et potius cecidisset nomen Elissae.
quid ? tunc sat compos, qui non ardentia tela
a Cannis in templa tuli Tarpeia Iovemque
detraxi solio ? sparsissem incendia montes
per septem bello vacuos gentique superbae
Iliacum exitium et proavorum fata dedissem.
cur porro haec angant ? nunc, nunc invadere ferro

[a] Dido.

When he had thundered out this speech, he launched his tall ships and sailed with many a groan over the sea. None dared to attack his rear as they departed, none dared to recall him. All thought it a gift from Heaven, that he should go of his own accord and at last set Italy free. Men prayed for wind and were content to see the shore with never an enemy upon it. So, when the gale ceases to blow and departs, leaving the sea once more to the mariners, their prayers are modest and ask no favouring breezes: it is enough for them that the storm has ceased, and they find the calm as good as a speedy voyage. While all the Carthaginian soldiers bent their gaze upon the sea, Hannibal kept his eyes steadily fixed on the Italian coast; the silent tears flowed down his cheeks, and again and again he sighed, like an exile driven to a dismal shore, who leaves behind his native land and the home he loves.

But when the winds rose and the ships began to move forward, while the hills grew less and less in the distance, till Italy disappeared and the land of Daunus was no longer visible, Hannibal thought thus as he gnashed his teeth: "Am I mad? Do not I deserve to return thus, as a punishment for ever leaving Italy? Better that Carthage had been burned with fire, and the name of Elissa[a] been blotted out for ever! Was I in my senses then when I failed to carry my fiery weapons from Cannae to the Capitol, and to hurl Jupiter down from his throne? I ought to have scattered fire-brands over the Seven Hills which none then defended; I ought to have consigned that proud nation to the destruction of Troy and the doom of their ancestors. Why should this thought, however, torment me? Who prevents

quis prohibet rursumque ad moenia tendere gressus?
ibo et, castrorum relegens monumenta meorum,
qua via nota vocat, remeabo Anienis ad undas.
flectite in Italiam proras, avertite classem.
faxo, ut vallata revocetur Scipio Roma."

Talibus ardentem furiis Neptunus ut alto
prospexit vertique rates ad litora vidit,
quassans caeruleum genitor caput aequora fundo
eruit et tumidum movet ultra litora pontum.
extemplo ventos imbresque et rupe procellas
concitat Aeolias ac nubibus aethera condit.
tum, penitus telo molitus regna tridenti
intima, ab occasu Tethyn impellit et ortu
ac totum Oceani turbat caput. aequora surgunt
spumea, et illisu scopulus tremit omnis aquarum.
primus, se attollens Nasamonum sedibus, Auster
nudavit Syrtim correpta nubilus unda;
insequitur sublime ferens nigrantibus alis
abruptum Boreas ponti latus; intonat ater
discordi flatu et partem rapit aequoris Eurus.
hinc rupti reboare poli, atque hinc crebra micare
fulmina, et in classem ruere implacabile caelum.
consensere ignes nimbique et fluctus et ira
ventorum, noctemque freto imposuere tenebrae.
ecce, intorta Noto veniensque a puppe procella
antemnae immugit (stridorque immite rudentum
sibilat) ac similem monti nigrante profundo
ductoris frangit super ora trementia fluctum.

---

[a] Neptune had been propitiated by Scipio (see l. 50) and now prevents Hannibal from returning to Italy.

[b] See note to i. 193. [c] See note to i. 408.

me from attacking in arms even now and marching a second time against the walls of Rome? I shall go. I shall march back over the remains of my former camps and tread a familiar track to the waters of the Anio. Turn the ships' prows back towards Italy and alter our course! I warrant that beleaguered Rome will summon Scipio ere long to return."

While Hannibal raged thus furiously, Neptune [a] looked forth over the deep and saw the ships turning back to shore. Then the sea-god, shaking his blue locks, churned up the sea from the bottom and drove the swollen tide above the coast-line. At once he summoned the winds from the rocky cave of Aeolus,[b] with rains and stormy blasts, and veiled the sky with clouds. Then with his trident he stirred up the inmost recesses of his realm, and smote the sea from East and West, and troubled the whole source of Ocean. High rose the foaming waves, and dashed on every rock till it shook. First, the cloudy South-wind, rising in the land of the Nasamones, caught up the waters of the Syrtis [c] and left it bare; the North-wind followed, bearing aloft on its dark wings part of the sea which it had carried off; and the black East-wind thundered with opposing blast and seized its share of the deep. Now thunder rent the sky, and now the lightning-flashes came thick and fast, and the inexorable sky rushed down upon the ships. Fire and rain, waves and angry winds, all worked together, and darkness covered the sea with night. But lo! a gust, launched by the South-wind, struck Hannibal's ship astern; it roared against the yard, while the cordage creaked and whistled with a fearful noise; then it carried a wave, mountain-high, from the darkling deep and broke it over Hannibal's

exclamat, volvens oculos caeloque fretoque:
" felix, o frater, divisque aequate cadendo,
Hasdrubal! egregium fortis cui dextera in armis
pugnanti peperit letum, et cui fata dedere
Ausoniam extremo tellurem apprendere morsu.
at mihi Cannarum campis, ubi Paulus, ubi illae
egregiae occubuere animae, dimittere vitam
non licitum, vel, cum ferrem in Capitolia flammas,
Tarpeio Iovis ad manes descendere telo."

Talia dum maeret, diversis flatibus acta
in geminum ruit unda latus puppimque sub atris
aequoris aggeribus tenuit, ceu turbine mersam.
mox, nigris alte pulsa exundantis harenae
vorticibus, ratis aetherias remeavit ad auras
et fluctus supra, vento librante, pependit.
at geminas Notus in scopulos atque horrida saxa
dura sorte rapit, miserandum et triste, biremes.
increpuere ictu prorae; tum murice acuto
dissiliens sonuit, rupta compage, carina.
hic varia ante oculos facies: natat aequore toto
arma inter galeasque virum cristasque rubentes
florentis Capuae gaza et seposta triumpho
Laurens praeda ducis, tripodes mensaeque deorum
cultaque nequiquam miseris simulacra Latinis.
tum Venus, emoti facie conterrita ponti,
talibus alloquitur regem maris: " hoc satis irae
interea, genitor; satis ad maiora minarum.
cetera parce, precor, pelago, ne tollat acerba
hoc Carthago decus, nullo superabile bello

[a] Claudius Nero, the conqueror at the Metaurus, is meant.

head. He shuddered and cried out, as he surveyed the sea and sky: "Fortunate were you, O brother Hasdrubal, and made equal to the gods in your death. You died gloriously, falling in battle by a soldier's hand[a]; and Fate permitted you to bite the soil of Italy as you died. But I was not suffered, either to breathe my last on the field of Cannae, where Paulus and many another hero fell, or, when I carried firebrands against the Capitol, to be struck down to Hades by the bolt of Jupiter."

While he lamented thus, two waves driven by opposite winds smote both sides of his vessel and held it fast beneath the dark heaps of water, as if a water-spout had sunk it. Then, driven up by boiling eddies of black sand, the ship came up again to the surface and hung above the waves, kept on an even keel by the opposite winds. But the fierce South-wind dashed two other vessels against the cliffs and jagged rocks—a pitiful sight to see. As they struck, their beaks crashed; and then the hulls, split by the sharp rocks, cracked as their framework broke up. Now a motley sight was seen: all over the water there floated, together with weapons and helmets and scarlet plumes, the treasure of Capua in her palmy days, the Italian booty set apart for Hannibal's triumph, tripods and tables of the gods, and images which the Romans had vainly worshipped in their affliction. Then Venus, appalled by the sight of the raging deep, spoke thus to the Ruler of the Sea[b]: "Sire, have done with your wrath for the time; your threats are terrible enough to secure greater objects. But now, I pray you, be merciful to the sea; or else cruel Carthage may boast

[b] Neptune.

progenuisse caput, nostrosque in funera Poeni
Aeneadas undis totoque eguisse profundo."
Sic Venus, et tumidi considunt gurgite fluctus.

. . . .

obviaque adversis propellunt agmina castris.
Dux, vetus armorum scitusque accendere corda
laudibus, ignifero mentes furiabat in iram
hortatu decorisque urebat pectora flammis :
"tu mihi Flaminii portas rorantia caesi
ora ducis ; nosco dextram. tu primus in ictus
ingentis Pauli ruis ac defigis in ossa
mucronem. tibi pugnacis gestantur opima
Marcelli. Gracchusque cadens tibi proluit ensem.
ecce manus, quae pulsantem te, belliger Appi,
moenia sublimis Capuae de culmine muri
excelso fusa moribundum perculit hasta.
ecce aliud fulmen dextrae, quo nobile nomen
Fulvius excepit non unum pectore vulnus.
huc prima te siste acie, cui consul in armis
Crispinus cecidit. me tu comitare per hostes,
qui nobis, memini, ad Cannas laetissimus irae
Servili fers ora ducis suffixa veruto.
cerno flagrantes oculos vultumque timendum
non ipso minus ense tuum, fortissime Poenum
o iuvenis, qualem vidi, cum flumine saevo

[a] That some verses, perhaps a great many verses, have been lost here seems to me certain. For the present episode is not completed ; and the following episode requires introductory matter which is lacking. There is no other instance in the poem of narrative so faulty. Further, it is known that Scipio and Hannibal met in conference before the battle ; and it is inconceivable that Silius should pass over an incident so dramatic.

that a son of hers proved invincible in war, and that the Aeneadae, my children, needed the sea and all its waves to put Hannibal to death."

Thus Venus spoke, and the swelling waves sank to rest.[a] . . . .
and they pushed their army forward, to meet the foe.

Hannibal, a veteran soldier, knew well how to heighten the ardour of his men by means of praise. In a fiery speech he roused their spirit to madness, and inflamed their hearts with ambition to excel.[b] "*You* it was," he said to one, "who brought me the dripping head of slain Flaminius; I recognize that hand.—And *you* rushed forward first to strike huge Paulus, and drove your point in to the bone.—And *you* bear the glorious spoils taken from brave Marcellus.—And *yours* was the blade which Gracchus wetted with his life-blood, as he fell.—I see too the hand which laid warlike Appius[c] low with a spear launched from the summit of the rampart, when he was attacking the walls of lofty Capua.—And yonder is another arm, like lightning in speed, which inflicted more than one wound on the breast of noble Fulvius.—*You* who slew the consul Crispinus in battle, come hither and stand in the front rank.—Keep by my side through the fray, *you* who at Cannae, as I remember well, rejoicing in your martial ardour brought me the head of Servilius fixed upon a pike.—Next, O bravest son of Carthage, I see *your* flashing eyes and countenance as formidable as even your sword; just so I saw you by the bloody stream of the famous

[b] The speech that follows gives a complete list of the Roman generals killed in the war. That all the soldiers who killed them should be living and present now is highly improbable.

[c] See xiii. 445 foll.

insignis Trebiae complexum ingentibus ulnis
mersisti fundo luctantem vana tribunum.
at tu, qui gelidas Ticini primus ad undas
Scipiadae patris tinxisti sanguine ferrum,
incepta exequere et nati mihi redde cruorem.
horrescamne ipsos, veniant si ad proelia, divos,
cum stetis, turmae, vidi contermina caelo
quas iuga calcantes summas volitare per Alpes,
cum videam, quorum ferro manibusque capaces
arsere Argyripae campi ? num segnior ibis
nunc mihi, qui primus torques in moenia telum
Dardana, nec nostrae facilis concedere laudi ?
te vero, te, te exstimulem, qui, fulmina contra
et nimbos tonitrusque ac summi numinis iras
cum starem, perferre sonos ac vana iubebas
nubila et ante ducem Capitolia celsa petebas ?
quid vos, quis claro deletum est Marte Saguntum,
exhorter, quos nobilitant primordia belli ?
ut meque et vobis dignum, defendite, quaeso,
praeteritas dextra laudes. divum ipse favore
vincendoque senex patriam post trina labantem
lustra et non visos tam longa aetate penates
ac natum et fidae iam pridem coniugis ora,
confisus vobis, repeto. non altera restat
iam Libyae, nec Dardaniis pugna altera restat.
certatus nobis hodie dominum accipit orbis."
Hannibal haec ; sed non patiens remorantia verba

[a] He was rescued by his son and survived the battle.

[b] An ancient city of Apulia, also called Arpi, said to have been founded by Diomede. It suffered from Hannibal in 217 B.C.

Trebia, when you clasped a Roman officer in your mighty arms and drowned him in the depths, in spite of his struggling.—*You* next, who were first to dye your sword with the blood of the elder Scipio [a] beside the cold stream of the Ticinus, now complete your task and give me the life-blood of his son. Need I fear to meet the gods themselves in battle, when you stand firm—my men, whom I saw treading peaks that reached to heaven and speeding over the Alpine heights,—when I see before me those who, sword in hand, set fire to the far-stretching plains of Argyripa [b]? —And *you*, who hurled the first missile against the Roman walls, unwilling that even I should outstrip you in the race for glory, shall I find you less active now?—And *you* above all, do *you* need encouragement, who, when I confronted the lightning and thunder, the storm and the wrath of Jupiter himself, bade me ignore the idle rattling of the clouds, and ran in front of me against the height of the Capitol?—Need I appeal to *you*, the men who destroyed Saguntum by your prowess and won renown from the first campaign of the war? I call on you: maintain your former fame in a manner worthy of me and of yourselves. I myself, favoured by the gods, have grown old in a career of conquest; and now, after thrice five years, I go back to my distressed country, and I hope, relying upon you, to see my home, so long unvisited,[c] and my son, and the face of the wife who has ever been loyal to me. Neither Carthage nor Rome can fight another battle. To-day must decide the struggle between us for the mastery of the world." Thus Hannibal spoke; but, when Scipio opened his

[c] Hannibal had never seen Carthage since he left it for Spain with his father about the year 238 B.C.

Ausonius miles, quotiens dux coeperat ora
solvere ad effatus, signum pugnamque petebant.
Haec procul aeria speculantem nube sororem
ut vidit divum genitor maestosque sub acri
obtutu vultus, sic ore effatus amico est:
"qui te mentis edunt morsus? da noscere, coniux;
num Poeni casus ducis et Carthaginis angit
cura tuae? sed enim reputa tecum ipsa furores
Sidonios. gentem contra et fatalia regna
Teucrorum quis erit, quaeso, germana, rebelli
fractis foederibus populo modus? ipsa malorum
non plus Carthago tulit exhausitque laboris,
quam pro Cadmea subiisti exercita gente.
turbasti maria ac terras iuvenemque ferocem
immisti Latio; tremuerunt moenia Romae,
perque bis octonos primus fuit Hannibal annos
humani generis. tempus componere gentes.
ad finem ventum est; claudenda est ianua belli."
Tum supplex Iuno: "neque ego, haec mutare laborans,
quis est fixa dies, pendenti nube resedi;
nec revocare acies bellumve extendere quaero;
quae donare potes (quoniam mihi gratia languet,
et cecidit iam primus amor) nil fila sororum
adversus posco: vertat terga Hannibal hosti,
ut placet, et cineres Troiae Carthagine regnent.
illud te gemini per mutua pignora amoris

[a] Romans. [b] The Fates.
[c] An invidious description of Rome.

lips to address the Roman soldiers, they resented the delay and refused to listen, demanding the signal for battle.

Juno watched these things from a cloud in the distant sky, and the Father of the gods marked her eager gaze and sad countenance. Then he addressed her with friendly speech : " What grief preys upon your heart ? Tell your husband what it is. Is it the plight of Hannibal that torments you, and anxiety for your loved city of Carthage ? Just consider in your own heart the madness of that people. Will there ever come a time, I ask you, sister, when they will cease to break treaties and wage fresh war against the Teucri [a] whose dominion is ordained by Fate ? Carthage herself has not suffered more and endured more than you yourself have done, in your exertions for the defence of that people. You stirred up land and sea ; you sent forth that proud young warrior against Italy ; the walls of Rome were shaken ; and for twice eight years Hannibal has been the foremost of all living men. The time has come to quiet the nations. We have reached the end, and the gate of war must be shut."

Then Juno made her humble petition : " I did not seat myself upon this overhanging cloud, in order that I might change events whose term is fixed already ; nor do I seek to recall the armies and prolong the war. I ask only what you have power to grant—since my influence has waned and your first passion for me has cooled ; I do not interfere with the spinning of the Three Sisters.[b] Let Hannibal retreat before the foe, since such is your pleasure, and let the ashes of Troy [c] reign at Carthage. But one thing I beg of you, I your sister and your spouse, in the name of

et soror et coniux oro : tranare pericla
magnanimum patiare ducem vitamque remittas
neve sinas captum Ausonias perferre catenas.
stent etiam contusa malis mea moenia, fracto
nomine Sidonio, et nostro serventur honori."
Sic Iuno, et contra breviter sic Iupiter orsus :
" do spatium muris, ut vis, Carthaginis altae :
stent lacrimis precibusque tuis. sed percipe, coniux,
quatenus indulsisse vacet. non longa supersunt
fata urbi, venietque pari sub nomine ductor,
qui nunc servatas evertat funditus arces.
aetherias quoque, uti poscis, trahat Hannibal auras,
ereptus pugnae. miscere hic sidera ponto
et terras implere volet redeuntibus armis.
novi feta viri bello praecordia. sed lex
muneris haec esto nostri : Saturnia regna
ne post haec videat, repetat neve amplius umquam
Ausoniam. nunc instanti raptum avehe leto,
ne, latis si miscebit fera proelia campis,
Romulei nequeas iuvenis subducere dextrae."
Dum statuit fata Omnipotens urbique ducique,
invadunt acies pugnam et clamore lacessunt
sidera. non alio graviores tempore vidit
aut populos tellus, aut, qui patria arma moverent,
maiores certare duces. discriminis alta
in medio merces, quicquid tegit undique caelum.
ibat Agenoreus praefulgens ductor in ostro,
excelsumque caput penna nutante levabat

[a] In 146 B.C. Carthage was destroyed by P. Cornelius Scipio Aemilianus, the younger Africanus, a grandson, by adoption, of the elder Africanus. [b] Italy.

the twofold tie between us: suffer the noble leader to pass safe through danger, and spare his life; let him not be taken captive, to carry Roman fetters. Also, let the walls of my city, though sorely battered, remain standing when the Carthaginian name has perished, and be preserved to honour me."

Thus Juno spoke, and Jupiter answered her briefly thus: "I grant to the walls of lofty Carthage the reprieve you seek. Let them stand, in answer to your tears and entreaties. But hear how far your husband is able to grant your requests. The days of Carthage are numbered, and another Scipio [a] shall come, to raze to the ground the towers which for the present are safe. Further, let your prayer for Hannibal be granted: let him be rescued from the fray and continue to breathe the air of heaven. He will seek to throw the world into confusion and to fill the earth with renewed warfare. I know his heart, which can bring forth nothing but war. But I grant him life on one condition: he must never hereafter see the land of Saturn [b] and never again return to Italy. Snatch him away at once from imminent death; or else, if he joins in fierce battle on the broad plains, you may be unable to rescue him from the right hand of the young Roman general."

While the Almighty Father thus fixed the doom of Carthage and of Hannibal, the armies began the battle, and their shouting challenged the stars. Never did the earth behold mightier nations in conflict or greater generals in command of their country's armies. High was the prize of victory set before them—even all that the wide canopy of heaven covers. The Punic leader came forth, glittering in purple; and the head he bore so high was made higher

crista rubens. saevus magno de nomine terror
praecedit, Latioque micat bene cognitus ensis.
at contra ardenti radiabat Scipio cocco,
terribilem ostentans clipeum, quo patris et una
caelarat patrui spirantes proelia dira
effigies ; flammam ingentem frons alta vomebat.
sub tanta cunctis vi telorumque virumque
in ducibus stabat spes et victoria solis.
quin etiam, favor ut subigit plerosque metusve,
Scipio si Libycis esset generatus in oris,
sceptra ad Agenoreos credunt ventura nepotes :
Hannibal Ausonia genitus si sede fuisset,
haud dubitant terras Itala in dicione futuras.
Contremuere aurae, rapido vibrantibus hastis
turbine, et horrificam traxere per aethera nubem.
inde ensis propiorque acies et comminus ora
admota ac dira flagrantia lumina flamma.
sternitur, in medium contemptrix turba pericli
quae primis se praecipitem tulit obvia telis,
gentilemque bibit tellus invita cruorem.
fervidus ingenii Masinissa et fervidus aevi
in primas Macetum turmas immania membra
infert et iaculo circumvolat alite campum.
caerulus haud aliter, cum dimicat, incola Thyles
agmina falcigero circumvenit arta covinno.
Graia phalanx patrio densarat more catervas
iunctisque adstabat nulli penetrabilis hastis.
immemor has pacti post foedus in arma Philippus

---

[a] For the colour see iv. 518.

[b] From the metal of his helmet.

[c] Philip V., king of Macedonia, had sent 4000 men and a sum of money to the aid of Carthage : he soon found out that he was " backing the wrong horse."

by his ruddy crest of nodding plumes. Dread and terror of his mighty name went before him ; and his sword that Rome knew so well shone bright. Over against him was Scipio, arrayed in glowing scarlet,[a] and displaying his dreadful shield, on which were engraved the figures of his father and his uncle, breathing fierce battle ; and his lofty front sent forth a mighty flame.[b] Though there was present so great a force of combatants and weapons, yet, for all, the hope of victory depended upon the leaders alone. Nay—so strongly were men moved by confidence in their leader or fear of his adversary—most believed that, if Scipio had been a son of Africa, universal empire would have fallen to the sons of Agenor ; but, had Hannibal been born in Italy, they doubted not that Rome would have ruled the world.

When the spears were hurled with speed and force, the air was shaken and a fearsome cloud spread over the sky. Next came the sword at close quarters, and face pressed close to face, and eyes blazed with baleful flame. Those who despised the danger and rushed forward to meet the first shower of missiles were all laid low, and the earth grieved as she drank the blood of her sons. Masinissa, hot by nature and hot with youth, hurled his huge frame against the front rank of Macedonian[c] horsemen, and dashed round the field with flying javelineers. Even so the woad-stained native of Thule[d] drives his chariot armed with scythes round the close-packed ranks in battle. The phalanx of Greeks was drawn up in close order after the fashion of their country, and no foeman could force a way through the thick hedge of their pikes. For Philip, forgetting his pledges and faithless to his treaty, had

[d] See note to iii. 597.

miserat et quassam refovebat Agenoris urbem.
rarescit multo lassatus vulnere miles
atque aperit patulas prostrato corpore late
inter tela vias. irrumpit mole ruinae
Ausonius globus et periuria Graia resignat.
Archemorum Rutilus, Teucrum Norbanus (et ambo
Mantua pubenti genetrix dimiserat aevo),
obtruncat Samium bellacis dextra Caleni,
at Clytium Selius, Pellaeum et vana tumentem
ad nomen patriae Clytium; sed gloria Pellae
haud valuit misero defendere Daunia tela.
Saevior his Latius vastabat Bruttia signa
Laelius increpitans: "adeone Oenotria tellus
detestanda fuit, quam per maria aspera perque
insanos Tyrio fugeretis remige fluctus?
sed fugisse satis fuerit. Latione cruore
insuper externas petitis perfundere terras?"
haec dicens Silarum, meditantem in proelia, telo
praevenit. hasta volans imo sub gutture sedit
et vitae vocisque vias simul incita clausit.
Vergilio Caudinus, acerbo Laüs Amano
sternitur. accendunt iras vultusque virorum
armorumque habitus noti et vox consona linguae.
quos ubi nudantes conspexit Hamilcare cretus
terga fuga: "state ac nostram ne prodite gentem,"
vociferans subit et convertit proelia dextra:
qualis in aestiferis Garamantum feta veneno
attollit campis ferventi pastus harena
colla Paraetonius serpens lateque per auras

[a] The capital of Macedonia and birth-place of Alexander. Presumably Archemorus and Teucer were Macedonians also.

[b] Hannibal had forced many of these to accompany him when he left Italy.

[c] See note to iii. 225.

sent them to the war, to prop up the falling city of Agenor. Worn out by many a wound, their ranks grew thin and, when corpses fell fast, wide passages opened up between the spears. In rushed a body of Romans carrying vast destruction with them, and broke the formation of the perjured Greeks. Archemorus was slain by Rutilus and Teucer by Norbanus—Mantua was the mother of both these youthful conquerors—the hand of warlike Calenus slew Samius, and Selius slew Clytius; Clytius, a native of Pella,[a] was filled with empty pride by the name of his native town, but the fame of Pella could not defend the hapless wretch from the Roman sword.

Fiercer even than these, Laelius for Rome made havoc of the Bruttian [b] ranks, taunting them thus: "Was the land of Italy so hateful to you, that you must needs flee from it over rough seas and furious waves on ships of Carthage? To have fled was surely guilt enough. Do you seek also to drench a foreign soil with Roman blood?" As he spoke thus he hurled his weapon, too quick for Silarus who was about to strike. The flying spear lodged in his throat, and the stroke robbed him of speech and life together. Caudinus was slain by Vergilius, and Laüs by fierce Amanus. The fury of the Romans was heightened by the faces of their antagonists, the familiar fashion of their weapons, and their kindred speech. When the son of Hamilcar saw the Bruttians exposing their rear in flight, he came up shouting, "Stand firm and prove no traitors to our nation!"—and his valour rallied the fugitives. Even so, on the parching plains of the Garamantes, an Egyptian [c] snake that has fed on the burning sands lifts its venomous neck on

undantem torquet perfundens nubila tabem.
continuo infesta portantem cuspide vulnus
impedit antevolans Herium, cui nobile nomen
Marrucina domus clarumque Teate ferebat.
atque illi, magnum nitenti et laudibus hostis
arrecto, capuli ad finem manus incita sedit ;
quaerebatque miser morienti lumine fratrem,
cum iuvenis subit et, leto stimulatus acerbo,
Pleminius saevum mucronem ante ora coruscat
ac fratrem magno minitans clamore reposcit.
huic proles Barcae : " germanum reddere vero
si placet, haud renuo. maneant modo foedera nostra,
Hasdrubalem revocate umbris. egone aspera ponam
umquam in Romanos odia ? aut mansuescere corda
nostra sinam ? parcamque viro, quem terra crearit
Itala ? tum manes inimicos sede repellat
aeterna socioque abigat me frater Averno."
sic ait et clipei propulsum pondere toto,
lubrica qua tellus lapsantes sanguine fratris
fallebat nisus, prosternit et occupat ense.
extendit labens palmas, Heriumque iacentem
amplexus, iuncta lenivit morte dolores.
tum Libys invadit mixtae certamina turbae
convertitque ruens per longum hostilia terga :
ut cum fulminibus permixta tonitrua mundum
terrificant, summique labat domus alta parentis,
omne hominum terris trepidat genus, ipsaque ob ora

high and hurls liquid poison far through the sky and drenches the clouds. Herius, who bore a noble name from the famous town of Teate [a] where he dwelt among the Marrucinians, was aiming a thrust with his spear, when Hannibal at once rushed before him and prevented him. Herius, eager to meet a foe so famous, made a mighty effort; but Hannibal drove his sword up to the hilt in the Roman's body. The dying man's eyes sought his brother, Pleminius; and up Pleminius came. Maddened by his brother's fate, he brandished his sword in Hannibal's face, and with loud threats demanded the life of the dead man. Hannibal replied thus: "Agreed, if you indeed are prepared to restore *my* brother to me! Only our bargain must be kept, and you must call back Hasdrubal from the shades.—Shall I ever forget the fierce hatred that I bear to Rome? Or shall I suffer my heart to be softened? Shall I spare a single son of Italy? Then may my brother keep my unloved spirit far from his eternal abode and drive me away from communion with him in Avernus!" Speaking thus he brought down the full weight of his shield upon Pleminius and felled him, where the earth, slippery with his brother's blood, made his footing insecure; then he attacked him with the sword. As Pleminius fell, he stretched out his hands to embrace the body of Herius; and the pangs of death were lightened because they died together. Then Hannibal plunged into the thickest of the fray; far and fast he rushed on, forcing the foe to turn their backs. So, when thunder and lightning together affright the heavens, and the high dwelling of the Mighty Father is shaken, every race of man on earth is terrified; the

[a] See note to viii. 520.

lux atrox micat, et praesens adstare viritim
creditur intento perculsis Iupiter igne.
  Parte alia, ceu sola forent discrimina campo,
qua misceret agens truculentum Scipio Martem,
aspera pugna novas varia sub imagine leti
dat formas. hic ense iacet prostratus adacto ;
hic saxo perfracta gemit lacrimabilis ossa ;
ast hos, turpe, pavor fusos proiecit in ora ;
horum adversa dedit Gradivo pectora virtus.
ipse super strages ductor Rhoeteius instat,
qualis apud gelidum currus quatit altior Hebrum
et Geticas solvit ferventi sanguine Mavors
laetus caede nives, glaciemque Aquilonibus actam
perrumpit stridens sub pondere belliger axis.
iamque ardore truci lustrans fortissima quaeque
nomina obit ferro. claris spectata per orbem
stragibus occumbit late inter tela iuventus.
qui muros rapuere tuos miserasque nefandi
principium belli fecere, Sagunte, ruinas ;
qui sacros, Thrasymenne, lacus, Phaëthontia quique
polluerant tabo stagna ; ac fiducia tanta
quos tulit, ut superum regi soliumque domosque
irent direptum : mactantur comminus uno
exitio ; redduntque animas, temerata ferebant
qui secreta deum et primos reserasse negatas
gressibus humanis Alpes. formidinis huius
plena acies propere retro exanimata ruebat.

[a] See note to ix. 367.

[b] The Hebrus is a Thracian river, and the Getae a Thracian people : Mars was supposed to live in Thrace.

[c] Weight is a common attribute of divinity in ancient mythology.

[d] The river Po.

[e] The Capitol.

fierce light flashes full in their faces, and each man in his panic believes that Jupiter stands in visible form before him and aims the fire at him.

Elsewhere, as if there were no fighting on the field except where Scipio drove the rout before him in furious warfare, the fierce battle displayed strange and diverse forms of death. One man lies prostrate, pierced by the sword; another, whose bones have been shattered by a stone, groans pitifully; some whom fear laid low lie prone in dishonour; others are brave men who offered their front to the slayer.[a] The Roman general presses on over the heaps of dead. Even so, by the cold Hebrus,[b] Mars, rejoicing in slaughter, stands erect in his chariot and drives it forward, melting the Getic snows with hot streams of blood; and the car, groaning beneath the god's weight,[c] breaks the ice that the North-winds have piled up. And now Scipio in his burning rage sought out and slew with the sword all the bravest and most famous. The soldiers renowned over the world for feats of slaughter were slain over all the field in this battle. The men who ravished Saguntum and began the abominable war by destroying the walls of that ill-fated city; those who polluted with gore the sacred lake of Trasimene and the pools of Phaëthon's river[d]; those who were bold enough to march against the throne and dwelling[e] of the King of Heaven, to sack it—all these were slain in hand-to-hand battle and shared the same doom. Slain also were those who boasted that they had desecrated the secret places of the gods and opened up the Alps where no foot of man had trodden till then. The Carthaginians, filled with fear for such guilt, turned in haste and fled, robbed of their senses. Thus, when

haud secus ac tectis urbis Vulcania pestis
cum sese infudit, rapidusque incendia flatus
ventilat et volucres spargit per culmina flammas:
attonitum erumpit subita formidine vulgus,
lateque ut capta passim trepidatur in urbe.
  Verum ubi cunctari taedet dispersa virorum
proelia sectantem et leviori Marte teneri,
omnes in causam belli auctoremque malorum
vertere iam vires tandem placet. Hannibal unus
dum restet, non, si muris Carthaginis ignis
subdatur, caesique cadant exercitus omnis,
profectum Latio; contra, si concidat unus,
nequiquam fore Agenoreis cuncta arma virosque.
illum igitur lustrans circumfert lumina campo
rimaturque ducem. iuvat in certamina summa
ferre gradum; cuperetque viro concurrere, tota
spectante Ausonia; celsus clamore feroci
provocat increpitans hostem et nova proelia poscit.
  Quas postquam audivit voces conterrita Iuno,
ne Libyci ducis impavidas ferrentur ad aures,
effigiem informat Latiam propereque coruscis
attollit cristis; addit clipeumque iubasque
Romulei ducis atque umeris imponit honorem
fulgentis saguli; dat gressum habitusque cientis
proelia et audaces adicit sine corpore motus.
tum par effigies fallacis imagine vana
cornipedis moderanda cito per devia passu
belligerae datur ad speciem certaminis umbrae.
sic Poeni ducis ante oculos exultat et ultro
Scipio Iunoni simulatus tela coruscat.
at, viso laetus rectore ante ora Latino

[a] Cp. iv. 517.

the scourge of fire has spread over the buildings of a city, and a gale fans the flying flame and scatters it over the house-tops, the people rush out into the streets, appalled with sudden fear; and there is widespread consternation, as if enemies had taken the city.

But Scipio was impatient of delay and weary of pursuing lesser adversaries in different parts of the field. He resolved to turn all his might at last against the cause of war and the originator of all Rome's calamities. While Hannibal alone survived, Rome had gained nothing, even if the walls of Carthage were set on fire and all her soldiers slain; on the other hand, if Hannibal alone fell, all her weapons and all her men would profit the people of Carthage not at all. Therefore he turned his gaze all over the field, seeking and searching for Hannibal; he longed to begin the crowning conflict, and would welcome all Italy to watch the contest. Rising to his full height, he challenged his foe with taunts and a shout of defiance, and demanded a fresh antagonist.

Juno heard his speech and feared it might reach the ears of the dauntless African general. Therefore she made haste to fashion a shape in the likeness of Scipio, and adorned its high head with a glittering plume; she gave it also Scipio's shield and helmet, and placed on its shoulders the general's scarlet mantle;[a] she gave it Scipio's gait and his attitude in battle, and made the bodiless phantom step out boldly. Next she made a phantom steed, as unsubstantial as his rider, for the phantom warrior to ride at speed over the rough ground to a mock combat. Thus the Scipio whom Juno had fashioned sprang forth before the face of Hannibal and boldly brandished his weapons. The Carthaginian rejoiced to see the

et tandem propius sperans ingentia, Poenus
quadrupedi citus imponit velocia membra
et iacit adversam properati turbinis hastam.
dat terga et campo fugiens volat ales imago
tramittitque acies. tum vero, ut victor et alti
iam compos voti, ferrata calce cruentat
cornipedem et largas Poenus quatit asper habenas :
" quo fugis, oblitus nostris te cedere regnis ?
nulla tibi Libyca latebra est, o Scipio, terra."
haec ait et stricto sequitur mucrone volantem,
donec longinquo frustratum duxit in arva
diversa spatio procul a certamine pugnae.
tum fallax subito simulacrum in nubila cessit.
fulmineus ductor : " quisnam se numine caeco
composuit nobis," inquit, " deus ? aut latet idem
cur monstro ? tantumne obstat mea gloria divis ?
sed non avelles umquam, quicumque secundus
caelicolum stas Ausoniae, non artibus hostem
eripies verum nobis." frena inde citati
convertit furibundus equi campumque petebat,
cum subito occultae pestis collapsa tremore
cornipedis moles ruit atque efflavit anhelo
pectore Iunonis curis in nubila vitam.
tum vero impatiens " vestra est haec altera, vestra
fraus," inquit, " superi ; non fallitis. aequore mersum
texissent scopuli, pelagusque hausisset et undae !
anne huic servabar leto ? mea signa secuti,
quis pugnae auspicium dedimus, caeduntur ; et absens

Roman general facing him; hoping soon to win a mighty prize, he threw his nimble limbs across his horse's back and quickly hurled his furious spear at the adversary. The phantom turned round and fled fast along the plain and past the fighters. Then indeed Hannibal, sure of victory and of attaining his high ambition, spurred his horse till the blood came, and roughly shook the reins that lay loose on its neck. "Whither do you flee, Scipio? You forget that you are retreating from our realm. For you there is no hiding-place on the soil of Libya." Speaking thus he pursued the flying phantom with drawn sword, until it led him astray to a spot far removed from the strife of battle. Then the delusive phantom vanished suddenly into the clouds. Fire flashed from Hannibal's eyes: "What god," he cried, "has masked his divinity and matched himself against me? or why does he hide beneath this phantom? Are the gods so jealous of my fame? But, whichever of the gods it is that favours Rome, he shall never snatch my victim from me nor rob me by craft of the real foe." Then in fury he turned his fleet horse's head and was riding back to the field, when suddenly, by the contrivance of Juno, the stalwart steed, smitten by a mysterious fever-fit, fell down and soon breathed forth its life into the air from panting lungs. Hannibal could endure no more: "From you, ye gods," he cried, "from you comes this second deception; but I see through your devices. Oh that I had been drowned at sea, that the rocks had been my tomb, and that the waves of ocean had swallowed me down! Was I saved for a death like this? The men who followed my standard and whom I led on to war are being slaughtered, and I am

accipio gemitus vocesque ac verba vocantum
Hannibalem. quis nostra satis delicta piabit
Tartareus torrens ?" simul haec fundebat et una
spectabat dextram ac leti fervebat amore.
Tunc Iuno, miserata virum, pastoris in ora
vertitur ac silvis subito procedit opacis
atque his alloquitur versantem ingloria fata :
" quaenam te silvis accedere causa subegit
armatum nostris ? num dura ad proelia tendis,
magnus ubi Ausoniae reliquos domat Hannibal armis ?
si velox gaudes ire, et compendia grata
sunt tibi, vicino in medios te tramite ducam."
annuit atque onerat promissis pectora largis
pastoris patresque docet Carthaginis altae
magna repensuros, nec se leviora daturum.
praecipitem et vasto superantem proxima saltu
circumagit Iuno ac, fallens regione viarum,
non gratam invito servat celata salutem.
Interea Cadmea manus, deserta pavensque,
non ullum Hannibalem, nusquam certamina cernit
saevi nota ducis. pars ferro occumbere credunt,
pars damnasse aciem et divis cessisse sinistris.
ingruit Ausonius versosque agit aequore toto
rector. iamque ipsae trepidant Carthaginis arces :
impletur terrore vago cuncta Africa pulsis
agminibus, volucrique fuga sine Marte ruentes
tendunt attonitos extrema ad litora cursus

---

[a] Like Turnus in the *Aeneid* (x. 681), he was contemplating suicide.

not with them; I hear their groans and their cries to Hannibal to help them. What river of Tartarus will ever purge away my guilt?" Even as he poured forth this complaint, he looked to the sword in his right hand [a] in his passionate desire for death.

Then Juno took pity upon him. Putting on the likeness of a shepherd, she suddenly emerged from a shady grove, and addressed him thus while he had in mind a dishonourable death: "For what purpose came you here, a man in arms, to our peaceful woodlands? Seek you the stern battle, in which great Hannibal is defeating the remnant of the Romans? If speed is your desire and you seek to get there quickly, I will guide you by a neighbouring path to the midst of the combat." He assented, and loaded the shepherd with promises of rich reward, saying that the rulers of mighty Carthage would give a great recompense and that he himself would be no less generous. Starting forward, he moved with great bounds over the surrounding plain; but Juno in disguise led him by a circuitous way, and, misdirecting him, earned no gratitude by saving his life against his will.

Meanwhile the Carthaginian army, deserted and affrighted, could see no sign of Hannibal nor of his famous achievements in the field. Some thought he had been slain by the sword; others, that he had abandoned the battle in despair, unable to cope with the ill-will of the gods. On came Scipio and drove them in flight all over the plain; and now even the towers of Carthage trembled. When her armies were routed, all Africa was filled with terror and confusion: flying, not fighting, panic-stricken men rushed with utmost speed to the most distant shores.

ac Tartessiacas profugi sparguntur in oras ;
pars Batti petiere domos, pars flumina Lagi.
sic ubi, vi caeca tandem devictus, ad astra
evomuit pastos per saecula Vesvius ignes,
et pelago et terris fusa est Vulcania pestis,
videre Eoi, monstrum admirabile, Seres
lanigeros cinere Ausonio canescere lucos.
  At fessum tumulo tandem regina propinquo
sistit Iuno ducem, facies unde omnis et atrae
apparent admota oculis vestigia pugnae.
qualem Gargani campum Trebiaeque paludem
et Tyrrhena vada et Phaëthontis viderat amnem
strage virum undantem, talis, miserabile visu,
prostratis facies aperitur dira maniplis.
tunc superas Iuno sedes turbata revisit.
iamque propinquabant hostes tumuloque subibant,
cum secum Poenus : " caelum licet omne soluta
in caput hoc compage ruat, terraeque dehiscant,
non ullo Cannas abolebis, Iupiter, aevo,
decedesque prius regnis quam nomina gentes
aut facta Hannibalis sileant. nec deinde relinquo
securam te, Roma, mei ; patriaeque superstes
ad spes armorum vivam tibi. nam modo pugna
praecellis, resident hostes : mihi satque superque,
ut me Dardaniae matres atque Itala tellus,
dum vivam, expectent nec pacem pectore norint."
sic rapitur, paucis fugientum mixtus, et altos
inde petit retro montes tutasque latebras.

---

[a] Spain.
[b] Cyrene.
[c] The Nile, standing for Egypt.
[d] See note to vi. 4.
[e] This observation received some confirmation recently when eruptions in Japan and Sumatra produced remarkable phenomena in Europe.
[f] The field of Cannae. The " river of Phaëthon " is the Po.

Some were scattered in flight as far as the land of Tartessus [a]; some sought the city of Battus,[b] and others the river of Lagus.[c] So, when Vesuvius, at length mastered by some hidden force, vomits forth to heaven the fires it has fed for centuries, and the visitation of the fire-god spreads over sea and land, the Seres in the east—a marvel beyond belief—see their wool-bearing trees [d] grow white with the ash from Italy.[e]

But at last Hannibal was weary; and Juno, the queen of heaven, made him sit down on a hillock hard by, whence he had a clear view of all that awful battle and could trace every detail. As he had once seen the field [f] by Mount Garganus, the marshes of the Trebia, the Etruscan lake, and the river of Phaëthon, all covered with corpses, so now—unhappy man—he witnessed the dreadful sight of his army overthrown. Then Juno returned ill-pleased to her home in heaven. And now the enemy came up close to the hill where he sat, and he said in his heart: "Though the earth yawn asunder, though all the framework of heaven break up and fall upon my head, never shalt thou, Jupiter, wipe out the memory of Cannae, but thou shalt step down from thy throne ere the world forgets the name or achievements of Hannibal. Nor do I leave Rome without dread of me: I shall survive my country and live on in the hope of warring against Rome. She wins this battle, but that is all; her foes are lying low. Enough, and more than enough for me, if Roman mothers and the people of Italy dread my coming while I live, and never know peace of mind." Then he joined a band of fugitives and hurried away, seeking a sure hiding-place among the high mountains in his rear.

Hic finis bello. reserantur protinus arces
Ausonio iam sponte duci. iura improba adempta
armaque, et incisae leges, opibusque superbis
vis fracta, et posuit gestatas belua turres.
excelsae tum saeva rates spectacula Poenis
flammiferam accepere facem, subitaque procella
arserunt maria, atque expavit lumina Nereus.
Mansuri compos decoris per saecula rector,
devictae referens primus cognomina terrae,
securus sceptri, repetit per caerula Romam
et patria invehitur sublimi tecta triumpho.
ante Syphax, feretro residens, captiva premebat
lumina, et auratae servabant colla catenae.
hic Hannon clarique genus Phoenissa iuventa
et Macetum primi atque incocti corpora Mauri,
tum Nomades notusque sacro, cum lustrat harenas,
Hammoni Garamas et semper naufraga Syrtis.
mox victas tendens Carthago ad sidera palmas
ibat et effigies orae iam lenis Hiberae,
terrarum finis Gades ac laudibus olim
terminus Herculeis Calpe Baetisque lavare
solis equos dulci consuetus fluminis unda,
frondosumque apicem subigens ad sidera mater
bellorum fera Pyrene nec mitis Hiberus,
cum simul illidit ponto, quos attulit, amnes.

---

[a] Carthage was required to surrender all her elephants she had also to pay 10,000 talents by instalments.

[b] "Scipio was by popular consent styled *Africanus*. Henceforth every land where troubles arose was viewed by Roman nobles as the potential source of a nickname of honour" (Heitland, *Roman Republic*, i. p. 340).

[c] He was a sick man, or he must have walked.

[d] Taken prisoner in Spain: see xvi. 72 foll.

Thus the war ended. At once and willingly the citizens opened their gates to Scipio. He took from them their excessive power and their weapons, and engraved conditions of peace upon tablets ; he broke down the power of their overweening wealth, and the huge beasts [a] laid down the towers they carried. And then the citizens saw a cruel sight, when their tall ships were set on fire ; the seas blazed up with a sudden conflagration, and Ocean was terrified by the glare.

Scipio had gained glory to last for ages ; he was the first general to bear the name of the country he had conquered [b] ; he had no fear for the empire of Rome. And now he sailed back to Rome and entered his native city in a splendid triumphal procession. Before him went Syphax, borne on a litter,[c] with the downcast eyes of a captive, and wearing chains of gold about his neck. Hanno [d] walked there, with noble youths of Carthage ; also the chief men of the Macedonians, with black-skinned Moors and Numidians, and the Garamantes whom the god Ammon sees as they scour the desert, and people of the Syrtis that wrecks so many ships. Then Carthage [e] was seen in the procession, stretching out her conquered hands to heaven ; and other figures also—Spain now pacified, Gades at the World's End, Calpe the limit of the achievements of Hercules in ancient times, and the Baetis that is wont to bathe the sun's coursers in its sweet waters. There too was Pyrene, the fierce mother of wars, thrusting her forest-clad height to heaven, and the Ebro, no gentle stream when it pours with violence into the sea all the streams it has brought down with it. But

[e] Images of conquered cities, mountains, and rivers were regularly carried in triumphal processions.

sed non ulla magis mentesque oculosque tenebat,
quam visa Hannibalis campis fugientis imago.
ipse, adstans curru atque auro decoratus et ostro,
Martia praebebat spectanda Quiritibus ora :
qualis odoratis descendens Liber ab Indis
egit pampineos frenata tigride currus ;
aut cum Phlegraeis, confecta mole Gigantum,
incessit campis tangens Tirynthius astra.
salve, invicte parens, non concessure Quirino
laudibus ac meritis non concessure Camillo !
nec vero, cum te memorat de stirpe deorum,
prolem Tarpei mentitur Roma Tonantis.

---

[a] For Phlegra see note to iv. 275.

[b] " Father of his country " was a Roman title of honour which very few Romans gained.

[c] For the divine paternity of Scipio see note to xiii. 637 foll.

no sight attracted the eyes and minds of the people more than the picture of Hannibal in retreat over the plains. Scipio himself, erect in his chariot and splendid in purple and gold, gave to the citizens the spectacle of his martial countenance. So looked Bacchus, when he drove his car, wreathed with vine-leaves and drawn by tigers, down from the incense-breathing land of the Indians ; and so looked Hercules, when he had slain the huge Giants and marched along the plains of Phlegra,[a] with his head reaching the stars. Hail to thee, father [b] and undefeated general, not inferior in glory to Quirinus, and not inferior to Camillus in thy services ! Rome tells no lie, when she gives thee a divine origin and calls thee the son of the Thunder-god who dwells on the Capitol.[c]

INDEX

N.B.—The names of common soldiers, Roman or Carthaginian, which seem to have been invented by Silius are omitted.

(The references are to the book and line.)

INDEX

INDEX

INDEX

INDEX

INDEX

INDEX